Korngold in America

THE OXFORD MUSIC/MEDIA SERIES
Daniel Goldmark, Series Editor

Tuning In: American Narrative Television Music
Ron Rodman

Special Sound: The Creation and Legacy of the BBC Radiophonic Workshop
Louis Niebur

Seeing through Music: Gender and Modernism in Classic Hollywood Film Scores
Peter Franklin

An Eye for Music: Popular Music and the Audiovisual Surreal
John Richardson

Playing Along: Digital Games, YouTube, and Virtual Performance
Kiri Miller

Sounding the Gallery: Video and the Rise of Art-Music
Holly Rogers

Composing for the Red Screen: Prokofiev and Soviet Film
Kevin Bartig

Saying It with Songs: Popular Music and the Coming of Sound to Hollywood Cinema
Katherine Spring

We'll Meet Again: Musical Design in the Films of Stanley Kubrick
Kate McQuiston

Occult Aesthetics: Synchronization in Sound Film
K. J. Donnelly

Sound Play: Video Games and the Musical Imagination
William Cheng

Sounding American: Hollywood, Opera, and Jazz
Jennifer Fleeger

Mismatched Women: The Siren's Song through the Machine
Jennifer Fleeger

Robert Altman's Soundtracks: Film, Music, and Sound from M*A*S*H to A Prairie Home Companion
Gayle Sherwood Magee

Back to the Fifties: Nostalgia, Hollywood Film, and Popular Music of the Seventies and Eighties
Michael D. Dwyer

The Early Film Music of Dmitry Shostakovich
Joan Titus

Making Music in Selznick's Hollywood
Nathan Platte

Hearing Haneke: The Sound Tracks of a Radical Auteur
Elsie Walker

Unlimited Replays: Video Games and Classical Music
William Gibbons

Hollywood Harmony: Musical Wonder and the Sound of Cinema
Frank Lehman

French Musical Culture and the Coming of Sound Cinema
Hannah Lewis

Theories of the Soundtrack
James Buhler

Through the Looking Glass: John Cage and Avant-Garde Film
Richard H. Brown

Sound Design Is the New Score: Theory, Aesthetics, and Erotics of the Integrated Soundtrack
Danijela Kulezic-Wilson

Rock Star/Movie Star: Power and Performance in Cinematic Rock Stardom
Landon Palmer

The Presence of the Past: Temporal Experience and the New Hollywood Soundtrack
Daniel Bishop

Metafilm Music in Jean-Luc Godard's Cinema
Michael Baumgartner

Acoustic Profiles: A Sound Ecology of the Cinema
Randolph Jordan

Four ways of Hearing Video Game Music
Michiel Kamp

Defining Cinema: Rouben Mamoulian and Hollywood Film Style, 1929-1957
Michael Slowik

Mobilizing Music in Wartime British Film
Heather Wiebe

Audiovisual Alterity: Representing Ourselves and Others in Music Videos
Michael L. Austin

Korngold in America: Music, Myth, and Hollywood
Ben Winters

Korngold in America

Music, Myth, and Hollywood

BEN WINTERS

Oxford University Press is a department of the University of Oxford.
It furthers the University's objective of excellence in research, scholarship,
and education by publishing worldwide. Oxford is a registered trade mark of
Oxford University Press in the UK and in certain other countries.

Published in the United States of America by Oxford University Press
198 Madison Avenue, New York, NY 10016, United States of America.

© Oxford University Press 2025

All rights reserved. No part of this publication may be reproduced, stored in a retrieval system, transmitted, used for text and data mining, or used for training artificial intelligence, in any form or by any means, without the prior permission in writing of Oxford University Press, or as expressly permitted by law, by license or under terms agreed with the appropriate reprographics rights organization. Inquiries concerning reproduction outside the scope of the above should be sent to the Rights Department, Oxford University Press, at the address above.

You must not circulate this work in any other form
and you must impose this same condition on any acquirer

Library of Congress Cataloging-in-Publication Data
Names: Winters, Ben, 1976– author.
Title: Korngold in America : music, myth, and Hollywood / Ben Winters.
Description: [1.] | New York : Oxford University Press, 2025. |
Series: Oxford music/media series
Identifiers: LCCN 2024055413 | ISBN 9780197684788 (paperback) |
ISBN 9780197684771 (hardback) | ISBN 9780197684818 (others)
Subjects: LCSH: Korngold, Erich Wolfgang, 1897–1957.—Criticism and interpretation. |
Korngold, Erich Wolfgang, 1897–1957. Motion picture music. |
Motion picture music—United States—20th century—History and criticism. |
Film composers—United States. | Expatriate composers—Austria. |
Composers—United States.
Classification: LCC ML410.K7356 W57 2025 |
DDC 781.5/42092—dc23/eng/20241120
LC record available at https://lccn.loc.gov/2024055413

DOI: 10.1093/9780197684818.001.0001

In loving memory of David John Winters (1946–2021)

Contents

Acknowledgments	ix
Introduction: A Composer in Transition?	1
1. Korngold and the Hollywood Studio System: A Productive Working Relationship	20
2. A Musician for Hire: Korngold's Contracts with Warner Bros.	53
3. A Hollywood Compositional Toolbox	83
4. Korngold, the Hollywood Dramatist	130
5. Korngold, Materiality, and Worldbuilding	174
6. Korngold between Two Worlds: Hollywood and the Concert Hall	210
7. Korngold's Hollywood Legacy: The Purer Realm of Phantasy	235
Bibliography	259
Index	267

Acknowledgments

This book has had a long gestation dating back at least as far as 2016 and in some respects even further. As a consequence, various ideas contained within the book were trialed in different contexts, including in various invited colloquia, and at international conferences before and after COVID-19 lockdowns. It would take too long to list every event, but I'm thankful to colleagues who engaged with those presentations in any way. I am particularly grateful to fellow film-music scholars Nathan Platte, Frank Lehman, and Aaron Fruchtman, who shared published and unpublished material with me at various points in the book's preparation.

The book would not have been possible without extensive archival work, and I'm grateful to The Open University for funding research trips to the Library of Congress and Warner Bros. Archives (University of Southern California), and for paying for the copying of sources to enable repeated study of archival documents; the assistance of Jacquie Green, in this regard, has been invaluable. I'm enormously indebted to Brett Service at Warner Bros. Archives and to Kate Rivers at the Library of Congress, both of whom provided patient assistance (not only when I was on site but in subsequent follow-up correspondence), and also acknowledge the help of Genevieve Maxwell at the Margaret Herrick Library and Ingeborg Formann at the Austrian National Library. Alex Dangerfield from Josef Weinberger Ltd. provided a perusal copy of *Die Stumme Serenade* that allowed me to check a minor detail at a late stage in the process. I also appreciate deeply the ongoing support of Kathrin Korngold Hubbard, on behalf of the Korngold family, in allowing me to copy items from the Korngold Collection at the Library of Congress.

Other colleagues have also provided feedback at various stages of planning and drafting, and among them I'd like to thank David Rowland and Helen Coffey. Special thanks must go to Peter Franklin and Alex Kolassa, both of whom read a complete draft of the book and offered many helpful suggestions. Needless to say, any errors or failings remain mine alone. I am also grateful for the support and encouragement of Norm Hirschy at Oxford University Press, and thankful for the assistance of project editor Rada Radojicic. Daniel Goldmark's ongoing enthusiasm for the project has been much appreciated. Finally, the two anonymous proposal reviewers and the reviewer of the completed draft helped me enormously to clarify aspects of the book's argument and structure. Their many helpful suggestions were very much appreciated.

X ACKNOWLEDGMENTS

I also need to acknowledge the ongoing love and support provided by my family through some difficult recent years—and want to thank, in particular, my mum, sister, and brother-in-law. I remember being particularly struck while examining correspondence relating to Korngold's last film for Warner Bros., *Deception*, of contemporary events happening simultaneously thousands of miles away, namely the birth of my father. It's with profound sadness, then, that following his death in January 2021, I cannot share this completed book with him. His loss is keenly felt in the family, and the book is dedicated in loving memory to him, and in gratitude for everything he did for me—thanks, Dad.

Introduction

A Composer in Transition?

In October 1934, the Vienna-raised Austro-Hungarian composer Erich Wolfgang Korngold set sail with his wife, Luzi, aboard RMS *Majestic* for America. He was traveling at the invitation of the Hollywood film studio Warner Bros. to work on their newest prestige picture, a version of Shakespeare's *A Midsummer Night's Dream*, to be directed by the acclaimed theatre impresario Max Reinhardt. Reinhardt had previously directed a successful Hollywood Bowl production of the play, and Korngold's agreed task was to adapt Felix Mendelssohn's 1826 overture and 1843 incidental music to function as the film's score.[1] This was a job for which the composer was well suited: during and after completion of his fourth opera, *Das Wunder der Heliane*, he had worked closely with Reinhardt on operetta adaptations and completions for Europe's stages. Indeed, at the age of thirty-seven, Korngold had enjoyed a long and successful career among the elite of the European music world, having risen to prominence in Vienna as a *Wunderkind* feted by Gustav Mahler, Richard Strauss, Giacomo Puccini, and others. His first operas, a pair of one-acters called *Der Ring des Polykrates* and *Violanta*, had been presented together in 1916 in Munich while the composer was still a teenager; his best-known opera, *Die tote Stadt*, received a double premiere in Hamburg and Cologne in 1920 and went on to a notable run at the Metropolitan Opera in New York, also launching the US career of soprano Maria Jeritza. In addition to his operatic successes, Korngold had written symphonic works that were premiered by Felix Weingartner and the Vienna Philharmonic; chamber works that were performed by prominent artists such as Artur Schnabel, Carl Flesch, and the Rosé Quartet; songs; incidental music; and numerous works for solo piano. Moreover, as the son of a prominent Viennese music critic, he had garnered a certain amount of critical approbation, arousing the jealousy of fellow composers such as Anton Webern—though such support was a double-edged sword that caused as many difficulties as opportunities. With the rise of Nazi Germany, however, and as a Jew, Korngold's opportunities for work were fast disappearing. Although he had started work on a fifth opera, *Die Kathrin*,

---

[1] Reinhardt had produced the play in numerous versions all over Europe. See Jay L. Halo, *A Midsummer Night's Dream* (Manchester: Manchester University Press, 2003), 37.

Korngold in America. Ben Winters, Oxford University Press. © Oxford University Press 2025.
DOI: 10.1093/9780197684818.003.0001

which would finally receive a 1939 premiere in Stockholm, the 1934 trip to America would ultimately lead to over a decade of film-scoring projects and to a permanent home in California that lasted until his death in 1957. In that sense, boarding the *Majestic* to America was a moment of significant career transition for the composer. Although he traveled back and forth between Hollywood and Vienna for the next three years, his acceptance of this opportunity ensured that his identity as a composer—for good or for ill—became indelibly associated with the dream factory of Warner Bros.

Telling the story of Korngold's move west, however, presents something of a problem for music historians looking to place the composer within commonly accepted models of historiography. Despite numerous calls to decenter music history and, in the wake of postmodernism, to challenge grand narratives predicated on modernist ideology, I would suggest there persists a kind of embarrassment about Korngold—a puzzle about where he fits—and, consequently, a tendency to overlook his contribution to music history. That puzzle may originate in his continued commitment to tonality in the 1920s while others were exploring modernist alternatives to organizing pitch, but he is given the ultimate stamp of tacit "disapproval" by choosing to associate himself with Hollywood. The music historian with strong modernist sympathies might therefore see this move west as the final, inevitable step for a composer who, despite initially flirting with modernism as a musical style in his youth and being acclaimed by Edward Dent in 1914 as "the founder of a new order of music,"[2] had finally embraced the mass culture that was seemingly the logical end point for musical romanticism. In such a scenario, with his ocean voyage west, Korngold departs into artistic irrelevancy as a composer whose attractive, audience-friendly musical language represents an abnegation of the critical role that a good modernist artist should occupy, and whose commercial alliance with Hollywood finally reveals the culturally bankrupt core of the romanticist project in the twentieth century.

Were we to tell this particular story, we might find a pleasing narrative relevancy in Korngold's choice of ship to facilitate his transatlantic passage. *Majestic* had started its life as a ship of the Hamburg America Line named *Bismarck* that, as a part of a trio of European superliners, promised much as the symbol of German modernity. Although launched in 1914, around the time of Dent's Korngold claim and the young composer's completion of his first operas, progress on the ship stalled due to world events, and she was still unfinished by the time the First World War ended. After the war, ownership was transferred to the British White Star Line, in compensation for the wartime loss of HMHS *Britannic*, and she was renamed *Majestic*. A maiden voyage in 1922 was followed by a period of success in the 1920s as the largest liner of her day. By 1934, however,

---

[2] Edward Dent, "Erich Korngold's New Sonata," *The Musical Standard*, January 31, 1914, 109.

with White Star forced to merge with its long-term rival Cunard as a result of the Depression, *Majestic* was on her last legs: although she was still the largest liner of the time, her best days were very much behind her, and she was a symbol of a fading once-glorious past. It is tempting indeed to see here a metaphorical reflection of Korngold's youthful promise as the "greatest hope for German music," his glory days in the 1920s as the composer of *Die tote Stadt*, and a fading reputation, such that by 1934 he was considered yesterday's man. That, at least, is one option. At the other end of the spectrum, though, the music historian beguiled by the legitimizing power of modernist rhetoric, but more suspicious of its exclusionary definitions that would seem to disavow a tonalist like Korngold, might be tempted to play another version of the modernism game, and to claim that Korngold was, in fact, a secret modernist all along—to suggest that despite flirting with mass culture he remained artistically relevant and critically engaged in the way a good modernist should. Such a move requires expanded definitions, or the pluralizing, of musical modernism and cinematic modernism alike to show Korngold as an artist continuing to reflect the conditions of modernity: although his music may not sound like a card-carrying modernist, nonetheless we might attempt to show how his film scores, and the films themselves, can be shown to have critical value on the same terms as those cultural products valued by modernism. Were we to adopt this second approach, though, one cannot help wishing that Korngold had somehow delayed his first trip to America until the new Art Deco–inspired French liner *Normandie* entered service in May 1935.

Ultimately, though, the shipping metaphor is nothing more than a historiographical conceit—and not a particularly reliable one either, since Korngold seemingly chose ships for his transatlantic passages according to their size; indeed, subsequently he did travel the Atlantic aboard *Normandie*.[3] Nonetheless, the temptation to search for narrative meaning in the vagaries of the shipping timetable perhaps points to some of the difficulties that face music historians in placing Korngold within prevailing narratives of music history. In contemplating a study of his music for Hollywood film, though, neither of the two perspectives presented above (albeit simplistically) would satisfy me, in the sense that both are in sway to the legitimizing power of a certain kind of modernist discourse. Thus, even a study that expands modernism's definition so that it can encompass aspects of popular culture not only buys into the ideology it might attempt to subvert but also might be accused of misrepresenting the appeal and character of popular culture. I have arguably been guilty of attempting in my own way to elevate Korngold's music into the pantheon of a more widely defined modernism,

---

[3] Luzi Korngold, *Erich Wolfgang Korngold: Ein Lebensbild* (Vienna: Elizabeth Lafite Verlag, 1967), 76. Other large ships in which Korngold crossed the Atlantic included the French Line's *Paris* and the Italian Line's *Rex*.

4 KORNGOLD IN AMERICA

without adequately interrogating the values I associate with the term.[4] The danger of doing so, however, is to blind oneself to the full gamut of Korngold's compositional character, to emphasize some characteristics at the expense of others, and potentially even to distort historical facts to better suit the story.

This book starts from the premise, then, that there is a prevailing tendency in the still relatively sparse English-language musicological literature on Korngold to see his career in rather under-nuanced terms, or to reduce it to an easily digestible narrative of rise and fall, or even of a failure of creative development. Such tendencies are, I would suggest, unduly influenced by a popularized version of modernist ideology—a kind of snobbery that has simplified the modernist project and used it as a battering ram with which to beat popular culture. Previous book-length studies of Korngold have been largely limited to biographical portraits aimed primarily, it seems, at resurrecting the composer's supposedly tarnished reputation, with many of the more interesting work found in small-scale chapters or articles.[5] Moreover, where Korngold is mentioned in survey histories, two broad attitudes are often found. The first, initially popularized by journalistic criticism with a somewhat reductive attitude to musical style—and echoed by contemporaries such as Ernst Toch with a modernist-influenced view of historical progress—is that Korngold was writing Hollywood film music all along. In such a view, the five operas he wrote in Vienna were merely film music *avant la lettre*; and that with the "culturally-bankrupt" products of Hollywood, Korngold found his true *métier*.[6] The second attitude appears to take Korngold's pre-Hollywood operatic career more seriously, perhaps as evidence of a rich artistic response to modernity in the first decades of the twentieth century; however, it then appears to regard his Hollywood career as, at best, nothing more than a continuation and transformation of a kitsch operatic style. This is arguably where Richard Taruskin's perspective is to be found.

In a 1994 essay entitled "The Golden Age of Kitsch," written in response to the first complete recording of Korngold's fourth opera *Das Wunder der Heliane*, Taruskin suggested that "At a profound level, the movies became the operas

---

[4] See, for instance, my chapter "Korngold's *Violanta*: Venice, Carnival, and the Masking of Identities," in *Music, Modern Culture, and the Critical Ear*, ed. Nicholas Attfield and Ben Winters (Abingdon: Routledge, 2018), 51–74.

[5] With the exception of my own 2007 monograph, *Erich Wolfgang Korngold's* The Adventures of Robin Hood: *A Film Score Guide* (Lanham, MD: Scarecrow Press, 2007), which was focused on one film score, other single-authored book-length studies in English are biographies: Brendan Carroll, *The Last Prodigy: A Biography of Erich Wolfgang Korngold* (Portland, OR: Amadeus Press, 1997) and Jessica Duchen, *Erich Wolfgang Korngold* (London: Phaidon, 1996).

[6] Toch, for instance, used to claim that Korngold had, in fact, always written for Warner Bros., in effect critiquing his earlier output in the same way as Heinrich Lemacher, who had claimed that *Die tote Stadt* was on the level of cinema music. See Peter Hayworth, *Otto Klemperer: His Life and Times*, vol. 1 (Cambridge: Cambridge University Press, 1996), 150–151. Harold C. Schonberg, too, later claimed that Korngold, suffering from a creative imagination that did not match his technique, found his *métier* in films. "Films—A New Dimension for Opera," *New York Times*, April 20, 1975.

of the mid- to late twentieth century."[7] Although Taruskin is primarily talking here about movies as spectacle and sensation, he also makes the assertion that "the movie sound track can be remarkably like an operatic score in its function" and thus claims that Korngold achieved the "transmutation of opera into film." Moreover, he states boldly that Korngold "never had to adapt his style in any way to the exigencies of the new medium."[8] Taruskin ultimately questions the distinction between the so-called kitsch status of movies and opera's apparent art status by suggesting that opera was just as capable of such hedonistic pleasure ("hypnosis," "narcotics," "intoxicants" are common words in this essay), yet he tars opera (and Korngold's operas in particular) with the "intoxicating" stain of cinema rather than suggesting anything more challenging to modernism's grip on musicology. Thus, he regards *Heliane* as furthering "the bourgeois trivialization of once-noble themes that is so often noted and condemned in [Richard] Strauss" and concludes somewhat patronizingly that Korngold was right to "adjust his sights to the less pretentious level of the Hollywood dream factory" and gain respect for an "honest, small deed."[9] Leaving aside his evident distaste for popular culture, his essentialism in equating functions in opera and film, as I will demonstrate throughout this book, seriously underestimates the demands and distinctiveness of film as a medium.

Although Taruskin's original essay is more than thirty years old, parts of it were nonetheless reproduced in the more recent *Oxford History of Western Music*,[10] and others have taken up similar attitudes, especially in the assumptions about the apparent similarities between opera and film. For instance, Michael Walter in a chapter for the *Cambridge History of Twentieth-Century Music* draws on the example of Korngold to suggest that film music in the 1930s was "a direct sequel to the tradition of nineteenth-century music," noting that Korngold set films as if they were opera librettos.[11] Although others have similarly argued there is a kernel of truth to these statements—David Neumeyer, for one, has suggested that "it is basically true that Korngold's scoring aesthetic was frankly operatic"[12]—nonetheless these rather glib narrative explanations

---

[7] Richard Taruskin, "The Golden Age of Kitsch," in *The Danger of Music and Other Anti-Utopian Essays* (Berkeley: University of California Press, 2008), 246.

[8] Ibid., 247–248.

[9] Ibid., 254–255.

[10] Richard Taruskin, *The Oxford History of Western Music*, vol. 4: *The Early Twentieth Century* (New York: Oxford University Press, 2005).

[11] Walter cites the 1981 edition of *Musik in Geschichte und Gegenwart* for this statement. See Michael Walter, "Music of Seriousness and Commitment: The 1930s and Beyond," in *The Cambridge History of Twentieth-Century Music*, ed. Nicholas Cook and Anthony Pople (Cambridge: Cambridge University Press, 2004), 302.

[12] "The Resonances of Wagnerian Opera and Nineteenth-Century Melodrama in the Film Scores of Max Steiner," in *Wagner and Cinema*, ed. Jeongwon Joe and Sander L. Gilman (Bloomington: Indiana University Press, 2010), 115.

6   KORNGOLD IN AMERICA

of Korngold's career do not stand up particularly closely to scrutiny. Although Bryan Gilliam found Taruskin's perspective to be compelling—in part because having swallowed some prevailing myths that I will dismantle in what follows, Gilliam regarded Korngold's method of scoring films as essentially unique—he nonetheless acknowledges that any equation between opera and film scoring has inherent complications.[13] Indeed, this is something that I shall return to period-ically throughout this book, resisting the urge to see film scoring as the logical continuation of operatic practice, no matter what the composer claimed. (In a 1940 article, Korngold had suggested somewhat cryptically that he did not dif-ferentiate between the two genres.[14]) Although Korngold undoubtedly drew upon his experiences in the opera house and theatre, his film scores reveal rather more in common with other practices of film scoring than many commentators would care to admit.

Existing perspectives, then, are in danger of essentializing the differences be-tween the dramatic mediums of opera and film. Moreover, they perhaps assume that Hollywood represented the logical end point for a style that failed to adapt to the conditions of modernity, rather than consider the possibility that it opened up new territory for a composer to explore such questions or to interrogate aspects of his compositional technique.[15] A perspective that sees Korngold's film scores as a continuation of his operatic career suggests a fundamental stalling, perhaps even implying that Korngold merely perpetuated a moribund operatic aesthetic, retreating from the culturally engaged world of European art to the backward-looking nostalgia of Hollywood, where such an aesthetic found a natural home. Here, then, Korngold is very much cast as the old *Majestic*, a ship trading on its

---

[13] Bryan Gilliam, "A Viennese Opera Composer in Hollywood: Korngold's Double Exile in America," in *Driven into Paradise: The Musical Migration from Nazi Germany to the United States*, ed. Reinhold Brinkmann and Christoph Wolff (Berkeley: University of California Press, 1999), 223–242.

[14] Erich Korngold, "Some Experiences in Film Music," in *Music and Dance in California*, ed. José Rodriguez, comp. William J. Perlman (Hollywood: Bureau of Musical Research, 1940), 137–139. Korngold, of course, is not the only composer to have attempted to shape his image through disclosures that may mislead as much as they inform. For instance, Taruskin suggests that Stravinsky's acknowledgment to André Schaeffner that the opening bassoon melody from *The Rite of Spring* was folk-derived was made in such a way as to imply it was a unique occurrence, whereas in fact *The Rite* is filled with folk-derived melodies. See Richard Taruskin, *Stravinsky and the Russian Traditions: A Biography of the Works Through Mavra*, vol. 1 (Berkeley: University of California Press, 1996), 891fn109.

[15] In a critically nuanced essay on Korngold's place in twentieth-century historiography, Leon Botstein portrays the composer as figure somewhat insulated from early to mid-twentieth-century politics, typifying a Viennese attitude that he suggests was characterized by self-deception, mis-placed nostalgia, and a taste for obscuring the truth. As a result, he notes the seamlessness with which Korngold transitioned from a sheltered, idealized Vienna to a Hollywood that was "the twentieth-century capital of the fabrication of illusions and dreams about life and the world." See "Before and After Auschwitz: Korngold and the Art and Politics of the Twentieth Century," in *Korngold and His World*, ed. Daniel Goldmark and Kevin C. Karnes (Princeton, NJ: Princeton University Press, 2019), 307.

past glories, marking time until its inevitable decommissioning. We find these perspectives expressed most clearly in a 2013 essay by Jane Davidson and Robert Faulkner that proposes the reasons why Korngold's talents were not enough to secure him "greatness"—namely, that his overprotective father's condemnation of modernism constrained his development in certain areas of creativity, that his early admirers' praise reinforced the sense that he had found his language rather than forcing him to search for it, and that the "disastrous" reception of *Das Wunder der Heliane* led to him concentrating on the "far less controversial pathway of rearranging operettas."[16] It is a view where assumptions of aesthetic greatness are left under-interrogated and where historical understanding of the complexities of critical positions and reception history are left unexplored. As a result, Davidson and Faulkner see Korngold as a cossetted, insecure artist who failed to achieve autonomy from his father and thus became "stuck in a [creative] rut." As a consequence, they likewise embrace the "operatic continuity" argument to suggest:

> It can be argued that just as Korngold saw his film soundtracks as operas without music [*sic*, singing], he essentially used the same kind of leitmotif characterization that he had in improvisations with his father for family guests more than 40 years earlier. He even used the same kinds of improvised techniques on a piano in the film studio to bring the characters . . . to life.[17]

Such claims made without compelling evidence merely reinforce an already-decided-upon conclusion: that Korngold failed to develop into a good modernist in the way a "great composer" should have done. No matter the potential value of the observations of Korngold's relationship with his father or with fellow artists—observations that, it must be said, are based only on the evidence provided by the biographical studies of Brendan Carroll and Jessica Duchen—here the underlying historiographical assumptions about the value of mass culture are laid bare.

That said, there have always been more nuanced perspectives on the music of Korngold and its relationship with twentieth-century music history, especially in the writings of Peter Franklin.[18] Recently, too, the publication of *Korngold*

---

[16] Jane Davidson and Robert Faulkner, "Music in our Lives," in *The Complexity of Greatness: Beyond Talent or Practice*, ed. Scott Barry Kaufman (New York: Oxford University Press, 2013), 367–389. More recent research on the reception of *Heliane*, however, reveals a more nuanced picture. See Charles Youmans, "'You Must Return to Life': Notes on the Reception of *Das Wunder der Heliane* and *Jonny spielt auf*," in Goldmark and Karnes, *Korngold and His World*, 37–65.

[17] Davidson and Faulkner, "Music in Our Lives," 378.

[18] For examples of Peter Franklin's work on Korngold, see "Deception's Great Music. A Cultural Analysis," in *Film Music 2, History, Theory, Practice*, ed. Claudia Gorbman and Warren B. Sherk (Sherman Oaks, CA: The Film Music Society, 2004), 27–41; or sections of *Seeing Through Music. Gender and Modernism in Classic Hollywood Film Scores* (New York: Oxford University Press, 2011) and *Reclaiming Late-Romantic Music: Singing Devils and Distant Sounds* (Berkeley and Los Angeles: University of California Press, 2014).

and His World represented a step forward in sustained serious scholarly attention,[19] and a 2022 article by Amanda Hsieh has contributed valuably to our understanding of Korngold's assimilated Jewish identity.[20] The time, then, is surely right for a reappraisal of Korngold's work for Hollywood, one that aims to regard his film scores critically in a way that does not fall into well-worn historiographical paths shaped by a simplified modernist ideology: thus, although I may draw attention to continuities in compositional technique or to the debt his scoring practice owed to his experience as an opera composer, having spent a great deal of time not only with the operas but also with the film scores' manuscript sources and the eventual films themselves, I do not see his movie work as a mere continuation of his operatic style. Nor, on the other hand, do I regard his activities in Hollywood as an enclave that needs to be separated from his pre- and post-Hollywood concert works and operas. Clearly, there are tensions here that, as Bryan Gilliam recognizes,[21] were felt by Korngold (or, at least, his wife in writing her biographical study of her husband); that at a certain point in 1944, Korngold in working on a third string quartet wished to return to writing music that Luzi describes as bringing him back to himself: that is, music for the concert hall, opera house, and theatre.[22] Yet, there are enough commonalities to suggest that the works written after his Hollywood career would not have been possible were it not for his Warner Bros. output.

In that sense, the state of Korngold scholarship might ostensibly appear somewhat similar to that associated with an earlier stage of Richard Strauss scholarship, in which the composer's later works were seen as failing to live up to the modernist "promise" of his earlier career.[23] In the case of Strauss, though, a reappraisal of the modernist paradigm in the wake of postmodernism allowed his output from *Der Rosenkavalier* onward to be seen as innovative rather than regressive,[24] and one option for Korngold scholarship would indeed be to argue that if the nature of the composer's relationship with Hollywood were better understood and an appreciation of the opportunities Hollywood offered the composer to grow as an artist is gained, a similar shift in thinking might be achieved. But here we find, once again, the same impulse to redraw the boundaries of modernism to allow Korngold entry, and thus to appeal to its legitimizing

---

[19] Goldmark and Karnes, *Korngold and His World.*

[20] Amanda Hsieh, "Jewish Difference and Recovering 'Commedia': Erich W. Korngold's 'Die tote Stadt' in Post-First World War Austria," *Music & Letters* 103, no. 4 (November 2022): 685–707.

[21] Gilliam, "Korngold's Double Exile in America."

[22] Luzi Korngold, *Erich Wolfgang Korngold*, 85.

[23] See, for instance, Norman Del Mar, *Richard Strauss: A Critical Commentary On His Life and Work*, 2nd ed., 3 vols. (Ithaca, NY: Cornell University Press, 1986). This was originally published between 1962 and 1972.

[24] Leon Botstein, "The Enigmas of Richard Strauss: A Revisionist View," in *Richard Strauss and His World*, ed. Bryan Gilliam (Princeton, NJ: Princeton University Press, 1992), 3–32.

rhetoric. This is something I want to try to actively resist, even as I am aware that advocating what might seem to be an "anti-modernist" position itself would have implicitly modernist overtones. Rather, I want in this book to ask whether Korngold's work in Hollywood tells us something new about his creativity and his compositional identity—rather than merely assuming it to be a compromised continuation of its most commercially attractive elements—but I want to attempt to do this without an acknowledged (or unacknowledged) agenda of reinscribing the legitimizing power of the modernist label. Thus, I want to gain a better understanding of the ways in which Korngold operated as a composer within a commercial film industry that can be regarded, in some respects, as the quintessence of twentieth-century modernity and that had both the desire to entertain and make money, and to also say something artistically meaningful. The result may reveal something about not only Korngold but also the relationship in the twentieth century between artistic endeavor and forms of mass entertainment. Needless to say, this is a tight rope to be traversed, and I may well appear to slip from time to time into apparently claiming for Korngold an elevated position that appears to more closely approach some modernist ideal of complexity or artistry, and that seems to separate him from others working in Hollywood film. I hope to avoid this, and to always interrogate the "modernist anxiety" that threatens to shape my arguments. In doing so, however, my ultimate aim is to better prepare the ground to allow these aspects of twentieth-century culture to be brought into dialogue. Thus, rather than claim that there are composers or practices within Hollywood that can be elevated above the mundane and approach an apparent modernist "respectability," I would be much more inclined to point to aspects of modernist culture that can be enjoyed for the qualities they share with the entertainment values of Hollywood.

Clearly, others have been grappling with similar questions for some time, albeit in a variety of different contexts. Recently, for example, attempts to revive the concept of the middlebrow as a way to challenge modernist historiography have been proposed, most notably by Christopher Chowrimootoo. In his study of Benjamin Britten's operas, Chowrimootoo presents a much broader study of twentieth-century modernism, one that

> tells a tale of composer, critics, and audiences torn between seemingly conflicting commitments—on the one hand to uncompromising originality and radical autonomy, and on the other to musical pleasure and communication with a new mass audience. It is a study of aesthetic and cultural ambivalence, and the creatively defensive postures that arose in response.[25]

---

[25] Christopher Chowrimootoo, *Middlebrow Modernism: Britten's Operas and the Great Divide* (Oakland: University of California Press, 2018), 3.

10   KORNGOLD IN AMERICA

As Chowrimotoo acknowledges, however, the concept of the "middlebrow"—which he borrows from Virginia Wolf's essay of the same way—nonetheless preserves the prestige associated with modernism while recognizing the pleasures that come from "tonality, melody, sentimentality, melodrama, and spectacle."[26] In the realm of film studies, though, Richard Rushton has sought to actively challenge modernism's influence over the discipline, and in so doing he advocates a perspective that may be particularly useful for musicology. Rushton's position, as outlined in his 2011 book, sought to question the assumptions that underline much film theory and to recognize its roots in the value judgments of "political modernism."[27] In the context of film studies, this ideological position distinguishes a cinema that offers spectators an illusion into which they are hoodwinked or manipulated from one that offers a representation of reality. Rushton's point was that such a distinction, in valuing film as something that "represented" reality and in judging film on how successfully it measured up to that reality (in terms of allowing a critical perspective on the social and political issues with which reality is concerned), ignored what he found most valuable about film: its ability to transform *our* reality and to be its *own* self-sufficient reality. A perspective that values art—whether it be a film, a film score, an opera, or a concert-hall work—not for its ability to reflect or critically engage with the problems of society but instead for its escapist function in creating a "new reality" might therefore allow us to look at Korngold's output anew. As such, Korngold can be perceived as doing something artistically meaningful but according to a somewhat different set of values from those associated with modernism.

In short, by freeing itself from the acknowledged or unacknowledged need to make Korngold and his music conform to a set of modernist-influenced values or functions, Korngold scholarship may be on the verge of a transition to something more nuanced and informed. Much of the early work on Korngold, after all, was undertaken by or reliant upon the work of enthusiasts outside the academy, where a somewhat less critically engaged but still pervasive view of the value of art has shaped the work. As a result, perhaps, myths have been created, and have been perpetuated even among professional musicologists reliant on that early secondary literature. Although Korngold himself was complicit in the creation of some of these myths—after all, he was arguably just as susceptible to the legitimizing power of modernist rhetoric as his advocates inside and out of the academy—the transition to a more nuanced understanding of the composer and his music can only take place once those myths are addressed.[28] These

---

[26] Ibid.

[27] Richard Rushton, *The Reality of Film: Theories of Filmic Reality* (Manchester: Manchester University Press, 2011).

[28] I am using the word "myth" in its colloquial sense as a synonym for "legend."

myths are deeply ingrained, and I want to spend a little while exploring them here before dismantling them in the chapters that follow.

Korngold Myths

Despite the relative paucity of in-depth academic studies in the English language, Korngold has always been regarded as an important figure in the development of the aesthetics associated both with the classic Hollywood film score of the 1930s and 1940s and with that style's perceived revival in the 1970s by figures like John Williams.[29] As such, Korngold is often presented as a significant composer for the history of film-score composition. Even here, though, there are dangers of misrepresenting Korngold's practice to better fit an image of the great artist (whether informed or not by an historiographical allegiance to modernism), and as with those who write about the composer's entire career, these perspectives may ultimately be grounded in certain anxieties about the place and value of popular culture in society. To some extent, these myths have been codified and enshrined by early advocates of the composer; however, as I will demonstrate throughout this book, they do not stand up to scrutiny when archival evidence is consulted.

One of the most persistent myths surrounding Korngold, for example, involves his engagement with the technology of film production. Multiple accounts in the secondary literature seem to stress the composer's innate, effortless ability to manipulate music to very precise degrees without the assistance of the technology utilized by other supposedly less talented individuals—or that, at least, is the implication. This is the apparent mark of Korngold's greatness as an artist: the myth tells us of his ability to transcend the world of the "hack" composer who in contrast worked with stopwatches, cue sheets, and click tracks.[30] Such technological aids to composition represent both the technology-mediated everyday world and the Hollywood industrial product, and by apparently avoiding them—the myth seems to say—Korngold effectively remained the great romantic (bourgeois) artist. As such, the myth aligns him with a certain conservative, backward-looking aesthetic and helps perpetuate a strict divide between modernism and mass culture, of the type that Andreas Huyssen's work has helped to problematize. Huyssen

[29] See, for example, Mervyn Cooke *A History of Film Music* (Cambridge: Cambridge University Press, 2008) or James Wierzbicki, *Film Music: A History* (Abingdon: Routledge, 2009).

[30] Cue sheets provided a detailed breakdown of a scene into precise shot lengths. A click track was a device used on the recording (or "scoring") stage to enable musicians to maintain a constant tempo, and thus synchronize more easily with an image. Holes would be punched in varying sized loops of film, and the punch would create an audible click when projected. See Milton Lustig, *Music Editing for Motion Pictures* (New York: Hastings House, 1980).

12 KORNGOLD IN AMERICA

showed persuasively how the aims of the historical avant-garde, in undermining ideas of art as natural, autonomous, and organic, and in utilizing technology to do so, nonetheless survived in altered form in mass-culture products like film. In so doing, he revealed the folly of maintaining strict divisions between mass culture and high art.[31] In many ways, Korngold's presence in film confronts this issue head on. As a figure, he is of course wonderfully problematic: for some prevailing discourses of twentieth-century modernism, he is an apparent throwback, one who stands for a conservative and aesthetically moribund artistic style; yet for many, his associations with that great art tradition, from which modernism ejected him, are his ticket to an elevated status above the world of mass-culture Hollywood. It is only by engaging with film as the technology-shunning "great" bourgeois artist, though, that he seems to achieve this. From the one perspective, he is arguably misunderstood (or rather, the ideological agenda of modernism in its Adornian guise rejects him out of hand); from the other, though, he is rescued from his association with the apparently grubby world of commerce in a way that simplifies and reduces both the complexities of Hollywood art and Korngold's engagement with it. This latter attitude is unfortunately ingrained in large parts of the Korngold and film-music literature. Michael Haas's study of Jewish composers banned by the Nazis, for instance, claims: "[whereas Alfred Newman and Max Steiner] supplied music by the minute and used stopwatches to measure to the second what was required . . . Korngold's practical mastery was unheard of . . . Most astonishingly, he knew instinctively how much music was needed for, say, twelve inches of film, and never used a stopwatch."[32] Similarly, Mervyn Cooke's history of film music notes: "While recording, Korngold scrupulously avoided click-tracks and stopwatches, preferring to rely on his innate musicality to aid the process of synchronization."[33]

It is difficult to castigate these writers, for they draw on a long tradition from existing biographical studies of the composer and his music. Jessica Duchen, for example, talks in her Korngold biography of "an unerring instinctual understanding of the relationship between music and time," claims that Korngold never used cue sheets, on which a scene's timing would be clearly laid out for a composer, and finally concludes that "Korngold refused mechanical aids of all types."[34] Likewise, according to Kathryn Kalinak's important early study of *Captain Blood*, Korngold "shunned the standard devices for synchronization,"[35]

---

[31] Andreas Huyssen, *After the Great Divide: Modernism, Mass Culture, Postmodernism* (London: Macmillan Press, 1980).

[32] Michael Haas, *Forbidden Music: The Jewish Composers Banned by the Nazis* (New Haven, CT: Yale University Press, 2014), 198.

[33] Cooke, *A History of Film Music*, 95.

[34] Duchen, *Erich Wolfgang Korngold*, 152.

[35] Kathryn Kalinak, *Settling the Score: Music and the Classical Hollywood Film* (Madison: University of Wisconsin Press, 1992), 96.

while Russell Lack talks about the composer "effortlessly" matching music to picture cues.[36] Moreover, the composer himself participated in this mythmaking, commenting somewhat ambiguously in a 1940 article for *Music and Dance in California* that "And if the pictures inspires me, I don't even have to measure or count the seconds or feet. If I am really inspired, I simply have luck." Although he did then go on to state (with characteristic tongue-in-cheek humor) that "And my friend, the cutter, helps my luck along," nonetheless he made pains elsewhere in the same article to stress his independence from the mechanical assistance used by others, noting, "I am not composing at a desk writing music mechanically, for the lengths of film measured out by an assistant."[37]

Undoubtedly, such repetition of historical "fact" generates its own truth and means that each successive writer is less inclined to doubt its veracity or to interrogate the attitudes that have shaped the discourse. It is likely that the so-called fact originates not so much in Korngold's own ambiguous statement about "luck" but rather in comments made by Luzi Korngold about her husband's first experiences with film when working on *A Midsummer Night's Dream*; that Erich had explained he would be unable to be conduct with mechanical aids (by which she refers to a click track).[38] It was codified in English, however, in the account written by Tony Thomas, an early cheerleader for the composer who had corresponded with Korngold and, after Korngold's death, with Luzi.[39] In his 1973 book *Music for the Movies*, Thomas states "[Korngold] never used timing sheets, cue marks, or earphones. If a sequence called for forty-two and two-thirds seconds, he would write a piece of music and conduct it so that it would fill forty-two and two-thirds seconds."[40] These statements thus point to many of the tensions that surround Korngold's position in Hollywood, and his reception in twentieth-century cultural history. They seem an attempt to perpetuate the "Great Divide" that Huyssen identified even if, in denying the interrelatedness of high art and mass culture, the attempt is doomed to failure: indeed, the effort to prop up the idea of Korngold as "Great Artist" has arguably resulted in the falsification of historical fact, because these statements of Thomas and those who have followed are simply not supported by manuscript and archival evidence. Examining materials from both the Library of Congress and Warner Bros. Archives, as I will discuss in both Chapters 1 and 3, reveals that not only did Korngold use cue sheets, but he also appears to have worked routinely with

---

[36] Russell Lack, *Twenty-Four Frames Under: A Buried History of Film Music* (London: Quartet Books, 1997), 128.

[37] Erich Korngold, "Some Experiences in Film Music," reproduced in Goldmark and Karnes, *Korngold and His World*, 250.

[38] Luzi Korngold, *Erich Wolfgang Korngold*, 67.

[39] Thomas's correspondence with both Korngold and Korngold's widow, Luzi, can be found in the Erich Wolfgang Korngold Collection, Music Division, Library of Congress, Washington, DC.

[40] Tony Thomas, *Music for the Movies*, 2nd ed. (Los Angeles: Silman-James Press, 1997), 172.

14 KORNGOLD IN AMERICA

timing aids on the Scoring Stage after 1938, in order to both assist with the setting of proper tempo and to help with music's synchronization with image. Moreover, such timing aids appear to have been intrinsic to his composition process and complement the other ways in which he engaged with the technologies associated with Hollywood film scoring, including the occasional use of multi-track recording and the embracing of new instruments dependent on twentieth-century technology.

Similar myths surround Korngold's Warner Bros. contracts with the result that the composer is often seen as a figure working in a fundamentally different way with Hollywood than other musicians employed at the time. Brendan Carroll's detailed biography, which for years was the only English-language biographical source worth consulting, talks of Korngold's 1938 contract with Warner Bros. as "the most generous and flexible ever granted to a [film] composer," and suggests that "More remarkable still, the music he composed would remain his property after the film was completed for use as he saw fit."[41] Unfortunately, no reference is provided for any of these claims, but I suspect they may have arisen in part from the books of Christopher Palmer and—ultimately—Tony Thomas. Thus, Palmer writes "Exceptionally, Korngold was given permission by Warners to make whatever use he pleased of his film compositions in other fields,"[42] while Thomas notes: "He had decided [in late 1937] to accept more assignments from Warner Bros. if they would meet his terms i.e., he would have carte blanche in scoring a film and the music could not be tampered with, and further, that the music would remain his property and not that of the studio. Warner Bros. was so anxious to get his name on a contract that they allowed him any condition."[43]

Here, it seems, expressed in its purest form, is the myth of the great artist only willing to collaborate with the supposed "grubby" world of commercial entertainment if accorded certain conditions and privileges, and of a movie studio desperate to associate themselves with the prestige his name represented. It is the vision of the kind of artist separated from mass culture that post-war modernism has heralded, and thus seems to reflect the desire for Korngold to be defended from his otherwise dubious association with film. In that sense, though, it is misleading—both historically and in helping us to understand the real nature of Korngold's artistic engagement with Hollywood—since there is remarkably little evidence in the contracts themselves to support any of it, as I will discuss in Chapter 2. Again, though, it is a myth repeated in otherwise reputable contexts. Bryan Gilliam, for instance, repeats that the "music was to be his and not the property of the studio, and his scores would remain untampered with. He could,

---

[41] Carroll, *The Last Prodigy*, 275.
[42] Christopher Palmer, *The Composer in Hollywood* (London: Marion Boyars, 1990), 67n3.
[43] Thomas, *Music for the Movies*, 176.

moreover, score as few films as he desired."[44] Likewise, Michael Haas suggests that Korngold's contract (note the singular) was "unique, and he was spared the assembly line methods of other studio composers. He could choose which films he worked on."[45] These statements are, in part, palpably incorrect, as I will demonstrate in Chapters 1 and 2.

I will also tackle other myths about the reception of Korngold's post-war works in Chapter 7, namely the assumption that his attempt to return to the concert hall was a critical failure and that a revival only began in the 1970s. Here, though, I want to mention one final received truth that demands more scrutiny than I can give it in this book. Many of the prevailing pictures of Korngold also present him as someone for whom contemporary politics or social consciousness was less important than centuries of romantic tradition. Korngold's statement upon his arrival in America in 1934 to work on arranging Mendelssohn's music, when asked his opinion by newspaper reporters of Hitler, that "I think Mendelssohn will outlive Hitler," has often been repeated.[46] Yet, as Luzi reported it, it seems to be the response of a tired traveler in a second language to a barrage of questions on the same subject, rather than as the considered statement of political apathy that is sometimes assumed. Similarly, Korngold's political "naivety" is sometimes demonstrated through the mess associated with his fifth opera, *Die Kathrin*. Its basis was a novella by Heinrich Edward Jacob, *The Maid of Achen*, which told the story of a French soldier and his love affair with a German maid-servant; however, this caused upset with Korngold's publisher Schott, ultimately requiring a change of nationality for the main character from French to Swiss and an approach that, as Luzi describes it, was freed from all politics. "Was he that ignorant of current events," Jessica Duchen asks, "Or was he, as ever, an idealist?"[47] Yet, Korngold, as an individual, was certainly socially conscious, and he was at least politically active enough to be elected on July 27, 1945, to the Executive Board of the Musicians Committee of the Hollywood Independent Citizens Committee of the Arts, Sciences and Professions (HICCASP). HICCASP was an organization of left-wing political persuasion that had changed its name from the Hollywood Democratic Committee in June 1945 to align itself with the New York–based Independent Citizens Committee of the Arts, Sciences and Professions (ICCASP), thus becoming its Hollywood chapter. It supposedly did so at the suggestion of Orson Welles owing to threats of exposure as "a Communist front," as was claimed in a later report on "Un-American Activities in California" for the Senate Fact-Finding Committee on Un-American

---

[44] Gilliam, "Korngold's Double Exile," 228.
[45] Haas, *Forbidden Music*, 266.
[46] Luzi Korngold, *Erich Wolfgang Korngold*, 64.
[47] Duchen, *Erich Wolfgang Korngold*, 142.

Activities,[48] but it appears to have included a wide variety of intellectuals and liberal thinkers united by their support for President Roosevelt's 1944 campaign. (Korngold later dedicated his Symphony in F Sharp to Roosevelt's memory.) According to Stephen Vaughn, by 1946 the organization supported a range of causes, including: universal disarmament and international cooperation, unemployment compensation and a minimum wage, civil liberties, and an abolition of segregation.[49] Korngold as an individual was perhaps not quite the politically naïve idealist, then, that suits the romanticized view of his artistry, and further work in this area is certainly warranted.

Taken as a whole, such myths misrepresent the realities of Korngold's film-scoring practice and his relationships with the institutions of Hollywood; they simplify the complexities of his creative life for the purposes of supporting already arrived at conclusions that often betray underpinning (and unarticulated) assumptions and values—most notably those concerning modernism. My aim in this book, then, is to attempt to address these myths as part of an honest assessment of Korngold's practice as a composer working in a collaborative, technological, and modern setting (the Hollywood film studio), and to do so free of—or, at least, conscious of—the legitimizing rhetoric of modernist historiography. As a result, where I find artistic value in Korngold's film scores and his works for the concert hall and opera house will not lie with their apparent social relevance or their ability to make their audiences reflect critically on the world—though those qualities can sometimes undoubtedly be demonstrated if we so choose—but instead, and in line with Rushton, in their ability to create worlds into which we as listeners may escape in moments of artistic reverie. This, I would suggest, is where artistic value of an alternative kind may be found in Korngold's music and the Hollywood films to which it contributed.

Outline of the Book

The image of Korngold presented in this book, then, is one that seeks to remain aware not only of the myths that surround him, but also of the value judgments

---

[48] "Fourth Report of the Senate Fact-Finding Subcommittee On Un-American Activities 1948," 253. See https://archive.org/details/1948CalifSenateFactFindingSubcommitteeUnAmericanActivitiesCommunistFrontOrgs462pp/page/n259/mode/2up?q=HICCASP (accessed July 20, 2023).

[49] Stephen Vaughan, *Ronald Reagan in Hollywood: Movies and Politics* (Cambridge: Cambridge University Press, 1994), 124. Korngold's political views are somewhat unclear, and, without more evidence, it is somewhat difficult to draw many conclusions from his election to the musicians' committee of HICCASP. Similarly, a 1943 letter from the Assembly for Democratic Austrian Republic, for instance, asks him whether he intends to support the restoration plans of Otto Habsburg noting that Korngold's name had appeared in connection with a committee headed by Habsburg. See LOC, Box C Folder 1. The letter, however, notes that other signatories had contacted the organization to suggest they had been misrepresented in this matter: that they were democrats who had no interest in the return of the Habsburgs but were only interested in Austria. Korngold's response is not on file, unfortunately.

and ideological imprint of modernism that have often shaped existing discourses concerning the composer. As a consequence, Chapters 1 and 2 present Korngold very much as a musician for hire—a contemporary kind of artist able to adapt to working alongside others amidst the commercial imperatives and time pressures of Hollywood modernity in the late 1930s and early 1940s. Chapter 1 reveals aspects of Korngold's relationships with studio personnel and outlines the processes of film production and postproduction with which he engaged on a regular basis. Chapter 2 explores Korngold's contracts with Warner Bros. and in so doing exposes the realities of commercial filmmaking for a twentieth-century composer. Both chapters reveal that Korngold was a musician fully enmeshed in the realities of the Hollywood studio system, an apparatus that required him to follow its methods of production, with rather surprising results for his existing reputation and supposed "great artist" exceptionalism. Moreover, these chapters show Korngold to be much more adaptable to existing methods of working in film than one might suppose. These are methods that would seem to belie notions that the film scores merely continued his existing operatic practice. Throughout these chapters, I have tended to avoid commenting on other aspects of Korngold's biography during these years, except where they directly impact on the composer's film work. Wherever possible, I have consulted original studio documents and manuscript sources—whether held at Warner Bros. Archives or in the Korngold Collection at the Library of Congress—rather than rely on secondary accounts of Korngold's activities. This archival information suggests that much of Korngold's work for Warner Bros. has been misrepresented by well-meaning advocates for the composer—whether family members like his wife Luzi or his son George, friends or admirers like Tony Thomas, or by later biographers and writers who rely upon their accounts. As a result, an accurate picture of Korngold's relationship with the studio system has been heretofore almost impossible to form. Even the oral history of his trusted orchestrator, Hugo Friedhofer, for the American Film Institute occasionally appears to mislead or to contradict other accounts. Needless to say, of course, I may well be equally guilty of misinterpreting what is often fairly insubstantial evidence. Documents, after all, are certainly not always the holders of objective facts we may sometimes suppose them to be. In these chapters, though, I have attempted to unpick as much as possible of the mythology that surrounds Korngold's everyday activities at Warners, and to rely on contemporary evidence rather than later recollection in reconstructing the practical realities of Korngold's contracts and salary, their impact on his art, and his engagement with the medium of film.

Chapters 3, 4, and 5 focus much more on the musical materials of Korngold's film scores themselves. Chapter 3 examines the tools Korngold possessed to create narratively compelling film worlds, including the use of synchronization technologies—his knowledge of which the mythology surrounding Korngold would seek to disavow. I also explore Korngold's recycling practices, a key aspect of continuity among all parts of his compositional career, and interrogate the stylistic and harmonic characteristics of his film scores in order to demonstrate that film scoring offered creative opportunities to engage with aspects of his own compositional identity. Chapter 4 interrogates Korngold's dramatic technique in film, arguing that although his approach to film scoring undoubtedly had some commonalities with the thematic structures he had employed in his operas, there are notable differences between the two genres and the techniques required. Indeed, there are passages of music in the films that would never be encountered in the operas. Chapter 5 then continues to explore the distinctiveness of film scoring by examining the ways in which Korngold's scores may function as materialized sound within the film worlds of which they are a part, prompting questions in their audiences about the narrative source of music that are more sophisticated than modernist discourse might assume. Despite this, I am not claiming that this is something necessarily restricted to Korngold's music in Classical Hollywood film, though undoubtedly his scores seem peculiarly amenable to such perspectives. I then explore the ways in which the scores of these films contribute to critical spaces where gender, disability, and race are brought into focus. Again, I do so not to bolster these scores' modernist credentials, but instead to show them as contributing to the creation of narratively compelling worlds. Throughout these three chapters, I have drawn extensively on the evidence of the original manuscript sources—though such sources are often incomplete and occasionally marked with non-contemporaneous markings where they have been used for later recordings. In referring to the source of a particular musical feature, though, I have eschewed film timings, since these can vary according to the home-entertainment format in which a film is viewed, and because in several cases films can exist in different cuts. Instead, and with the assumption that these film-score manuscripts in the future are likely to be either more readily accessible in digital form, or to be published—in either facsimile or critical editions[50]— when referring to musical features I have used cue numberings to locate them. I have, however, used musical examples adapted from various manuscript sources in order that the reader without access to these primary documents can follow the progression of my argument.[51]

Chapters 6 and 7 then focus on the ways in which Korngold fostered a dialogue between Hollywood and the concert culture from which he came, and to which he would make a cautious return. Chapter 6 concentrates, firstly, on three films for Warner Bros.—*The Constant Nymph, Escape Me Never*, and

---

[50] The planned Erich Wolfgang Korngold Werkausgabe (Berlin-Brandenburg Academy of Sciences and the Academy of Sciences and Literature, Mainz) promises editions of the film scores.
[51] Many of these manuscript sources include an abundance of cautionary accidentals. I have kept these in place for clarity.

Deception—all of which are concerned in some way with concert culture, before examining the ways in which Korngold brought his experiences of Hollywood scoring directly to bear on his compositional practices for the concert hall. All his post-Hollywood works employed material written for film in a way that showed no artificial distinction made between music destined to be enjoyed in the movie theatre or the concert hall. Chapter 7 then examines something of the positive reception history of these works to add a much-needed corrective to the prevailing view of Korngold's post-war concert career as representing a critical failure. The tendency to see Korngold's post-Hollywood career in such stark terms ignores the ways in which his final films and his concert works bring together what modernist ideology would attempt to keep apart: Hollywood and classical concert culture. As such, by emphasizing the much more nuanced reception of these works alongside a consideration of Korngold's activities, we have the beginnings of a solution to one of the intractable historiographical problems facing music historians: how to "place" Korngold in twentieth-century music history without succumbing to the modernist anxiety that would either encourage us to dismiss the relevance of much of his output or to distort the content of his works and his working practices such that they better align with perceived modernist ideals.

By the end of his life, Korngold clearly rejected the tenets of musical modernism, and it is about time we took that stance seriously and admit that his music can still hold value despite that open rejection. Such an approach necessarily involves an implicit critique of the perspective that sees modernism's ability to encourage critical engagement with contemporary social and political realities as the only way in which one can ascribe value to twentieth-century music. Yet, once we abandon some of the baggage associated with modernism— with its image of the artist as the lone critical voice working independently of, and often in opposition to, institutional and commercial structures—we may find ourselves learning far more about Korngold's working practices as a result. The first step, then, in achieving this transition for our view of the composer is to attempt to examine Korngold's working life in Hollywood free of the mythologies that prevailing modernist anxieties have helped to reinscribe, and it is with this in mind that I turn first to examine Korngold's working relationships at Warner Bros.

1

Korngold and the Hollywood Studio System

A Productive Working Relationship

One of the more evocative items in the Library of Congress's "Erich Wolfgang Korngold Collection" is a simple stencil-design card that sends a "grand person" a birthday wish.[1] Surrounding the typically awful rhyme inside is a whole gaggle of signatures representing Korngold's colleagues at Warner Bros. Music Department in the mid-1940s. Department chief Leo Forbstein's signature is front and center, but the many other signees include: orchestrators Hugo Friedhofer, Milan Roder, Simon Bucharoff, Ray Heindorf, and Manuel Emmanuel;[2] composers Heinz Roemheld, Adolph Deutsch, Eugene Del Cioppo, and Clifford Vaughan; arranger Bill Ellfeldt; copyists Jaro Churain, Joe Wiesenfreund, Leo Damiani, Art Grier, and Charles Eggett; other department staff such as Ed Plantamura and Nina Sampson; music editor Hal Findlay; music librarian Vito Centrone;[3] and pianist Victor Aller. Although the names of Franz Waxman and Max Steiner, two composers working at Warner Bros. at the time, are notable by their absence, it is still a remarkable collection of key personnel in the Music Department. At first glance, then, the card—which was evidently intended for Korngold on his forty-eighth birthday—might be considered simply to be a reflection of the esteem in which the composer was held at the studio.[4] As such, it reinforces the impression that he was on good terms with numerous colleagues throughout his career at Warner Bros.: his wife, Luzi, tells the story of Korngold in 1935 inviting the technical personnel who had worked until 5 in the morning on the dubbing of one of his first films, *Captain Blood*, to breakfast at Sardi's in Hollywood.[5] There seems little reason to doubt Korngold's egalitarian

---

[1] Erich Wolfgang Korngold Collection, Music Division, Library of Congress, Washington, DC (hereafter LOC), Box E Folder 12. It is grouped with correspondence from 1945.

[2] Manuel Emmanuel never worked on a Korngold score at Warner Bros.

[3] Vito Centrone also sent a separate birthday card dated 1945. LOC, Box E Folder 12.

[4] May 1945 was also potentially a busy time when Korngold and his orchestrators Simon Bucharoff, Milan Roder, and Hugo Friedhofer were working on the numerous changes to *Of Human Bondage*.

[5] Luzi Korngold, *Erich Wolfgang Korngold: Ein Lebensbild* (Vienna: Elizabeth Lafite Verlag, 1967), 71. Sardi's was a restaurant and nightclub at 6315 Hollywood Boulevard (some 4 miles from

Korngold in America. Ben Winters, Oxford University Press. © Oxford University Press 2025.
DOI: 10.1093/9780197684818.003.0002

popularity with his colleagues, and the 1945 birthday card seems to confirm that this was a lasting state of affairs, not merely an initial effort to ingratiate himself.[6]

Collaborative working relationships with members of the Music Department were, however, vital to the timely preparation of the film's music, and the birthday card is perhaps most illuminating in revealing the number and variety of creative collaborators with whom Korngold worked on a regular basis. Indeed, a further idea of the range of people working on the "sound" of a Warner Bros. film is apparent from a copy of the *Sea Hawk* score that Korngold presented to orchestra contractor Izzy Friedman at Christmas 1940.[7] This contains a set of technical credits, apparently prepared by Korngold's amanuensis and secretary, Jaro Churain, and is instructive for its egalitarian approach to questions of attribution and credit. Korngold, one assumes, wished to fully acknowledge the contributions of his colleagues:

Music by: Prof. Erich Wolfgang Korngold	Conductor: Prof. Erich W. Korngold
Musical Director: Leo Forbstein	Orchestration: Hugo Friedhofer & Ray Heindorf
Contractor for Orchestra: Izzy Friedman	Milan Roder & Simon Bucharoff
Film Editor: George Amy	Music Mixer: Dave Forrest
Sound: Maj. Nathan Levinson	Music Librarian: Vito Centrone
Master Copy (Conductor Parts) Jaro S. Churain also Sec. to Prof. Erich W. Korngold	
Duping: Gerald Alexander	Moviola: Phil Scores, Operator: Ed. Higgins[8]
Ditto Printing[9]: Joe E. Bryant	Orchestra: 54 Men, Copyist: 15 men, Proofreader

In interrogating our assumptions about the working life of an artist, though, and their relationship with collaborators, the legend of Nietzsche's

---

the studio) that had opened in 1933 and catered to the stars. See https://calisphere.org/item/c8b1f 0275622c5b45b675fae3983177f/ (accessed August 23, 2021).

[6] Intriguingly, Jane Davidson and Robert Faulkner see this popularity as indicative of the composer's need to be accepted by others and link it with a perceived personal, social, and sexual repression. They are, however, basing their views on some pretty flimsy biographical evidence, and attempting to explain an already reached conclusion: that Korngold failed to achieve "greatness." Jane Davidson and Robert Faulkner, "Music in Our Lives," in *The Complexity of Greatness: Beyond Talent or Practice*, ed. Scott Barry Kaufman (New York: Oxford University Press, 2013), 386.

[7] This was sold by Schubertiade Music & Arts. See https://www.schubertiademusic.com/collecti ons/autographs-manuscripts-archive/products/17487-korngold-erich-wolfgang-1897-1957-fried man-irving-izzy-1903-1981-the-sea-hawk-inscribed-presentation-copy-of-dye-line-film-score-with-amqs-and-original-photographs (accessed October 17, 2024).

[8] Eddie Higgins also sent Korngold a birthday telegram in 1939. LOC, Box B Folder 1.

[9] Ditto Printing refers to the copies of scores and parts produced by a Ditto (or Banda) machine. They have a distinctive blue or purplish tint.

artist-philosopher-hero arguably still holds powerful sway. As R. J. Hollingdale has characterized it, the view of Nietzsche as "an isolated and embattled individual," although palpably false, has shaped our view not only of what his philosophy espouses but of the nature of Nietzsche the man and his relationship with others.[10] Moreover, the "legend" has arguably influenced our assumptions about the ways in which an artist should work—particularly the autonomous figure of twentieth-century modernism. In order to fully understand the conditions of Korngold's artistic production in these years, though, we need to attempt to honestly appreciate his relationships with the people with whom he worked and the working practices of Hollywood studio system itself, free of that modernist anxiety I spoke of in the Introduction. My aim, then, is to resist the temptation to make a claim for Korngold that by downplaying his creative interactions aligns him with the Nietzsche legend's modernist ideal of the suffering loner. Instead, I want to highlight the extent to which Korngold worked alongside others when writing scores for Warners and to outline the ways in which he engaged with working practices that were, to a degree, dictated by the technological processes of the studio system. In some instances, these are principally creative musical relationships, as his collaborations with orchestrators reveal. In other cases, however, they encompass interactions with the management structures of Warner Bros.: with Leo Forbstein as Head of the Music Department, and ultimately with studio executives like Hal B. Wallis, who was titled Executive in Charge of Production. The Hollywood studio system, though, always maintained a tension between art and commerce, and at Warner Bros. a fine balance was preserved between creativity and economics. Figures like Wallis and Forbstein were not merely bureaucrats. Forbstein was musically trained,[11] and Wallis had strong creative opinions on every aspect of the filmmaking process. It is not a simple matter, then, to distinguish creative relationships from managerial or economic ones. The picture that emerges of Korngold from the archival evidence is of an individual who engaged fully with the complexities of Hollywood production. Although he was clearly a figure who garnered considerable respect, that respect did not always necessarily result in the kinds of creative freedom we may sometimes imagine (idealistically) a composer with an existing high-art pedigree working within a commercial sphere should enjoy. As such, Korngold's relationship with Warner Bros. is in some ways typical of a composer's relationship with a movie studio at this time, and in other respects more unusual.

---

[10] R. J. Hollingdale, "The Hero as Outsider," in *The Cambridge Companion to Nietzsche*, ed. Bernd Magnus and Kathleen Higgins (Cambridge: Cambridge University Press, 1996), 71–89.

[11] For example, Scott MacQueen notes that Forbstein prepared the overture and exit music for the roadshow prints of *A Midsummer Night's Dream* since this was done in June 1935, by which time Korngold had returned to Europe. See "Midsummer Dream, Midwinter Nightmare: Max Reinhardt and Shakespeare versus the Warner Bros.," *The Moving Image: The Journal of the Association of Moving Image Archivists* 9, no. 2 (Fall 2009): 84.

Table 1.1 shows the approximate working period for each of the films produced while Korngold was employed at Warner Bros. between 1934 and 1946.[12] Initially, his movie work was restricted to Winter "seasons" (1934–1935, 1935–1936, and 1936–1937), though for the second of these he had returned to Hollywood not to work for Warners but at the behest of Paramount Pictures in connection with the film *Give Us This Night*. During these early years, Korngold's winter sojourn in Los Angeles was undoubtedly a sideshow to his continuing Viennese career as a composer of opera and arranger of operetta, and he perhaps justified it as a temporary move, just as his youthful idol Gustav Mahler had done when accepting his role as guest conductor at the Metropolitan Opera in New York. Although thoughts of US citizenship were declared by Korngold as early as November 1936, perhaps in recognition of diminishing operatic opportunities in Germany, events in Europe somewhat forced his hand, and following his permanent emigration to the United States in February 1938, his movie work became more regular—though never full time. (Indeed, he was free for substantial periods during the year.) Korngold's usual working period for writing a film's score was twelve weeks; however, this might be longer if he was also involved in "prescoring." In other words, in addition to providing musical score in post-production, he was sometimes required to contribute music while a film was still in production. Prescoring was necessary when music was shown being performed onscreen, and such music would need to be written and recorded prior to filming, with onscreen actors subsequently miming to the "playback." Korngold's involvement in a film would also typically extend until the film was previewed, and sometimes past that point, since preview performances were an opportunity for the studio to try out a film prior to release, and to make changes in response to audience feedback. Alterations necessitating Korngold's input might encompass perceived shortcomings in the music; more usually, though, they would involve changes made to the film, including cuts or re-edits, that required corresponding adjustments in music. Longer periods noted in Table 1.1, or non-contiguous dates, then, are a reflection either that Korngold was required to respond to a subsequent change in the film after initial scoring was complete, or an indication that he was involved in prescoring.

Although the progress of each film project was somewhat different depending on the amount of prescoring required, and the number of changes made following a preview, nonetheless the production of music followed a more-or-less standard model in the late 1930s and early 1940s. Korngold, it must be made clear, did not transform this process of scoring—despite early efforts on *A Midsummer Night's Dream* to mold it to better suit his method of working.

---

[12] I have included Korngold's work for Paramount in this table, but not his work on *Magic Fire* for Republic Pictures, which took place in 1954, eight years after his work for Warners concluded.

24   KORNGOLD IN AMERICA

Table 1.1 Film working periods, 1934–1946.

Film	Korngold's approximate working period
A Midsummer Night's Dream (dir. Max Reinhardt/William Dieterle, 1935)	November 1934–April 1935
Give Us This Night (dir. Alexander Hall, 1936) (Paramount)	August 1935–February 1936[a]
Captain Blood (dir. Michael Curtiz, 1935)	November–December 1935
Rose of the Rancho (dir. Marion Gering, 1936) (Paramount)	Unknown, but after August 1935 and before January 1936
Anthony Adverse (dir. Mervyn LeRoy, 1936)	February–April 1936
Hearts Divided (dir. Frank Borzage, 1936)	Prior to June 1936[b]
The Green Pastures (dir. Marc Connelly/William Keighley, 1936)	April 1936
Another Dawn (dir. William Dieterle, 1937)	November 1936–March 1937[c]
The Prince and the Pauper (dir. William Keighley, 1937)	February–April 1937[d]
The Adventures of Robin Hood (dir. Michael Curtiz/William Keighley, 1938)	February–April 1938
Juarez (dir. William Dieterle, 1939)	November–December 1938; February–April 1939
The Private Lives of Elizabeth and Essex (dir. Michael Curtiz, 1939)	April–September 1939
The Sea Hawk (dir. Michael Curtiz, 1940)	January 1940; April–July 1940
The Sea Wolf (dir. Michael Curtiz, 1941)	January–February 1941
Kings Row (dir. Sam Wood, 1942)	October–December 1941
The Constant Nymph (dir. Edmund Goulding, 1943)	January 1942; April–May 1942
Devotion (dir. Curtis Bernhardt, 1946)[e]	December 1942–March 1943; May 1943
Between Two Worlds (dir. Edward A. Blatt, 1944)	October 1943; December 1943–March 1944
Of Human Bondage (dir. Edmund Goulding, 1946)	December 1944–June 1945
Escape Me Never (dir. Peter Godfrey, 1947)	September–October 1945; January–April 1946
Deception (dir. Irving Rapper, 1946)	May 1946; July 1946; September 1946

Table 1.1 Continued

ᵃ *The Film Daily* on August 15 reported Korngold still in New York at the Hotel St Moritz but due to leave shortly for Hollywood. Korngold's materials for the film are held in a leather binder inscribed with the date October 1935 (LOC, Box 29 Folder 2); however, his contract with Paramount did not end until February 15, 1936.

ᵇ *The Film Daily* (May 7, 1936) announced Korngold would be leaving New York for Europe on May 9 aboard SS *Paris*.

ᶜ *The Film Daily* (October 22, 1936) announced Korngold arriving from Italy on SS *Rex*.

ᵈ *The Film Daily* (May 4, 1937) announced Korngold sailing for Europe that day on SS *Paris*. He arrived back in New York on February 3, 1938, aboard *Normandie*. See Ben Winters, *Erich Wolfgang Korngold's* The Adventures of Robin Hood: *A Film Score Guide* (Lanham, MD: Scarecrow Press, 2007), 77. Korngold's date of entry into the United States, however, is listed as February 4, 1938, on an Affidavit of Identity dated August 1, 1939. LOC, Box 93 Folder 1.

ᵉ *Devotion*'s release was delayed owing to legal action brought against the studio by Olivia de Havilland, who starred in the film as Charlotte Brontë. De Havilland objected to the studio's interpretation of the length of her exclusive contract. See Daniel Bubbeo, *The Women of Warner Bros.: The Lives and Careers of 15 Leading Ladies, with Filmographies for Each* (Jefferson, NC: McFarland, 2010), 63.

Instead, Korngold adapted his methods to the production and post-production realities of Hollywood. It is arguably in this very adaptability that part of his identity as a contemporary musician of the twentieth century lies (in contrast to the idealized romantic that is often portrayed in the literature): one who was, by necessity, fully engaged in the technological modernity of the Hollywood product and willing to adjust his working methods to meet the demands of commercial film production. In what follows, then, I explore firstly Korngold's involvement with the processes of film-score composition and the associations he maintained with the individuals within the Music Department. With so many individuals and stages involved, a standard process was necessary to preserve efficiency. I then turn my attention specifically to his working relationship with Executive in Charge of Production, Hal B. Wallis, a connection that reveals the shifting balance of power Korngold enjoyed throughout his time at the studio. What emerges throughout the chapter challenges some of those foundational myths concerning the composer about which I commented in the Introduction.

Working in the Department

In composing film scores for Warner Bros., Korngold was required to engage with systems that were dictated by schedules and budgets. As such, there was precious little room for the kinds of idealized artistry that the "artist hero" of the Nietzsche legend represents. Instead, Korngold's art was applied within the constraints imposed by processes that were often outside of his control. In Korngold's day, the Music Department at Warner's Burbank studios (the old First

26   KORNGOLD IN AMERICA

National Studio lot) occupied a series of one-story buildings surrounding the Scoring Stage, which was also known as Building 6.[13] It is not possible to establish from the studio records exactly where Korngold worked, though he would have been based around the area known as "Sound Alley," which in addition to the Scoring Stage also included the Music Building (with the Music Library), the New Dupe Building, the Recording Building, and a number of offices and bungalows in the vicinity.[14] On his first film for Warners, *A Midsummer Night's Dream*, he seems to have worked in a bungalow provided by Jack Warner, according to Luzi Korngold's memoirs.[15] He is also said to have made use of a nearby projection room, which Luzi reports Korngold occupied at night, beginning at 9 in the evening and lasting until 1 or 2 in the morning.[16] For his other films, though, it is difficult to say how often the composer was on the studio lot, typically, and how much work was carried out from his home on Toluca Lake Avenue, a mere one mile away. The degree to which his working habits and location shifted over the twelve years of his career with Warner Bros. is also open to question. As work began for *Anthony Adverse*, for instance, Wallis appears to have worried about Korngold, and in particular his overlap with work on *Give Us This Night* at Paramount—though this was not unusual for a producer who kept close control over his staff and their activities. He wrote to Forbstein on February 10, 1936, to ask: "Is KORNGOLD spending any time over here on 'ANTHONY ADVERSE'? He is on salary now, and I don't want him over at Paramount all the time. Let me know if he is reporting in over here, and if he is doing anything."[17] Later agreements with the studio allowed for the installation of a piano at his house (see Chapter 2), and his principal orchestrator Hugo Friedhofer reports that Korngold would take home sketches made in the projection room to refine.[18] Nonetheless, in order to check with the running of the film, for meetings with studio personnel, and for scoring sessions, he would certainly have made

---

[13]   The Scoring Stage is still in operation but was renamed as the Eastwood Scoring Stage in 1999, replacing its former name: the Leo Forbstein Scoring Stage. E. J. Stephens and Marc Wanamaker, *Early Warner Bros. Studios* (Charleston, SC: Arcadia, 2010), 118.

[14]   Ibid. Also see Steven Bingen, *Warner Bros.: Hollywood's Ultimate Backlot* (Guildford, CT: Globe Pequot, 2018), 89–92.

[15]   Luzi Korngold, *Erich Wolfgang Korngold*, 66. It is unclear whether Luzi meant that Jack Warner gave Korngold his own bungalow, or whether he gave Korngold use of *Jack's* own private bungalow, a "magnificent second home on the Burbank lot," as Hal Wallis described it in Hal Wallis & Charles Higham, *Starmaker: the Autobiography of Hal Wallis* (New York: Macmillan, 1980), 28. Later, Luzi refers to "our" bungalow (68) when Erich was preparing for recording sessions and Luzi was helping to train the elves in the room next door.

[16]   The projection room may have been one of projection rooms 6, 7, and 8, which were located with the cutting room in a building on the north side of "Sound Alley."

[17]   See Warner Bros. Archives (hereafter WBA), "ANTHONY ADVERSE" STORY—MEMOS & CORRESPONDENCE 12/4/35–2/26/36 1703 Special. In fact, Korngold was not placed on salary until February 16 since his contract with Paramount ended on February 15.

[18]   Linda Danly, ed., *Hugo Friedhofer: The Best Years of His Life. A Hollywood Master of Music for the Movies* (Lanham, MD: Scarecrow Press, 2002), 44.

the short trip to the studio on a regular basis. He would likely have entered from the main employee entrance at Barham Gate on Barham Boulevard (now Gate 2 on Olive Avenue) and made the short trip along Third Street and up Avenue D toward the Scoring Stage and its surrounding buildings.

Any prescoring work completed in advance of filming would involve Korngold's time in terms of both composition and recording. This was particularly the case with films whose subject matter concerned composers, such as *Deception* and *Escape Me Never*, where a "music plot" was produced to document all the scenes that would require prescoring.[19] *Escape Me Never*'s story, for example, centered around the fictional composer Sebastian Dubrok, and the required prescoring work related to Dubrok's ballet *Primavera*, the composition of which is a major part of the film's narrative. Korngold needed to compose and record the ballet before scenes featuring its performance could be rehearsed and filmed. Exceptionally, too, Korngold might look at and comment on a script, as appears to have been the case with the equally music-rich *The Constant Nymph*.[20] Whenever a film required prescoring work, Korngold might also be required on set—though this would simply require him to stroll over to one of the sound stages or to visit the exterior locations on the back lot. For *A Midsummer Night's Dream*, the daily production and progress reports reveal he was on set daily from December 6, 1934, through to January 12, 1935: on this last day, he was there for thirteen hours. Despite the fact that his interference with the shoot had not always endeared him to the studio's management, in later years his presence on set appears to have been welcomed. On January 14, 1946, for instance, producer Henry Blanke wrote to Al Alleborn in connection with *Escape Me Never*, a film on which Korngold's role was significantly expanded: "When we get to shooting the Lavender Woman on the London street at Ext. Sebastian's Lodgings, don't forget to have Prof. Korngold on the set as he has to be there to determine the key in which the singing has to take place so that it will dovetail with the Int. of the lodgings. On second thought [*sic*] it may be advisable to get the Lavender Woman, who is already set, together with Korngold one day before shooting."[21]

Once work on post-production began, and Korngold started the process of composing his score, he worked through a number of processes with a variety of individuals. I will explore this practice in greater detail in Chapter 3 in connection with Korngold's compositional technique. Here, however, I will concentrate on the nature of the collaborative relationships required. The processes of "spotting" (that is, deciding where each music cue should occur) are undocumented,

---

[19] WBA, "ESCAPE ME NEVER" STORY- MUSIC PLOT 1885B. *Deception* has a set of "Revised Final Music Notes"; see WBA, "DECEPTION" MUSIC 1053.
[20] LOC, Box 3 Folder 11.
[21] WBA, "ESCAPE ME NEVER" STORY-MEMOS & CORRESPONDENCE 1 OF 3 1/3/46–7/ 12/46 1885B.

28 KORNGOLD IN AMERICA

with one notable exception early in his career (that of *Captain Blood*, of which more below). However, once Korngold had an idea of where music was likely to occur, he could ask for detailed breakdowns of the timing of events found in certain scenes to assist him in his initial compositional work. These breakdowns were likely provided by a music editor and were known as "cue sheets" or "cue timing sheets" with the word "cue" referring to a discrete section of music in a score.[22] Cue sheets consisted of precise measurements of timings, in seconds (or, sometimes, more accurately in feet and frames), of events found in a particular scene, identified with the reel of film in which they take place. When cue sheets were measured in feet and frames, they were likely prepared using a Moviola, an editor's film-previewing device that incorporated a frame counter. The timing of events could thus be precise to 1/24th of a second, since 35mm film at this time ran at the standardized speed of twenty-four frames per second. Events could be marked as occurring at so many feet and frames after the beginning of the reel or a standardized start point, with each foot of 35mm film consisting of sixteen individual frames. Whether such documentation was specifically requested by Korngold, or prepared as a matter of course, the surviving documentation does not indicate. The fact that Korngold annotated these "cue sheets," though, demonstrates that he engaged with them closely during the composition process, and in some cases they appear to be written entirely in Korngold's own hand.

When spotting decisions had been finalized, each cue (whether provided as pre-score, arranging a pre-existing piece of music, or newly composed) would be given a cue identifier, which would be retained throughout multiple manuscripts and other documentation. These cue identifiers were necessary for the smooth running of the collaborative processes of composition, orchestration, copying, recording, and rights clearances, since cues could pass through a number of hands. Korngold cues were identified according to two general systems, which were used interchangeably or simultaneously: the first merely numbered the cues consecutively; the second used letters to indicate order according to the reel of film in which the cue featured. Thus, in the second method, the first cue in Reel 5 would be labeled 5A (or 5-A, V-A, or Reel 5 #A, etc.), whereas the third cue in Reel 11 would be labeled 11C. Occasionally, a cue might be known as "Reel 2 part 2" instead of 2B. Often, the cue identifiers written by Korngold in pencil

---

[22] It is likely these were prepared by Hal Findlay, who did the same job for Max Steiner. See Steven C. Smith, *Music by Max Steiner: The Epic Life of Hollywood's Most Influential Composer* (New York: Oxford University Press, 2020), 203. Alternatively, since a Moviola would undoubtedly have been used in their preparation, it is possible that Phil Scores provided them. A manuscript for *The Sea Hawk* credits him and Ed Higgins in connection with the Moviola. See https://www.schube rtiademusic.com/collections/autographs-manuscripts-archive/products/17487-korngold-erich-wolfgang-1897-1957-friedman-irving-izzy-1903-1981-the-sea-hawk-inscribed-presentation-copy-of-dye-line-film-score-with-amqs-and-original-photographs (accessed October 17, 2024).

would be amplified by a stamped inked indicator in much larger font. These numbering systems would be retained in all subsequent manuscript sources and documentation for consistency.[23]

Korngold would then begin composition of a cue, itself informed by the rough sketching of music he may have already undertaken.[24] Upon completion of the cue in a reduced "short score" format, and after it had been copied by Jaro Churain, it would be passed to an orchestrator, before moving on to copyists who would prepare orchestral parts. The cue would then be recorded by the Warner Bros. orchestra at a scoring session conducted by the composer, which took place on the Scoring Stage. Undoubtedly, the separate cues that make up Korngold's film scores were neither composed, orchestrated, nor recorded in strict order—and although Korngold may have started with Reel 1 of a film, there are indications that an earlier cue could draw upon material already written for a later one: in *The Adventures of Robin Hood*, for example, manuscripts of cues 5E and 7C instruct orchestrators to insert material from the later love scene (cue 8B).[25] Moreover, the short timeframe available for composition, orchestration, and recording—and the spread-out nature of the scoring sessions themselves—suggest that orchestrators would be working on one cue while Korngold composed another. In other words, once spotting was complete, the stages of composition, orchestration, copying, and recording were not distinct processes where one stage needed to be completed in its entirety before moving on to the next.

The number of orchestrators working on any film ranged from a single orchestrator (Korngold himself for *A Midsummer Night's Dream*) or just two (Hugo Friedhofer and Milan Roder for *The Prince and the Pauper* and *The Adventures of Robin Hood*) up to eight (Milan Roder, Simon Bucharoff, Bernard Kaun, Leonid Raab, Ernst Toch, Hugo Friedhofer, Jerome Moross, and Joe Dubin for *Devotion*). How orchestrators were assigned to any project is, admittedly, not made clear

---

[23] Sometimes, however, additional numbering systems would also be used. For *Of Human Bondage*, in addition to identifying cues with a mixture of numbers and alphanumerics, each cue in the full score is also stamped with a five-digit figure that ranges from 27957 to 28005. A similar five-digit number is used in the full score of *Captain Blood* (15716 to 15762, with the later numbers used for revised cues), *The Green Pastures*, *Hearts Divided*, *Another Dawn*, *Escape Me Never*, and *Deception*. With a film like *Anthony Adverse* the numbers are more complex: they range from 15619 for an Italian March, and 15706–15708 for the prescoring cues written by Aldo Franchetti that predate Korngold's involvement in the film (see Chapter 3) with the main numbering of Korngold's cues ranging from 16009 to 16065. 16009 is for cue number 3, so it is likely that this sequencing started with 16007, though cue numbers 1 and 2 are missing. Evidently, the need to ensure that material was tracked was vital, given the number of persons involved and the potential for revision; however, it is curious that many films do not contain these five-digit numbers.

[24] This is often said to have followed a period of improvising to a showing of the film. See, for example, Danly, *Hugo Friedhofer*, 42. This is an abridged version of Friedhofer's oral history for the American Film Institute: Irene Kahn Atkins, *Oral History with Hugo Friedhofer*, American Film Institute/Louis B. Mayer Foundation (unpublished).

[25] Winters, *Korngold's* The Adventures of Robin Hood, 88.

30 KORNGOLD IN AMERICA

by studio documentation, though Music Department chief Leo Forbstein must have had a large say. Once an assignment to an orchestrator had been made, and after any initial conversations with Korngold had taken place, the orchestrator would provide a full score in pencil for that cue, marked with the appropriate cue identifier to match earlier sources. Generally, orchestrators would also identify themselves on their full-score manuscripts, often using the legend "Arr. by x," though their handwriting is usually sufficiently clear to distinguish them without this label. Milan Roder's hand, in particular, was a model of clarity and is much easier to read than Hugo Friedhofer's somewhat spidery writing. Orchestrators would also seemingly use their own stock of manuscript paper, which sometimes included that provided by other Hollywood studios: thus, some of the full score for *Anthony Adverse* is written on manuscript paper bearing the names of MGM or Columbia, while Milan Roder's work for the same film sometimes used paper with a printed stamp bearing Hugo Friedhofer's name, which was then crossed out. Occasionally orchestrators collaborated on a cue, splitting it between them. On *Juarez*, for instance, Simon Bucharoff and Milan Roder both worked on cue 9D while Bucharoff and Freidhofer worked together on 15D; on *The Sea Hawk*, Roder and Ray Heindorf collaborated on cue 2A.

Korngold, however, had a particularly long-lasting relationship with his principal orchestrator, Hugo Friedhofer, which encompassed the vast majority of his films, beginning with *Captain Blood* and running through to *Escape Me Never* in late 1945/early 1946. The closeness of the working relationship is relatively well known, and is detailed in Friedhofer's oral history for the American Film Institute.[26] Moreover, the association persisted despite the fact that Friedhofer officially left Warners in the autumn of 1942 for two years to work for Alfred Newman at Twentieth Century-Fox, an opportunity that allowed him to compose his own film scores. He continued to orchestrate at Warner Bros. during this time for both Korngold and Max Steiner, contributing to Korngold's scores for *Devotion* and *Between Two Worlds*.[27] In addition to orchestrating most of the extant cues on *Captain Blood*,[28] Friedhofer did the bulk of the orchestration for *Anthony Adverse*, *The Prince and the Pauper*, *The Private Lives of Elizabeth and Essex*, *The Sea Wolf*, *Escape Me Never*, and *The Constant Nymph*. In all these cases, he worked alongside Milan Roder, whom Friedhofer describes as "a sort of freelance orchestrator around town."[29] Friedhofer arguably underplays Roder's importance to the sound of Korngold's scores, though. Although Roder's contribution on the films listed above was relatively slight, on some films Roder wrote

---

[26] Atkins, *Oral History*.
[27] Ibid., 82, 205.
[28] The orchestrated full score held at WBA is missing roughly a quarter of the cues.
[29] Danly, *Hugo Friedhofer*, 70.

KORNGOLD AND THE HOLLYWOOD STUDIO SYSTEM   31

far more—and he was evidently well known to Korngold, as attested by his various birthday greetings to the composer preserved in the Korngold Collection. On *The Adventures of Robin Hood*, for example, Roder shared a number of cues with Friedhofer[30] and orchestrated a large stretch of the score in Reels 6 and 7—though it was only Friedhofer who received screen credit (for the first time in a Korngold film). On *Another Dawn*, Roder orchestrated fully two-thirds of the cues, with Friedhofer supplying the rest. Roder also orchestrated a sizeable amount of both *Juarez* and *Kings Row*, and a large chunk of *Devotion*, and also contributed in a smaller way to *Between Two Worlds* and *Of Human Bondage*. He was also often involved in orchestrating the trailer cues, which were used to advertise coming attractions. For instance, he supplied the four trailers for *The Adventures of Robin Hood* and may have even designed them, given the lack of manuscript material for the trailers in Korngold's hand.[31] For other projects, though, clear evidence exists to suggest Korngold himself designed the trailer music: one can see short scores in Korngold's hand designated "Trailer 1, 2, 3 etc." or "Trailer Part 1, 2, 3 etc." for *Juarez*, *The Sea Wolf*, *The Constant Nymph*, *Escape Me Never*, and *Of Human Bondage*. In any case, trailers were usually prepared from material already written and were often assembly jobs that re-used orchestrations rather than requiring bespoke arrangements.[32] Nonetheless, it seems that Roder was far more involved with this kind of trailer material than Friedhofer, given the frequency with which he supplied the orchestrations.[33]

Roder and Friedhofer remained a constant presence throughout Korngold's Warner Bros. career, and Korngold worked almost exclusively with them until 1939, whereupon he began to widen the circle of his collaborators. For 1939's *Juarez*, Korngold teamed up for the first time with Simon Bucharoff, who was given the chance to orchestrate a handful of cues (less than 10% of the total). Bucharoff also contributed to *The Sea Hawk*, though the bulk of the heavy lifting was again done by Friedhofer and Roder. This mammoth score consisted of eighty-six cues (when trailers and intermission music for the premiere or roadshow version of the film were included), and Table 1.2 reproduces a rare summary listing of orchestrators provided by Jaro Churain for the copy of the score Korngold presented to Izzy Friedman.[34] By the time of *Devotion* in 1942,

---

[30] Cues 1C, 1D, 2B, 3E, 7C, 10C, 11B. See Winters, *Korngold's* The Adventures of Robin Hood, 90–91.

[31] Ibid., 24.

[32] For *Robin Hood*'s trailer, Roder admittedly reorchestrates film cues originally orchestrated by Friedhofer. Ibid., 93.

[33] Friedhofer mentions he had done "a couple" of trailers for Max Steiner and mentions doing so on a film he remembers as *Desperate Journey* (dir. Raoul Walsh, 1942); however, in fear of being restricted to being "a trailer composer" he opted to go back to Twentieth Century-Fox. Atkins, *Oral History*, 130–131, 206.

[34] Kim R. Holston states that *The Sea Hawk* was not a roadshow, so whether the music was planned with the assumption that it would be, or whether this extra music was provided to be played

32 KORNGOLD IN AMERICA

though, Simon Bucharoff was evidently trusted to orchestrate a larger proportion of the score. Of the sixty-one numbered cues (a couple of which are missing from the archives), he orchestrated at least twenty, with Roder orchestrating nineteen cues, and Friedhofer, having now left for Twentieth Century-Fox, handling only five. Bucharoff subsequently orchestrated almost half of *Between Two Worlds* (1943–1944) and was the main orchestrator for *Of Human Bondage* (1944–1945). He also contributed to *Deception* (1946), though as large parts of the full score for this film are missing from the archives the extent of his role is difficult to assess.

Another collaborator who worked on *Deception* was Ray Heindorf, someone who had also contributed a great deal to *The Sea Hawk*, as Table 1.2 shows. Heindorf had orchestrated the main title for *Captain Blood*, and Friedhofer claims in his oral history that Korngold rated his talent highly.[35] His contributions to Korngold's scores were rather sporadic, though: he also orchestrated the main title to *The Sea Wolf*, along with at least four other cues, and orchestrated eight cues out of seventy-two in *Kings Row*. As Korngold grew to trust a wider circle of orchestrators, though, perhaps in consultation with Forbstein, the names working on his scores expanded even further. Four cues for *Kings Row* were provided by Bernhard Kaun, while *Between Two Worlds* added the talents of Leonid Raab and utilized the arranging skills of jazz trombonist Leo Arnaud, who also arranged the songs in *Escape Me Never*. On *Devotion*, in addition to the faithful Friedhofer and Roder, the now-familiar Simon Bucharoff, and Bernard Kaun (who supplied a single cue), Korngold also used Raab, Jerome Moross, and fellow Viennese émigré Ernst Toch.[36] This last name is particularly significant as Toch had enjoyed a sizeable reputation in the world of European modernism before fleeing Nazi Germany to America, via London. He had already secured Academy Award nominations for his film scores, including one for *Peter Ibbetson* (dir. Henry Hathaway, 1935), and perhaps as a result of this, and his undoubtedly very different attitude toward European modernism, the relationship between the two composers appears to have been somewhat strained.[37]

---

live at the premiere, is unclear. See *Movie Roadshows: A History and Filmography of Reserved-Seat Limited Showings, 1911–1973* (Jefferson, NC: McFarland, 2013), 6. Danish souvenir programs exist for *The Sea Hawk* along with many other Korngold-scored films suggesting an element of theatrical presentation.

[35] Danly, *Hugo Friedhofer*, 67. Heindorf contributed to the jazz arrangement heard in *Deception* of the Wedding March from Wagner's *Lohengrin*. Its authorship was described in sources as "arr[anged] Heindorf-Wagner-Corny," indicating a possible nickname for Korngold.

[36] The fairground music cues in Reel 7 were orchestrated by Joe Dubin.

[37] Toch had also been assigned to compose *The Charge of the Light Brigade* by Warners, but when that fell through, he had been replaced by Max Steiner. Nathan Platte, "Max Steiner in the Studios, 1929–1939," in *The Routledge Companion to Screen Music and Sound*, ed. Ronald Sadoff, Miguel Mera, and Ben Winters (New York: Routledge, 2017), 264.

Table 1.2 *The Sea Hawk* scoring duties[a]

No.	Reel	Orig. sketch by Erich W Korngold	Master Copy by Jaro B. Churain	Scoring by								Time
				H. Friedhofer		R. Heindorf		M. Roder		S. Bucharoff		
				Pages	Bars	Pages	Bars	Pages	Bars	Pages	Bars	
1–7	I	30	30	*	*	37	131	14	86	*	*	7:50
8–16	II	47	47	*	*	9	37	40	222	*	*	9:09
17–21	III	30	30	*	*	42	180	15	61	*	*	8:24
22–25	IV	25	25	26	104	*	*	26	149	*	*	8:23
26–28	V	19	19	46	177	*	*	11	47	*	*	5:46
29–32	VI	17	17	24	92	10	47	4	24	*	*	6:19
33–37	VII	22	22	49	198	*	*	5	25	*	*	8:12
38–43	VIII	25	25	*	*	29	144	24	124	*	*	8:29
44–51	IX	21	21	12	60	15	71	8	39	*	*	8:55
52–56	X	17	17	30	119	*	*	10	46	*	*	6:23
57–64	XI	32	32	30	118	*	*	23	88	5	27	9:57
65–69	XII	27	27	46	201	*	*	*	*	14	55	8:13

(*continued*)

Table 1.2 Continued

No.	Reel	Orig. sketch by Erich W Korngold	Master Copy by Jaro B. Churain	Scoring by								Time
				H. Friedhofer		R. Heindorf		M. Roder		S. Bucharoff		
				Pages	Bars	Pages	Bars	Pages	Bars	Pages	Bars	
70–83	XIII	37	37	67	287	*	*	13	46	*	*	9:51
Total: 83	13	349	349	330	1366	142	610	193	957	19	82	105:51
				684 Score Pages, 3005 bars, 1 hour, 45 mins, 51 sec.								
84–86	trail.	15	15	*	*	*	*	11	95	*	*	3:04
Total: 86	13	364	364	330	1366	142	610	204	1052	19	82	1:08:55

[a] The numbers in the third and fourth columns appear to relate to the numbers of pages of score in each reel. "Sketch" in this context refers to a complete short score.

KORNGOLD AND THE HOLLYWOOD STUDIO SYSTEM   35

An unusual (and undated) document in the Korngold Collection lists the orchestrators for the first five reels of *Devotion*, the biopic of the Brontë sisters. Significantly while the names of scenes are written in an unknown hand, the list of orchestrators is penned by Korngold.[38] Whether this represents the assignment of duties or merely the recording of a situation decided by Forbstein is unclear. Only four cues were assigned to Toch—including the scene of Miss Branwell in the village (1B), and an early meeting between Emily Brontë and Mr. Nicholls (3D)—though Toch also contributed to the main title (from Rehearsal Figure 11 onward). He was initially set for cue 2B (the scene at the inn featuring a drunk Branwell Brontë) but was replaced by Hugo Friedhofer (a cross is against his name on the Library of Congress list), and it seems Korngold signaled to Toch that they were not musically sympathetic.[39] As a result, on March 26, 1943, Toch wrote a rather formal letter to Korngold in German, evidently concerned about the amount or type of work he had been given, and indicating that Korngold had suggested there was a fundamental incompatibility between the two musicians.[40] Toch was not used again for any future Korngold project. Other music-department collaborators included Murray Cutter, and Jack Scholl, both of whom contributed to *Deception*.[41] In short, the process of orchestration involved substantial collaboration between Korngold and numerous creative artists.[42]

The next stage in the process after the creation of an orchestrated full score involved the preparation by a copyist of a reduction, generally described as a "piano-conductor" score. This could be easily reproduced in multiple copies and used by those involved in the recording.[43] Orchestral parts bearing the various identifying numbering systems were also prepared and could be written on a variety of manuscript paper.[44] Recording of the score (which took place in so-called scoring sessions) occurred on the Scoring Stage at the north end of Avenue D at the intersection with First Street, with Korngold conducting the Warner Bros. orchestra using the orchestrator's full scores. Further changes to cues were

---

[38]   LOC, Box D Folder 23.

[39]   Toch's full score for the cue, with Korngold's annotations, can be found in LOC, Box 73 Folder 4.

[40]   LOC, Box D Folder 22.

[41]   Scholl wrote the music to a radio commercial to words by M. K. Jerome for a fictitious cleaning product called Drawrof. Scholl had also written the lyrics for the choral numbers in *The Sea Hawk* (including "Strike for the shores of Dover," which was officially titled "The Freedom," and the final cue 13J).

[42]   If necessary, Korngold could even step in to orchestrate a cue himself. In *The Sea Wolf*, for instance, he orchestrated a number of short cues, such as 11C ("Van Weyden dies").

[43]   For some films, multiple copies of these sources are extant.

[44]   On rare occasions, the manuscript paper of the orchestral parts could be reused for another film. The reverse side of some orchestral parts for cue 46 in *Captain Blood* were reused for Heinz Roehmheld's score for the film *I Married a Doctor* (dir. Archie Mayo, 1936). Moreover, some of the manuscript paper used for parts for *Another Dawn* in WBA bears the inscription "Property of Selznick International Pictures, Inc. and/or Pioneer Pictures, Inc. No. 112."

also made on the Scoring Stage, often notated in the full score in Korngold's red pencil, and as a result, working days could be long. On *The Adventures of Robin Hood*, a violinist noted on their part that the recording on Sunday April 3, 1938, did not finish until midnight,[45] while the number of recording hours for *The Sea Hawk* in sessions between April 20 and June 18, 1940, totaled 58.[46] Surviving orchestral parts annotated by the clarinetist and saxophonist Teddy Krise often reveal further information. For instance, on *Another Dawn*, the dates that Krise noted on his parts indicate that scoring sessions took place on January 11, 1937, followed by January 13, 20, 23, and 26, and February 9 and 18.[47] Since Krise appears to have been involved in nearly all the cues recorded, it seems that these were perhaps the only scoring sessions for this particular film. Moreover, the dates reveal that although some of the earliest parts of the score were recorded first, recording did not proceed in strict order: thus, cue numbers 30–34 were recorded on January 23 and 26 before cue numbers 20–24, which were recorded on February 9.[48]

An Executive Relationship: Korngold and Hal Wallis

As we have seen, Korngold's working practices involved frequent collaboration and cooperation with members of the Music Department, under the overall supervision of department chief Leo Forbstein; however, Korngold was also required to work closely with studio executives. Although he had a social relationship with studio head Jack Warner, undoubtedly the most senior figure with whom the composer engaged on a regular basis was Hal B. Wallis. At the time when Korngold worked for Warners, the studio operated under a producer-unit system, in which production was divided into specialist units headed by an individual producer who from 1937 would receive "Associate Producer" credits. Thus, Associate Producer Lou Edelman made "headliners" (drawn from contemporary news events), while Bryan Foy looked after the studio's B pictures, and Henry Blanke produced prestige pictures such as biopics. Directors, stars, and other personnel also clustered around these units. Overseeing the whole

---

[45] Winters, *Korngold's* The Adventures of Robin Hood, 151. The fact that the time was recorded might seem to suggest that working so late was an unusual occurrence for the orchestra.

[46] See https://www.schubertiademusic.com/collections/autographs-manuscripts-archive/products/17487-korngold-erich-wolfgang-1897-1957-friedman-irving-izzy-1903-1981-the-sea-hawk-inscribed-presentation-copy-of-dye-line-film-score-with-amqs-and-original-photographs (accessed October 17, 2024).

[47] The orchestral parts are held in WBA.

[48] For Krise's recording dates for *Robin Hood*, see Winters, *Korngold's* The Adventures of Robin Hood, 150–151.

enterprise, however, was Wallis, who had ultimate control of all these producer units, though understandably he paid particular attention to the prestige films on which Korngold typically worked. His input on a film could be forensic, and gaining the trust of Wallis was essential to the success of a composer's career at Warner Bros.

Korngold is mentioned in Wallis's autobiography as part of a series of reminiscences about the importance of music to the pictures made by Warners in the 1930s, where he is contrasted (typically, it must be said) with Max Steiner:

> Reinhardt's conductor and arranger [for *A Midsummer Night's Dream*] was a roly-poly opera composer named Erich Wolfgang Korngold, an imposing name for an imposing and enchanting human being. He came to Hollywood to supervise the score of *Dream* and we became very good friends.
>
> I used him again on *Captain Blood.* His rousing music caught the spirit and tempo of the pirate days magnificently . . . While Korngold was in Hollywood [working on *The Adventures of Robin Hood*] he heard that the Nazis were in Vienna and had seized his home. . . . Korngold's misfortune became our good fortune. He stayed on to do memorable work for us. . . . I was impressed with his genius from the time I first met him at Reinhardt's castle near Salzburg in 1934. . . . Korngold's work was on an operatic level; Max Steiner was expert in commercial program music. They were both indispensable to the success of our pictures in the thirties.[49]

Undoubtedly, the contrast Wallis notes between Korngold and Steiner may be an example of the kind of mythologizing that surrounds the discourse of the "art music" composer in a commercial world—though Wallis's admiration for both composers is evident in his comments.[50] Such mythologizing threatens to obscure more than it reveals, however, in that it resists proper interrogation of a composer's creative role: in maintaining neat dividing lines between an authentic genius and the work of an "expert" commercial musician, it ignores the important ways in which a figure like Korngold might adapt his art to suit his surroundings. It is possible that this image of elevated artistry shapes, in part, Wallis's respectful recollections, though it is equally apparent that an element of friendship characterized their relationship. In a more contemporary source, Korngold refers in his 1940 article "Some Experiences in Film Music"

---

[49] Wallis and Higham, *Starmaker*, 36–37.
[50] See the Introduction. Also see my chapter "The Composer and the Studio: Korngold and Warner Bros.," in *The Cambridge Companion to Film Music*, ed. Mervyn Cooke and Fiona Ford (Cambridge: Cambridge University Press, 2016), 51–66.

38 KORNGOLD IN AMERICA

to his harmonious relationship with "the executive producer," who "always calls me in for the running of the picture's final cut and I am invited to voice my opinion for or against proposed changes, and I may make suggestions myself."[51]

Despite Wallis's remembered fondness for the composer, though, archival evidence suggests their relationship was not always so harmonious—or, at least, that it followed the normal tensions that characterized any working relationship in the high-pressure environment of a Hollywood movie studio. Korngold, of course, would be unlikely to mention this in a published article in which he is participating in the construction of his own public image. It appears, though, from contemporary documents that it took a while for composer and executive producer to fully trust one another. During their first project together, *A Midsummer Night's Dream*, Wallis sought to establish the balance of power. Despite the composer's potential star quality, which Warners would recognize and exploit in surrounding publicity for the film,[52] Wallis had noted as part of a long memo dated December 31, 1934:

> Another thing I am concerned about is the fact that KORNGOLD is stepping in too much as to how people should speak and how it is going to fit in with his music, and I would rather not have him on the set at all if this is going to be the case. He knows nothing whatever about pictures, and I don't want him to have any say at all in how the people are to speak, or whether they are to speak like fairies or anything of the kind. All I want him to concern himself with is the music.[53]

Wallis had been worried about aspects of the "artistic" and artificially theatrical nature of director Max Reinhardt's vision, particularly as it related to sound. As he put it, "The dailies are beautiful so far as composition, photography, and action is concerned, but we must hear these people and know what they are talking about, and we must also keep them moving."[54] Moreover, Wallis had been concerned by Korngold's requests to special-effects guru Fred Jackman to accomplish a shot in a certain timeframe in order to fit with his music. In a memo

---

[51] The article has recently been reproduced with an introduction by Daniel Goldmark in *Korngold and His World*, ed. Daniel Goldmark and Kevin C. Karnes (Princeton, NJ: Princeton University Press, 2019), 247–254.

[52] Korngold makes an onscreen appearance in the short film, *A Dream Comes True*, which documents aspects of the production. See Nathan Platte, "Dream Analysis: Korngold, Mendelssohn, and Musical Adaptations in Warner Bros.' *A Midsummer Night's Dream* (1935)," *19th-Century Music* 34, no. 3 (Spring 2011): 232–233.

[53] Ibid.: 217.

[54] Memo from Hal Wallis to Henry Blanke and William Dieterle, December 31, 1934, WBA, "A MIDSUMMER NIGHT'S DREAM" Memos and Correspondence. All other memos concerning *Dream* mentioned in this chapter can be found in these eight folders.

of December 27, 1934, to Henry Blanke, Wallis was clear about the extent of Korngold's role and the degree to which he was permitted to interfere with creative decisions taken by others:

> It is my understanding that in arranging the schedule for the pre-scoring job, KORNGOLD cut out a certain amount of music, and this of course should not have been done. I realize that we had to have play-back music on the set for certain portions of it, but to ask JACKMAN to stick within the limitations of a certain number of bars of music for the trick shots that he is going to do is going to hurt the picture. In other words, in order for him to fit in with KORNGOLD's music we are going to sacrifice some great effects, and this we absolutely will not do. ... Unless you can you have this understood with [co-director, William] DIETERLE very clearly I am going to have to call a meeting with everyone concerned, as I don't want DIETERLE telling anybody that he has so many feet in which to do a certain thing, as the picture is not going to be made on that basis.

By January 16, 1935, Korngold was still causing problems by insisting that a muffled recording of James Cagney (Bottom) singing be used for playback in opposition to the wishes of Nathan Levinson, George Groves, and Dave Forrest—and, above all, Wallis. Reinhardt's co-director William Dieterle had evidently hedged his bets and agreed to try the scene with both the muffled recording and a clearer one, which evidently did not satisfy Korngold; however, Dieterle used the muffled recording first and was happy with it, whereupon Levinson repeated his concerns about the film's sound and the recording of dialogue. On January 24, Wallis summoned Blanke to a meeting the following morning to talk about Cagney's singing scene. It is not hard to imagine that Blanke received a dressing down for not controlling Dieterle, who was evidently too respectful of the wishes of Korngold for Wallis's liking.

Korngold also appeared to overstep the mark in other ways: on January 28, studio manager Bill Koenig informed Blanke that Korngold had "notified Miss [Nini] Theilade [the Fairie attending Titania] that she will have to stay until we finish with her. This is not true ... Tell Mr Korngold not to bother her about staying after [February 10], as this is the date we have definitely agreed upon." By February 6, Wallis demanded a meeting with Forbstein, Blanke, and Korngold to "get it all straightened out." Even after his work on the film was complete, Wallis's (perhaps only mild) irritation with Korngold continued. A memo from Wallis dated September 9, 1935, to Major Levinson of the Sound Department reads: "Despite our instructions to the effect that 'MIDSUMMER NIGHT'S DREAM' wasn't to be run for anyone without the okay of MR WARNER or myself, I found KORNGOLD up in my projection room, running the first reel of the picture ... Why did you want this run for KORNGOLD, and who okayed it?"

In the early years of their relationship, then, Wallis appeared to maintain closer supervision of Korngold's activity (often via department head Leo Forbstein) than is apparent in later films, possibly as a direct result of some of the difficulties encountered on *Dream*. For example, Wallis had to insist that Korngold score *Another Dawn* in 1937, an assignment that Korngold was contractually obliged to take in spite of his evident reservations. In a remarkable memo to Forbstein dated November 23, 1936, Wallis laid down the law in typically forthright fashion in a way that belies the supposed special status that biographers later insisted Korngold enjoyed: "I want KORNGOLD to start working on scoring 'ANOTHER DAWN' immediately. I don't want him to see any more pictures. There is no reason for him to look at some pictures to make a selection, as the only picture I want him to do is 'ANOTHER DAWN,' so let's get down to business."[55]

In fact, the mechanisms via which Korngold could be assigned to a project varied over time, and they reveal something of his growing importance to the studio.[56] By March 10, 1941, for instance, Korngold's letter to Hal Wallis about his ideas for *The Constant Nymph* reveals a much stronger working relationship that could even bypass Forbstein as department chief:

> I do not know whether or not you will entrust me with the musical assignment for this film. But since I have read the original script and have also seen the English picture,[57] I ask your indulgence for the purely musical suggestion I would like to submit to you.... How would it be this time to have the creation of an *opera*, whose overwhelming final love duet would unravel before our eyes in its first performance, and which would re-awaken in the conducting composer his love for the Constant Nymph—suddenly and irresistibly?[58]

Neither the opera proposal, nor Korngold's other plot suggestions, were taken up, but he did eventually receive the assignment, and as such produced a symphonic poem for the film's fictional composer (Lewis Dodd) to write. The composer's involvement with *Kings Row* also seems to have been at the direct behest of Wallis, perhaps as a result of difficulties with the original plans for the end of the film.

---

[55] WBA, "ANOTHER DAWN" STORY—MEMOS & CORRESPONDENCE 1 of 2 1706B.

[56] Nathan Platte reveals the irritation felt by Max Steiner when, having scored the Paul Muni vehicle *The Life of Emile Zola* (dir. William Dieterle, 1937), he lost to Korngold the scoring of *Juarez*, a similar biopic also directed by William Dieterle and starring Muni. See *Making Music in Selznick's Hollywood* (New York: Oxford University Press, 2018), 155.

[57] It is unclear whether Korngold refers to the 1928 silent version directed by Adrian Brunel starring Ivor Novello as Lewis Dodd, or more likely the 1933 film directed by Basil Dean with Brian Aherne playing Dodd.

[58] WBA, "THE CONSTANT NYMPH"—MEMOS & CORRESPONDENCE 1/20/40–7/11/341, 1of 2.

In June 1941, Leo Forbstein had written to Victor Blau of the Legal Department asking about the intention to use a musical setting of "Invictus" by Bruno Huhn, noting, "While the script does not call for visual uses of this number, the director, Mr [Sam] Wood may want to show voices singing, or may want to use it only instrumentally."[59] This matter had not been resolved by August 21, when Jack Warner cabled Blau: "HAVE READ YOUR CORRESPONDENCE REFERENCE INVICTUS. . . . WE IN DIFFICULT SPOT AS COMPLETE END OF OUR PICTURE KING'S ROW HAS BEEN BULT UP TO THESE LYRICS AS WELL AS MUSIC AND WOULD BE PATCHED UP JOB IF WE HAD TO WRITE OUR OWN MUSIC IRRESPECTIVE BEING ABLE TP [sic] BUY IT FOR $150.00."[60] Korngold may have been suggested by Wallis as a way out of Warner's "difficult position." In any case, Korngold's name does not appear in studio correspondence until September 25, 1941, when Wallis asked Leo Forbstein specifically: "I asked you the other day to get in touch with KORNGOLD about starting to work on 'KINGS ROW,' and you were going to talk to him and let me know. I have not heard from you. What has happened?"[61] Forbstein's reply is not on file, but there is a handwritten letter from Korngold to Wallis dated October 13, in which he thanks Wallis for the assignment, praises the film—which he says he knows pretty well—and asks Wallis whether "you want me with you, when you are running "Kings Row" for the first time (as you did in the past)."[62]

Although their relationship undoubtedly developed in later years, Wallis appeared to maintain an initial mistrust of Korngold's talents in his first forays into film scoring, though that may be entirely appropriate for a composer considered inexperienced in the movie industry. Having agreed to score *Captain Blood*, for instance, Korngold was provided with a detailed set of music spotting notes by Wallis dated November 11, 1935. These are the only extant set of notes in connection with a Korngold-scored film, and this occasion may conceivably have been the only time that Wallis provided them for the composer.[63] Certainly, there is evidence that Wallis provided music notes for composers on other productions—those for *Casablanca* are often remarked upon[64]—though they pale in comparison with the very detailed and extensive spotting notes written by David O. Selznick for his composers, and which Nathan Platte has discussed

---

[59] WBA, 735–747A "KINGS ROW" 1121.

[60] Ibid.

[61] WBA, "KINGS ROWS" STORY MEMOS 1 of 2, 2022A.

[62] Ibid.

[63] There are music spotting notes for *Escape Me Never* termed a "Music Plot," though these have Production Manager Tenny Wright's name attached to them and are much less detailed. WBA, "ESCAPE ME NEVER" STORY—MUSIC PLOT 1885B.

[64] See, for example, Rudy Behlmer, *Inside Warner Bros. (1935–51)* (London: Weidenfeld and Nicolson, 1986), 216, and Aljean Harmetz, *Round up the Usual Suspects: The Making of Casablanca - Bogart, Bergman and World War II* (London: Weidenfeld and Nicolson, 1993), 259–260.

in great detail.[65] The *Captain Blood* notes were sent to Forbstein, Korngold, Amy, Hal McCord, and Levinson, and although they were not followed to the letter, they undoubtedly shaped Korngold's work. On November 11, Wallis had also written to supervisor Harry Joe Brown about some added shots, and in talking of the scene following the dumping of the plantation-owner and chief antagonist Colonel Bishop overboard by Blood and his men, Wallis makes clear the importance of his conception of music: "NOTE: The following scenes are to be augmented with music which builds finally to an ecstatic climax." He then offers a basic outline of music's relationship with the narrative in this scene:

> MED SHOT (STOCK) MEN
> Climbing the rigging. (The music is building now.)
> . . .
> CLOSEUP BLOOD
> He looks toward the rigging
> (music builds more and more.)
> . . .
> The ship is under way. CAMERA PANS from the water line up
> to the top of the rigging.
> (The music builds.)
> LONG SHOT THE SHIP (STOCK)
> as it sails away.
> (The music hits a climax.)[66]

Moreover, with *Captain Blood*, Wallis continued to monitor Korngold's work closely as scoring proceeded. The recording had finished on Sunday, December 8. On Tuesday, December 10, though, Wallis reviewed the film prior to its planned preview on the Wednesday and produced two pages of cutting notes, with extensive mentions of music. The first page is reproduced in Kalinak's *Settling the Score*.[67] The second page includes the following instructions:

> Lose the chord when ERROL FLYNN is standing by the rail and says "Here come the Spaniards! That's what we've waited for!" End that chord before he speaks, and then there's another chord right after that on another piece of dialogue, and take that one out entirely.

---

[65] On *Since You Went Away* (dir. John Cromwell, 1941), for instance, Platte notes that Selznick "had largely determined the film's spotting before Steiner even arrived." Platte, *Making Music*, 231.

[66] WBA, "CAPTAIN BLOOD" STORY—MEMOS 4 of 4. SPECIAL 1788.

[67] Kathryn Kalinak, *Settling the Score: Music and the Classical Hollywood Film* (Madison: University of Wisconsin Press, 1992), 77.

KORNGOLD AND THE HOLLYWOOD STUDIO SYSTEM   43

Lose the music where COL. BISHOP starts off the deck and goes out to the Cince Logus.... [*sic*] That whole first chord, lose that whole strain there.

The music when BLOOD's ship sails, we keep all the music in, but every time BLOOD gives a command or there is any dialogue from WOLVERSTONE or PITT, or any of them, drop the music way down and bring the voices up, and then raise the music when the dialogue is over.

Hold the music down on the dialogue between BLOOD and his men in the cabin, when they strike the English ship, and bring it right up as soon as the dialogue stops and we go into the silent action ... [*sic*] bring the music up and we hear it full, but under the dialogue, let's hear the dialogue.

Hold the music down where LEVASSEUR says "My Captain, what a pair we would make!," and through this whole scene now, subordinate the music.

Lose the little piece of music in the scene with DeHAVILAND [*sic*] and STEPHENSON on the boat.... [*sic*] on the deck of the boat.

Put in the singing voices that we made where the men are raising the anchor with the Captain. Don't use the old sound track; Get singers in and have them sing in the same rhythm and tempo that the music is scored in this spot.

Take out the couple of chords of music where he passes the girl on the desert island, and where after WILLOUGHBY says "Who might [page 3] that be do you suppose?" and the girl says "That is CAPTAIN BLOOD." Take out the little chord of music there.

In the dawn sequence that starts with the miniature, we take out the music. The music starts with the first bugle.

Where FLYNN is talking with the girl, where he makes the bargain and says "I'm no longer your slave," take out those sound effects. Leave the music.

On all music leading up to the actual start of the battle, where the boats are creeping up to the French boats and they are preparing and all of that, hold the music down until BLOOD says "Tear down the French flag and hoist our own colors!," and when the English flag goes up, let that phrase come up with the flag, and from then on carry the music, but every time that there is dialogue, or commands, or dialogue between principals, hold the music way down and let the dialogue come up.[68]

This kind of extensive engagement with music, it subsequently transpired, was unusual for a Korngold-scored film and together with the spotting notes suggest an executive not yet ready to fully trust his inexperienced composer. At least one of the cutting notes appears to relate to an instruction in the spotting notes that was not followed. In referring to the necessity to subordinate the music in the scene in which Levasseur and Blood discuss their partnership ("My Captain,

---

[68] WBA, "CAPTAIN BLOOD" STORY—MEMOS 4 of 4. SPECIAL 1788.

44 KORNGOLD IN AMERICA

what a pair we would make!") Wallis's original instruction (spotting note 26) had been to "stop the music." In other words, had Korngold stuck to the original instruction in the spotting notes, the change specified in the cutting notes would not have been necessary.

Wallis also requested extensive music changes to the very film Korngold was seemingly reluctant to score, *Another Dawn*, belying the truth of one of the foundational myths of Korngold's work for Warner Bros.: that his music would not be "tampered" with. When comparing the surviving versions of the film with the manuscript sources, it becomes apparent that large parts of the score were cut, likely as a direct result of Wallis's cutting notes of February 24, 1937.[69] This is a remarkable document since—in contradistinction to the cutting notes associated with other films on which Korngold worked—most of the three pages of notes concern music. Wallis admittedly often simply asks for the music to be "held down" so that dialogue can more easily be heard, though this itself perhaps reveals Korngold's relative inexperience at this time in writing music to underscore Hollywood dialogue; however, on many occasions he also asks the notes' recipients (editor Ralph Dawson, editorial supervisor Hal McCord, supervisor Harry Joe Brown, and George Groves of the Sound Department) to "take out" or "lose" music, or even to "rescore." It is this latter instruction that likely accounts for an additional scoring session held on March 3. Some of the changes are no longer apparent since the scenes themselves appear to have been cut, including a sequence between Roark and Julia in an automobile—such is the difficulty in trying to reconstruct the process of scoring.[70] Of the scenes that survive in the cut of the film available in home entertainment formats, however, there are a large number that originally had Korngold's music, and which now no longer do.[71] Wallis's notes are so draconian in comparison with the relatively minor changes that occurred in the composer's later scores that they warrant quoting at length:

and then when Flynn goes to get the horse for Francis, stop the music, and when Flynn laughs, don't have any music. Then start the music again when the scene starts after the laughter and the reaction of Francis on that horse business.

When Flynn and Hunter say, "Let's go into the other room and see if the girls have finished their unpacking," there is a music start there now. Take out the

---

[69] Wallis was in the habit of dictating these cutting notes at home on a Dictaphone machine. See Wallis and Charles Higham, *Starmaker*, 40.

[70] It is also not always apparent whether the versions of the films available today on home entertainment formats bare much resemblance to various contemporaneous edits. This is particularly the case with roadshow films, where extra footage (in addition to extra music) may have been available.

[71] Warner Bros. Archive Collection DVD.

music to the fadeout and don't have any more music until the next sequence at the post.

… when we dissolve to the two of them seated on the settee, dissolve into the same scene that is in there now, it's better with music, but do it with just a few instruments as it would be actually played. Don't do it with an orchestra. Rescore this section up to the point of where it goes into the love scene and then let the music dissolve into the love scene as played with an orchestra as it is now.

When we fade in on the post again and they are playing Cricket, lose that whole piece of music. Play it silent. Play it the way it is with sound effects.

Lose the music in the sequence where Flynn is trying to tie his tie.

After Hunter leaves Francis at the door and says good-night to her, take out those first few bars of music and just pick it up where that phrase starts …

In rescoring the garden sequence, we will retain the present scene but do it with violins, cut out all the brass and drums, and when Francis points off and says, "Look," and we pan around the garden, we'll dissolve there into the love scene played very softly and carry that right through.

When Francis and Flynn are sitting on the settee where they kiss, rescore that section from there on until the fade out. Don't have the music built up into such a crescendo after the kiss …

We will have music scored under the long shot of the desert and over the insert and the music stops when Julia comes in.

FORGET THE INSERT. We'll dissolve from a long shot of the desert—a peaceful shot of the desert—to the living room and Julia comes in and Flynn says "I'm making an application for transfer" and we'll score the exterior shot and just the cross-over of Julia and where she sits down and starts to talk we'll lose the music …

Lose the music in the morning where he says "Has Colonel Roark reported yet" where he walks over to the map. Take it out entirely.

Lose the music in the last part of the sequence just before the fade out.

Take out all the music where Hunter is coming over to see Francis in her room.

We stop the music where we leave Flynn and Francis and we start the music again when we cut back to them. …

Take the music out with the knock on the door …

When the orderly says "The Colonel wants to see you in his quarters" hold on him as long as you do now and then lap dissolve to the shot where you see Flynn coming in to Hunter and Hunter is standing at his desk and take out all of the music.

We will score the insert only. Take out all the other music. Just score the insert and don't score it with that heavy music …

46 KORNGOLD IN AMERICA

> Take the music out in the scene with Hunter and Flynn where they toss the coin...
>
> When we cut to Hunter up in the plane, cut the music out and let's just hear a loud roar of the plane...
>
> Rescore the finish in the morning and don't build it up so heavy.[72]

Although not all of the above changes were made, significant portions of Korngold's score simply disappeared from the film. The story centers around a woman (Julia) who, still in love with a dead aviator, marries an army officer (Col. John Wister) out of friendship and returns with him to the fictional colony of Dikut. There she falls in love with his deputy (Capt. Denny Roark). For the scene in which newly married Julia first hears Roark laugh—thus reminding her of the love she lost (Duncan Hitchen) and confirming her attraction to him—Korngold had included an entirely appropriate sequential repetition of the first phrase of the love theme.[73] This section plays to silence in the surviving cut, as do many of the other sequences indicated above, including those for the cricket game and the scene in which Errol Flynn's character (Roark) is frustratedly adjusting his bow tie. Although Wallis's notes are certainly not as extensive as those often found for Selznick's pictures, Korngold had been considered by Selznick as a potential composer for *The Prisoner of Zenda* around this time, an assignment that was ultimately undertaken by Alfred Newman. Platte suggests that it "is hard to imagine Korngold welcoming Selznick's hands-on instructions or Selznick indulging Korngold's 'Great Composer' exceptionalism"—yet it appears as though Korngold at this time was well used to such matters in his interactions with Hal Wallis.[74]

Undoubtedly, Wallis grew to trust Korngold's instincts and experience more in later years. 1939's *Juarez*, for example, suffered a disastrous preview performance,[75] and thus warranted an extensive set of cutting notes. Unlike *Another Dawn*, however, the music largely escaped Wallis's ire. Undoubtedly, the extensive cuts asked for by Wallis changed aspects of Korngold's score, yet aside from adjusting the balance of the music, the notes mention cutting music only once, in stark contrast to the *Another Dawn* notes of two years previously.[76] Having said that, music exists in manuscript form for scenes that survive in the film without music, so Korngold material was certainly cut at some point, though whether

[72] WBA, "ANOTHER DAWN" STORY—MEMOS & CORRESPONDENCE 1 of 2, 1706B.

[73] This is presented in E major and then in B flat major (for Korngold, a typical tritone harmonic relationship). See Reh. Fig. 12 in cue number 12.

[74] Platte, *Making Music*, 118.

[75] Bernard F. Dick, *Hal Wallis: Producer to the Stars* (Lexington: University Press of Kentucky, 2004), 53.

[76] LOC, Box B Folder 21. The note reads, "Take out the run of music when he blows the light out, but let the rest of it continue"; however, since it is not clear to which surviving scene this note refers, it is possible that the film changed further and that this scene no longer survives.

on Wallis's explicit instructions it is impossible to say.[77] Extant cutting notes are relatively rare for Korngold's films, and the only mention of music in Wallis's cutting notes for *The Sea Wolf* (dated February 20, 1941) was a note to "Clean up the music a little in the fight in the forecastle."[78] Evidently, the situation with *Another Dawn*'s score was unlikely to occur again. Nonetheless, other scores reveal cuts that might suggest the presence of no longer extant cutting notes. In a large number of scenes in *Kings Row*, for instance, Korngold's manuscripts provide much more music than survives today: some cues stop apparently halfway through, whereas in other cues there are gaps in the film where what was provided would have filled the time between two patches of music. It would seem logical to assume, then, that this music was recorded, and subsequently cut—though on whose instructions it is folly to speculate.[79]

A couple of weeks after Wallis cut so much from the *Another Dawn* score, he was perhaps forced by outside factors to reassesses the prowess of Korngold as a film composer. On March 4, 1937, the score for *Anthony Adverse* won the Academy Award in the Music (Scoring) category for the Music Department, an award that was gratefully accepted by Leo Forbstein on the department's behalf.[80] As Hugo Friedhofer later claimed, "if you've got an Academy Award and couple of nominations under your belt, [producers] begin to trust you."[81] Perhaps as a result of this public acknowledgment of Korngold's skill as a film composer, an attempt was made after the scoring of *Another Dawn* was complete to market some of Korngold's music from the film as a popular song. On March 18, 1937, Wallis wrote to lyricist Al Dubin, copying in Forbstein and composer/lyricist Art Schwartz, asking him to write lyrics for a Korngold melody "so that we can issue the song commercially, as I feel that it can be very popular and will be a big plug for the picture."[82] Evidently, Wallis didn't indicate which melody should be used, and Dubin wrote back to tell him:

---

[77] For instance, cue 10D, a scene between Carlota and Maximilian, was originally scored with the love theme. Only when Bazaine hands over his message, however, does the music in the surviving film start (Reh. Fig. 7 in the cue).

[78] WBA, "THE SEA WOLF" STORY—MEMOS & CORRESPONDENCE 1 OF 3.

[79] Cue 3B, for example, in which Parris bids Dr. Tower goodbye and sees first Cassie and then Drake, cuts the middle part of the cue (from Reh. Figs. 9 to 13) when Drake utters his line "How's Cassie?" The cue then picks up at Reh. Fig. 13 after Drake informs Parris that Louise is the girl he wants to marry. Other cuts were made to 1D, 1E, 1F, 1G, 2A, 2B, 3D, 4C, 4D, 4E, 5A, 6B, 10C.

[80] Although this caused tension between Korngold and Forbstein, it was standard practice for the time. Forbstein, recognizing the delicacy of the situation, attempted to give the award to Korngold privately, which prompted a terse letter in response, LOC, Box A Folder 13. The tension clearly did not last long, and their friendship blossomed in later years, with the pair exchanging birthday greetings and presents. Forbstein was evidently a horse-racing fan, and Korngold appears to have bought him a "horse plaque" birthday gift from the Hollywood Trophy Company in October 1941 at a cost of $11.63 engraved with a message: "DEAR LEO: MAY THIS HORSE WIN EVERY RACE FOR YOU. ERICH." LOC, Box C Folder 6.

[81] Atkins, *Oral History*, 101.

[82] WBA, "ANOTHER DAWN" STORY—MEMOS & CORRESPONDENCE 1 of 2, 1706B.

48   KORNGOLD IN AMERICA

> Received your note requesting a lyric for "Another Dawn." Have spent the afternoon trying to get the music for same, but Forbstein informs me that there is no melody in there suitable for a commercial song.
>
> I finally had Schwartz get music from Korngold, but he sent over an intermezzo, and I hesitated to ask him to boil this down to the length of a popular song as I know he is a great artist and operatic composer and might have felt offended.
>
> Would suggest that you ask him to extract from his melody what he wishes used as a verse and chorus for a song and then he may be able to do something, though I am sure that no one but an operatic singer could sing a song with such a range, and it would naturally limit the radio plugs, but nevertheless, I am willing to do it; though you must not expect too much from the song insofar as commercial value is concerned.[83]

Schwartz also wrote back to Wallis the same day, noting that in its present form, "[the number] is very rough as the tempo changes and the theme wanders. I am having the number boiled down and we will see how it sounds in a more commercial form."[84] Wallis, though, was unperturbed, and wrote to Forbstein the following day asking him to "follow through on the matter of the song. . . . as I feel that the song has possibilities and that we can do something with it."[85] By March 31, the day of a press preview of the film with buffet supper afterward (instead of the more customary open preview), the Music Department had a commercial song titled "Another Dawn" with melody by Korngold and lyric by Dubin; however, the composer was not entirely happy and spoke to Wallis about it. As Wallis informed Forbstein: "Korngold told me he had another change to make on the commercial number 'ANOTHER DAWN.' There were a few phrases to be cut out or something. He was going to fiz[z] it up. Will you follow through on this and see that he completes this so that you can send it in to New York for publication. Also, when it is completed, I would like to hear it."[86]

It is perhaps unsurprising that Korngold was not entirely pleased, given his lack of experience with such forms. For all his melodic gifts, his experience with Viennese theatrical life, and his recent work with Oscar Hammerstein for the Jan Kiepura and Gladys Swarthout vehicle at Paramount, *Give Us This Night*, Wallis had not requested an operatic *Schlager*—in other words, the sort of number that could be extracted and marketed in phonographic form as sung by a classically

---

[83] Ibid. Indeed, Dubin's comments are indicative of the respect in which Korngold was held by his colleagues.

[84] Ibid.

[85] Ibid.

[86] Ibid.

trained singer, and a form of which Korngold was undoubtedly a master[87]—but something that could be recorded by popular performers. It would thus require a more forgiving vocal part. The completed song—held in the archives, marked "tempo di tango" and dated March 24—uses for its verse the "Bedouin" love song melody Korngold had written for the scene in which Rourke (Errol Flynn) and Julia (Kay Francis) are left alone to become better acquainted.[88] It is music that Rourke asks Julia to listen to, though the performing musicians are never seen, and its narrative source remains ambiguous. The chorus of the song uses as its music Julia's theme, also heard in the same scene (of which, more in Chapter 4). The sentimental lyrics, though, in using a simplistic and unimaginative rhyme scheme and in invoking moonbeams and dreams, are perhaps not Dubin's finest work. Nonetheless, the song was registered for copyright and listed as published on April 15, 1937, by Music Publishers Holding Corp., New York—twenty-five years to the day, perhaps appropriately given its apparent lack of commercial success, since the Titanic sank.

Wallis was, in all likelihood, looking to extract maximum value for money from his star composer, and the idea of Warners releasing a commercial song based on Korngold's music was to resurface in 1947 in connection with *Escape Me Never*—and to far greater success, it must be said.[89] Two original songs were written for use in the film in late 1945: "O Nene" and "Love for Love." The former had Italian lyrics written by Aldo Franchetti (for which he was paid the princely sum of $1), and an English translation by Ted Koehler. Koehler also supplied the lyrics for "Love for Love." Commercial recordings were subsequently made of "Love for Love" by Andy Russell with Paul Weston and his Orchestra, by Fran Warren with Claude Thornhill's Orchestra, by Vaughan Monroe and his Orchestra, and by Hal MacIntyre and his Orchestra (with a vocal by Frankie Lester).[90] The reasons why Korngold's commercial song-writing efforts were apparently more successful in the mid-1940s than a decade previously are not

---

[87] A notable example of this was the Lute song, "Glück, das mir verblieb" from *Die tote Stadt*. See Benjamin Goose's "Opera for Sale: Folksong, Sentimentality, and the Market," *Journal of the Royal Musical Association* 133, no. 2 (2008): 189–219.

[88] WBA, "ANOTHER DAWN" PUBLICITY—MISCELLANEOUS.

[89] Korngold had, admittedly, produced more popular numbers before. "Du bist mein Traum," for instance, was taken from the operetta he had arranged for Richard Tauber, *Das Lied der Liebe*. It had been published in English as "You Haunt My Heart" and recorded by James Melton as RCA Victor 18466-A and in 1941 by Lanny Ross as Victor 27723.

[90] Andy Russell's version was released by Capitol Records in October 1947 as the B-side of "Muchachita" (Armengol-Fernandez-Arnheim). Capitol Records 15006. See https://www.discogs.com/Andy-Russell-Muchachita-Love-For-Love/release/6020687 (accessed February 8, 2021). Vaughn Monroe's version (RCA Victor 20-2514) was released with a B-side of "Baby Be Good" (Ryerson-Eaton-Moore). See https://www.discogs.com/Vaughn-Monroe-And-His-Orchestra-Love-For-Love-Baby-Be-Good/release/2110512 (accessed February 8, 2021). Fran Warren's version was released on Columbia 37940, and Hal MacIntyre's on MGM 10090 with "Jumpin' Jubilee" (Hurd) as a B-side. https://www.discogs.com/it/Hal-McIntyre-And-His-Orchestra-Love-For-Love-Jumpin-Jubilee/release/5970904 (accessed February 8, 2021). All were released in 1947.

50 KORNGOLD IN AMERICA

easily accounted for, though the fact that "Love for Love" and "O Nene" had both been written to be performed as songs in the film rather than adapted from other material is surely significant. Nonetheless, Wallis's desire to explore the possibilities of marketing Korngold as a "song composer" in 1937 perhaps speak to the wariness that appears to characterize the early relationship between Korngold and Warner studio executives. Korngold was also asked to help out with other composers' projects early on in his career, as a contracted asset who could be used wherever he might be needed. Once work on *Anthony Adverse* finished in early April 1936, for instance, Wallis immediately assigned him to uncredited work on *The Green Pastures*, the score of which consisted mostly of African-American spirituals sung by the Hall Johnson choir.[91] It is also likely that the small amount of work Korngold did to assist Bernard Kaun and Heinz Roemheld on *Hearts Divided* was completed in this period, given that the film was previewed on June 3, 1936, a month before *The Green Pastures*, and the score was being recorded in mid–late April 1936. Consulting the manuscript full score for *Hearts Divided*, it seems that Korngold's contribution was restricted to a solitary cue in Reel 9 ("The Separation"). It is perhaps telling that Korngold's uncredited involvement with both *The Green Pastures* and *Hearts Divided* came early in his career with Warners, and suggests that Wallis was making full use of the composer's contracted time.

It seems, then, that Korngold's working relationship with Wallis was one characterized by initial wariness from the latter followed by growing trust. Korngold, though, also had direct contact with the producers working under Hal Wallis such as Henry Blanke, who appears to have recognized the value of the composer's opinion. When working on *The Sea Hawk*, for instance, a memo dated April 25, 1940, from Blanke to Hal Wallis suggested that both Korngold and director Michael Curtiz should attend that evening's running of the edit. Indeed, there is precious little evidence in the archives of any conflict between Korngold and these associate producers working at Warners. Only with *Devotion*'s producer, Robert Buckner, is there a suggestion of tension. On February 4, 1943, Buckner wrote to Korngold, via a Warner Bros. memo, gently and respectfully admonishing him for expressing opinions about the project, which was yet to finish shooting:

Dear Mr. Korngold:
I understand that there are parts of our picture DEVOTION which you do not like, and while you are of course fully entitled to your private opinions,

---

[91] On April 6, 1936, Hal Wallis asked Forbstein to "[b]e sure that the day after KORNGOLD finishes 'ANTHONY ADVERSE' he does whatever little music is necessary for 'GREEN PASTURES.'" WBA, "GREEN PASTURES"—Memos and Correspondence.

I would greatly appreciate it as a personal favor if you [would] not make your criticisms too public, since I have had certain reactions from them which are detrimental to the best interests of the picture.

It is somewhat embarrassing and difficult to write this note, but under the circumstances I sincerely hope you may see the dangers of too free negative criticism from the studio's point of view, particularly from those who are actively engaged in working upon it.

We are counting a great deal upon your fine work to help make this the very good picture which we believe it will be, and this note is purely between ourselves.[92]

The memo is instructive as much for what it discloses about Korngold's apparent influence within the studio by 1943 as for what it reveals about his judgement of the film. The fact that Korngold had expressed these opinions before the film was cut might even indicate he had seen some of the "dailies" (the raw unedited footage). Moreover, that Buckner felt the need to state that the note was "purely between ourselves" might indicate Korngold's active involvement in studio politics and the various creative tensions that were part and parcel of a Hollywood studio. Despite the tensions, though, the composer's reputation and abilities clearly warranted Buckner treating him with considerable respect—at least on the evidence of this one piece of written communication.

***

Producing the music for a film at Warner Bros. in this period was a complex, multi-stage process involving numerous creative interactions. Moreover, the evidence reveals that Korngold was a figure who engaged fully in this collaborative world, not an outsider who could, or did, rely on his "great composer" reputation to sidestep the more prosaic activities or relationships that required his attention. No matter how contested that reputation was within contemporary critical circles, it was, as Wallis's memoirs hint, accepted within Hollywood. Yet, it did not prevent Korngold from needing to develop productive working relationships with a range of colleagues; nor did it preclude the occasional moment of tension or need to compromise his artistic vision. The picture of Korngold's working life, then, is far from that idealized romantic-modernist "artist-philosopher" of the Nietzsche "legend" often favored by Korngold's own mythmaking and sometimes advocated by biographers. It suggests a composer fully enmeshed in a commercial world for whom working relationships were valued ones to be cultivated. It also suggests a composer able to turn his hand to a variety of

---

[92] LOC, Box D Folder 23.

assignments, to take instruction, and to make compromises to suit the project on which he worked. At the same time, though, no diminishing of artistic voice is implied here. I do not mean to suggest that this commercial or "system" worldliness should dissuade us from viewing Korngold's film scores as documents of artistic expression. Nor do I want to view them as somehow "triumphing" over commercial restrictions. Instead, I see Korngold's film scores as balancing the need to satisfy a number of priorities: the technical and generic restrictions of the medium, including the priorities of his creative collaborators; the need for artistic expression, to fulfil aspects of both the composer's own inherited view of artistry and, in all likelihood, his father's long-held sense of his son's destiny and place within an Austro-Germanic lineage; and, finally, the financial imperative to support his family. A fuller understanding of the ways in which Korngold's work in this arena was shaped by financial considerations and the more prosaic nature of schedules, however, requires a more in-depth look at his contractual agreements with Warner Bros., and it is these to which I now turn.

2

A Musician for Hire

Korngold's Contracts with Warner Bros.

Korngold's relationship with the Hollywood studio system encompassed a variety of working interactions that ranged from exchanges with studio executives and employees to the ways in which he engaged with the mechanics of the medium itself. Chapter 1 explored some of the interpersonal exchanges that arose through the normal patterns of Korngold's film-scoring work, both with orchestrators and other music-department staff, and with a studio executive like Hal Wallis. Here, though, I want to concentrate on the composer's contracts with Warner Bros., and the apparently mundane aspects of his everyday working arrangements with the studio as an institution that such documents reveal. Although he was never employed on a permanent full-time contract, Korngold signed regular agreements between 1934 and 1946, and each of them reveals something about his developing relationship with Warners. Periods of intense activity could be followed by months with no film work whatsoever, and Korngold was as a result never quite as enmeshed in the day-to-day grind of the studio system as fellow Warner Bros. staff composers Max Steiner and Adolph Deutsch—or orchestrators like Hugo Friedhofer and Simon Bucharoff. Nonetheless, in all other respects, Korngold was a composer under contract and, as such, had as much or as little autonomy as any other musician working in the collaborative atmosphere of a Hollywood movie studio in the 1930s and 1940s. This is significant in redressing one of the more persistent myths about Korngold, which concerns the apparently special terms under which he operated at Warner Bros. and which has shaped the prevailing view of the composer and his relationship with Hollywood. I set out in the Introduction the background behind the claims made for Korngold's 1938 contract. An examination of the archival copies of all the extant contracts, however, reveals no suggestion that Korngold enjoyed *carte blanche* and no contracted promises that his music would not be tampered with; indeed, the evidence provided by an examination of manuscript sources suggests quite the opposite in the case of films like *Another Dawn*, a score that as we have seen in Chapter 1 was subject to numerous cuts by studio executives. Moreover, all Korngold's agreements, including the 1938

Korngold in America. Ben Winters, Oxford University Press. © Oxford University Press 2025.
DOI: 10.1093/9780197684818.003.0003

54 KORNGOLD IN AMERICA

contract, contain the standard copyright clauses shared with other composers writing for Warner Bros.

Individually, then, Korngold's contractual agreements with the studio indicate nothing particularly unusual for a freelance artist willing only to sign on for two or three films at a time. What is perhaps more surprising is the progression of terms, or lack thereof. On the one hand, Korngold—seemingly without a personal lawyer who might advise him[1]—appears to have negotiated minor changes and the provision of benefits, such as the installation of a piano at his house and traveling expenses if required; on the other, despite an initial pay hike, from the time Korngold signed his first agreement for two or more films on May 1, 1936, to his last agreement with Warner Bros. some ten years later, his payment *did not increase at all*, remaining at a guaranteed $12,500 per film for twelve weeks' work.[2] In the case of *The Sea Wolf*, indeed, he was paid only $7,500. This persistence of terms seems somewhat remarkable for a composer of Korngold's stature whose reputation within the movie industry only grew in these years, and compares unfavorably with other musicians employed on full-time contracts at the studio, who in contrast could depend on regular pay rises. It is also surprising given the high inflation of the war years in the United States, which ran at times in double-digit percentage figures. It certainly does not suggest a movie studio desperate to bend over backwards to secure or retain his services, or indeed a composer anxious to make money. Rather, it indicates either a composer somewhat independently wealthy for whom the acquisition of money was apparently not a motivating factor for large parts of his film-scoring career, a composer unaware of his true financial value, or merely one unwilling to engage in the process of contract renegotiation.[3]

Claims of independent wealth had, admittedly, long been part of the composer's public image. In a 1937 interview published in *The Etude Music Magazine*, Verna Arvey wrote: "Fortunately, for Korngold, he is said to be wealthy in his own right. He does not need the films, or the money they bring."[4] Indeed, this might appear to reinforce that idea of the artist somewhat separated from the commercial sphere. In that sense, Korngold and his biographers might be understood to have colluded in projecting an image that they imagined would

---

[1] At least, there is no legal correspondence to indicate this.

[2] Korngold became a US citizen in 1943, yet this appears to have had no discernible effect on his earning potential or his contractual agreements with Warners.

[3] Certainly, Korngold appears to have been generous in his charitable donations. Documents in the Korngold Collection reveal that he had donated money to the American Jewish Committee in 1942 and the Associated Refugee Artist's Guild of America in May 1939, and he made donations to the United Jewish Welfare Fund in 1939 and 1940 ($500 and $300, respectively). He also contributed to a concert for Russian War Relief in 1945 conducting his *Passover Psalm*. See Erich Wolfgang Korngold Collection, Music Division, Library of Congress, Washington, DC (hereafter LOC), Box C Folder 7; Box H Folder 32; Box E Folder 12.

[4] See https://digitalcommons.gardner-webb.edu/etude/851/ (accessed October 21, 2024).

elevate him to a modernist ideal—of the artist separated from popular culture, or at least from its money. Yet, as I will continue to emphasize throughout this book, such an attitude is rooted arguably in a modernist anxiety about the devaluation of art; and, although Korngold's beliefs about artistry may have been shaped by that attitude, it is one that his music and the realities of his artistic production consistently challenged. A proper appreciation of the commercial conditions under which he operated as a musician for hire, though, is crucial to an understanding of that delicate relationship between his artistry and the financial imperatives that shaped his working patterns. For instance, it is simply not true that Korngold did not need the money that scoring provided (though it may have been the case in 1937). On several occasions he asked for an advance on his next film's salary, indicating that the income he derived from film scoring became an important revenue stream. That he did not negotiate higher fees as he grew in experience is thus all the more surprising.

Initial Agreements: 1934–1936

Korngold's introduction to the world of film came via his old friend, the director and theatrical impresario Max Reinhardt, with whom the composer had long collaborated on operetta arrangements in Europe. When Reinhardt arranged with Warner Bros. to produce a film of his Hollywood Bowl production of Shakespeare's *A Midsummer Night's Dream*, he suggested Korngold for the score, thus introducing Korngold to his first negotiations with the studio. As Nathan Platte has remarked, the concept of the score, in being largely an arrangement of Mendelssohn's overture and incidental music, appeared to be a curious "step backward" reminiscent of the "light classical pastiche scores of the so-called silent era."[5] Yet, it signaled the entry of Warner Bros. into a world of high-prestige pictures—a step away from the hard-boiled crime pictures and backstage musicals that were its stock in trade in the early 1930s. One could be forgiven, then, for assuming that Korngold's involvement in the process would be on terms as fundamentally different from his fellow composers working in the industry as the subject matter of the new film was from the studio's standard fare. The contracts and pay records for *Dream*, though, reveal a rather more prosaic story. Korngold signed a contract dated October 31, 1934, to write/arrange the music for the film, following an initial cabled offer dated October 19 that made clear certain terms and the balance of power in the relationship: "WE TO OWN WORLD'S COPYRIGHT AND ALL RIGHTS OF EVERY

---

[5] Nathan Platte, "Dream Analysis: Korngold, Mendelssohn, and Musical Adaptation in Warner Bros' *A Midsummer Night's Dream* (1935)," *19th-Century Music* 34, no. 3 (Spring 2011): 211–236.

56 KORNGOLD IN AMERICA

NATURE WHATSOEVER IN ALL MUSIC WRITTEN BY YOU DURING EMPLOYMENT BY US INCLUDING RIGHT TO MAKE ALL CHANGES, additions [added in pencil] AND ADAPTATION WE DEEM NECESSARY STOP.... AS TO GRAMOPHONE MUST BE UNDERSTOOD WE TO HAVE ALL GRAMOPHONE RIGHTS HOWEVER WHEN YOU IN NEW YORK WE MAY YIELD ON THIS POINT AFTER HEARING YOUR ARGUMENTS IT BEING UNDERSTOOD HOWEVER THAT THIS IS COMPLETELY WITHIN OUR DISCRETION."[6]

The prospective movie composer was promised $4,000 in remuneration plus a further sum of $4,000 in "full payment of any and all traveling expenses, board and lodging incurred by composer," for which he received an advance of $1,500.[7] The remainder would be paid in twelve weekly installments of $541.67. The "twelve weekly installments" would quickly become the method by which Korngold was paid for all his film projects at Warners. Although $541.67 a week compares extremely favorably, of course, with the income of ordinary workers, for whom an increase in wages under the National Recovery Act of the previous year was tempered by a decline in working hours,[8] it is more instructive to compare it with studio orchestrator Ray Heindorf's weekly salary at this time of $500.[9] As such, the initial terms of Korngold's weekly agreement with Warner Bros. cannot be described as unusually generous.

The services required of him were described as "Arrange, re-arrange and adapt the musical composition 'A MIDSUMMER NIGHT'S DREAM' by Ludwig Felix Mendelssohn-Bartholdy for use in and in connection with Producer's production entitled 'A MIDSUMMER NIGHT'S DREAM,' and to compose original musical compositions for use in said production."[10] As was typical for a composer working in the Hollywood studio system, Korngold agreed to the following clause: "Composer conveys to Producer free and clear of any and all claims for royalty or other compensation.... all right whatsoever in and to all and every [*sic*] the works that he shall write, conceive, compose or produce during the full term hereof." A memo from Jack Warner to producer Henry Blanke dated December

---

[6] USC Warner Bros. Archives (hereafter WBA), "A MIDSUMMER NIGHT'S DREAM" LEGAL—CORRESPONDENCE 2 of 2.

[7] WBA, Folder 12627A Erich Wolfgang Korngold, composer. Agreement dated October 31, 1934.

[8] See, for instance, Bryant Putney, "Wage Rates and Workers' Incomes," *Editorial Research Reports 1938*, vol. 1 (Washington, DC: CQ Press), http://library.cqpress.com/cqresearcher/cqresrr e1938012000 (accessed May 18, 2020). Average hourly wages in manufacturing industries, for instance, were 55 cents in June 1934. With an average working week of 34.7 hours, this equates to around $19 a week.

[9] See contract dated May 24, 1933, in Heindorf's employee file at WBA (NB Heindorf's name is spelled consistently as Heindorff in Warner Bros. records). Tax records published by the IRS indicate that for 1934 the average yearly net income in California was $3,065.77, https://www.irs.gov/pub/irs-soi/34soireppt1ar.pdf (accessed October 28, 2021), 59.

[10] WBA, Folder 12627A Erich Wolfgang Korngold, composer. Agreement dated October 31, 1934.

A MUSICIAN FOR HIRE   57

11 indicates, however, that there was some subsequent disagreement between composer and studio about what was required and for what he was being paid:

> Am surprised Dr Korngold now wants to hold us up for $2500 to conduct his score. When I agreed to send for Korngold it was understood that he would do everything whether it is in the contract or not. He certainly should take enough interest on [*sic*] what he is doing to conduct his score.
>
> I have informed [studio manager, Bill] Koenig to forget Korngold and Forbstein will conduct the orchestra as we see fit. Also am surprised that Korngold is going into legal technicalities on what he should and should not do when it was explicitly understood he was to do everything.[11]

Korngold's father, Julius, had trained as a lawyer, and one wonders whether Korngold consulted him having realized that the contracted terms were rather vague. Nonetheless, it seems as if respect for Korngold's stature did not warrant exceptions to the harsh realities of studio legalities and finances. That said, work on the film went on much longer than anyone had anticipated. Despite the original contract, the period of time during which Korngold was employed on *Dream* was extensive. He was put on the payroll on November 5, 1934, and was paid for twelve weeks at $541.67 (a total of $6,500.04, which when added to his $1,500 advance satisfied the terms of the original agreement). He was, however, employed at a new weekly rate of $666.67 for a further twelve weeks (from February 1, 1935, until April 27, 1935), providing him with another $8,000.04, resulting in a total payment of $16,000.08. This was more in total than he was paid for any other film at Warner Bros. for the remainder of his career, and was as a result of the lengthy period of time he devoted to the project.

Upon completion of his work on *Dream* in April 1935 prior to its eventual premiere in October, Korngold returned to Vienna. He had, however, signed an agreement with Paramount Pictures dated April 29 committing himself to return.[12] The agreement was to provide music for a film featuring the singer Jan Kiepura, with whom Korngold had worked in Europe.[13] It commenced on August 7 and had an initial completion date of December 1 with payment of $12,000 due thereafter; however, two further extensions were added, bringing Korngold's contracted time with Paramount until February 15, 1936, and giving him an extra $7,000 for the first extension of nine weeks, and a further $833.32 for the last two weeks. This contract, for a total of $19,833.32, thus covers the

---

[11] WBA, "A MIDSUMMER NIGHT'S DREAM" 2078, Folder 2 of 4.

[12] Paramount Pictures contract summaries, Margaret Herrick Library, Academy of Motion Picture Arts and Sciences, Folder 1356/Erich Wolfgang Korngold, 71409998.

[13] Kiepura had sung the role of The Stranger in the first production of the composer's fourth opera, *Das Wunder der Heliane*.

58 KORNGOLD IN AMERICA

work he did on both *Rose of the Rancho* and *Give Us This Night* in 1935–1936; however, at some point in late 1935 the chance to score *Captain Blood* for Warners also presented itself. The film's budget dated July 29, 1935, listed only a relatively modest $15,000 for musicians and nothing at all for "song writers" (though later memos indicate that including composer fees in this category was not the norm at this point), and Luzi Korngold later recalled:

> In the course of the winter, when Erich was already on the orchestral recordings for the Paramount film *Give Us This Night,* Warner Bros. made themselves known. They wanted Erich to write music for the just completed film *Captain Blood* (based on the novel by Sabatini). Erich refused. Firstly, he was still too busy with his work at Paramount, and secondly he would have had absolutely no intention to write any more film music. After daily desperate telephone calls, he was finally persuaded to at least see the film.[14]

Luzi reports that Korngold was pressed further by Warners until he relented, noting that the money on offer was "in no way tempting."[15] No contracts or agreements are extant in connection with Korngold's role on *Captain Blood*, though payroll records indicate that starting November 8, 1935, he was paid $1,000 a week until the end of the month, and thereafter at $500 until his services terminated on December 11.[16] Indeed, it appears that Korngold was paid only a total of $4,500 for his work on that film, which might seem odd given it contained a great deal more of his original music than *Dream*. Yet, since he was only working for five and a half weeks, he was being paid more per week than he had the previous winter. Moreover, he was still being employed by Paramount at this time, with substantial payments owed to him that would be made at the beginning of January 1936.

Clearly, though, the composer was not yet ready to commit to Hollywood on more than an *ad hoc* basis. *Captain Blood* had been released in time for Christmas 1935, and while still working on *Give Us This Night* for Paramount in February 1936, Warners invited him to work on *Anthony Adverse*.[17] The composer was

---

[14] Luzi Korngold, *Erich Wolfgang Korngold: Ein Lebensbild von Luzi Korngold* (Vienna: Elisabeth Lafite, 1967), 71 (My translation).

[15] "[D]as materielle Angebot war keineswegs verlockend." Luzi Korngold, *Erich Wolfgang Korngold*, 72.

[16] Korngold's contract with Paramount—which originally stated that his provided services need not be exclusive from November 10 to December 1, 1935—had to be amended to allow non-exclusive work from October 30.

[17] Korngold's modest amount of work for Paramount on *Rose of the Rancho* was evidently completed before that film opened in the week of January 7, but it seems his much more extensive role on *Give Us This Night*, which was the project he had been contracted for in the first place, was still being finished in February 1936, despite the leather folder containing his short score bearing a date of October 1935. LOC, Box 29 Folder 2.

once again put on the payroll at Warners on February 1, and was paid the initial relatively modest rate of $416.67 per week. The start of this payment period, unusually, was prior to the end of filming for *Anthony Adverse*, which had begun on November 6, 1935, and finished only on February 14. Yet, the bulk of prescoring work had already been undertaken long before Korngold was on the payroll—not least by freelancer Aldo Franchetti, who provided opera segments for the fictional work *La Duchessa di Ferrara* sung by Olivia de Havilland's character, Angela. On February 16, the day after his contract with Paramount formally finished, the beginning of Korngold's "12 weeks guarantee" period on *Anthony Adverse* began at $833.34 per week, as post-production work started on scoring the film, with a "contract terminated" note in the payroll dated May 9.[18] All told, then, Korngold was paid $10,833.42 for his work on *Anthony Adverse* for 14 weeks' work, though after early April he had also done a small amount of uncredited work for the studio on *The Green Pastures* and *Hearts Divided*. Korngold's weekly rate at Warner Bros. had thus fluctuated between an average of $666.67 for the lengthy work on *Dream*, $1,000 a week for the brief but intense *Captain Blood*, and $773.82 for a more normal working period on *Anthony Adverse*.[19]

The First Multi-Film Contract: 1936

As his work on *Anthony Adverse* was nearing its end, Korngold put his signature for the first time to a multi-film contract that guaranteed him a predictable income over a much longer period of time. Although such a move offered him improved pay and conditions in return for a longer commitment to the studio, it would be a mistake to assume that it represents a fundamental shift in his prestige with Warners. Indeed, in the case of *Another Dawn* it meant the composer was also forced into scoring a project he appeared somewhat reluctant to undertake.

The agreement, held at Warner Bros. Archives, is dated May 1, 1936, and it is for two films: a project called *Danton*, based on the life of the French revolutionary leader, or alternatively another film directed by Max Reinhardt; and "one other picture."[20] It offered the composer a much-improved weekly rate in addition to expenses to cover his travel from Vienna: "the Producer shall

---

[18] WBA, Folder 12627A Erich Wolfgang Korngold, composer, 3103D.

[19] According to his Paramount contract, he was paid instalments of $2,000 on September 16, September 30, October 14, and October 28, 1935, with a further $4,000 paid on January 6, 1936. There then followed nine weekly payments of $777.78 a week followed by two additional weeks at $416.66. Korngold was also paid a flat $3,000 by Paramount for traveling expenses. His payment dates from Paramount thus filled in the gaps when he was not receiving a weekly payment from Warners, thus ensuring a regular income. Paramount Pictures contract summaries, Margaret Herrick Library, Academy of Motion Picture Arts and Sciences, Folder 1356/Erich Wolfgang Korngold, 71409998.

[20] WBA, Folder 12627A Erich Wolfgang Korngold, composer, 3103D. Agreement dated May 1, 1936. Neither *Danton* nor an alternative Reinhardt project materialized.

60 KORNGOLD IN AMERICA

pay to the Composer as traveling expenses, only for himself, the sum of Two Thousand Five Hundred Dollars. . . . in addition, the sum of $12,500 for each of said two pictures . . . in consecutive weekly instalments of $1,041.66." If more than twelve weeks were required, Korngold would be paid pro rata at a weekly rate of $1,145.85. He would be given thirty days' written notice in connection with the first film (the Reinhardt-directed picture), and the second film would not start earlier than one week after completion of the first, and not later than eight weeks after the twelve-week minimum period for the first. The contract also stipulated that Korngold would have the use of a full-time copyist and orchestrator, and it included both a non-compete clause and a standard agreement to transfer all royalty claims to the producer.[21] In addition, exhibit A of the contract gave the producer the right to "use said work, in whole or in part, in whatever manner said purchaser may desire." The only amendment Korngold made was to clause 15 where he struck through three words: "It is specifically understood and agreed, that Producer shall have the right ~~at any time~~ to lend, rent, or transfer the services of Composer to any other producer of recognized standing for only one (1) of two (2) said motion pictures." Finally, Korngold would receive his own title credit card. Admittedly, this was unusual, and general counsel Roy J. Obringer later had to remind Eddie Selzer about the billing:

> Our contract with ERICH WOLFGANG KORNGOLD provides that he is to be given credit on a separate title card on the screen and in all paid publicity within our control, giving him full credit for all original musical compositions and for all arrangements made by him and based upon musical compositions composed by any composers other than Mozart and Beethoven. We further agree that he is to be given credit for all original musical compositions and for all arrangements on our theatre billing and paid advertising where the director's name is used in such billing, and in addition, credit is to be given Korngold on a separate title card on our trailer picture or advertising, provided the name of the director is likewise used thereon.
>
> NOTE: This same billing pertains to all Korngold pictures.[22]

A project did not present itself, however, until later in the year, when Korngold began work on the Errol Flynn vehicle *Another Dawn*, directed by William Dieterle. As indicated in its production reports, *Another Dawn*—which finally

[21] A non-compete clause indicated he could not work for one of the studio's competitors. Transfer of royalty claims was also standard, and his Paramount contract had likewise stipulated that original material was "to become property of Corporation." Paramount Pictures contract summaries, Margaret Herrick Library, Academy of Motion Picture Arts and Sciences, Folder 1356/Erich Wolfgang Korngold, 71409998.

[22] Memo To Mr Selzer from Mr Obringer, January 27, 1937. WBA, "PRINCE AND THE PAUPER" Production Story File.

began filming on September 25, 1936, after lengthy delays—finished shooting on November 12, after which a day of retakes was required on November 21.[23] Korngold arrived from Austria with his family in New York on October 22 and appears to have been placed on salary on October 31, though the note in the payroll record indicates that it is in connection with the aborted *Danton* project. A separate payroll notice indicates that the end of his guaranteed twelve weeks of work occurred on January 23, 1937. As mentioned in Chapter 1, however, in contradistinction to the mythology that surrounds the composer's privileged position, Korngold's involvement in *Another Dawn* appears to have been somewhat forced upon him, and this early picture assignment seems to have been one where composer and studio were still adjusting to each other.

The decision to use Korngold on *Another Dawn*, in all likelihood, was made after the budget of September 21, which allotted only $5,900 for music ($5,000 for musicians, and $900 for song clearances). Later, the practice at Warner Bros. was to include the composer's fee under "song writers and song clearances" in the budget, though quite when that change was made is unclear. In any case, Korngold's fee by this point, as agreed in the May contract, was a guaranteed $12,500, and there is no mention of this in the budget calculations. By November 16, the decision to use him had still not been made. Wallis's executive assistant Walter McEwan wrote to Eddie Selzer indicating that Jack Warner had okayed the film's billing but asked him to "hold up putting this billing through for a little while until we definitely determine whether or not KORNGOLD is going to do the music on it since, if he does, we will of course be required to put his name on the credit sheet. I will let you know about this in the next couple of days."[24] The following day, Hal Wallis wrote to Forbstein asking him "What did you do about having KORNGOLD work on 'ANOTHER DAWN'?" Evidently some persuasion was necessary, as revealed in Chapter 1. Director William Dieterle was another whose hand was somewhat forced on the matter, and he later recalled to Wallis that "I don't have to tell you again how much I disliked the story, but I made the picture for your sake."[25] Clearly, though, with the demise of the *Danton* project, Warners were committed to paying Korngold and needed to use him. *Another Dawn* was the best option.

The second picture of the May 1, 1936, agreement became *The Prince and the Pauper* (production no. 134, directed by William Keighley), and Korngold's payroll notices on this started on 1 February, 1937.[26] In other words, the working

---

[23] WBA, "ANOTHER DAWN" PRODUCTION—DAILY PROGRESS REPORTS, 2869A.

[24] Memo to Selzer from MacEwan, November 16, 1936. WBA, "ANOTHER DAWN" STORY—MEMOS & CORRESPONDENCE 1 of 2, 1706B.

[25] Dieterle to Wallis, July 21, 1938, reproduced in Rudy Behlmer, *Inside Warner Bros. (1935–1951)* (New York: Simon & Schuster), 72.

[26] WBA, Folder 12627A Erich Wolfgang Korngold, composer, 3103D.

62 KORNGOLD IN AMERICA

period overlapped with that of *Another Dawn*. Korngold's involvement may not have been planned for in the budget of December 7, 1936, though—which allocated a total of $6,300 for musicians, song writers, and song clearances—but it had been decided by January 21. On this date, Wallis wrote a memo to Forbstein, Nathan Levinson of the Sound Department, and Editorial Supervisor Hal McCord stating that *The Prince and the Pauper* needed to be shipped from the studio by April 1 in order "to release the picture at Coronation time, which may have considerable to do with making the picture a tremendous success."[27] As a consequence of this desire to cash in on the coronation of British monarch George VI on May 12 and its obvious parallels with the coronation scene in the film, the anglophile Wallis states: "I am asking those of you to whom this note is addressed to see that the cutting is kept up to date, that KORNGOLD looks at the reels as they are cut, and that no time is lost in getting the reels put through the sound department. We will have approximately eight weeks to work on the picture, and this should be sufficient."[28] According to the copyright cue sheet, scoring was complete on March 23, in time to meet Wallis's deadline, and a preview held at Warner's Hollywood Theatre on Monday, April 5, at 8.25 pm. Korngold's twelve-week guarantee salary ended on April 24, though whether he was actively employed on *The Prince and the Pauper* up to this point seems unlikely.

A New Agreement: The 1938 Contract

The next project was to be *The Adventures of Robin Hood*, directed by William Keighley and Michael Curtiz, and starring Errol Flynn and Olivia de Havilland, and Korngold—having returned to Vienna in May 1937—had already begun preparatory work on the score. On January 21, 1938, Korngold received a cable from Wallis and Blanke asking him to return to Hollywood and upon arrival in New York took receipt of the script from studio story editor Jacob Wilk. He appears to have signed a separate agreement for this one film dated February 4—though the document itself is unfortunately missing from Warner Bros. Archives. As is well known, Korngold was reluctant to take on the project once he saw a rough cut on February 11.[29] Nonetheless, he relented—no doubt swayed by the political situation at home in Austria. Luzi's biography, however, implies something unusual in the conditions of his acceptance: "Finally, he

[27] WBA, "PRINCE AND THE PAUPER" 2166.
[28] Ibid.
[29] See Ben Winters, *Erich Wolfgang Korngold's* The Adventures of Robin Hood: *A Film Score Guide* (Lanham, MD: Scarecrow Press, 2007), 77–78. The complete production process of that score is covered in this book.

promised Forbstein he would at least attempt to write the 'Robin Hood' music. He didn't want a contract. His conditions were: work from week to week, paid from week to week. 'If I see that I'm no longer inspired, I can stop with a good conscience; everything I've already written will belong to you,' he explained. His proposal was accepted."[30] Yet, in all other projects Korngold had also been paid "from week to week," and the material likewise belonged to the studio. Luzi's account, though, suggests that Korngold could stop without being in breach of his contract. Moreover, the fact that he was intending to make use of his own prior musical material (the symphonic overture *Sursum Corda* and a theme he had written for his arrangement of Leo Fall's operetta, *Rosen aus Florida*) might have required special dispensation to grant the studio full rights to the material.[31] Without the missing agreement, though, it is difficult to be certain how unusual its terms were. Evidently, though, Korngold warmed to his task, and by April 13 when the film's dubbing was complete, Obringer could send a memo to comptroller C. H. Wilder to indicate that the unpaid balance of Korngold's guaranteed $12,500 was due.[32] It is notable that the figure of $12,500 per film, carried over from the 1936 contract, now seems the norm.

Korngold's extended family had joined him and Luzi in Los Angeles during the period in which he was working on *Robin Hood*. Now, with his future tied firmly to Warner Bros. and to the United States, Korngold signed a new agreement dated May 8, 1938, for a further two more pictures over the next year, commencing September 15, with an option to extend.[33] This appears to be the contract that Brendan Carroll refers to as "the most generous and flexible ever granted to a composer."[34] The contract was on much the same salary terms as before, though. He was still committed to receiving a guaranteed $12,500 per film for twelve weeks' work, just as he had agreed for his 1936 contract and the separate *Robin Hood* contract. The only change in remuneration was a negative one. If he was required after the twelve-week minimum period, Korngold would receive his regular payment of $1,041.66 rather than the higher rate $1,145.85 of the 1936 contract. The 1938 contract, admittedly, abandons the non-compete clause, granting Korngold the right to make one outside picture for another studio, though stipulating he may not do so for more than sixteen weeks without the consent of the producer. This was not particularly unusual for a musician working in Hollywood at this time, and it was in any case not as generous as his earlier Paramount contract, which noted that his services need not

---

[30] Luzi Korngold, *Erich Wolfgang Korngold*, 77–78 (my translation).

[31] See Winters, *Korngold's* The Adventures of Robin Hood, 97–104.

[32] WBA, "THE ADVENTURES OF ROBIN HOOD" Story—Memos & Correspondence 1 of 8 2/11/38–11/3/38.

[33] WBA, Folder 12627A Erich Wolfgang Korngold, composer. Agreement dated May 8, 1938.

[34] Brendan Carroll, *The Last Prodigy: A Biography of Erich Wolfgang Korngold* (Portland, OR: Amadeus Press, 1997), 275.

64 KORNGOLD IN AMERICA

be exclusive. No such outside work was done, however, and Korngold remained a Warner Bros. composer for the next eight years. The contract also allowed him to continue with Max Reinhardt's "spectacles and/or festivals." Again, Korngold received a full-time orchestrator and copyist, but once again a standard clause about ownership was included:

> *The Composer does hereby agree to, and does herby grant, bargain, sell, assign and transfer to Producer, free and clear of any and all claims for royalty*, except as to all prior agreements between the Composer and any European or American societies for composers, or any organizations acting on their behalf, and as to these, Producer has knowledge and agrees that nothing herein contained shall conflict with or alter such prior royalty agreements, or other compensation, and except as hereinafter in this paragraph provided for, *all rights whatsoever in and to all and every the works he shall write, conceive, compose or produce during the full term hereof*, and particularly, though without limiting the foregoing general language, the motion picture, talking picture, radio, television, phonograph, publication and dramatic rights thereunder and thereto, and does further authorize and empower Producer to secure copyrights to the same and to do all things in connection therewith which Composer might otherwise himself do or perform [my italics].[35]

It is possible the mention of the prior agreements between the composer and any European or American societies for composers (in other words, ASCAP, the American Society of Composers, Authors, and Publishers) might have caused the confusion noted in the secondary literature about Korngold somehow owning the rights to his film scores. A similar clause had been inserted by hand in the original *Dream* contract: "The composer does hereby agree to, and does hereby grant, bargain, sell, assign and transfer to Producer, free and clear of any and all claims for royalty and compensation, *except as hereinafter provided for*, all right whatsoever in and to all and every [*sic*] the works that he shall write, conceive, compose or produce during the full term hereof [handwritten emendation in italics]."[36] This addition was retained in the 1936 contract. Similarly, the revised clause as worded in the 1938 agreement appears in all subsequent contracts; however, as a much later letter from general counsel R. J. Obringer to Herman Starr of the Music Publishers Holding Company dated May 26, 1948, reveals, there was nothing particularly surprising or unusual about this clause.[37] The letter noted that staff composer Adolph Deutsch's contract did not allow

---

[35] WBA, Folder 12627A Erich Wolfgang Korngold, composer. Agreement dated May 8, 1938.
[36] WBA, Folder 12627A Erich Wolfgang Korngold, composer. Agreement dated October 31, 1934.
[37] Found in WBA, Adolph Deutsch Composer Expired (MPHC was the music publishing arm of Warner Bros.).

him, expressly, to retain performing rights in the way that Korngold's did, but goes on to mention that "It is my understanding, however, and I believe it would follow as a matter of law, that when entering into a contract with a composer the Producer need not have much concern about the reserved performing rights on the part of the composer because assuming that the composer is an ASCAP member and theretofore entered into an agreement with ASCAP for small performing rights, our contract was consequently entered into subject to the rights of ASCAP." It then notes of the Korngold case that Deutsch's (missing) part of the correspondence apparently raised: "Under paragraph 6 of the Korngold contract, Korngold granted and assigned to us free and clear of any and all claims for royalty 'except as to all prior agreements between the Composer and any European or American societies for composers or any organization acting on their behalf' all rights, etc. Here Korngold did make an express reservation, or at least made our employment subject to any agreements he at the time had made with any societies for composers." That then might suggest a special case; however, it is clear that Max Steiner did exactly the same thing: "With respect to Steiner, he did [the film] ROUGHLY SPEAKING under contract dated April 1, 1941 (mailed to Mr. Wallace on May 1, 1941) and in paragraph 7 it was expressly provided that 'nothing contained in this agreement shall be deemed to grant to the Producer any rights heretofore granted by the Composer to the American Society of Composers, Authors and Publishers, or to be in any way inconsistent the terms of the agreement heretofore entered into between the Composer and the American Society of Composers, Authors and Publishers.'" Moreover, the letter concludes that "Therefore, from the above it is apparent that both Korngold and Steiner made express reservations of small performing rights in favor of ASCAP, and if Deutsch was an ASCAP member prior to the signing of our contract there would be an implied reservation."

In other words, it would appear there was nothing particularly unusual about Korngold's contract in this way, and it merely put into words a legal right that was implied: that a composer's contract with Warner Bros. could not supersede previously agreed contracts with performance-rights organizations. It thus assured Korngold of separate royalty income from ASCAP brought about by performances of his existing works and any new concert works he should write in the same period as covered by his Warner Bros. contract.[38] Nowhere is

---

[38] One ASCAP "royalty record" is extant in the Korngold Collection at the Library of Congress. Dated 1941 and recorded on the back of Korngold's membership card, it contains very little detail, merely recording four quarters of $185 received and a total for the year of $740. See LOC, Box C Folder 6. The Korngold Collection also includes one communication from Universal Edition (the publisher of some of Korngold's early works) dated January 29, 1940, which states that they cannot pay him the RM80 due to him for the year 1939 without the approval of the foreign exchange office, and that they require a tax clearance declaration from the last tax office responsible for him in Vienna.

66 KORNGOLD IN AMERICA

it apparent that Korngold retained any ownership of the new film material he wrote for Warner Bros.

Indeed, Korngold's royalty income from Europe was no doubt drying up, in part as a result of the political situation in Austria and Germany. Korngold even appears to have resorted to a little subterfuge in order to transfer rights to his opera *Die tote Stadt* from the fictional Paul Schott—a character that Korngold and his father had created and to whom they attributed authorship of the libretto they themselves had written. Documents in the Library of Congress reveal a letter apparently written to Korngold by the mysterious Paul Schott in Zurich dated January 27, 1938, just before Korngold began work on *Robin Hood*.[39] The letter transfers to Korngold and his legal successors all copyrights relating to *Die tote Stadt* and *Waltzes from Vienna* in apparent exchange for 5,000 Swiss francs. It is clearly a necessary fabrication, given that elsewhere in the collection is a page of headed Warner Bros. notepaper in which someone (presumably Korngold himself) tries out various versions of the fictional Paul Schott's signature, which matches the signature used in the letter.[40]

The first film on which Korngold was involved under the terms of the new 1938 agreement was the William Dieterle–directed historical epic, *Juarez*, starring Paul Muni as the title character, Bette Davis as the "mad" Carlota, and Brian Aherne as her husband, the Hapsburg Emperor Maximilian I. Payroll records indicate that Korngold was paid from November 21, 1938, for five weeks until December 24, and then was taken off the payroll until actual compositional work on *Juarez* started, filming of which had begun only on November 7. Principal photography finished on February 6, 1939, with retakes lasting until February 23 while, according to payroll records, Korngold's work in earnest began on February 13—at which point he was to be paid the remainder of his fee in seven weekly installments.[41] The studio ran into significant legal troubles once the film was released, though, in a case that also reveals something profoundly important about the legal status of Korngold's musical material. The trouble arose when a plagiarism charge against *Juarez* was leveled by Miguel Torres in connection with his 1934 Spanish-language film, *Juárez y Maximiliano*. Torres had also produced an English-language remake named *The Mad Empress* starring Lionel Atwell and Medea de Novara (who reprised her role as Carlota from the 1934 version) and, as a compromise, Warner Bros. agreed to distribute the new English-language film later that year. As part of this compromise deal, and since Torres's film had apparently failed to secure certain copyrights, Warner

---

[39] LOC, Box A Folder 32.
[40] LOC, Box F, Folder 7.
[41] WBA, Folder 12627A Erich Wolfgang Korngold, composer, 3103D. On February 6 Dieterle invited Korngold and his wife Luzi to a dinner party at his house on the 11th to "salute the completion of the picture." LOC, Box B Folder 1.

Bros. proposed to eliminate the film's original score by James Bradford, remove his name from the title card, and replace the score with music of their own—including portions of Korngold's cues for *Juarez*. This was done in collaboration with Torres, as Blanke reported to Jack Warner on July 18, 1939, noting in a memo the previous day to Jimmie Gibbons that "After we get through working on 'THE MAD EMPRESS' this afternoon and tonight, I want you to run the picture tomorrow morning at 10 o'clock with Mr Forbstein and Mr Torres so that Mr Torres can point out to Mr Forbstein the pieces of music that have to be eliminated and have to be substituted by something else which Mr Forbstein has to put in on account of Torres not having applied for certain rights to use certain music now contained in the picture."[42] As a result, a number of Korngold's action and ceremonial cues from Reels 4, 5, 9, and 11 of *Juarez* were re-used in *Mad Empress* without Bradford's (or any other composer's) name attached.[43] There is no record of any correspondence with Korngold seeking his permission to use the music, because Warners understood that such permission was unnecessary. The *Juarez-Mad Empress* case reveals that for all Korngold's artistic pedigree, his film music remained the property of Warner Bros. to do with as they pleased.

Korngold's second film of 1939 was the historical costume epic, *The Private Lives of Elizabeth and Essex*, which starred Bette Davis and Errol Flynn as the title characters. The revised budget of April 19, 1939, allows for Korngold's salary in its figure of $12,500 against "song writers and song releases" while $30,000 was budgeted for the necessary musicians.[44] Korngold was put on the payroll on June 26, whereupon he was paid for twelve weeks' work, finishing on September 16;[45] however, he was certainly required several weeks prior to his official payroll notice date in order to participate in prescoring the song to be sung to the Queen by Lady Penelope Gray (Olivia de Havilland) and Mistress Margaret Radcliffe (Nanette Fabares). Moreover, a memo dated April 23, 1939, from Norman Reilly Raine, the film's original script writer, refers to "three more verses" that he can send the composer, perhaps indicating that Korngold had already started work by this earlier date.[46] In any case, he was certainly working by

[42] WBA, "JUAREZ" LEGAL, 2874.

[43] This is when compared with the seventy-two-minute version of *The Mad Empress* available today. A longer, ninety-five-minute version was originally available and may have contained even more of Korngold's score. In any case, trying to establish exactly the relationship between the two scores is difficult when certain manuscript sources are missing.

[44] A total of $42,500 for the film's music in the budget compared favorably with Errol Flynn's budgeted "star" salary of $41,300, while director Michael Curtiz was allocated $41,600. Curtiz's payment went up to $45,500 in a budget change dated May 4, 1939. Bette Davis earned $35,000. WBA, "THE PRIVATE LIVES OF ELIZABETH AND ESSEX" STORY MEMOS & CORRESPONDENCE 5/1/39–12/4/39 2 OF 2, 1880.

[45] WBA, Folder 12627A Erich Wolfgang Korngold, composer, 3103D.

[46] LOC, Box B Folder 29. Raine's role in writing the original draft of the screenplay prompted him to write a memo to Wallis once the picture had finished, complaining of the changes made to his script. Memo dated September 28, 1939, in WBA, "THE PRIVATE LIVES OF ELIZABETH AND ESSEX" STORY MEMOS & CORRESPONDENCE 5/1/39–12/4/39 2 OF 2.

68 KORNGOLD IN AMERICA

mid-June. The Daily Production and Progress Report for Tuesday, June 13, for instance, notes "KORNGOLD ASSISTING ON DUDLEY CHAMBER'S [*sic*] SONG" with the accompanying memo of the following day from Frank Mattison to T. C. Wright, noting, "Our 6-1/2 pages are a little misleading for this covers the singing number done by Miss DeHAVILLAND and Miss FABARES, which I am sure will be re-shot with a different song and different lyrics."[47] Reports for June 14 indicated that "Mr Lord has arranged some new lyrics for Miss FABARES and Miss DeHAVILLAND to sing and turned them over to Mr. Korngold who will make another arrangement, and we hope to be able to get them pre-recorded at some early date so that we may pick this up when we have an easy day."[48] The revised prescoring was recorded on Saturday June 17, still over a week before Korngold's salary officially started. It seems, then, that Korngold had accepted that his payment for each of these films would essentially constitute a flat fee of $12,500 whether or not twelve weeks or more work was required. Given he made no attempt to renegotiate this, it seems it either suited him, or he was unwilling to enter into the necessary dialogue to change the situation.

The 1939 Contract Renewal and the 1940 Contract

Even before his scoring duties for *Elizabeth and Essex* were complete, though, Korngold's renewal to his year-long contract was exercised. A letter dated August 10, 1939, sets out the same terms and payment as the 1938 contract.[49] His first film under the new agreement was *The Sea Hawk*, pairing him once again with director Michael Curtiz and established star Errol Flynn. Korngold's involvement was needed early in the New Year as the script contained a song to be sung by Dona Maria (Brenda Marshall) to Queen Elizabeth I (Flora Robson). As with *Elizabeth and Essex*, this would require prescoring and thus Korngold's involvement while filming was still in progress. The completed song was recorded prior to the scene's filming on February 5, 1940, as the day's production report (written the following day) makes clear: "Monday the company was called at 9:00AM, had their first shot at 10:25 and finished shooting at 6:30 last night. The company shot 2 script scs. [scenes] in 10 set-ups for a total of 2'30", over 2-1/2 pages of dialogue, working in the INT. QUEEN'S PRIVATE CHAMBER on Stage 3. Started JOHN BURTON in the cast. . . . Mr. Curtiz did not have a good day yesterday owing to the recording of the girl [Brenda Marshall] singing to a playback."[50]

---

[47] WBA, "THE PRIVATE LIVES OF ELIZABETH AND ESSEX" PRODUCTION—DAILY PROGRESS REPORTS, SPECIAL 1485.

[48] Ibid.

[49] WBA, Folder 12627A Erich Wolfgang Korngold, composer, 3103D.

[50] Memo to Mr T C Wright from Mr Frank Mattison, February 6, 1940, #296—WBA, "THE SEA HAWK" #296—CURTIZ 1486. The scene was shot early in the filming schedule as Flora Robson

A MUSICIAN FOR HIRE   69

Korngold's regular weekly payment of $1041.66, however, did not start until April 15, 1940,[51] though this in itself was still five days before filming finished, according to Production Manager T. C. (Tenny) Wright's "closing notice," and ten days prior to an April 25 memo from Henry Blanke to Hal Wallis suggesting that both Korngold and Curtiz should attend that evening's running of the edit. Further changes were no doubt made in response to Wallis's May 3 cutting notes, since although the recording (a total of fifty-eight recording hours) started on April 20, it did not finish until June 18, 1940.[52] Korngold's twelve-week-guarantee period finished on July 6.

With *The Sea Hawk*, Korngold had only written one film score under the 1939–1940 agreement. Perhaps, as a result, when he signed a new contract dated September 12, 1940, it asked him for three scores over two years, at least one of which would be produced in the first year. Again, though, his remuneration stayed at $12,500 per film for a guaranteed twelve weeks' work. Once again paragraph 6 assigns all rights to the producer, but paragraph 15 now adds "and Producer agrees to permit Composer to use any of his own music and any 'free' music now written, in scoring pictures." More than anything in the 1938 contract, I suspect this 1940 clause may have been misread—perhaps even by Korngold himself—and might have resulted in the oft-reported "fact" that somehow Korngold retained the rights to his music produced for Warner Bros. Instead, the contract merely gave him permission to do what he already done in *The Adventures of Robin Hood*, where his previously written concert work *Sursum Corda* was recycled, and to still be paid for the work. The September 1940 agreement did provide the composer with an extra perk, however: a piano for use in his home. Korngold's emendations to the contract are slight but include a minor change to the clause connected with the possibility of outside film work, for which he was again allowed to undertake one example: "Conditioned solely upon receipt of such notice of such bona fide outside offer, Producer hereunder may, by notice to the Composer given not later than three [crossed out five] days after receipt of such notice from Composer, elect to engage the services of Composer for one (1) additional motion picture production to be produced during the term hereof."[53] Such clauses were academic, in any case, as Korngold

---

wanted to finish all her scenes within a week (from February 1–8). The song used was based on "Das Mädchen" from the *Zwölf Eichendorff Lieder* (1910–1911), though it was recomposed in a number of respects.

[51] WBA, Folder 12627A Erich Wolfgang Korngold, composer, 3103D.

[52] See the score credits in the bound copy of the score presented to Warner Bros. orchestra contractor Izzy Friedman, sold by Schubertiade Music & Arts. See https://www.schubertiademusic. com/collections/autographs-manuscripts-archive/products/17487-korngold-erich-wolfgang-1897-1957-friedman-irving-izzy-1903-1981-the-sea-hawk-inscribed-presentation-copy-of-dye-line-film-score-with-amqs-and-original-photographs (accessed October 21, 2024).

[53] WBA, Folder 12627A Erich Wolfgang Korngold, composer, 3103D.

70 KORNGOLD IN AMERICA

worked solely for Warner Bros. during these years. Only in his later work for Republic Pictures on *Magic Fire* (dir. William Dieterle, 1955) would Korngold work again for another studio—though a letter in the Library of Congress reveals he was considered for RKO's horror film *Some Must Watch*, which became *The Spiral Staircase* (dir. Robert Siodmak, 1946).[54]

On November 25, 1940, Korngold was advanced $4,166.66 against the first picture under the 1940 contract, to be paid in four weekly installments of the standard $1,041.66 (with a note in payroll records to make Motion Picture Relief Fund deductions).[55] That next contracted picture was *Kings Row*, and Korngold's payroll records indicate he was paid for the remaining eight weeks between October 6 and December 3, 1941, in connection with that film; however, an emendation was also made to Korngold's contract in January 1941. As Mr. Booth wrote to Mr. Obringer in a memo dated January 28, in addition to the three pictures mentioned in his contract, Korngold would also write the music for *The Sea Wolf* "for which he is to be paid the flat sum of $7,500. Mr Korngold has been working on 'THE SEA WOLF' for 3 weeks, but he does not desire to be paid any compensation until he completes his work, which should possibly be in another three or four weeks."[56] Thus, the next film on which Korngold worked after *The Sea Hawk* was *The Sea Wolf*, starring Edward G. Robinson, Ida Lupino, and John Garfield, and directed—once again—by Michael Curtiz. Korngold's involvement, as Booth's memo to Obringer notes, began in early January 1941, sometime after production finished on January 8. With three days of reshoots taking place on January 10, 11, and 18, Korngold's involvement was clear enough to change the billing for the film on January 17. As Robert S. Taplinger noted in a memo to Mort Blumenstock dated the same day, "The additions are music credits, heretofore unavailable, and effect [*sic*] the billings as follows: On the Main Title, the names of Hugo Friedhofer, Ray Heindorf and Leo F. Forbstein have been added to the general credit card. Erich Wolfgang Korngold's name is on a separate card."[57] Korngold's work was completed according to a memo from Booth to Obringer on February 20, 1941.[58]

The Sea Wolf premiered at the Sebastiani Theatre in Sonoma on March 21, 1941,[59] and the film was approved for release on April 14, 1941. By this point, initial work on *Kings Row* was underway, though a memo from Tenny Wright to

---

[54] Letter from George Chasin, September 28, 1945, LOC, Box E Folder 12.

[55] WBA, Folder 12627A Erich Wolfgang Korngold, composer, 3103D. MPRF was a charitable organization founded in 1921 to provide "a safety net of health and social services" for the entertainment industry. https://mptf.com/history/ (accessed May 19, 2020).

[56] WBA, Folder 12627A Erich Wolfgang Korngold, composer, 3103D.

[57] WBA, "THE SEA WOLF" PICTURE FILE 2 OF 2 2879.

[58] WBA, Folder 12627A Erich Wolfgang Korngold, composer, 3103D.

[59] Studio executives, stars, and press were ferried from Los Angeles to San Francisco, where the opening scenes of the film were set, on board the new ship of the United States Line, SS *America*, which had had its maiden voyage the previous August.

all departments on April 9 announced that "'KINGS ROW' has been postponed and will now start as of Monday, April 21, 1941."[60] On April 18, Wright was working through the budget with Hal Wallis, and clarified those aspects of the music budget Wallis had queried: "Concerning the $9,000 charge for 'Song Writers and Song Releases,' for our information, this item used to be an Overhead Account, but now the salaries of Max Steiner, and other Composers and Arrangers, who work on background music for the picture, are direct picture charges, and are shown under the classification of 'SONG WRITERS & SONG RELASES.'"[61] Since Korngold had already been advanced a third of his $12,500 fee for this film in November of 1940, it seems possible that the $9,000 budgeted anticipated his likely involvement, though it might be thought odd that Wright had not named him if that were the case. At any rate, no mention is made of Korngold in studio correspondence surrounding *Kings Row* until September 25, 1941, and only with a letter of October 13 from Korngold to Wallis, thanking him for the assignment, is his participation confirmed.

The second official picture of Korngold's 1940 contract was *The Constant Nymph*, a film that required Korngold's extensive involvement in the production owing to the central role of music in the narrative, based as it was on Margaret Kennedy's music-heavy novel and play. As a result, Korngold was first paid for four weeks' prescoring work beginning January 5, 1942, prior to being paid for eight weeks for the scoring of the picture beginning April 6 and ending May 30, 1942.[62] The film had a remarkably long gestation period, though, and initial pre-production work had been undertaken as far back as 1940 before a memo from Tenny Wright on June 24, 1940, asked all departments to stop all preparation and to spend no more money. By the time Korngold's 1940 contract expired in September 1942, then, he had only written two out of the contracted three films stipulated therein (*Kings Row* and *The Constant Nymph*), with *The Sea Wolf* undertaken under a different agreement. There is no evidence in Korngold's file at Warner Bros. Archives to suggest that this caused any issues, or that Korngold was pressured to accept another assignment in the way he had been earlier in his career with *Another Dawn*.

The 1942 Contract Extension and 1943 Contract

On September 12, 1942, Warner Bros. had modified and extended Korngold's contract of September 12, 1940, which was due to expire, to January 20, 1943.

---

[60] Memo to all departments from T. C. Wright. WBA, "KINGS ROW" PICTURE FILE 2 OF 2, 2875.

[61] WBA, "KINGS ROWS" STORY MEMOS 2 of 2, 2022A.

[62] WBA, Folder 12627A Erich Wolfgang Korngold, composer, 3103D.

72 KORNGOLD IN AMERICA

On September 19, though, they wrote to the composer stating that "we do not have a motion picture in which we desire to assign you to render your services under said contract."[63] As such, Korngold was free to undertake conducting duties on Broadway in connection with *Rosalinda*, the arrangement of Strauss's *Die Fledermaus* that Korngold had made for Max Reinhardt before the war. The first performance took place on October 28, 1942.[64] An undated telegram draft in the Korngold Collection dates from this period:

> DEAREST LEO [Forbstein]
> HAVE FINISHED CONDUCTING ROSALINDA WHICH WILL RUN TWENTY MORE WEEKS WITHOUT ME AND I PLAN TO ARRIVE SATURDAY HOLLYWOOD IF YOU HAVE A PICTURE READY FOR ME STOP THE OPERA COMPANY OFFERS ME A CONCERT WITH MY OWN COMPOSITIONS ON MONDAY THE THIRTIEST [sic] STOP ONLY IN CASE YOU HAVE NO PICTURE READY FOR ME AND IF IT WOULD BE TO YOUR ADVANTAGE TO POSTPONE THE START OF MY CONTRACT UNTIL DECEMBER FIFTH I WOULD CONSIDER ACCEPTANCE OF CONCERT IN WHICH PARTS OF MY NEW OPERA ARE SUPPOSED TO BE PRESENTED PLEASE WIRE ME AT ONCE YOUR ANSWER HOTEL ASTOR SINCERELY YOURS.[65]

Entries in the payroll records indicate that a new project was soon found, and Korngold was paid $12,500 for his work on *Devotion*, the Brontë-sisters biopic starring Ida Lupino, Olivia de Havilland, and Paul Henreid. He was certainly earning his usual weekly $1041.66 on December 7, 1942, though since payment completed on February 5, 1943, it is probable that it began in mid-November. The payroll record notes in connection with the closure notice "and have understand[ing] that no further payments to be made on 'Devotion,' regardless of time he renders services."[66] Significantly, though, work on *Devotion*, which had started filming on November 11, had barely started. According to the daily production reports, shooting did not finish until February 9, 1943, after which there were three days of retakes: on February 20, 22, and 24.[67] In other words, Korngold was paid a flat rate of $12,500 almost entirely in advance for his work on *Devotion*, with only a modest amount of prescoring work done while he was on salary. This includes the scene in which a drunk Branwell Brontë sings Korngold's own setting of "Though Art Not So Unkind As Man's Ingratitude"

---

[63] Ibid.
[64] See https://www.ibdb.com/broadway-production/rosalinda-1235 (accessed October 14, 2021).
[65] LOC, Box D Folder 2.
[66] WBA, Folder 12627A Erich Wolfgang Korngold, composer, 3103D.
[67] WBA, "DEVOTION"—DAILY PRODUCTION PROGRESS REPORT.

from *A Midsummer Night's Dream*, and in all likelihood the ball attended by the Brontë sisters. With regards to the ballet extract seen toward the end of the film, *La Esmerelda* by Pugni, a performance of which is attended by Charlotte Brontë in London, no prescoring was necessary since there is no close synchronization of the ballet dancing and no close-ups of the musicians performing. *La Esmerelda* is a real work by Cesare Pugni (1802–1870), and it was suggested by the Research Department in response to a query from producer Robert Buckner;[68] however, the original music evidently could not be located, so Korngold supplied his own in post-production as part of cue 10C.

Recording of *Devotion*'s score was not completed until May 4, 1943, whereupon Korngold's role on the film ended. A memo to Jack Warner dated May 5, though, references some apparently last-minute "music changes" and notes that the Lab had already made up "local prints, fine grains and foreign negatives on the picture" but expected to have the domestic negative complete by Friday May 7. It continues: "Because of the changes in Reels 5 and 10, the domestic negative will be held up a day[;] however, McCord has told the Lab not to make any changes in the prints already made or the foreign negatives and fine grains."[69] In the end, though, such disparities between the foreign and domestic negatives were academic since the film was not released until 1946 owing to a legal dispute between Warner Bros. and Olivia de Havilland, which the latter eventually won (the so-called "De Havilland Law").[70]

Meanwhile, another contract dated February 1, 1943, and modified on March 5, was issued to the composer.[71] The term was once again for two years to commence on January 1, 1944, and to terminate on December 31, 1945, or upon completion of the contracted number of films, which this time was for just two. Compensation remained at $12,500 per film. Also dated February 1, 1943, is an agreement between Korngold and the Music Publishers Holding Corporation (MPHC), which was a subsidiary of Warner Bros. The existence of this agreement is recorded in a summary list of agreements held in Warner Bros. Archives, though the document itself is missing from the file, but it perhaps allowed the composer to regain the rights to the symphonic poem entitled *Tomorrow* that Korngold had provided for *The Constant Nymph*, allowing it to be published by Warner's publisher, Witmark & Sons, as Korngold's Op. 33 on August 30, 1943.[72]

---

[68] Memo to Robert Buckner from Research Department (February 2, 1943). WBA, "DEVOTION"—RESEARCH, 1012.

[69] WBA, "DEVOTION"—STORY MEMOS/CORRESPONDENCE.

[70] Daniel Bubbeo, *The Women of Warner Brothers: The Lives and Careers of 15 Leading Ladies, with Filmographies for Each* (London: McFarland, 2010), 63.

[71] WBA, Folder 12627A Erich Wolfgang Korngold, composer. The March 5 amendment was a letter noting that the term of employment would terminate on December 31, 1945, or upon completion of the second film.

[72] *Catalog of Copyright Entries: Musical Compositions, Part 3* (Washington, DC: Library of Congress Copyright Office, 1943), 1257.

74   KORNGOLD IN AMERICA

Korngold's next score was *Between Two Worlds*—starring Paul Henreid, Eleanor Parker, and John Garfield—and it appears to have been treated as the first one written under the 1943 contract, which came into force on January 1, 1944. A memo dated March 21, 1944, from Leo Forbstein to Dick Pease indicated that Korngold had been working on the film for the past twelve weeks, though separate payroll records suggest that Korngold had been paid the end of his twelve-week guarantee on February 12, 1944, and that the balance of his services were to be "rendered without compensation."[73] Owing to the requirement to prescore scenes in which the character of Henry (Paul Henreid) is playing the piano, Korngold must have been involved long before the payroll records indicate, however. Indeed, after filming started on October 7, 1943, the production progress reports indicate that the scenes of Henry performing appear to have been filmed on October 12 (script scenes 38 and 39) and December 9 (script scenes 159 and 160). For the latter, the close-ups of a pianist's hands on the keyboard performing to playback were filmed, with pianist Ray Turner on set between 5 and 6 pm—presumably to act as a hand double for Henreid. Clearly, though, Turner is performing Korngold's music; as with *Devotion*, then, the composer was engaged in work while not actually officially on the payroll. Such instances reveal the difficulties in using the payroll records and the contracts alone to accurately trace Korngold's working patterns, but they do indicate the fact that the composer seems prepared at times to have offered his services without too much concern about the compensation offered.

The second film of the February 1943 contract appears to have been *Of Human Bondage*, starring Paul Henreid and Eleanor Parker, and directed by Edmund Goulding. The beginning of Korngold's twelve-week guarantee began on December 11, 1944, with a pro rata payment thereafter of $1041.55 per week or $173.61 per day for a period of less than a week.[74] The film had finished shooting on October 19, 1944, according to the daily production and progress reports,[75] and Korngold's short score is inscribed "The End 14. I. 1945" after the final cue of the film and before the trailer music.[76] In any case, initial scoring work must have been completed by February 7 at which point a preview took place, with Korngold probably in attendance.[77] It is not known how successful

[73] WBA, Folder 12627A Erich Wolfgang Korngold, composer.
[74] Ibid.
[75] WBA, #631 "OF HUMAN BONDAGE" 1488.
[76] LOC, Box 11 Folder 4.
[77] Documentation on this film is somewhat scant. The February 7 preview's list of attendees includes "composer." Korngold is named on the April preview list of attendees, but his name is crossed out with an indication that he was in New York. An unsigned letter to Korngold indicates that the preview at the Wiltern Theatre had produced an "excellent" reaction from the audience, "and will require only a few minor changes before it is finally approved. Everyone commented that your music was an important factor in securing the right mood for this picture." WBA, "OF HUMAN BONDAGE"—story 2145.

this preview performance was, though it seems it was probably not a triumph, since a second preview was held in April and numerous changes were made to the score. The April preview appears to have been a much more successful event, although Korngold was in New York at the time and could not attend. The film's cue sheet, however, indicates a final recording date of June 21, 1945, suggesting yet more alterations to the score were needed after the preview.[78] At any rate, the full score indicates clear retakes to cues 4A, 3A, and 11E, and there are similar retake pages for 3A, 4A, and 11E in Korngold's hand that have been inserted into a copyist's short score, along with other numerous minor changes.[79] The exact sequence of events and changes is somewhat difficult to trace, though clearly the production was a troubled one, and in any case the film was not released until July 1946.

A Return to Single-Film Agreements: 1945–1946

In composing scores for both *Between Two Worlds* and *Of Human Bondage*, Korngold had satisfied the terms of his 1943 contract. His remaining film work for Warners once more returned to the *ad hoc* arrangements of his earlier film projects, committing the composer only to the films named in the agreements. Thus, while awaiting *Of Human Bondage*'s release, Korngold worked on a film that, as with *The Constant Nymph* and, to a certain extent, *Between Two Worlds* required extensive amounts of prescoring. *Escape Me Never* was another Margaret Kennedy property centered around a composer (played by Errol Flynn) and his composition of a ballet called *Primavera*, the musical material of which Korngold was required to supply as prescoring. On December 11, 1945, Korngold signed an agreement with both the MPHC and the studio, though again a copy of the agreement with the MPHC no longer appears to exist in Warner Bros. Archives. The copy of the studio agreement residing in the archives is not signed either and is in the form of a letter, so it is unclear whether Korngold was bound by its clauses, but the agreement noted in detail the new range of roles the composer would be required to provide:

> You agree to render services . . . as a musical adviser and supervisor, and as well render your services in the composing and recording of piano and orchestra playbacks. You further agree that during the term hereof you will render services in composing, conducting, arranging, rearranging, directing and adapting musical compositions (words and music) created and composed by you, as

[78] WBA, 1370A "OF HUMAN BONDAGE" 11246.
[79] LOC, Box 11 Folder 5A.

76 KORNGOLD IN AMERICA

well as musical compositions to be furnished you by us. Likewise, you agree to render services for us during the term hereof in connection with the actual scoring of our aforesaid motion picture, and to render such other services as may be requested by us pertaining to the work of a composer, conductor, arranger and adaptor.[80]

The letter also noted that Korngold's term of employment had already begun on November 8, 1945. Indeed, Korngold's role in writing the ballet meant that he was informed of the studio's plans as far back as September 26, when Henry Blanke wrote to Leo Forbstein to tell him that shooting would begin on October 15, more or less in continuity, and noting that "this is for your and Korngold's information."[81] The payment terms in the contract were, as ever, a guaranteed twelve-week period of $1,041.66 per week. If employment extended beyond twelve weeks, Korngold would be paid at the same rate, but:

it is agreed that should your services be required hereunder from and after the expiration of a period of fifteen (15) weeks from the commencement of the term hereof, we shall not be obligated to pay you any compensation whatsoever during the period commencing at the expiration of said fifteen (15) weeks['] period and ending at the time of the first preview of the aforesaid motion picture, and should you render services for us hereunder subsequent to the date of said first preview of said motion picture, then and in that event we agree to compensate you for such additional services on a per diem basis at the rate of One Hundred Dollars ($100) per day.[82]

Clause five of the agreement also made it clear that he could not expect any further payment in connection with *Of Human Bondage*, the second film made under the provisions of the 1943 contract, which was still awaiting release.[83] Meanwhile, clause six once again laid out the standard transfer of ownership typical of film-score composition:

You hereby grant, bargain, sell, assign and transfer to us, free and clear of any and all claims for royalty . . . all rights whatsoever in and to all and every the works that you shall write, conceive, compose or produce during the term hereof. . . . It is further agreed in so far as the work done and performed by you . . . may consist of songs and /or lyrics that we . . . shall have the sole, exclusive,

---

[80] WBA, #400 "ESCAPE ME NEVER" 12736A.
[81] WBA, "ESCAPE ME NEVER" STORY-MEMOS & CORRESPONDENCE 2 OF 3 9/20/45–12/29/45, 1885B.
[82] WBA, #400 "ESCAPE ME NEVER" 12736A.
[83] Ibid.

absolute and unlimited right, license, privilege and authority to copyright, print, reprint, copy and vend . . . throughout the world . . . You hereby grant to us the right to assign to the Music Publishers Holding Corporation, or any other publisher designated by us, for publication any work or works done and performed by you hereunder, and for which you shall be paid the royalties provided for by the agreement made simultaneously herewith by and between you and the said Music Publishers Holding Corporation. . . . You hereby represent and warrant that any and all musical and/or literary material that may be composed, written or prepared by you . . . shall be wholly original with you and shall not be copied, in whole or in part, from any other work.[84]

Thus, the agreement with MPHC of the same date is explained. Other clauses in this letter of agreement included a right to make use of and control his name and likeness, the promise that if he was required to work anywhere other than Burbank, first-class transport would be provided (including Pullman accommodation if available), and that "In the event that by reason of mental or physical disability or otherwise you shall be incapacitated from fully performing and complying with your obligations . . . we . . . shall be entitled to refuse to pay you any compensation during the period of such incapacity."[85] In such an event, however, Korngold would be entitled to extend his twelve-week minimum term.

In addition to writing *Escape Me Never*'s ballet, Korngold had certainly been working already on the songs to be sung in the film by Gemma (Ida Lupino), the separate publication of which had been accounted for in the contract. A memo to Tenny Wright from Al Alleborn dated December 11, 1945, reported the previous day's activity (the twenty-fourth day of shooting) and mentioned: "We had a meeting in the Music Department regarding the music in the picture, especially the song IDA LUPINO sings [presumably 'Love for Love']. Dudley Chambers, Korngold, director and the producer were present. Everything is arranged to make the record on Wednesday afternoon. Miss LUPINO will take this record home and rehearse it, and we plan on shooting the song when we move in on Stage 17 toward the end of the week."[86] Moreover, as the contract made clear, Korngold's role on this film would extend beyond simply composing the ballet music, the songs, and the score, to a more consultative one. This included coaching actor Albert Bassermann, who needed to conduct in one scene. On December 18, 1945, Henry Blanke wrote to Alleborn asking him, "Will you please check with Prof. Korngold to have Albert Bassermann start as soon as possible to learn conducting the entire ballet number. We can never tell when

---

[84] Ibid.
[85] Ibid.
[86] WBA, #656 "ESCAPE ME NEVER" P GODFREY, 1488A.

78 KORNGOLD IN AMERICA

the camera will be on him at this stage of the game. Therefore, he'd better learn conducting the whole thing."[87]

The ballet scenes themselves were filmed by a separate unit directed by LeRoy Prinz. By December 18, 1945, rehearsals for the ballet could begin, and these continued daily until December 22, and resumed after Christmas on December 26. They involved two figures, Malcolm Beelby (sometimes spelled Beelbe in archival records) and Chas Kisco. On January 3 Al Alleborn reported to Tenny Wright about the Prinz unit's day on January 2, revealing that the ballet itself was evidently complete and awaiting recording: "Company rehearsed on Stages 7 and 19, starting at 9:00 AM and finished at 5:00PM. The pre-recording of this number was cancelled due to the illness of Mr. KORNGOLD, who was home sick. However, this does not hold up the rehearsal because they are rehearsing to a piano track."[88] On February 1, 1946, a day after filming completed, Blanke sent Korngold a continuity sheet, presumably to aid in the scoring process—though the document itself is no longer extant. Extensive changes were made to the film after the first preview, however: Obringer reported to Jay Goettman on April 26 that Korngold had provided eight days of services after the first preview, and further revealed that "Under the contract, he is entitled to $100 for each day; however, he has agreed to settle for $500."[89] Such comments confirm that on multiple occasions, Korngold was apparently underpaid for the work he did for Warners.

Korngold's last film for the studio was the music-rich melodrama *Deception*, which was directed by Irving Rapper and starred Bette Davis, Paul Henreid, and Claude Rains. Like *Escape Me Never* it was a film about musicians, and as such required extensive involvement of the composer during the film's pre-production. As with *Escape Me Never*, a separate letter of agreement was signed for this one film. Initially, though, Korngold was hired only to write the Cello Concerto that is composed by the character Hollenius (Claude Rains) and performed by Karel Novak (Paul Henreid), with the job of scoring the film left somewhat up in the air. The agreement of July 15, 1946, on which date the term of his employment also officially began, sets out Korngold's compensation as a weekly rate of $1,041.66 for five consecutive weeks followed by a further sum of $5,208.30 (a total of $10,416.60). Some changes were made to the agreement, though the original is unreadable: "You hereby represent and warrant that any and all musical and/or dramatic material that may be composed [deletions here] by you during the term hereof shall be wholly original with you [deletions here], and

---

[87] WBA, "ESCAPE ME NEVER" STORY-MEMOS & CORRESPONDENCE 2 OF 3 9/20/45–12/29/45, 1885B.

[88] Memo January 3, 1945, to T C Wright From Al Alleborn. WBA, #656 "ESCAPE ME NEVER" P GODFREY, 1488A. The press book for the film reports a local flu epidemic that, it seems, affected not only Korngold but also Bassermann. WBA, PRODUCTION "ESCAPE ME NEVER" MISCELLANEOUS, 685B.

[89] WBA, Folder 12627A Erich Wolfgang Korngold, composer.

that we shall have the right to use, adapt, translate and change the work or works done and performed by you hereunder."[90] Indeed, a memo from Roy Obringer to Jay Goettman dated July 17, 1946, confirms that a deal had been concluded with Korngold and that the additional $5,208.30 was "for rights in and to the work heretofore done by him."[91] An accompanying agreement states that Korngold will be credited as the composer of "CELLO CONCERTO" but notes that "in the event that you shall write the score ... then, in lieu of the credit. ... you will be accorded credit in the manner set forth in paragraph 22."[92]

Clearly, the composition of a cello concerto to be heard in the film was somewhat different from previous scoring work Korngold had undertaken for Warner Bros., particularly as the composer agreed to provide this separately from the work of scoring and could thus negotiate the rights, which, in contrast to all his other film work, he would indeed hold. Perhaps this is the source of the misunderstanding about Korngold's supposed special status among film composers. Despite the somewhat special nature of the Cello Concerto, though, Korngold could still call on departmental colleagues for assistance, and the concerto as heard in the film was thus orchestrated by Korngold's longstanding collaborators Ray Heindorf and Simon Bucharoff. Korngold evidently soon agreed to write the score, too, and a letter from W. S. Wallace of the Trust Department to Mr. S. Schneider, dated September 30, 1946, confirms that the July 15 agreement had been modified so that in addition to the contracted services related to the concerto, Korngold would also render his services "in scoring said picture," for which he was paid an extra three weeks of salary, commencing September 9, 1946.[93] Two copyright cue sheets for the film indicate end scoring dates of October 2 and October 14, 1946, respectively.[94] That said, it is also abundantly clear that Korngold had been involved with the film long before any letter of agreement was signed. Correspondence dating from May 1946 between Joe McLaughlin (who worked on copyright in the Music Department) and Helen Schoen of the Copyright and Music Clearance Division of Warner Bros. in New York referenced conversations with Korngold and Forbstein about the costs of clearing pieces of music for inclusion in the film, including the Haydn Cello Concerto in D, and the Saint-Saëns Concerto in A minor.[95] Since Korngold was

[90] Ibid.

[91] Ibid.

[92] Ibid.

[93] Ibid.

[94] WBA, 1417A "DECEPTION" 1126A.

[95] Ibid. A letter of May 7, 1946, notes that "Leo [Forbstein] and Korngold were 'weeping' so much about the price ... Oh well, they can't say we didn't try." The Haydn (Hob. VIIb:2), despite being written in the late eighteenth century, was at this time available in a version arranged by François-Auguste Gevaert and published in 1890. It seems to be this edition that publishers wanted $750 to allow Warners to reproduce in performance in *Deception*. For full details of this contested piece of music, see George Kennaway, "Haydn's (?) Cello Concertos, 1860–1930: Editions, Performances, Reception," *Nineteenth-Century Review* 9, no. 2 (2012): 177–211. The arrangement of the Haydn

80 KORNGOLD IN AMERICA

still working on *Escape Me Never* until the end of April, it appears there was virtually no gap between his working periods on these last two films.

***

The contracts and payroll records, supported by various other pieces of evidence in the archives, thus present us with an overview of Korngold's working life as a musician for hire at Warner Bros. Despite their complexity, one thing is clear: had Korngold entered into a full contract with the studio it would have undoubtedly offered him greater financial security, though at the cost of at least some independence in film choice. Orchestrator and composer Ray Heindorf's contracts, for instance, included mandated pay rises of $100 a week in the second year of each renewal. Starting at $400 a week in 1933 (with a pay rise after twenty-six weeks to $500), by the time of his 1938 contract his weekly salary was $800 rising to $900 the following year. In addition, the contract allowed for an option to extend at either $1,000 or $1,100 a week.[96] Orchestrator Hugo Friedhofer, by contrast, received a mere $350 a week and did so without any pay rises between 1936 and 1942.[97] Moreover, Korngold was not given an especially generous salary when compared with other figures working in the Music Department. Leo Forbstein, as head of the department, had started in 1929 with a salary of $450 per week and in correspondence dated April 7, 1944, surrounding a new contract, the extent of his remuneration was made clear:

> Commencing June 19, 1933 he was employed for yearly periods at the rates of $500, $700, $800 and $1,000 per week. In 1938 a term contract was entered into for a period of three years commencing June 20, 1938, at the rate of $1500 per week, with an option for an additional three year period at the same rate of salary. Such contract in its entirety will expire June 19, 1944. Applicant desires to place Mr Forbstein under a further term contract commencing on the expiration of his present contract, that is, on June 20, 1944. . . . five straight years with options and at the uniform rate of $1750 per week through such term.[98]

Forbstein was an executive, and thus entitled to a much higher rate of pay; however, other composers with weekly contracts at Warners were paid substantial amounts. Max Steiner started off earning an astonishing $1,500 per week in 1937, and in 1941 was bumped up to $1,650 per week. By April 1945 when he signed a new five-year contract, he was earning $1,750 a week, which became $2,000 per week in 1946 (with scope to earn up to $2,500 in the seventh year of that particular contract).[99] Steiner made significant charitable donations to the

---

heard in the film, however, is attributed to "Korngold-Gevaert," since a minor plot point concerns the version of the finale cadenza played by Henreid's character.

[96] See contracts dated May 24, 1933, and May 16, 1938, in Ray Heindorf's file at WBA.

[97] See the "Temporary payroll folder" and "Off payroll notice" in Hugo Friedhofer's file at WBA.

[98] See the folders "Forbstein, Leo" and "Forbstein, Leo (Director)" at WBA.

[99] See WBA, "Max Steiner Payroll 1 of 2" and "Max Steiner Payroll 2 of 2."

United Jewish Welfare Fund: a payroll memo from May 23, 1944, asks for $50 at a time to be deducted from his weekly salary until the total reached $2,500.[100] Korngold was perhaps not in a position to do the same, but did donate $500 to the same organization in 1939, and $300 the following year (indeed, he received a letter from Al Lichtman asking whether he might equal his previous year's contribution).[101] Adolf Deutsch was earning a rather less impressive $600 per week from 1937 to 1943, $650 per week from 1943 to 1944, and $700 per week from 1944 until the termination of contract in 1945.[102] Franz Waxman earned a little more, at $750 per week from 1942 to 1945, and $1,000 from 1945 to 1947.[103] The situation enjoyed by other department colleagues including composers under contract—who renegotiated higher rates at contract renewal time, or had mandated pay rises built into their contracts—thus contrasts markedly with Korngold's weekly salary (when he was working), which remained the same throughout a ten-year period. In the year ending December 1941, he was paid a total of $15,833.36 by Warners.[104] In the same calendar year, the full-time head of the Music Department, Leo Forbstein, earned an astonishing $78,000—the equivalent of around $1.6 million in 2024.[105]

Korngold, then, was by no means poorly paid. But it is striking that in spite of his high-art pedigree his compensation was not only less than a studio executive like Forbstein, but also substantially less than his fellow composer, Max Steiner—both in terms of weekly rate and, because he was not on a full-time contract, total yearly salary. Yet, as Steven C. Smith notes, given that Steiner could score ten films a year (or twelve in 1939), he was "a bargain" for the studio in that he would be paid less per film than an A-list freelancer.[106] It is also true that by avoiding a full-time contract, Korngold could leave himself free for other work. Yet, other composers working within the industry were able to negotiate sabbaticals within the financial security provided by full-time "staff composer" contracts: Miklós Rózsa's autobiography mentions the revised contract he was

---

[100] Memo 5/23/44 To Cy Wilder from Edward Selzer. WBA, "Max Steiner Payroll 1 of 2." Aaron Fruchtman, drawing upon evidence from Steiner's financial records held in the Steiner Collection at Brigham Young University, details that a total of $2,050 was deducted in 1944 and 1945 for this purpose. He also lists Steiner's other sizeable donations to the United Jewish Welfare Fund between 1939 and 1952, and mentions the claim that Jack Warner demanded that his Jewish employees donate to this fund but states he can find no evidence to support it. At any rate, it is clear that Steiner made substantial donations to Jewish and non-Jewish charities alike. See "Max Steiner's Jewish Identity and Score to *Symphony of Six Million*," *Journal of Film Music* 9, nos. 1–2 (2016): 83–84.

[101] See LOC, Box H Folder 32. Korngold also appears on a list of sponsors in connection with a 1943 United Jewish Welfare Fund event (along with Forbstein and, among other Hollywood royalty, Samuel Goldywn, Louis B. Mayer, and David O. Selznick, but not Steiner). See LOC, Box D Folder 1.

[102] WBA, "Adolph Deutsch."

[103] WBA, "Franz Waxman Composer Expired."

[104] See end-of-year statement from Comptroller C. H. Wilder in LOC, Box C Folder 6.

[105] See a statement dated November 3, 1943 in WBA, "Forbstein, Leo (Director)."

[106] Steven C. Smith, *Music by Max Steiner: The Epic Life of Hollywood's Most Influential Composer* (New York: Oxford University Press, 2020), 201.

able to negotiate at MGM in the early 1950s, which allowed him three months unpaid leave each summer.[107] Korngold undoubtedly retained a measure of control over the work he did, though not nearly as much as existing myths suggest. He never did have *carte blanche* to score precisely what film he wanted, with the exception of the single film agreements for *A Midsummer Night's Dream*, *Robin Hood*, *Kings Row*, *Escape Me Never*, and *Deception*, all of which were made outside of existing agreements. Moreover, Rózsa was later supposedly able to negotiate a staff-composer contract with MGM that allowed him first refusal on their "most prestigious films."[108] In other words, the kinds of freedom that Korngold enjoyed were also available to others on much more generous terms. When working on a film, too, Korngold was subject to many of the same restrictions as his fellow composers in the industry, and his music would remain the property of the studio to do with as they wished, as was clear in the case of *Juarez* and its reuse in *The Mad Empress*.

The contractual and financial detail revealed here, then, suggests that although Korngold was well compensated for his contributions to film, his work was not valued at an exorbitant rate when compared with his contemporaries, claims about the "most" generous of contracts notwithstanding. Perhaps only in the fact that he was permitted to sign short-term agreements for two or three pictures at a time did he enjoy any special privileges, something he paid for in the lack of progression in terms enjoyed by his colleagues on permanent contracts. In that sense, Korngold engaged with Hollywood not as a lofty outsider prepared to dabble in the murky waters of movie-making only if compensated in a way that recognized his exalted status, but instead as a jobbing twentieth-century freelancer mindful of the need to earn a living, for whom Hollywood represented an important and convenient income stream. Yet, it also offered him numerous opportunities to further explore his own artistry, and dramatic challenges to overcome. For this, Korngold had a well-developed compositional toolbox that he could draw upon to craft his scores, and it is to the processes and techniques of composition that I now turn.

---

[107] *Double Life: The Autobiography of Miklós Rózsa* (Tunbridge Wells: The Baton Press, 1984), 156.

[108] Ibid., 144.

3

A Hollywood Compositional Toolbox

Film is routinely regarded as a meaningful art form, open to powerful hermeneutic inquiry and welcoming of individual artistic expression. In connection
with this latter quality, though, it is often explored via the persona of a film's director or, less commonly, a screenwriter or producer. To think of a film score
as a vehicle for a composer to explore aspects of personal self-expression is,
perhaps, somewhat less common—especially in the case of scores of the studio
era. To some degree, that reflects relatively recent changes in attitudes toward
the role of individual creativity in Hollywood. Quite rightly, studies of studio-
era filmmaking have sought in recent years to redress a perceived imbalance
by challenging those auterist models of creativity that dominated film production discourse in earlier decades and instead to stress collaboration. A similar
challenge to auterist models of musical creativity in film composition that, in
laboring under a kind of modernist anxiety, feel the need to emphasize compositional autonomy has arisen in recent years. Thus, my own work has sought to
complicate a simplified understanding of compositional creativity in studio-era
filmmaking and to shine a light on those creative contributions by orchestrators
and other music personnel. Likewise, Nathan Platte's study of studio-era music-
making in the context of David O. Selznick's films has revealed the complexity
of these creative relationships between producers and music personnel, and has
immeasurably enriched our understanding of the historical realities of collaborative endeavor.[1] With these lessons in mind, however, and having explored these
kinds of creative and contractual collaborations between Korngold and others
at Warner Bros. in the first two chapters, the question still arises: might we read
Korngold's film scores as sites for personal artistic expression, while resisting a
modernist desire to stress his artistic autonomy? The notion that composers are
required to subordinate themselves to the demands of a film's narrative is a significant factor that might preclude such a perspective, as is the fact that scoring
is generally carried out in post-production.[2] This would seem to suggest that the

---

[1] Nathan Platte, *Making Music in Selznick's Hollywood* (New York: Oxford University Press, 2017).

[2] "Compositional voice" is often the site for contested debate when it comes to film composers.
Frank Lehman, responding to claims that film composer Hans Zimmer lacks a distinctive compositional voice, has argued that "Part of Zimmer's appeal to filmmakers is that he is *not* as stylistically
chameleonic as, say, John Williams. . . . Zimmer cannot help but speak in his own, immensely distinctive voice." See "Manufacturing the Epic Score: Hans Zimmer and the Sounds of Significance," in
Music in Epic Film: Listening to Spectacle, ed. Stephen C. Meyer (New York: Routledge, 2017), 33.

Korngold in America. Ben Winters, Oxford University Press. © Oxford University Press 2025.
DOI: 10.1093/9780197684818.003.0004

84 KORNGOLD IN AMERICA

constraints placed upon composers by not only the narrative decisions made by filmmakers but also filmmakers' aesthetic demands (which composers are generally not at liberty to ignore) rarely result in work that is capable of functioning as "genuine" artistic self-expression. Here is where the commercial and practical realities of film-score production would seem to distance themselves from the worlds of opera or concert-hall composition, which are less prone (if not immune) to "outside" interference. Yet, to assume that film scores are incapable of such artistic work because of the circumstances of their production would itself be somewhat short-sighted, and arguably just as fallacious as the other extreme in assuming they are the product of a single creative auteur unaffected by the realities of creative collaboration.

In this chapter, then, I want to suggest that—mindful of the apparent restrictions placed on his compositional process by the circumstances of production, and the richness of his creative interactions with others—scoring films did indeed offer Korngold opportunities to explore and develop his own creative identity as a composer; and that, in their role of "worldbuilding"—by which I mean creating a convincing, consistent, and compelling musical component to the narrative—the scores may contribute hugely to the value of the films of which they are a part. (This is somewhat ironic in that, with the exception of *The Adventures of Robin Hood*, none of the movies that Korngold scored are perhaps particularly well regarded today as films.[3]) In some ways, though, these opportunities were conditioned by those very practicalities of film scoring that would seem to deny scores the ability to function as self-expression; indeed, writing film scores appears to have encouraged Korngold to develop his attitude towards concepts of originality and reuse, something that had its logical fruition in his post-Hollywood works, as we will discover in Chapter 6. First, I will explore the ways in which Korngold engaged technologically with the medium of film, and which afforded him opportunities to develop his skills as a film-score composer. This challenges fundamentally some of the mythology about which I commented in the Introduction. I then turn my attention to Korngold's penchant for recycling material and for engaging with the compositional material of others. In many ways, of course, this supports the image of the musician for hire I presented in the first two chapters—in ways that would be instantly familiar to composers from earlier ages such as J. S. Bach and G. F. Handel— but it also represents a continuation and expansion of behavior he had already demonstrated in his pre-Hollywood career. As such, I would argue it represents no fundamental compromise of artistic behavior but a serendipitous alignment

---

[3] *Robin Hood* appeared on both the American Film Institute's "100 Years ... 100 Thrills" and "100 Years ... 100 Heroes and Villains" lists. Although such lists provide only a narrow snapshot of a film's critical reputation, *The Adventures of Robin Hood* is the only Korngold-scored film to appear on any of the AFI's lists. See https://www.afi.com/afi-lists (accessed July 31, 2023).

of commercial exigency and artistic impulse. Finally, I want to investigate the ways in which the films for which he wrote music allowed Korngold to explore his own identity as an artist—in terms of both his ability to engage with a variety of musical styles and dramatic scenarios, and the timbral and harmonic characteristics of his music. As a result, I suggest that film scores were no mere cultural *cul-de-sac* that prevented Korngold from growing creatively or that encouraged him to retreat from the challenges of contemporary artistic life into the safe, unthreatening and above all uncontroversial world of Hollywood. Rather, they afforded opportunities to challenge himself as a creative artist, and to contribute to the creation of cinematic worlds that although shaped by the restrictions that a medium like film provided can be considered products of artistic endeavor.

First, however, it is worth revisiting Korngold's normal working method of preparing post-production music, which remained largely consistent throughout his time working for Warners. Ordinarily, any prior research work connected to the musical content of a film would have been undertaken by the studio's Research Department, headed by Hermann Lissauer, and completed long before Korngold was assigned to a film.[4] Sometimes, however, Korngold undertook his own initial research or asked for extra material to supplement this: in the case of *The Adventures of Robin Hood*, he examined sixteenth-century dance tunes in Vienna's public libraries prior to his arrival in Hollywood,[5] and for *The Sea Hawk*, his secretary Jaro Churain asked the Research Department for sixteenth-century national songs of both England and Spain, presumably at Korngold's request.[6] Once ready to start composing, though, Korngold's first step appears to have been to sketch material in response to a rough cut. By "sketch," I mean the kind of fragmented compositional ideas that are often the subject of musicological "sketch studies," with Beethoven's the best known and most extensively studied. This is somewhat different from the way in which the word is used in Hollywood, where it refers to a complete "short score" of several staves;[7] however, it is useful to distinguish between Korngold's private sketch material and the short score that he would hand over to Churain for copying. Thus, the

---

[4] As noted in Chapter 2, for *Devotion*, the Research Department was asked by producer Robert Buckner to investigate the possible ballets that Charlotte Brontë (Olivia de Havilland) might have seen in London in the 1840s. As a result, Music Department chief Leo Forbstein asked Victor Blau to clear the use of Pugni's *La Esmerelda* for the film; Letter dated February 5, 1943, from Forbstein to Blau. Warner Bros. Archives (hereafter WBA), Folder 12627A Erich Wolfgang Korngold, composer. As Helen Schoen confirmed to Nina Sampson, though, since no copy could be found, Korngold composed a replacement; Letter dated October 18, 1943 to Helen Schoen from Nina Sampson in WBA, 1172A "DEVOTION." The poster displayed in the film still identifies it as Pugni's *La Esmerelda*, however.

[5] Ben Winters, *Erich Wolfgang Korngold's* The Adventures of Robin Hood: *A Film Score Guide* (Lanham, MD: Scarecrow Press, 2007), 73–74.

[6] Letter dated January 29, 1940, WBA, "THE SEA HAWK"—RESEARCH.

[7] Nathan Platte, for instance, uses the term "sketch" in its usual industry sense. See *Making Music in Selznick's Hollywood.*

86   KORNGOLD IN AMERICA

amount of sketch material extant for each film varies considerably—from a mere ten pages for *Anthony Adverse* or twenty-seven pages for *The Adventures of Robin Hood* to seventy-nine pages for *Of Human Bondage* and 142 pages for *Between Two Worlds*—and it is commonly loosely organized: sketches may be collections of fragments on a single stave or may operate over two, three, or four staves for a couple of pages. They might constitute an early draft of an entire scene, as with cue 8B from *The Adventures of Robin Hood* or cue 1C in *Between Two Worlds*, where Korngold is clearly engaging closely with the image (noting such elements that will be useful for synchronization). In other instances, though, sketches might comprise mere fragments of thematic material, sometimes labeled with a character or actor name. Korngold writes "Garfield," for instance, against a theme used for John Garfield's character in the extensive sketches for *Between Two Worlds*,[8] and a number of the character themes for *Anthony Adverse* are present in single-stave sketches. The composer's often impenetrable hand is even less clear in these sketch materials than in other manuscript sources, though since they were for his private use that should be no surprise.

After spotting decisions had been made, cue timing sheets would be prepared. As I noted in Chapter 1, sometimes these are in Korngold's hand or contain Korngold's handwritten notes. The surviving cue sheets in the Korngold Collection at the Library of Congress are a mixture of typed and handwritten documents, and they can reveal the importance of the visual and auditory content of a scene for Korngold's music. For the duel between Robin Hood and Sir Guy of Gisborne in *The Adventures of Robin Hood*, the cue sheet's precise indication of the location and duration of visual stasis in this most dynamic of scenes is an essential factor in the cue's construction.[9] Even if, for the sake of musical continuity, Korngold occasionally ignores some of these moments of stasis, knowledge of shot lengths (likely measured at this point in his film-scoring career in basic fashion with a stopwatch) was evidently necessary to the cue's compositional process. The use of cue sheets was not restricted to action-adventure films, though. They exist for the historical costume drama *Devotion*, which is a biopic of the Brontë sisters, and although no cue sheets survive for the earlier historical costume drama *Anthony Adverse*, an interview article for a 1937 issue of *The Etude Music Magazine* noted: "even Korngold, while he worked on 'Anthony Adverse' . . . had to work with stop watch in hand; for in such cases accurate and precise timing is of paramount importance."[10] Although cue sheets are only

---

[8] The sketch materials for *Between Two Worlds*, though, contain a number of later notes in an unknown hand that are not always accurate. The theme for the Rev. William "Bunny" Duke is accompanied by an incorrect annotation: "Faye Emerson's theme." LOC, Box 3 Folder 7.

[9] See Winters, *Korngold's* The Adventures of Robin Hood, 84 for a reproduction of this cue sheet.

[10] See http://thompsonian.info/korngold-etude-Jan-1937.html (accessed October 14, 2021).

extant for a fraction of the films on which Korngold worked,[11] there seems little reason to doubt that they formed a normal part of his working method whatever the nature of the film.[12] They were part of Korngold's compositional process at least as early as 1938 and probably earlier, and continued throughout his career.[13] Moreover, they demonstrate that precise timing during composition was achieved by mechanical means, contrary to much of the mythology surrounding the composer.

The next stage involved Korngold preparing an autograph pencil short score consisting of three, four, or occasionally more staves, divided clearly into cues, whose content often matched quite closely the eventual recorded score.[14] This autograph short score could also include special music provided for a premiere or roadshow version, and occasionally trailer music.[15] According to Hugo Friedhofer's oral history, he—and presumably the other orchestrators who collaborated with Korngold—would not work directly from this short-score

---

[11] Cue sheets exist in the Korngold Collection for *The Adventures of Robin Hood, The Private Lives of Elizabeth and Essex, The Sea Hawk, The Sea Wolf, Devotion,* and *Magic Fire.*

[12] Even in his earliest project for Warner Bros., archival evidence indicates that some technical timing assistance was necessary. In the files for *A Midsummer Night's Dream,* along with apparent recordings of dialogue and prescoring, there are also requests for "A record of beats every foot a beat. 60 beats altogether" and "In front of the piano playback 4 beats, each one as long as one bar of the piano playback, approx. 1½ foot distance in between each beat." WBA, "A MIDSUMMER NIGHT'S DREAM" Folder 4 of 4, Story File #2078.

[13] The extant cue sheets for *Magic Fire* are primarily concerned with planning recording sessions, though they nonetheless reveal a concern with synchronization of Wagner's music with shots or lines of dialogue in the film. LOC, Box 10 Folder 6.

[14] Friedhofer's oral history suggested that Korngold only ever wrote a "piano part"; see Linda Danly, ed., *Hugo Friedhofer: The Best Years of His Life. A Hollywood Master of Music for the Movies* (Lanham, MD: Scarecrow Press, 2002), 40. However, although only two staves are used in parts of the short score for *Captain Blood* and *Anthony Adverse,* the default on later scores is three staves or more.

[15] "Roadshowing" was an exhibition practice derived from theatrical traditions in which a film would be presented for a limited run with bookable seats at selected high-prestige venues, prior to going on general release. Such roadshow versions of films often included special musical accompaniments in the form of overtures, entr'actes, intermission, and exit music. See Ben Winters, "Historical Sound-Film Presentation and the Closed-Curtain Roadshow Overture," in *The Oxford Handbook of Cinematic Listening,* ed. Carlo Cenciarelli (New York: Oxford University Press, 2021), 139–155. Warners appeared to have used similar practices for a number of the prestige pictures involving Korngold's music, as a result of which recorded or live orchestral overtures were prepared. Korngold's autograph short score for *The Constant Nymph,* for example, sets out the content of the overture in a combination of written instructions to draw material from the score and trailer music, and manuscript connecting passages. Overtures were also prepared for *A Midsummer Night's Dream, Juarez,* and *The Private Lives of Elizabeth and Essex.* Although, according to Kim R. Holston's definition in *Movie Roadshows: A History and Filmography of Reserved-Seat Limited Showings, 1911–1973* (Jefferson, NC: McFarland, 2013) of these only *A Midsummer Night's Dream* was actually roadshowed, contemporary press certainly reports that *Juarez* was roadshowed in New York at the Hollywood Theatre on a five-week, reserved-seat basis (with tickets at $2.20) from April 25, 1939. It was released nationally on June 10. See *Boxoffice,* May 27, 1939, 22-H. The film also received a premiere in Hollywood, on April 25, at Warner's Beverly Theatre. Although the pages from the *Juarez* full score that were used for the roadshow overture (from cues 6A, 9E, 10D) are missing from the archives, Brendan Carroll has uploaded a recording of the overture lasting 5:38 to YouTube: https://youtu.be/-Xtp1f-bLPk?si=RKxNLOqZBrRzI9Bo (accessed September 5, 2023).

88 KORNGOLD IN AMERICA

manuscript, but rather from a copy prepared by Korngold's amanuensis, Jaro Churain, who could presumably better read his hand.[16] Although Korngold's "compositional" work continued after these short scores were passed to orchestrators—through processes of review and refinement carried out on the Scoring Stage—and although other copyists' scores were prepared to assist in documenting the recording process, the main crux of the compositional process is apparent in these autograph short-score manuscripts.

The short scores also reveal that efficient preparation and recording of the music was aided immeasurably by a change in Korngold's technique that occurred in early 1939 when working on the music for *Juarez*. It was a profound change that reveals the importance of technology to Korngold's process, and as such challenges some of those foundational myths about the composer I mentioned in the Introduction. It reveals the extent to which Korngold, as a creative artist, was thoroughly immersed in the technical modernity of Hollywood.

Synchronization Possibilities

Korngold's work on the sixteen reels of *Juarez* in early 1939 proceeded as with the previous project, *The Adventures of Robin Hood*, with one notable exception. For the first time, the short scores contain circular markings in blue pencil indicating regular punches to be made in the celluloid (see Figure 3.1), so that as a work print was projected during scoring sessions, a series of flashing lights would appear onscreen, functioning as a metronome either to give Korngold as conductor the correct tempo before the start of the cue,[17] or to act as a warning prior to onscreen events that required precise alignment with a musical gesture. These markings are absent from Korngold's manuscript materials prior to this date, but are present from this point onward in *all* his scores for Warner Bros. (both his manuscript short scores and orchestrated full scores). In short, this moment represents a significant change in Korngold's use of timing aids that would make synchronization much easier and scoring sessions run much more smoothly. No surviving correspondence indicates why this change in scoring technique was made—though as Korngold became more familiar with the possibilities

---

[16] For the most part, these copies have unfortunately disappeared. The only ones that seem to have survived almost complete are those for *The Adventures of Robin Hood*, *Kings Row*, and *Deception*, though fragments in Churain's hand also exist for *Of Human Bondage* and *Captain Blood*. Identifying Churain's musical hand is difficult, though fragments of his handwriting exist. The *Robin Hood* piano-conductor score seems to be mostly in Churain's hand (though other hands appear to be present, which may be those of studio copyists like Charles Eggett or Anthony Macario). Churain's exact role in the process remains somewhat difficult to confirm.

[17] As the film was running through the projector at 24 frames per second (or 1,440 frames per minute), a punch every 24 frames would flash once a second, the equivalent of a metronome mark of 60 beats per minute (bpm).

Figure 3.1 Punch markings in Korngold's short score (cue 2A) of *Juarez*. Box 8 Folder 4. Erich Wolfgang Korngold Collection, Music Division, Library of Congress, Washington, DC. Courtesy of the Korngold Family Estate.

offered by the medium's technology, it is possible he elected to make use of it voluntarily. Far more likely, however, is that either Music Department chief Leo Forbstein, or Executive in Charge of Production Hal B. Wallis himself, suggested or demanded it in order to save considerable time on the Scoring Stage. The last day of scheduled recording for *Robin Hood* had taken the musicians up until midnight on Sunday, April 3, 1938, and although there was a whole reel of music to record on that day, they were evidently up against a tight deadline.[18] Perhaps Korngold insisted on multiple takes to achieve a close alignment of music and picture without being aware of the ability of technology to help, or maybe he was reluctant to make use of it. For a studio that prided itself on economic use of time—and an executive in Wallis who pursued the waste of time and money with almost religious zeal[19]—it seems inconceivable that this situation would have been allowed to continue. In any case, once the change had been made in Korngold's use of the technology, it was a permanent one. Moreover, it is significant that such markings exist not only in the orchestrated full scores alongside the conducting annotations Korngold routinely made in preparation for the sessions, but also in the short scores themselves. Thus, it appears that Korngold's method of composing may have changed fundamentally from November 1938

---

[18] See Winters, *Korngold's* The Adventures of Robin Hood, 151. Another day of recording was required on April 11 to record revisions following the Pomona sneak preview on April 7. Ibid., 79.

[19] On *Anthony Adverse*, for instance, in a memo of December 21, 1935, to T. C. Wright, Wallis exploded: "I find that we have built almost a complete theatre.... somebody has criminally wasted thousands of dollars." WBA, "ANTHONY ADVERSE" STORY—MEMOS & CORRESPONDENCE 12/4/35–2/26/36, 1703 Special.

90 KORNGOLD IN AMERICA

as he realized the possibilities for much closer audiovisual synchronization than would have been possible in earlier projects.

In *Juarez*, the markings in both short score and full score are limited to blue circles and crosses without frame rates to accurately specify the spacing of the timing punches. These frame rates, however, would appear in all future films and allowed for precise audiovisual alignment.[20] Moreover, Korngold also begins engaging around this time with more precise frame rates in the cue sheets. The *Robin Hood* cue sheets are precise only to a third of a second (and mostly only to the second). By the time of *The Sea Hawk*, however, Korngold could rely on much more accurate timings. The scene in Reel 11 in which the film's hero, Geoffrey Thorpe, and his men escape captivity warranted eleven pages of cue sheets in which the spacing of events have been indicated in feet and frames, a much more rigorous timing system than could have been provided by a mechanical stopwatch.[21] In addition, a page of manuscript paper exists in the Korngold Collection (Figure 3.2) that sets out events rhythmically—including camera shots—in 4/4 time. The 14½ frame mark indicates that punches would presumably be made every 14 or 15 frames of film, resulting in a flash of light every 0.6 seconds (the equivalent on a metronome of 100 beats per minute). As a result, this translates a standard cue sheet into peculiarly musical terms, with one event marked at a semiquaver level and thus rendered with a precision of 0.15 seconds. Such a timing aid was probably requested by the composer, and prepared by a music editor, and was likely much more extensive than the solitary page that survives (a note at the bottom says "see next"). Significant events that required precise synchronization—such as the cuts between shots of the guard on the ship's deck above and the prisoners below, which are ultimately aligned with changes of musical texture—are marked at the appropriate point in the bar. Ultimately, though, and with the benefit of onscreen punches now available to him, Korngold chose to compose this section in cue 11F in a different way. Rather than opt for a constant 4/4 meter and a more-or-less steady frame rate, he reduced it from sixteen bars to nine and made extensive use of fermatas and punches (at various frame rates marked in the full score) to ensure precise synchronization with onscreen events. Such an approach allowed significant events

---

[20] I have previously detailed several sequences in *Kings Row* that rely on punch markings for synchronization in "The Composer and the Studio: Korngold and Warner Bros.," in *The Cambridge Companion to Film Music*, ed. Mervyn Cooke and Fiona Ford (Cambridge: Cambridge University Press, 2016), 59–63.

[21] LOC, Box 16 Folder 11. Each foot of 35mm film consisted of 16 frames, and since it was projected at 24 frames per second, the separation of events could theoretically be rendered accurate to 1/24th of a second. Although a standard mechanical stopwatch beating at 18,000 beats per hour ticks five times a second, a certain amount of gear lash means that it is rarely possible to time events to a fifth of a second. The studio may have used more specialist stopwatch equipment with faster beat-rates, but timing using the film stock itself would have been more reliable.

A HOLLYWOOD COMPOSITIONAL TOOLBOX 91

Figure 3.2 Cue sheet for Reel 11 of *The Sea Hawk*. Box 16 Folder 11, Erich Wolfgang Korngold Collection, Music Division, Library of Congress, Washington, DC. Courtesy of the Korngold Family Estate.

to align with a downbeat, which undoubtedly made it easier to conduct on the Scoring Stage. Where Mr. Pitt (Alan Hale) strikes the stunned timekeeper, for instance, the cue sheet marks it on a quaver beat; Korngold's final version has it occurring on a downbeat.

The freedom that punches gave Korngold to compose while still achieving precise synchronization contrasts with the process used in the earlier *The Adventures of Robin Hood*. In cues 4C (the attack by Robin and his Merry Men on the treasure caravan) and 11C (the duel between Robin and Sir Guy of Gisbourne)—which are both cues that rely on close audiovisual synchronization—minor cuts to the music were required to ensure a proper fit to picture. These cuts are marked in the piano-conductor score used during scoring sessions by those undertaking the recording. Whether they were a result of last-minute changes made in the edit, or as a direct consequence of a scoring and recording process that did not yet take full advantage of timing technologies, it is impossible to say for certain, but the latter seems most likely. As the composer became more *au fait* with the technology, though, punch markings including frame rates become ever more common in his manuscript materials. In the short score manuscripts for *Of Human Bondage*, which Korngold worked on from December 1944, they can be found throughout in the composer's hand. Korngold then also added these indications himself to the prepared full scores to assist him on the Scoring Stage, since he would conduct from these manuscripts. In the case of *Of Human Bondage*, the technology also allowed him to write many fewer numbered cues, since large stretches of silence in the music could be accommodated without the need to separate and start a new cue. Thus, after each period of silence, and to prepare for the resumption of music, Korngold would mark a series of warning punches to prepare him for the next music entry. Undoubtedly, this helped him streamline the process of composition and recording.

Other notational practices to aid synchronization that became more common post-*Juarez* include the extensive use of blue or red pencil to indicate dialogue cues and changes of shot. These are found both in the short score manuscripts and in the full scores. Indeed, the placement of hard cuts, dissolves, and dialogue can even be found in the initial sketches for some scenes, suggesting that Korngold was now thoroughly immersed in the grammar of the medium from

Figure 3.3 Details from cue 5A of *Escape Me Never*. Box 6 Folder 6A and Folder 3A. Erich Wolfgang Korngold Collection, Music Division, Library of Congress, Washington, DC. Courtesy of the Korngold Family Estate.
(a) Sketch of opening.

Figure 3.3b Short score of opening.

his earliest compositional thoughts. Figure 3.3 shows pages from the initial preparatory sketches and manuscript short score from cue 5A "Whistling" of *Escape Me Never*. Composer Sebastian Dubrok (Errol Flynn) has just bid "Auf Wiedersehen" to the young girl of whom he has asked directions while traveling through the Dolomites with his brother Caryl and companion Gemma. In the initial sketch (Figure 3.3a), Korngold notes the melody but also marks in pencil (overlaid in blue) "Cut Flynn" and then indicates two further changes of camera shot. The next stage, a short score, adds tempo information in the form of four warning punches thirteen frames apart (or c. 111 bpm)—see Figure 3.3b. Later in the same cue, Korngold also notes significant dialogue in blue ("It gives me something to shoot at," itself a slight variant of the actual dialogue: "I'm keeping it for something to shoot at") as Sebastian talks of the inspiration provided by his father's musical manuscript—see Figure 3.3c. (At this point, Korngold introduces a variant of the main motif from Sebastian's own ballet, the composition of which is a key narrative device in the film.) Likely, these markings are to remind Korngold of the necessity for close synchronization of these moments. Figure 3.3d shows two of the "cuts" recorded in Figure 3.3a and a subsequent "dissolve." All three editorial cuts are prepared with a warning punch sixteen frames beforehand, indicating that Korngold is not only considering precise synchronization of music and image when composing (itself hardly a surprise) but is also marking these manuscripts with the very imprint of the technology that will help him achieve this synchronization on the Scoring Stage.

There is even evidence that Korngold used a click track in recording *Of Human Bondage* when creating an extra four bars to be inserted prior to cue 10B (the cue in which Mildred Rogers explodes with rage at Philip, calling him a "cripple"). A click track was a series of audible clicks used on the Scoring Stage

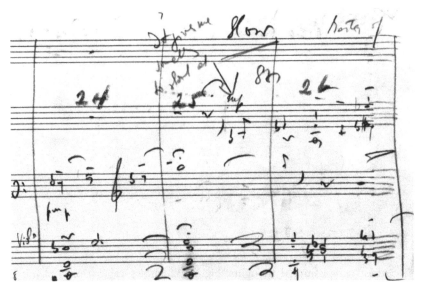

Figure 3.3c Significant dialogue.

Figure 3.3d Changes of camera shot.

to help musicians synchronize with image. At this time, it would have been an optical click track created using loops of blank film stock punched with regularly spaced holes in the sound track area that produced an audible click as each hole passed the optical sound head.[22] The manuscript short score for 10B indicates

---

[22] See Milton Lustig, *Music Editing for the Motion Pictures* (New York: Hastings House, 1980), 42–47.

Figure 3.4 Click-track indications in *Of Human Bondage*. From "Of Human Bondage Holograph Short Score in Pencil" Box 11 Folder 5A. Erich Wolfgang Korngold Collection, Music Division, Library of Congress, Washington, DC. Courtesy of the Korngold Family Estate.

that this cue was to be made "Wild" (that is, not recorded to picture) and was thus to be done "to clicks"—see Figure 3.4. A series of vertical strokes at the beginning of the image suggest two bars of clicks at "9 frames" (160 bpm). This, though, is the only extant evidence that Korngold worked with a click track, and it seems that he would only have used one in a recording "made wild" because the picture was not available to give him his usual onscreen visual punches. Nonetheless, that Korngold even used a click track surely provides the final nail in the coffin to bury the myth that he had "no need" of mechanical timing aids. That is not to say that Korngold necessarily worked in exactly the same fashion as Warner Bros. colleagues. Friedhofer, for instance, in his Oral History for the American Film Institute, seems to suggest that Korngold and Steiner worked in fundamentally different ways by noting that "Steiner, after running the picture once—at the most twice—would depend entirely on the cue sheets.... [whereas] Korngold did all his [compositional] work in the projection room—just improvised to the film."[23] However, as I have shown, it would be a mistake to assume that the "improvisation" was the end point, or that Korngold did not use

---

[23] Danley, *Hugo Friedhofer*, 42.

96   KORNGOLD IN AMERICA

cue sheets; he obviously did. Despite his innate gifts, the precision with which Korngold's music is matched to the film was still achieved with the assistance of mechanical means. As such, Korngold emerges as an artist interested in, and capable of engaging with, the most contemporary of Hollywood technologies.

What is perhaps most striking when consulting these manuscripts, though, apart from Korngold's rather difficult-to-read hand, is the degree to which the composer made use of a musical shorthand to improve efficiency. Where bars could be copied and pasted from elsewhere (even if transposition was necessary), the composer was all too aware and thus, as a result, could save much needed time. This is evident from the earliest scores; thus, in *Captain Blood*, Korngold's short score of the opening titles starts to indicate the reuse of previously written material as early as bar 12 (where the first four bars of the main theme are repeated).[24] The effect when looking at the short score of *The Sea Hawk*, which Korngold had bound in two volumes in an outer Art Deco folder and presented as a 1940 Christmas present to Jack Warner, is of an often constructivist approach to assembly whereby the composer works with recurring elements of his own preexisting material to generate a huge musical canvas. That urge to reuse was not only an important characteristic of Korngold's approach to film-score composition but also one that had a much longer history in his compositional practice.

Recycling and Reuse

When a report foolishly got abroad that the music from his unproduced opera [*Die Kathrin*] was the music he was contributing to "The Adventures of Robin Hood," Professor Erich Wolfgang Korngold shivered the timbers on the Warners lot with a mixture of rage and mirth . . . [he] railed at the idiocy which would entertain [such a thought]. But more than that, his personal feelings [were] very badly damaged. "Could anyone think I would use something I had already written?" he asked, with an appalled expression. "Even if such a thing were possible, it would be cheating." (Thornton Delehanty, "A Score for 'Robin Hood,'" *The New York Times*, May 22, 1938)

Korngold's appalled expression referred to here by Thornton Delehanty may well have been hiding an amused smirk as he deliberately and humorously misled a reporter, because although his score to *The Adventures of Robin Hood* and his fifth opera, *Die Kathrin* are assuredly not "the same thing," the film score does contain large amounts of music he had "already written"—and the fanfare that opens the film (associated with the character of the chief antagonist, Prince

---

[24] LOC, Box 27 Folder 1.

John) also shares much in common with military fanfares used in *Die Kathrin*. One perspective on this issue might acknowledge that Korngold approached his film scores fully aware of the time pressures the job brought and the need to sometimes make use of his own pre-existing material to meet deadlines.[25] Musical reuse was common within the industry, after all, and not merely confined to smaller studios.[26] Another perspective, however, might wonder whether the composer's use of pre-existing material was a deliberate creative choice—as the act, even, of a quasi-postmodernist *bricoleur*. It is likely that the truth lies somewhere between the two: that the necessity of scoring to tight deadlines presented the composer with situations wherein he could creatively explore his relationship with pre-existing material. Indeed, it is important to acknowledge that this is something Korngold had long done, whether formally in terms of his operetta arrangements or through his habit of recasting material in different contexts, or even in quoting very small amounts material by other composers in his operas.[27] Film presented far more opportunities to work with pre-existing material, though sometimes this was demanded incontrovertibly by circumstances.

Korngold's decision to use several symphonic poems by Liszt when working on *Captain Blood*, for example, was undoubtedly motivated by the short timeframe available to score the picture, and because he was still working at Paramount on *Give Us This Night*.[28] The *Captain Blood* short score, which is held in a leather-tooled binder with gold lettering confirming the dates of composition (November 10–December 8, 1935), is even written on Paramount manuscript paper. The time available to produce the music was exceedingly short when compared with later Korngold scores, and studio correspondence from the time emphasized the somewhat frantic nature of the work. On Friday December 6, 1935, Hal Wallis wrote to Major Levinson stressing that duping (the duplication of film print elements) had to be finished by Monday night if they wanted to meet the planned Christmas release date, as the picture needed to be previewed

---

[25] Indeed, this was also common to other composers with back catalogues of concert-hall works. David Cooper comments on Bernard Herrmann's tendency to "self-plagiarism" in reusing prior concert material in his film scores and radio dramas as "demonstrating his pragmatism and efficiency." *Bernard Herrmann's* The Ghost and Mrs Muir: *A Film Score Guide* (Lanham, MD: Scarecrow Press, 2005), 3.

[26] Reuse of scores was particularly common at smaller studios like Republic and Universal; however, as Nathan Platte makes clear, a prestige producer like Selznick when faced with a problematic scene saw no difficulties in asking his composers to reuse music that worked in another of his productions—as with his suggestions to use *Little Lord Fauntleroy* (1936) music in *A Star is Born* (1937) or to reuse a number of cues by Roy Webb, Franz Waxman, and Daniele Amfitheatrof at the climax of Rózsa's score to *Spellbound* (1945). See Platte, *Making Music in Selznick's Hollywood*, 112, 254–258.

[27] Haydn in *Der Ring des Polykrates* and Meyerbeer in *Die tote Stadt*. See Winters, *Korngold's* The Adventures of Robin Hood, 17–18.

[28] Hugo Friedhofer's oral history suggests somewhat antithetically that the reason Korngold worked on *Captain Blood* in the first place was because "he had time on his hands" between the prescoring and scoring of *Give Us This Night*. AFI Oral History, 58–59.

98 KORNGOLD IN AMERICA

on Wednesday night and "a day or two allowed for possible cuts." Wallis asked Levinson's department to work in twenty-four-hour shifts, but he also notes that scoring was still proceeding: "FORBSTEIN scores the last two reels of the picture by Sunday [December 8] so, by Sunday night, you should have completed everything but the two reels, and you should have crews waiting here Sunday night to get the sound track that is scored on Sunday and let them work all night Sunday night and Monday to complete the two reels, which are difficult, and it will probably need that much time."[29]

Scoring finished on time and the film was released, as planned, at Christmas 1935, but in order to meet that deadline, Korngold resorted to using two symphonic poems by Liszt, *Mazeppa* and *Prometheus*, at a number of points.[30] As a consequence, his title credit was changed to "musical arrangements by." This is the only time that Korngold used extensive extracts from previously published classical works in a score that was credited to him as an original composition,[31] but similar behavior on a smaller scale was warranted in later films. Korngold's next project for Warners after *Captain Blood*, for instance, also required him to work with a small amount of pre-existing material—albeit of a different nature and under rather different circumstances. *Anthony Adverse* had long been in production prior to the composer's involvement and, as a result, Korngold had nothing to do with the prescoring of the extensive opera sequences that formed a part of the narrative. For the first, an arranged extract from Monteverdi's *L'Orfeo* was used: the Act 1 chorus "Lasciate i monti." The studio's solution for the second, however, was to use an opera excerpt they had bought for $500 from Aldo Franchetti—who did occasional freelance jobs for the Music Department— subsequently labeled *La Duchessa di Ferrara*.[32] It was used for the opera house sequence in which Anthony (Frederic March) sees Angela (Olivia de Havilland) sing on stage under her professional name, Mademoiselle George. As a consequence, Korngold's score was required to work with Franchetti's extant material in a couple of cues. Korngold's short score cue number 50 (15A), which is heard as we see the advertising poster outside the Paris Opera, incorporates the first four bars of Franchetti's fanfare-like opening.[33] Korngold even confirms in his manuscript short score in red pencil "Orchestration Opera (Franchetti) first 4 bars." After this point, though, Korngold continues the cue with his own material, even notating the sound of violins tuning up. There then follows Franchetti's

---

[29] WBA, "CAPTAIN BLOOD" STORY—MEMOS 4 of 4.

[30] For details, see Winters, *Korngold's* The Adventures of Robin Hood, 42–44.

[31] In providing the score for Paramount's *Give Us This Night*, it was necessary to incorporate an excerpt from Verdi's *Il Trovatore*, namely the Act III aria "Di quella pira."

[32] There is a well-documented and rather interesting legal dispute in the archives about this extract. WBA, "ANTHONY ADVERSE" PICTURE FILE 2869.

[33] Remarkably, Franchetti himself receives onscreen credit not only in the film's opening titles but also in the world of the film: his name is mentioned on the poster outside the opera house.

rather Puccinian opera scene, which includes an "offstage" aria for Angela. (Since this was prescored it is missing from the manuscript and thus unnumbered in the short score's sequence of cues.) Franchetti's extensive material was not quite enough, though, to underscore the entire length of the opera sequence, and after the first climax and burst of applause, Korngold provided a twelve-bar instrumental "Opera Interlude" as cue 51 (15B) to cover Angela's entrance onstage. After an initial descending sequence, this interlude repeats and varies Franchetti's fanfare before dovetailing with the remainder of Franchetti's own prescored material: a reprise of Angela's aria as a vocal ensemble. Korngold then takes over responsibility for the score in cue 52 with Angela's theme, as Anthony disconsolately leaves the opera house knowing that his marriage to Angela is over.

Although Korngold made relatively little use of pre-existing material written by others in *The Adventures of Robin Hood*—of the historical songs turned up by the extensive activities of the Research Department, only "Sumer Is Icumen In" was used[34]—for *Juarez*, Korngold's use of source material was more extensive. The musical design of the film had been considered as far back as August 1938, when the project was still known as *The Phantom Crown*. Herman Lissauer had written to Leo Forbstein to tell him of the "considerable store of music of the period" he had come across, and in October Forbstein had asked the Legal Department to look into the rights to use period songs.[35] Numerous songs were considered at various points, with Forbstein asking about "Adios Mama Carlota," "A Media Noche," and a "Sugar Cane Song" in November 1938, with a January 16 follow-up indicating that "Marcha Zaragoza" had been deleted from the film.[36] In the end, though, the score used only "La Paloma," "Adios Mama Carlota" (as cue 14A), and a "Sugar Cane" song with the lyrics "Cana de azucar! Frescacana" as cue 6E. Forbstein was later asked by Victor Blau of the Legal Department to provide further information about the featured songs, and in a letter dated April 27, 1939, he indicated that "Mr Korngold developed the 'French Anthem' [Napoleon III's theme] from PARTANT POUR LA SYRIE and the 'Austrian Hymn' [Maximilian's theme] from GOTT ERHALTE FRANZ DEM KAISER [the Austrian National Anthem]. Attached hereto you will find both the original music and Mr Korngold's themes for your information. THE MARSEILLAISE was not used."[37] In addition to notating the relevant themes, the attached information also revealed that Korngold's theme for Benito Juarez was adapted from the Mexican Anthem and

---

[34] See Winters, *Korngold's* The Adventures of Robin Hood, 72–73.

[35] Including the songs "La Golondrina," "Cielito Lindo," and "Jarabe Tapatios."

[36] This piece was possibly the source of Korngold's contemporary comment to the press that "All of the music written in Mexico during that period of struggle . . . is unmistakably Viennese." LOC, Box H Folder 1.

[37] WBA, 9222-34 "JUAREZ" 1116A.

that Lincoln's theme was "developed" from an "American War Song." Lincoln's theme was, in fact, merely "The Battle Hymn of the Republic" and as source material for this Korngold was given the main title from the recently completed short film *Lincoln in the White House* (dir. William McGann, 1939). Along with a copy of "Partant Pour La Syrie" it is grouped with the sketch material for the film held in the Korngold Collection.[38] Undoubtedly, the most significant of these "developments" of existing material might be thought to be one for Juarez himself, since it dominates the film; however, the resemblance between Korngold's theme for the character and the Mexican anthem by Jaime Nunó is incredibly slight. It appears that Korngold merely took the opening arpeggio from the anthem as the initial idea, and subsequently developed it—hardly enough to warrant grouping alongside the use of the "Battle Hymn of the Republic" or even "Partant Pour La Syrie." Nonetheless, it is an indication that Korngold's compositional practice for film did not ignore relevant models; just as he had modeled Maid Marian's theme in *Robin Hood* on sixteenth-century dance tunes from William Chappell's *Old English Music* collection,[39] so Juarez's theme retains a link (however slight) to a pre-existing source. Other examples of similar practices in later scores include the integration of Beethoven piano sonatas into the scores of *Kings Row* and *Deception*. Although other films feature characters performing works of the Western classical tradition—in *Devotion*, for instance, we hear Schubert's G-flat Impromptu D.889/3 (transposed to G major and notated as cue 6D)—in both *Kings Row* and *Deception*, Korngold appropriates the Beethoven material in surrounding cues, much in the manner he had done when using Franchetti's material in *Anthony Adverse*.

Korngold, then, occasionally worked with others' compositional material in his scores; however, he made much more extensive use of his own pre-existing compositional output. Self-borrowing was something that Korngold had long practiced prior to his Hollywood career, and he had previously developed the specific habit of reworking recently published Lieder into new instrumental compositions: thus, "Schneeglöckchen" from the *Eichendorff Lieder* was reused for the opening theme of the finale from the Violin Sonata, Op. 6; the central movement of the Piano Quintet, Op. 15, reworked the songs "Mond, so gehst du wieder auf" and "Sterbelied" from *Vier Lieder des Abschieds*, Op. 14; and the fourth movement of the Op. 23 Suite for Piano Quartet was a literal rearrangement of "Was Du mir bist" from the Op. 22 songs, and entitled "Lied" as a result.[40] In that sense, Korngold was carrying on a well-established tradition

---

[38] "Partant pour la Syrie" was the anthem of the Second French Republic (1852–1870).

[39] The tenor part of "A Round of Three Country Dances in One" from Thomas Ravenscroft's 1609 collection *Pammelia*, and the tune "Robin Hood and the Stranger" (Cambridge University MS D.d.9.33 fol. 81ᵛ). See Winters, *Korngold's* The Adventures of Robin Hood, 73.

[40] Korngold also revised songs, of course: thus, "Österreichischer Soldatenabschied" was reworked as "Gefasster Abschieds" in Op. 14.

of the sort that Gustav Mahler had practiced in placing his *Wunderhorn* songs in new symphonic contexts, and he continued to do so when developing material for the film scores. Moreover, there seems to be little evidence to suggest that these cases of self-penned musical reuse in film were motivated by excessive anxiety about generating new material caused by looming deadlines, as had been the case with *Captain Blood*'s use of Liszt: rather, it seems a feature of his compositional character to reframe material in different contexts, one that he was able to continue exploring in his Hollywood output. Thus, for *The Adventures of Robin Hood*, Korngold made extensive use of his own earlier symphonic overture *Sursum Corda* to provide both thematic material for Robin and a love theme, and to underscore several battle scenes. He also drew on material he had written to complete a Leo Fall operetta, *Rosen aus Florida*. The segment written to signify Austria in a "beauty contest of nations" subsequently became the March of the Merry Men, one of the score's most important and oft-used themes.[41] Although this strategy might be assumed to be in response to the size of the task facing him, it is also the case that he had considered using *Sursum Corda* before even seeing the film and its many action scenes, apparently at the suggestion of his father.[42] Moreover, further examples are readily apparent. In the case of cue 3A in *Juarez*, in which the newly arrived Carlota and Maximilian ride through Mexico in a carriage, the passage is clearly based upon the early Eichendorff song setting "Angedenken" of 1911.[43] Likewise, in the opening titles (1A) to *The Private Lives of Elizabeth and Essex*, Korngold quotes bars 43–53 from his 1916 orchestral song *Kaiserin Zita-Hymne*, while rhythmic aspects of the song's introductory and concluding gestures also inform the cue. Perhaps the composer simply recognized the regal commonalities between the two projects, and the opportunity to use a song that was not assigned an official opus number: in any case, it blends seamlessly with the musical language and rhetoric of the rest of the title music.[44] Korngold also reused part of his unpublished 1913 cantata *Der Sturm* for the battle between Irish and English forces (cue 8B) in the same film.

The Sea Hawk likewise prompted the reuse of previous Korngold material. The song sung to the Queen by Dona Maria clearly originated in "Das Mädchen" from the *Zwölf Eichendorff Lieder* (1910–1911), though the revised version heard in the film was subsequently re-published as "Alt Spanisch" in Korngold's

---

[41] See Winters, *Korngold's* The Adventures of Robin Hood, 103–104.

[42] Ibid., 97–102.

[43] This is sometimes also known as "Andenken." It was then transformed into Korngold's setting of Eichendorff's "Der Kranke" (the sick man) from the Op. 38 Lieder (1948)—itself a hermeneutic connection with Carlota's mental illness.

[44] As Frank Lehman notes, the two phrases drawn from *Kaiserin Zita-Hymne* share harmonic characteristics of the rest of the main titles and form part of what he labels (following Mark Richards) a discursive theme. See "Form und thematische Struktur in den Vorspannmusiken E. W. Kornoglds," in *Musik im Vorspann*, ed. Guido Heldt et al. (Munich: Richard Boorberg Verlag, 2020), 11–52.

Op. 38 Lieder. Similarly, *The Sea Hawk*'s theme for Thorpe's monkey seems to be modeled closely on incidental music Korngold composed for Hans Müller's 1923 play, *Der Vampir* (Act II, No. 5), which also features a theme very close in character to the one that was used for the Queen.[45] *Between Two Worlds* drew on several entries from Korngold's back catalogue. The theme for Pete Musick appears to be modeled on the opening phrases of "Liebesbriefchen" from *Sechs Einfache Lieder*, Op. 9, a connection that itself carries strong hermeneutic import: Pete (George Tobias) is a character who cannot help but speak of his wife and their newborn child, while the Elisabeth Honold text set in Korngold's Op. 9 talks of separation from a love ("Fern von dir denk' ich dein, Kindelein": "I think of you, my little child, from far away"). Similarly, the theme for Benjamin (Gilbert Emery) in the same film draws on the opening of Sterbelied (Requiem) from the *Vier Lieder des Abschieds*, Op. 14 (Four Songs of Farewell); although it continues differently, it shares its first bar with the orchestral song. As with Pete's theme, the allusion is entirely compelling: Benjamin's theme is first heard in its entirety when he bids his wife farewell, as both face the realities of their afterlife.[46] Finally, the second part of theme associated with Rev. William "Bunny" Duke (Dennis King) is modeled on a prominent melody from Act III of Korngold's fourth opera, *Das Wunder der Heliane*, an opera concerned with themes of death and resurrection.[47] The opportunity to reuse his own previously published music in new, often hermeneutically relevant, contexts was something, then, that Korngold actively embraced.

Importantly, too, the same Korngold music could be reused between scores, much in the way that productions could reuse sets built on sound stages or the street locations on the Burbank backlot. In this way, Korngold fully embraced the recycling ethos of the studio system. Admittedly, this was not something confined to Korngold: it was standard studio-era practice to repurpose music in different contexts, even in big-budget A pictures. Max Steiner, for example, could happily reuse the main title from *The Lost Patrol* for *Casablanca* (albeit with some minor tweaks to the melody) or, as Nathan Platte has revealed, transform a melody from *Crime School* via *They Made Me a Criminal* into the "Tara" theme from *Gone With the Wind*.[48] Korngold was, at least, reusing material owned by the same studio (Steiner in repurposing music from an RKO picture in Warner's *Casablanca* was presumably taking a risk) and could thus be open about instructing orchestrators accordingly. *Juarez* and *The Sea Hawk*, for instance, share several sections of musical material. Cue 12B in *The Sea Hawk*, in which Thorpe and his men prepare the stolen Spanish galleass for escape,

---

[45] See Act 1, No. 2. Reh. Fig. 1+3 in Cello.
[46] We hear the first three notes in the card trick scene.
[47] See, for example, Reh. Fig. 283+3.
[48] Platte, *Making Music in Selznick's Hollywood*, 173–178.

features material first used in cue 5C from *Juarez*—in which General Porfirio Diaz (John Garfield) announces his plan to break through the encircling French forces; the two cues even share the same orchestrator, Simon Bucharoff. In this instance, Bucharoff re-orchestrates the same material from Korngold's short score rather than reusing the older cue verbatim; however, in the full score of cue 8E of *The Sea Hawk*, where Thorpe and his men are ambushed in the Panamanian jungle by the Spaniards, a note from Milan Roder simply asks the copyist to "copy from score 15 (Juarez) 10 bars beginning with last bar on page 9 with blue pencil changes (no Cimble) [*sic*]." Score 15 (or cue 4C) in *Juarez* is likewise battle music orchestrated by Roder, and thus entirely appropriate for reuse in its new context. The flood cue from *The Green Pastures* (cue no. 3) also found a new home in *The Sea Hawk* as cue 2E. In the manuscript short score of the latter, Korngold writes "II/E Continuation ('Green Pastures' Flood)," at which point copyist ditto pages are pasted in. This store of previous film-score material that Korngold could call to mind effortlessly and redeploy as necessary is particularly striking.

Besides the direct lifting of passages, character themes from one film might turn up in another.[49] A theme that was introduced in cue 11 of *Another Dawn* ("Talk in the Bedroom")—and subsequently cut from that film as a result of Hal Wallis's requested changes (see Chapter 1)—was reframed as Mons. Heger's theme in *Devotion* (see Example 3.1). The theme as it features in manuscript sources for *Another Dawn* is related to the martial music used in the ride-out cues (cues 12 and 19) but seems most plausible as an abandoned one-off light-hearted theme for Denny's sister, Grace (Frieda Inescort)—a character who has no musical theme in the version of the film that survives. In its altered form in *Devotion* the theme has a new, more coquettish, rhythm, though in preserving the uncertain shifting harmonic character of the melody, it now serves to express Mons. Heger's difficult-to-read character for Charlotte: will he leave his wife for her or not? This particular reuse may have transpired because Korngold knew the music had been cut from *Another Dawn*, but it is not the only example of thematic reuse. Willoughby's theme as heard in *Captain Blood* was reprised as the London theme in *Devotion*, doubling for the person of Thackeray (Sidney Greenstreet), while the theme for Queen Elizabeth's sorrow in *The Private Lives of Elizabeth and Essex* found a new home in the music for *Deception*, as part of the Cello Concerto composed by Hollenius: we even see the same actress onscreen (Bette Davis) when hearing it in context during the rehearsal scene.[50] The theme

---

[49] Other examples are close enough to suggest they are cut from the same cloth. The fanfare for Prince John in *Robin Hood* shares much with not only the theme for the King in *The Prince and the Pauper*, but also the theme for Philip's medical career in *Of Human Bondage*.

[50] We first hear it in the score when seeing an announcement of the rehearsal in the paper.

Example 3.1 "Unheard" thematic reuse (a) *Another Dawn*, cue 11 (b) Mons. Heger's theme in *Devotion*, cue 6E.

for Father Xavier (Henry O'Neill) in *Anthony Adverse* also had another outing in varied form as the Brussels music in *Devotion* (see Example 3.2).[51]

In addition to these inter-film recyclings, Korngold was, as noted above, adept at recognizing the possibility of musical reuse within a score, a practical solution to the time-intensive task of composing for films. Thus, many of his short scores use a shorthand instructing orchestrators to copy an aspect of a previous section, an instruction often reproduced in the full-score manuscript for the benefit of copyists. The result is sometimes pages of almost blank full score, with a single skeletonized line of music for reference. The climactic duel between Thorpe and Wolfingham in *The Sea Hawk*, for instance, consists of three cues: 13C, 13D, and 13E. As Table 3.1 reveals, although 13C is entirely original, 13D and 13E are largely made up of music copied from earlier in the film, namely Reel 2 Part H (in which Thorpe duels with Captain Lopez) with a number of short insertions and repetitions, including a distinctive xylophone-dominated passage that shares much with the duel from *Robin Hood*. Undoubtedly, such practices constituted a more efficient use of everybody's time; however, they also suggest that Korngold

---

[51] The opening of the Brussels music in cue 6B of *Devotion* also seems to bear a close resemblance to the opening of Korngold's opera, *Die Kathrin*.

Example 3.2 Varied thematic reuse (a) Father Xavier's theme in *Anthony Adverse* (cue 10) (b) Brussels music in *Devotion* (cue 6B).

adopted, on occasion, a conscious cut-and-paste approach to composition.[52] The construction of cue 13E in *The Sea Hawk*, in particular, reveals an assemblage using prior material and a way of extension using interpolated bars. Fragmentation, repetition, and development of thematic material had always been part of Korngold's composition arsenal. Arguably, the processes and time pressures of Hollywood offered the composer the opportunity to develop further these methods of formal musical construction.

Reuse of material is often one of the sticks with which composers working within the film industry are beaten. The underlying assumption is that recycling

---

[52] It might bear some similarity to the cut-and-paste approach of Igor Stravinsky, even if it was not necessarily used to the same aesthetic ends or in the same practical sense. See Gretchen Horlacher, *Building Blocks: Repetition and Continuity in the Music of Stravinsky* (New York: Oxford University Press, 2011).

106 KORNGOLD IN AMERICA

Table 3.1 *The Sea Hawk* duel's construction and its reliance on earlier material.

Cue	Content	Action
13C	32 bars of original material (featuring some internal repetition)	Duel begins
13D	Bars 1–23 from 2H Four bars of new material Bars 26–30 from 2H Bars 32–33 from 2H ("N.B!" written in full score) Bars 36–37 from 2H ("N.B!" written in full score) Three bars of new material (with one bar subsequently cut)	Table thrown over Thorpe and Wolfingham lock swords Wolfingham crashes through glass doors
13E	Bars 1–6 from 2H Five bars of new material Bars 12–23 from 2H Nine bars of new material Bars 13–19 from 2H One bar of new material Bars 1–2 from 2H (with new violin and piccolo lines) repeated Seven bars of new material	Long shot of duelists through archways Thorpe and Wolfingham lock swords

involves a lesser amount of creativity that, in reflecting the commercial-driven imperatives of the industry, comes into direct conflict with romantic notions of originality that are largely perpetuated in many idealized views of music composition. Yet, Korngold had always explored such practices, and the processes he used in film scoring represent merely the next logical step in this artistic journey. As we will discover in Chapter 6, this resulted in a significant challenge to existing norms and practices of artistic production: the reuse of film-score material in genres for the concert hall.

Stylistic Plurality

Korngold is often associated with a late-romantic harmonic lushness, and he was certainly on comfortable ground in film when writing love scenes, for which he utilized the Straussian harmonic language long familiar to him. The romance scenes between Maria and Denis in *Anthony Adverse*, for instance, are suffused with a *fin-de-siècle* Viennese richness: Rehearsal Figure 7 in cue 2A features swooping C minor seventh chords over a pedal B♭ prefaced with chromatic diminished sevenths. Similarly, *Captain Blood*'s scenes between Blood

Example 3.3 Straussian neighbor-note chromaticism in *Captain Blood* (cue 11).

and Arabella Bishop make expressive use of a kind of chromatic neighbor-note voice leading that seems particularly redolent of Strauss (Example 3.3). Yet, it is clear that although this Straussian idiom was an entirely natural and comfortable one for Korngold, he had always been prepared to employ more varied musical styles. The opportunity to explore stylistically distinct music is something we find already in several of Korngold's pre-Hollywood operas, where moments of meta-theatricality—in which he was required to compose music that worked as quotation or that was otherwise stylistically distinct from the music that surrounded it—are apparent.[53] This includes such items as the "Totentanzlied" in *Violanta*, the "Lautenlied" and the "Pierrot Lied" from *Die tote Stadt*, and the "Wanderlied" from *Die Kathrin*, all of which are required to be perceived as phenomenal performance, to use Carolyn Abbate's term.[54] The result is frequently a rich, stylistically allusive operatic practice—one in which character identity seems to be in constant flux and subject to negotiation.[55] Evidently, that applies as much to the composer's own identity as to his operatic characters, and one feels the composer was actively exploring and negotiating the Austro-Germanic

---

[53] William Cheng has stressed the meta-theatrical aspect of the "Pierrot Lied" in *Die tote Stadt* in its ability to stand apart from the opera's reality as one of four nested levels of narrative. Amanda Hsieh has argued that all the performance numbers of the opera's Act II, Scene iii, can be considered as such. See William Cheng, "Opera en abyme: The Prodigious Ritual of Korngold's Die tote Stadt," *Cambridge Opera Journal* 22, no. 2 (July 2010): 115–146, and Amanda Hsieh, "Jewish Difference and Recovering 'Commedia': Erich W. Korngold's 'Die tote Stadt' in Post-First World War Austria," *Music & Letters* 103, no. 4 (November 2022): 685–707.

[54] Carolyn Abbate, *Unsung Voices: Opera and Musical Narrative in the Nineteenth Century* (Princeton, NJ: Princeton University Press, 1991). Korngold also composed a foxtrot for his incidental music to *Der Vampir* to function meta-theatrically.

[55] Amanda Hsieh has focused on the *commedia dell'arte* nature of the *Pierrot Lied* in *Die tote Stadt* and its contrasts with the Catholic symbolism that surrounds the rest of the opera's music as a site for articulating audible Jewish difference in Catholic Austria. See Hsieh, "Jewish Difference."

108   KORNGOLD IN AMERICA

cultural world as an assimilated Austrian Jew, one not immune to the abuse of the antisemitic press.[56] Perhaps significantly, such stylistic variety was altogether absent from Korngold's most troublesome and arguably least "successful" opera, *Das Wunder der Heliane*, in the late 1920s—an opera that maintains its weighty metaphysical tone throughout.

Film undoubtedly offered Korngold a chance to rediscover the stylistic eclecticism that is apparent from his earlier operatic career, and which is arguably an important facet of his response to modernity. Indeed, the narrative situations, historical settings, and character types generated by films set in medieval or Elizabethan England; eighteenth- and nineteenth-century Europe, Africa, and America; turn-of-the-century Europe and America; and the present day were far more varied than those he encountered in the opera house, and they demanded a plethora of stylistic responses. He might be required to write material as stylistically distinct as: a Tango for the "Bedouin"-inspired jazzy lounge music heard in *Another Dawn*; pseudo-historical pastiche for narratives set in medieval, Elizabethan, or Tudor England (*The Adventures of Robin Hood*, *The Prince and the Pauper*, *The Private Lives of Elizabeth and Essex*, *The Sea Hawk*); a contemporary popular song ("Love for Love") for *Escape Me Never*; music with a self-consciously modernist or expressionist harmonic language for *The Sea Wolf*; not to mention the Straussian-style love scenes that were his stock in trade. It is a pity that Korngold did not take up the scoring assignment for *The Spiral Staircase* (dir. Robert Siodmak, 1946), discussions about which are evident in a letter from George Chasin of The Small Company, after conversation with Dore Schary, the film's producer.[57] In the end, Roy Webb took the assignment. One can only imagine what Korngold might have done with a film often classed as a blend of horror and *film noir*, and one frequently cited as a precursor to the slasher film. Nonetheless, the films he did work on offer us scores with a wide stylistic range. The demands of the narrative motivated this variety to some extent; however, the composer appears to have embraced the creative opportunities made possible by these scenarios.

Korngold's stature as a humorist, for instance, was explored extensively in his film scores, though humor can also be found in his pre-Hollywood theatrical work. There are many moments of levity in his "comic" opera, *Der Ring des Polykrates*, and even some light-hearted sections in the otherwise serious *Violanta* or *Die tote Stadt* (such as in the Act 2 Pierrot scene). By way of contrast, however, there is no humor whatsoever in his fourth opera, *Das Wunder der Heliane*, which is self-consciously serious throughout. In arranging operetta

---

[56] With regards to the antisemitic reception of *Violanta*, see my chapter "Korngold's *Violanta*: Venice, Carnival, and the Masking of Identities," in *Music, Modern Culture, and the Critical Ear*, ed. Nicholas Attfield and Ben Winters (Abingdon: Routledge, 2018), 56.
[57] LOC, Box E Folder 12.

in Europe in the late 1920s and early 1930s, Korngold had undoubtedly developed his comic abilities further, something reflected in his final operetta-like opera *Die Kathrin*—and some of his early orchestral music, such as the finale of the Op. 5 Sinfonietta, is avowedly light-hearted. Film, though, offered him many more opportunities to become a veritable musical humorist, and it is perhaps significant that his only post-Hollywood theatrical work, *Die stumme Serenade*, was comic. Korngold discovered, in particular, that the fleeting nature of physical comedy found in films could be punctuated and emphasized by well-placed musical gestures: in *Escape Me Never*, Gemma sticking out her tongue to the "selfish pig" Sebastian is matched with an acerbic stopped-horn *sforzando* mordant (the manuscript notes "tongue" in blue pencil along with an indication for a synchronization punch). Similarly, in *Devotion*, Branwell Brontë's drunken fall against the gate of the vicarage in cue 2E is paralleled by lurching *sforzando* brass augmented triads. On other occasions, however, the comedic tone embraces entire cues. The earlier scene at the inn (2B and 2C) in *Devotion*, for instance, also scores Branwell's drunkenness with lopsided stomach-churning parallel chords.[58] When the aspiring artist presents his caricature sketch to its intended recipient (in hopes of securing money for another drink) the point-of-view shot of the sketch presents the same musical phrase in trumpets armed with Harmon or "wah-wah" mutes.

The golf game from *Another Dawn* (cue 5) presented an opportunity to which Korngold responded with rather more subtle character humor. John (Ian Hunter) wants to "try his hand" at the game. A busy and confidant xylophone and strings opening that is all false bravado and shifting melodic and harmonic sequence is followed by an immediately less-assured clarinet solo accompanied by chromatically shifting pizzicato and xylophone chords—as John's caddy, recognizing the danger of the situation, gives him some sage advice about keeping his eye on the ball. As John swings his club, the opening of the melody is stated and then repeated an octave higher in a piece of comedic mickey-mousing; his misplaced swipe at the ball is accompanied by a harp glissando and stacked thirds chords. The caddy's amusement is again matched by octave-spaced fragments of the opening melody in bassoons, oboes, and clarinets. As John has another attempt, the opening melody—once again complete—is given to flutes in thirds, now much less sure and assertive than the percussive xylophone and strings that opened the cue. The comic punchline is provided when he is hit on the shin by Julia Ashton's errant golf ball, which arrives from offscreen with punctuating augmented sixth chords (with chromatic grace notes). Julia's arrival prompts a

---

[58] A score extract from this cue is reproduced in my chapter "New Opportunities in Film: Korngold and Warner Bros.," in *Korngold and His World*, ed. Daniel Goldmark and Kevin Karnes (Princeton, NJ: Princeton University Press, 2019), 118.

110   KORNGOLD IN AMERICA

version of her theme in the score, but when she agrees to give John a few tips, the opening bravado returns along with an assertive statement of the melody— now with a little confident brass punctuation at the end—as John limbers up. The results and the musical strategy, though, are all too similar as John skies his ball ("Fore, Saint Peter!" Julia cries). It is a remarkably adroit use of music and shows an awareness of the comic potential of instrumental sonority to under- score characterization and enhance the comedy of a scene that is not exactly "so- phisticated" in its content. Such comedy in film, though, is often reliant on the close synchronization between music and image, in a way that is distinct from stage drama. As such I return to the subject of synchronization, and the ways in which it distinguishes film from opera in Chapter 4.

Timbral Choices

Korngold's reputation as a master orchestrator is certainly a significant aspect of his reception history, though it is often given a negative twist by critics (that he was "merely" so).[59] Yet although, as was common in the studio system, Korngold did not orchestrate his own film scores, owing to the short timeframes available for scoring, he nonetheless had a significant say in instrumental and timbral choices, as his pencil instructions to orchestrators reveal. Moreover, certain Korngold timbral signatures, apparent in his pre-Hollywood works, persist across the film scores. He had long been fond of bell sonorities, and made prominent use of them in the Catholic procession depicted in Act III of *Die tote Stadt*. A cacophony of bells features near the beginning of Act III of *Das Wunder der Heliane*, and bells are heard at the opening of Act III of *Die Kathrin* to evoke the church bells of a Swiss mountain landscape. It is perhaps unsurprising, then, that Korngold utilizes bell sonorities throughout his film scores.[60] The narratives of *Escape Me Never*, *Between Two Worlds*, *Kings Row*, *The Constant Nymph*, and *Of Human Bondage* all end with bells present (in a particularly prominent way in the case of *Escape Me Never*, *Kings Row*, and *Between Two Worlds*) while *Devotion*'s final scene features a version of the "sisters" theme in bells,[61] which reflects Emily Brontë's affinity with the funeral bells mentioned in her brother's poetry. Indeed, nearly every film score features bells at some point, whether notated in the manuscripts or present

[59] Richard Taruskin, for instance, has claimed "[t]here was no hypnotist in music more expert than . . . Korngold. He commanded the resources that Wagner had pioneered with a routined virtu- osity even greater than Wagner's . . . The Straussian celesta . . . mutates in Korngold's orchestra into an indefatigably churning section of keyboard and mallet instruments . . . that oozes endless aro- matic goo." See "The Golden Age of Kitsch," in *The Danger of Music and Other Anti-Utopian Essays* (Berkeley: University of California Press, 2008), 252.

[60] Bells are often identified as "chimes" in the manuscript materials.

[61] The original orchestrated version of this cue by Simon Bucharoff did not feature bells, which must have been added on the Scoring Stage.

in the sound mix: a bell is prominent in *Deception*'s opening title; the first non-score sound of *The Constant Nymph* is a bell; chiming clocks occur in *The Prince and the Pauper*, *The Private Lives of Elizabeth and Essex*, and *Of Human Bondage*; while nautical bells feature in both *The Sea Hawk* and *The Sea Wolf*. Processional or ceremonial bells can also be heard in *The Adventures of Robin Hood* and *The Prince and the Pauper*, while the approach of the Examiner's launch in *Between Two Worlds* is also signaled by a bell—indeed, in occurring on four occasions and evoking mounting nervousness in the characters awaiting judgment, it ceases to function as an indexical sign for the launch and instead becomes a sonic symbol for the approaching Examiner himself. In that sense, the film scores represent a continuation and intensification of Korngold's long-standing interest in these sonorities. Significantly, though, in utilizing extensively a sound that functions convincingly both as part of a musical score and as part of a film's diegetic sound world, the composer draws attention to the slipperiness of the distinction between these two categories—something I will explore further in Chapter 5.

Just as his predilection for bell sonorities persisted across his career, Korngold's fondness for tuned keyboard percussion instruments—as demonstrated by the core combination of celesta, piano, harmonium, glockenspiel, and xylophone used in *Die tote Stadt* and *Das Wunder der Heliane*—was also continued in orchestration choices for the film scores. The celesta features prominently in *Of Human Bondage*, where it is associated with Mildred Rogers (Eleanor Parker), and the piano and xylophone feature prominently in all the scores alongside occasional use of the electric organ, harmonium, and marimba. In addition, however, coloristic possibilities were undoubtedly nourished further by the newly invented instruments that the Warner Bros. orchestra made available to him, something that immediately shaped his operatic output. Thus, when it came time to orchestrating his fifth opera *Die Kathrin* (which Korngold had begun in the early 1930s but only completed in summer of 1937, after his Hollywood career had started), he was able to add to his arsenal the vibraphone, an instrument with an electric motor that had been invented in the 1920s and previously utilized in vaudeville and jazz. Korngold, though, had gained first-hand experience of the instrument via the Warner Bros. orchestra.[62] It features in *Another Dawn*, on which he worked before completing the orchestration of the opera, and it soon became a firm favorite.[63] In *Devotion*, for instance, we hear it prominently in the scene in which Emily Brontë recounts her dream to Arthur Nicholls (cue 3F). The original

---

[62] James Blades, *Percussion Instruments and their History*, rev. ed. (Westport, CT: The Bold Strummer, 2005), 408–409. Famously, Alban Berg had used the instrument in *Lulu* to invoke a 1930s jazz idiom and also associates it with the title character; in *Die Kathrin*, Korngold utilizes it outside of the obvious night-club scene of Act 2 to lend a shimmering atmosphere to textures, especially to the scenes between Kathrin and François and to François's "Wach auf, du schöne Sünderin!" in Act 3.

[63] Korngold also used the vibraphone in his post-Hollywood concert works such as the concertos for violin and for cello.

cue was orchestrated by Hugo Friedhofer, but Korngold himself orchestrated a retake of this section, in which he introduced solo marimba and added the solo vibraphone E-minor chords that end the scene. Indeed, Korngold often made use of marimba alongside vibraphone: in evoking Wolf Larson's crippling headaches in *The Sea Wolf* (cue 3A), for example, vibraphone and marimba play ascending and descending half-diminished seventh broken chords.

In addition to the vibraphone, Korngold also embraced the Novachord, an electronic instrument that featured elaborate controls that allowed the player to control the tone and sound envelope of its tuned tube oscillators in a way that prefigured the synthesizer technology of the 1960s, such that some have argued it to be the world's first polyphonic synthesizer—see Figure 3.5.[64] The Novachord had been developed by Laurens Hammond, who had demonstrated it at the Ritz-Carlton hotel in February 1939, and an article in *The Science Newsletter* of that month reported on another demonstration in Washington, DC, at which the instrument "[poured] forth the varied notes of a piano, violin, Hawaiian guitar, harpsichord, clavichord, trumpet and French horn." Describing its vacuum tube construction, and the controls that determined the tone color and the attack envelope, the article concluded that the instrument offered "distinct new possibilities for varied orchestral effects and for greater diversification of home entertainment."[65] The instrument first reached a wide audience at the 1939 New York World's Fair, where composer Ferde Grofé and his New World Ensemble performed at the Ford pavilion and at an outdoor stage in the Garden Court. Theodore Koster and Frank White also gave at least one organ and Novachord recital in the IBM Gallery of Science and Art,[66] and the instrument was also used to provide part of the soundtrack for a General Motors documentary film about the company's Futurama exhibit, *To New Horizons*.[67] The opening sections covering the past and present were filmed in black and white and had orchestral accompaniment (including an extract from Dvořák's "New World" Symphony); however, as the film shifted to "this wonder world of 1960," the orchestral score was replaced by the Novachord—literally the sound of the future. Hollywood, too, also embraced the instrument: Franz Waxman used it to great effect in *Rebecca* (1940), where two Novachords and an electric organ combined as a separate "ghost orchestra" that was used to represent the title character herself.[68] Waxman worked on the score in early 1940, and around the

---

[64] See Thom Holmes, *Electronic and Experimental Music: Technology, Music, and Culture*, 5th ed. (New York: Routledge, 2016), 31–32.

[65] "Electric Musical Instrument Imitates Orchestra Pieces," *Science News Letter*, February 25, 1939.

[66] "Today's Program at the Fair," *New York Times*, May 17, 1940.

[67] https://www.youtube.com/watch?v=aIu6DTbYnog (accessed: March 14, 2018).

[68] David Neumeyer and Nathan Platte, *Franz Waxman's* Rebecca: *A Film Score Guide* (Lanham, MD: Scarecrow Press, 2012), 115.

Figure 3.5 1938 Hammond Novachord No. 346: Image courtesy of D. A. Wilson, Hideaway Studio.

same time, Hanns Eisler used the instrument in his score for the documentary short, *White Flood*.[69] A Novachord also appears to feature in Adolph Deutsch's score for *The Maltese Falcon* (1941). Yet, the apparatus was both enormously expensive to produce and difficult to play, and production only lasted until 1942.

Despite its esoteric and short-lived nature, this newest of instruments was adopted enthusiastically by Korngold. He first made use of a Novachord during January and February 1941 when working on *The Sea Wolf*, where it features prominently in the opening title, with orchestrator Ray Heindorf providing a few indications of settings: "vox humana (wide vibrato)" is written from the third bar of Reh. Fig. 12. The decision to use the instrument was certainly Korngold's, though. In cue 7C "Van Weyden," for instance, Korngold indicates in his manuscript short score elements of orchestration, including xylophone, marimba, and in bar 4, the Novachord (see Figure 3.6), where the instrument's timbral qualities blend with sustained chords. Elsewhere, Korngold took the opportunity to highlight its unearthly sound. In cue 2A, its lower register intones the theme

---

[69] Peter Schweinhardt and Johannes C Gall, trans. Oliver Dahin, "Composing for Film: Hanns Eisler's Lifelong Film Music Project," in *The Oxford Handbook of Film Music Studies*, ed. David Neumeyer (New York: Oxford University Press, 2014), 138.

Figure 3.6 Korngold's indication of the use of the Novachord (bar 4) in cue 7C of *The Sea Wolf*. Box 17 Folder 1, Erich Wolfgang Korngold Collection, Music Division, Library of Congress, Washington, DC. Courtesy of the Korngold Family Estate.

that signifies Wolf Larson and his ship, the *Ghost* as it makes its first appearance out of the fog (see Figure 3.7). The instrument was next used in *Kings Row* and *The Constant Nymph*, where it was employed sparingly, but it was given much more prominence in *Devotion*. Here, the film's supernatural elements ensured that the distinctive timbre of the Novachord could be highly effective. Most strikingly, though, its otherworldly qualities lent a strongly atmospheric tone to the fantastical narrative of *Between Two Worlds*. The majority of the film, after all, takes place aboard an ocean-going ship of souls as travelers make an apparently literal journey to the afterlife.[70] Its unmistakable sonority is most obvious in cue 6A, when it is played solo in the scene between Lingley and Maxine; in cue 9A, when Lingley makes his exit—where we hear it in a low register; in 10A, when Maxine appears all in black ready for her "trial" (where it is heard in its highest register); and finally in 10B during the card game between Prior and the Examiner, at which point it intones a high F augmented chord with heavy vibrato. The Novachord was likewise used throughout *Of Human Bondage* and *Deception*, and gradually became simply another sonority for Korngold— one to either blend with other instruments or to be heard prominently. Its

---

[70] The Novachord is present in the main title (1A), but it is more prominent at the beginning of cue 1B "Loudspeakers." Frequently, its tone is combined with woodwind (12D), celesta (3A, 12B/1) harp (3A, 8E), violas and bassoons (1G2), violas and celli (12C), all strings (11B), and solo violin (8B). At other times, it is simply presented on its own (2D, 3B, 3E).

Figure 3.7 The Novachord in cue 2A of *The Sea Wolf*. Box 17 Folder 1, Erich Wolfgang Korngold Collection, Music Division, Library of Congress, Washington, DC. Courtesy of the Korngold Family Estate.

ubiquity in the later Warner Bros. scores suggests that Korngold had embraced its possibilities wholeheartedly.[71]

Korngold's writing for film also took occasional advantage of multi-track recording techniques. He had first experimented with these during *The Adventures of Robin Hood* where in the coronation procession near the end of the film (cue 10E) extra brass fanfares for three trumpets and two trombones were recorded separately on the Scoring Stage and dubbed over the existing

---

[71] The full score of cue 2B in *Of Human Bondage* includes a note in pencil "033000 small vib only," which indicates the instrument's tone-control settings. These six rotary switches were situated on the left-hand side of the central "balancer" on the control panel, and had four positions (0, 1, 2, and 3) corresponding to off, and three loudness positions. The service manual describes the switches as follows: "'Deep Tone' is a low pass filter which emphasizes the lower frequencies; 'First Resonator,' 'Second Resonator' and 'Third Resonator' are tuned circuits which emphasize particular ranges of frequency; 'Brilliant Tone' is a high pass filter which emphasizes the higher frequencies; and 'Full Tone' passes all frequencies equally." See https://archive.org/details/original-hammond-novachord-service-manual/page/1/mode/2up (accessed: August 7, 2024).

116   KORNGOLD IN AMERICA

recording.[72] At other moments in this score, extra sweeteners have also been dubbed over the top. In cue 8A, for instance, when a disguised member of the Merry Men throws a bucket of water over a guard, the harp glissando appears to have been layered over the existing recording.[73] Subsequently, *The Sea Hawk* also used multitracking in cue 4B for the throne room fanfares as a way to achieve the sound of eight trumpets using the four available in the Warner Bros. orchestra. The eight trumpet parts are marked in Milan Roder's full score "1st take" and "2nd take." Later, *Deception* used multitracking techniques in the cadenza of the Cello Concerto, whose performance constitutes the climax of the film. Originally written with double-stopped sixths in rapid semiquavers, it was evidently unplayable by cellist Eleanor Aller and required multitracking to create the effect.[74] When the work was published as Korngold's Op. 37, the double-stops are found only sporadically in the passage, and performers wisely do not attempt to replicate the version heard in the film. In a real sense, then, the work as conceived perhaps only exists in its recorded filmic version, enabled by the technologies of the medium. The use of multitracking in *Deception* arguably constitutes the creation of a new kind of cello instrument—one that is dependent on the very technology of recording Korngold encountered in Hollywood.

Harmonic Characteristics

Korngold's harmonic language throughout his career was a constantly shifting aspect of his compositional persona, yet one that he could vary according to dramatic requirements—whether song texts, opera librettos, or film narratives. His music could, on occasion, be largely diatonic and use functional harmony; at the other end of the spectrum, he could employ a chromatic language that drew on semitonal dissonances and eschewed stable key centers. In between these two extremes is where we find the bulk of Korngold's harmony, in a style commonly referred to in the literature as "late-Romantic" or "post-Romantic."[75] What

---

[72] The extra brass parts were identified as "10 E Trumpets" YM 5663-9927-1. See Winters, *Korngold's* The Adventures of Robin Hood, 149. They were notated in Korngold's hand in the manuscript short score, though many are missing from the full score. See Ben Winters, "Korngold's Merry Men: Music and Authorship in the Hollywood Studio System" (DPhil diss., University of Oxford, 2006), 334.

[73] Winters, "Korngold's Merry Men," 286.

[74] The parts in WBA for *Deception*, Reel 10 Part D "Fugato" (also identified as 29649), indicate two separate lines in that section of the cadenza, marked "I. Soundtrack" and "II. Soundtrack."

[75] Peter Franklin, while aware of the terminological slipperiness of the term "late-Romantic," nonetheless opted to retain its broader associations with hyperexpressivity and "quasi-commodified emotional experiences." See *Reclaiming Late-Romantic Music: Singing Devils and Distant Sounds* (Berkeley and Los Angeles: University of California Press, 2014), xiv.

Hollywood offered him, though, was a way to explore and develop all aspects of this spectrum, not merely the middle ground that encourages easy labeling.[76] Although a full exploration of the harmony of Korngold's film scores lies outside the scope of this book, nonetheless it is possible to use one particular feature to illuminate a part of this whole. Indeed, in so doing, my aim here to is to nuance the sometimes necessarily simplistic characterizations or descriptions of Korngold's style that have prevailed in parts of the literature. For example, as part of the concluding chapter to a book that included an influential exploration of Korngold's music for *Captain Blood*, film scholar Kathryn Kalinak referenced in passing "the sound of a Korngold fanfare" as an example of personal style in Hollywood film scoring.[77] This statement is revealing in itself in indicating the aspect of Korngold's film music perhaps most likely to invite attention; yet, it is also useful in providing us with a lens through which to explore the scope of Korngold's harmony in a little more detail than is often possible. Using the fanfare as a starting point, we can examine Korngold's fondness for parallel voice-leading, his use of harmonic sequence, and his use of chromatic mediant chord progressions.

The Sea Hawk, for instance, is a score dominated by fanfares, a factor that is impressed upon a watching audience by a main title that in invoking the main character of Geoffrey Thorpe is suffused with them. Although the main title itself is largely triadic, its voice-leading involves minimal amounts of motion. In contrast, however, the fanfares heard at the start of cue 4B reveal a different approach to voice-leading, one in which voices move in sustained parallel motion—sometimes called "harmonic planing" (Example 3.4). This parallel motion is something that Korngold had employed in various pre-Hollywood works;[78] however, it is particularly noticeable in his film scores. It is found in character themes, such as those for Denny Roark and Achaban in *Another Dawn*, or Louise Gordon in *Kings Row*. Moreover, it can also be deployed in non-thematic parts of scores in ways that are particularly noticeable. Cue 6D in *The Sea Hawk* is one such instance. The scene shows Don Alvarez and Lord

---

[76] In contrast to any "easy labelling," Frank Lehman has helpfully suggested that much of Korngold's film music can be thought of in terms of a "roving diatonicism." Yet, there are undoubtedly examples of his music that would also fit other categories Lehman uses, such as "common-practice tonality," "functional chromaticism," "roving chromaticism," and "tethered chromaticism." See *Hollywood Harmony: Musical Wonder and the Sound of Cinema* (New York: Oxford University Press, 2018), 205–207.

[77] Kathryn Kalinak, *Settling the Score: Music and the Classical Hollywood Film* (Madison: University of Wisconsin Press, 1992), 203.

[78] Examples can be found as early as the 2nd Piano Sonata, Op. 2 (1910), which features parallel-third-less triads in its first movement. Moments in the operas are also heavily reliant on this kind of parallel voice-leading—for example, the parallel minor triads that form the hate motif in *Violanta* at Reh. Fig. 18-2, the parallel fourths found at Reh. Fig. 258 in *Die tote Stadt*, the parallel major seventh chords at Reh. Fig. 218-2 in *Das Wunder der Heliane*, and the mysterious parallel triads at Reh. Fig. 99 in *Die Kathrin*.

Example 3.4 Parallel triadic writing in *The Sea Hawk* (cue 4B).

Wolfingham consulting an astronomical expert with the information they have gleaned from a visit to Thorpe's chart maker. Using a large globe, they discover the destination of Thorpe's secret mission to be the isthmus of Panama. The unusual transformations found in this remarkable passage of triadic harmony are presented in parallel motion (Example 3.5). Other prominent moments of parallel triadic writing include Bunny's prayer in *Between Two Worlds* (Example 3.6a), or cue 12C in the same film, which uses surging closely spaced root-position triads in a low register to reflect Ann's perplexity after being told by Scrubby that her husband has returned to life from their voyage to the afterlife (Example 3.6b). The battle music in *Another Dawn* (cue 21) is also founded on parallel major triads with ascending roots of G, A, B♭, C, C♯, E♭, E. Parallel-seventh writing is frequently encountered in, for instance, the London montage scene of *Devotion* (cue 9D), which shows the printing of *Jane Eyre*; or in the chase music from Reel 2 of *Robin Hood* (cue 2C) in which parallel major seventh chords with missing third are heard. More dissonant harmonies are also often presented in parallel motion to emphasize their starkness. In *Of Human Bondage*, Mildred's violent destruction of Philip's lodgings (cue 10C) is accompanied by parallel triads with added minor sixth and major seventh—a kind of chromatic mediant chord formed by the superimposition of triads a major third apart—that descend chromatically (Example 3.6c).[79] Similarly, the self-consciously modernist two-piano arrangement of Lewis Dodd's composition *Tomorrow* in *The Constant Nymph* also makes prominent use of parallel voice-leading to highlight its semitonal dissonances (Example 3.6d).

Fanfares can reveal other harmonic characteristics. Although those of the archery tournament in *The Adventures of Robin Hood* (cues 6A–6E) are

---

[79] It is strikingly reminiscent of the outburst of rage in Act II Scene II of *Die tote Stadt* after Frank tells Paul "Ich bin dein Freund nicht mehr" (Reh. Fig. 140).

Example 3.5 Parallel transformational harmony in *The Sea Hawk* (cue 6D).

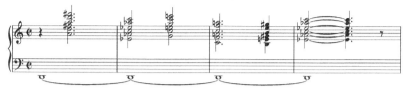

Example 3.6 Parallel voice-leading in (a) *Between Two Worlds*, cue 7D (b) *Between Two Worlds*, cue 12C (c) *Of Human Bondage*, cue 10C (d) *The Constant Nymph*, cue 30.

ostensibly diatonic, the scene nonetheless reveals Korngold's fondness for freely modulating harmonic sequence—chromatic realignments about which Frank Lehman has commented in connection with *The Sea Hawk*.[80] Thus, although the sequence of fanfares in cue 6A relies on functional dominant-tonic harmony, Korngold uses a descending chromatic bass line alongside

---

[80] Lehman identifies the romantic theme from *The Sea Hawk* as the epitome of something he labels "intraphrasal chromaticism." *Hollywood Harmony*, 265n11.

120 KORNGOLD IN AMERICA

pivot chords, enharmonic relationships, chromatic mediants, and tempo-rary tonicizations to traverse chromatic space with an astonishing freedom. Example 3.7 summarizes the triadic content of the cue. After four bars of dominant preparation, the cue presents four iterations of essentially the same modulating harmonic sequence, separated by one passage of seventh chords. In each repeating sequence, Korngold uses pivot chords with a single use of a chromatic mediant—a non-diatonic progression where the two chords in the progression are related by a major or minor third and share a single pitch class in common (such as F♯m and E♭m, which share the note G♭/F♯; or F minor and D minor, which share the note F). The seventh chord progressions can also be described as chromatic mediants, and all chromatic mediants are marked "CM" in Example 3.7. By the end of just over a minute of music, Korngold has remarkably tonicized all twelve chromatic pitches—indicated by an underlined chord symbol in the reduction presented in Example 3.7. A sim-ilar freely modulating harmonic sequence can be found in the opening march from *The Private Lives of Elizabeth and Essex* as Essex returns to England (cue 1C). Example 3.8 shows an ever-shifting passage of triadic harmony from the middle of the cue that makes use of common-tone transformations, highlighting the uncertain nature of political intrigue in the court to which Essex will be subject.

Chromatic mediants are a key facet of the *Robin Hood* archery tournament's traversal of harmonic space, albeit as connecting tissue in a passage of otherwise common-practice harmony, and they form an essential part of Korngold's har-monic language. A chromatic mediant where the roots are related by a minor third, though, is also associated with the octatonic collection—a scale formed of alternating semitones and tones. Indeed, this label is arguably appropriate to the fanfares associated with the Queen in *The Private Lives of Elizabeth and Essex* (Example 3.9).[81] Moreover, Korngold seems to have invoked octatonic space on other occasions in connection with fanfares.[82] One such instance is cue 4B of *The Sea Hawk* in a scene that introduces Queen Elizabeth's court after the film's opening scenes on the high seas. The parallel triads referred to above (Example 3.4) are in fact built on chromatic mediant relationships

---

[81] These bear some resemblance to the octatonic "Rebel fanfare" motif first used in John Williams's score to *Star Wars* (dir. George Lucas, 1977). As a result, I hear more resemblance in the score of *Star Wars* to *The Private Lives of Elizabeth and Essex* (or the similarly octatonic-flavored *The Sea Hawk*) than the oft-cited main title of *Kings Row*.

[82] An undated fanfare in the Erich Wolfgang Korngold Collection, Music Division, Library of Congress, Washington, DC, Box 6 Folder 10, may be part of initial sketches Korngold made for the Warner Bros. film *Don Juan* that was eventually scored by Max Steiner. It also makes use of octatonic harmony in its first line, juxtaposing triads of E♭, C, and A. Notably, too, the sketch also demonstrates that same commitment to parallel voice-leading seen in other fanfares heard in the films. Other octatonic fanfares can be found in *Juarez*, where the fanfare associated with the Crown Prince Augustin consists of alternating B and G♯ triads.

(Example 3.10). Harmonically, the overall trajectory of the cue is from the E major that ends the previous cue to C major, with a straightforward functional ending in that key, but within this there are prominent triadic moves by the minor third. Thus, the E, C♯, G major triads belong to one octatonic collection, the F♯, D♯, and A major triads to another, and the A♭, F, and B major triads to the third. Octatonicism is, however, a wider characteristic of Korngold's harmony in *The Sea Hawk*; thus, an octatonic progression of seventh chords is used to introduce the love theme in the climactic reunion scene between Thorpe and Dona Maria

Example 3.7 *The Adventures of Robin Hood*, cue 6A triadic content and analysis.

Example 3.7 Continued

Example 3.8 Freely modulating triadic harmony in *The Private Lives of Elizabeth and Essex* (cue 1C).

Example 3.9 Queen's fanfare from *The Private Lives of Elizabeth and Essex* (cue 1B).

in cue 12D: F7-D7-B7-A♭7-F7.[83] The harmonically distinct sound of octatonic space can also be found in the chase music in *Robin Hood* (cue 2C)—where triads of B♭, C♯, E, and G outline a complete octatonic (Oct$_{1,2}$) collection[84]—and, in a particularly memorable case, the escape scene of *The Sea Hawk* (cue 11E), where tritone-separated major triads also suggest octatonicism.[85]

In addition, the overall tonal direction from E to C major in cue 4B of *The Sea Hawk* and the prominent triadic moves by major third, marked with circles in Example 3.10, might suggest applying the label hexatonic. (As Fred Lerdahl has explained, the triadic/hexatonic space is the formal twin of the triadic/octatonic space, and in the same way that the octatonic collection contains major triads separated by a minor third, the hexatonic collection—formed from alternating minor seconds and minor thirds—contains three major triads separated by a major third.[86]) Korngold invokes triadic hexatonic space in a more consistent way, though, in the chromatic shifts of *The Sea Hawk*'s love/romantic theme, as Lehman has noted,[87] and even in the apparently diatonic fanfares of the

---

[83] The love theme is sometimes referred to as the romantic theme since it is also associated with love for the sea and for England. Another octatonic progression is heard in cue 4A after Thorpe drops a log into the sea (A7-C7, E♭7-F♯7) to attract the attention of Dona Maria.

[84] Similarly, the battle music in *Another Dawn* (cue 21 "The Battle" and 23 "The Battlefield") also features octatonic harmony. Admittedly, Korngold does not always "spell" these progressions in the way I have described them. Korngold had also used octatonic harmony or chromatic mediant progressions earlier in his output, too, including in the *Schauspiel-Ouvertüre* (for example, Reh. Fig. 4+3), the Piano Concerto (such as the passage between Reh. Figs. 23 and 25), *Violanta* (Reh. Figs. 58-2 and 66—though with chromatic infilling), and *Die Kathrin*, Reh. Fig. 99, to name but a few examples.

[85] Tritone-separated triads are also found in Korngold's score for *A Midsummer Night's Dream*, cue 28 ("Donkey") in which triads of E and B♭ are juxtaposed. That said, tritone separated chords can also be found in the opening titles to *The Sea Wolf*, where augmented sixth chords built on ♭II (E♭) with added ninth are alternated with A7 chords. The F♯ does not belong to the Oct$_{0,1}$ collection, however.

[86] Fred Lerdahl, *Tonal Pitch Space* (New York: Oxford University Press, 2001), 258.

[87] Lehman, *Hollywood Harmony*, 265n11.

Example 3.10 Chromatic mediant harmony in *The Sea Hawk* (cue 4B).

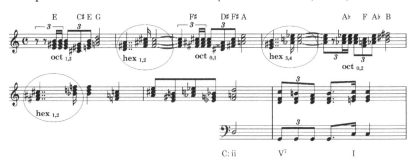

main titles (1A) in which Korngold effectively traverses a wide harmonic vista by taking a quick trip across hexatonic space: after initial B♭ statements of the fanfare and a brief tonicization of C minor, he tonicizes the dominant (F), after which there is a brief excursion to D♭ major, back to F and then A major, before a chromatic slip back to F functions as the dominant for a return to the B♭ fanfare.[88] The notes of the triads of D♭, F, and A outline a hexatonic scale (Hex$_{0,1}$), and its distinctive harmonic flavor is found at a number of points in *The Sea Hawk*.[89] Likewise, the Fm maj7 chord that occupies such an important narrative role in *Between Two Worlds*, and about which I will comment in Chapter 5, also belongs to hexatonic space, while the structural major third steps in the modulating sequence in *Robin Hood*'s archery tournament could also be conceptualized in similar terms.[90]

Often, however, Korngold freely mixes chromatic mediants in a passage rather than employing octatonic or hexatonic collections consistently. Therefore, the music may proceed by means of chromatic mediants that appear initially entirely octatonic only to introduce a triad a major third away. Cue 3D in *The Private Lives of Elizabeth and Essex*, in which the Queen is talking with Margaret Radcliffe, is a particularly potent example of this. At Reh. Fig. 10, when the Queen commands Margaret to approach, Korngold takes a fragment of the song that Penelope and Margaret had sung to the Queen, which doubles as a theme for Margaret, and uses it to sequentially traverse chromatic mediant triadic space: major chords of B♭, D♭ (enharmonically spelled), and E are followed by a

---

[88] Admittedly, it is the main titles' B section that accomplishes the most astonishing journey in its "series of hexatonic cycles at multiple levels of its structure" (ibid.).

[89] During the escape scene (cue 11E) where the chain is passed through the loops of the prisoner's belts, we hear a progression of C, E, and A♭ triads.

[90] Korngold had previously used the hexatonic juxtaposition of triads a major third apart in his earlier works, such as in the 3rd Piano Sonata (for example, 1st movement, bs. 15–16), the finale of the Sinfonietta (Reh. Fig. 7), or Reh. Fig. 145-2 in *Die tote Stadt*.

Example 3.11 Traversing chromatic mediant triadic space in cue 3D of *The Private Lives of Elizabeth and Essex* (a) Reh. Fig. 10 (b) Reh. Fig. 24.

final chord of G♯ (Example 3.11a) breaking the minor-third pattern by moving to a chromatic mediant with a root a major third away. Likewise, at the end of the cue, at Reh. Fig. 24 we hear the same fragment presented sequentially over major triads a minor third apart: G, B♭, D♭. The last two chords in the sequence, though (F and A) are related by major third (Example 3.11b). The unusual progression found in the globe scene (6D) also uses a mixture of octatonic (tritone) and hexatonic (major third) relationships. It is at once a typically Korngold moment of pure harmonic strangeness and shimmering texture that would not be out of place in more recent science-fiction film, as its use of the tritone-related triads would suggest (Example 3.12).[91] Triadic harmony using chromatic mediant root motion had long been a feature of Korngold's harmonic language and is arguably something he inherited from his familiarity with the output of Richard Strauss.[92] The opening to Korngold's 1927 opera *Das Wunder der Heliane*, for example, is essentially based on chromatic mediant root movement.[93]

The fanfare does not offer a gateway to examining every Korngold harmonic signature of interest, though. The composer's fondness for quartal harmony—a

---

[91] In Neo-Riemmanian operators, this could be described as a PRPR transformation.

[92] See my chapter "Influence," in *Richard Strauss in Context*, ed. Morten Kristiansen and Joseph E. Jones (Cambridge: Cambridge University Press, 2020), 311–319.

[93] The opening F♯ chord is followed by superimposed A and D triads, thus encompassing both the minor/major third root movement simultaneously, and proceeds to F and A♭ triads, before using an Fm triad as preparation for the E♭ of the opening choral entry. Chromatic mediant root movement can also be found in *Die tote Stadt*: for example, Reh. Fig. 144-2, where the triadic progression F-D-B♭-C♯ occurs.

Example 3.12 *The Sea Hawk*'s globe scene (cue 6D).

harmonic characteristic of much early twentieth-century modernism, and found in his most famous opera, *Die tote Stadt*[94]—is not readily apparent in any film fanfares; however, it is seen often in his score to *The Sea Wolf*. It is most prominent in Wolf Larson's theme, which is essentially quartal in character (even if it is supported by the occasional non-quartal bass note—see Example 3.13a). Likewise, Korngold's use of whole-tone and pentatonic harmony is not found in any fanfare, but these characteristics are particularly apparent in his score for *Devotion*, where Branwell Brontë's music is marked by whole-tone writing. The first bars of his moors theme (e.g., cue 1C) starts with whole-tone harmony (the 1, 3 collection) underpinned by a non-whole-tone collection D that resolves onto a D major triad with added quartal sixth and ninth, and proceeds to a chord formed from the second whole-tone collection (the 0, 2 collection) resolving to G major with added sixth and ninth (see Example 3.13b); likewise, the version of Branwell's drunken theme in cue 2E is also based on the two transpositions of the whole-tone scale, and the augmented triads that result.[95] Pentatonicism had likewise long been part of Korngold's compositional toolbox,[96] and characterizes some of Charlotte's music in *Devotion*: for example, in cue 7D, as Charlotte faces having to return home from Brussels owing to Branwell's illness, she panics and we hear her theme fragmented and treated to sequential repetition in various iterations of major pentatonic scales (Example 3.13c).

Korngold was also not averse to using diatonicism where it suited the narrative situation. Thackeray's theme in *Devotion*, for instance, presented in its simplest form when he reveals his identity to Charlotte, uses largely common-practice harmony (Example 3.14). Employing only a few decorative tonicizations using

---

[94] Parallel-fourths writing is found elsewhere in his output, such as the first movement of the String Sextet, Reh. Fig. 4+14, and in *Violanta* (the Venetian "Unsre Barke" at Reh. Fig. 8, which bears a resemblance to the Venetian theme written for *Escape Me Never*).

[95] Likewise, one can find whole-tone melodies in Korngold's operatic output, such as in *Violanta* (Reh. Fig. 14 "Er träumt von ihren weißen Gliedern, worauf der Mond die Laute spielt"). Whole-tone writing is also apparent in Act II of *Die tote Stadt*, where it characterizes the Pierrot players, for example at Reh. Fig. 165, and can also be found in *Das Wunder der Heliane* in, for example, the Porter's theme (Act I, Reh. Fig. 6+1).

[96] As the opening of Act II Scene 1 of *Die tote Stadt* demonstrates.

Example 3.13 Other harmonic characteristics (a) quartal harmony in *The Sea Wolf*, cue 1A; (b) whole-tone harmony in *Devotion*, cue 1C; (c) Pentatonic harmony in *Devotion*, cue 7D.

diminished sevenths, and one fleeting use of the Lydian second (a non-diatonic F chord in bar 2), it is otherwise an entirely diatonic E♭ major cue that even makes use of a cadential 6/4 chord. Its mock pomposity, though, is perfectly matched to Sydney Greenstreet's portrayal of Thackeray, and as a result one feels this is

Example 3.14 Near common-practice harmony in *Devotion* (cue 10A).

Korngold very much writing in quotation marks, much as the Lute song in *Die tote Stadt* is self-consciously styled as nostalgic.

***

All these tools in Korngold's compositional toolbox—whether they be harmonic, stylistic, or timbral in nature, or rooted in his recycling and synchronization practices—were ultimately in the service of creating compelling film-narrative worlds that can be regarded as fundamentally musical in nature. The concept of worldbuilding is often associated with fantasy cinema,[97] and yet each of the films scored by Korngold has a particular sonic character that is at least partially defined by the consistent aesthetic choices the composer made (in conjunction with the decisions taken by his creative collaborators elsewhere in Warner Bros.): the swashbuckling worlds of *Robin Hood* or *The Sea Hawk* would, I suggest, be very different without Korngold's music, and, as I will emphasize in the chapters to come, Korngold's music is thoroughly integrated into the audible characteristics of their onscreen worlds. I have long maintained that it makes little sense to separate musical score narratively from the worlds it accompanies,

---

[97] Daniel White has, for example, explored worldbuilding in the context of fantasy-film narratives. See *The Music of* Harry Potter *and* The Lord of the Rings: *Sounds of Home in the Fantasy Franchise* (Abingdon: Routledge, 2024).

suggesting that the tendency to do so is rooted in an implicitly modernist attitude that sees music's proper role as a self-consciously critical one in relationship to the rest of the narrative.[98] Instead, I want to advocate a role for music in Classical Hollywood cinema that sees it as constitutive of onscreen worlds, and as fundamental to their identity. Korngold had a long history of creating compelling fictional worlds, primarily through his operatic works, and there are certainly aspects of continuity in his film work with his previous output: just as Korngold's harmonic signatures in the film scores can be traced to aspects of his pre-Hollywood works, so too can his recycling practices, his ability to write stylistically distinct music, and his interest in orchestral timbre. Perhaps what is particularly noteworthy about the film scores is the way in which Korngold deploys these tools with a bravura confidence: he is able to call upon a wide variety of compositional resources without any sense that his aesthetic language has been unduly restricted by the demands of the medium. Moreover, in providing him with new technological opportunities to explore methods for synchronization that allowed more precise audiovisual alignment than was ever possible (or for that matter desirable) in the opera house, Hollywood afforded him the chance to create musical worlds that are much more recognizable to us—and, for some, perhaps more compelling as a result—than the heightened theatricality of the stage. In that sense, in terms of personal creativity, film offered him numerous opportunities to explore aspects of his own compositional identity, yet the selection of the relevant compositional tool was not dictated purely by the need for personal expression but instead by the requirement to create compelling worlds into which we as spectators willingly immerse ourselves. The next chapter, then, explores in more detail the ways in which Korngold deployed the tools of his compositional toolbox for dramatic purposes. Although film required him to apply and refine a thematic technique first forged in the opera houses of Europe, there are also notable differences between the two genres of opera and film that nonetheless should not be overlooked.

[98] See Ben Winters, "The Non-diegetic Fallacy: Film, Music, and Narrative Space," *Music & Letters* 91, no. 2 (May 2010): 243.

4

Korngold, the Hollywood Dramatist

"Never have I differentiated between my music for the films and that for the operas and concert pieces. Just as I do for the operatic stage, I try to invent for the motion picture dramatically melodious music with symphonic development and variation of the themes."[1] This statement was made in a chapter entitled "Some Experiences in Film Music" that Korngold wrote for a 1940 book, *Music and Dance in California*.[2] Although it offers a relatively rare insight into the composer's craft of supporting film narrative, it might suggest, as many have implied, that Korngold was simply transplanting his operatic technique to a new medium; that, as Richard Taruskin has claimed, he achieved "the transmutation of opera into film."[3] The passage preceding the above quotation is instructive here, however: "I have often been asked whether, in composing film music, I have to consider the public's taste and present understanding of music. I can answer that question calmly in the negative." As such, the statement reads rather less as a considered comparison between two genres and more as a plea for a composer's integrity, as a way of elevating film scoring to the level of operatic and concert culture. Given the defensive tone, we should perhaps be wary of taking its claims to equivalence too literally. Undoubtedly, Korngold's experience as an opera composer with an advanced post-Wagnerian thematic technique prepared him for his Hollywood career and shaped the approach he took to scoring drama. At the same time, though, the demands of a film narrative were somewhat different from the opera librettos he had previously set, typically containing many more characters requiring musical representation and far more varied narrative situations. Thus, whereas the operatic structures Korngold created used recurring themes that, with certain exceptions, tended to resist straightforward signification, the themes found in his film scores are often much more easily connected to characters, emotions, or occasionally places or objects—even if they admit interpretative ambiguity and are capable of that

---

[1] Erich Korngold, "Some Experiences in Film Music," in *Korngold and His World*, ed. Daniel Goldmark and Kevin C. Karnes (Princeton, NJ: Princeton University Press, 2019), 251.
[2] Erich Korngold, "Some Experiences in Film Music," in *Music and Dance in California*, ed. José Rodriguez, comp. William J. Perlman (Hollywood: Bureau of Musical Research, 1940), 137–139.
[3] Richard Taruskin, "The Golden Age of Kitsch," in *The Danger of Music and Other Anti-Utopian Essays* (Berkeley: University of California Press, 2009), 248.

Korngold in America. Ben Winters, Oxford University Press. © Oxford University Press 2025.
DOI: 10.1093/9780197684818.003.0005

"symphonic development and variation" that Korngold claimed. In addition, though, Korngold was required to generate non-thematic material in his film scores, especially for atmospheric effects or action sequences (though such scenes could also feature appropriate thematic material, duly fragmented and subject to sequential repetition). The results, coupled with the need for a much more fragmented structure that could not rely on the long stretches of developmental space found in opera, somewhat belies the composer's statement that he did not differentiate composing for the two genres. That should not mislead us, however, into assuming that film did not offer the composer a challenge or an opportunity to develop as a dramatist; rather, it required a more condensed dramatic technique that generated recurring musical material that would signify quickly on the smaller scale to clarify aspects of character identity, and to quickly establish settings of narrative time and space. As such, Korngold was required for each film to develop a plethora of stylistically appropriate themes that were amenable to transformation according to narrative situation.

Contemporary film-music critic Bruno David Ussher, for one, was aware and appreciative of Korngold's thematic structures. In a glowing and lengthy review of *The Private Lives of Elizabeth and Essex* he suggested that in comparison with the large number of motifs used in *Juarez*, *Elizabeth and Essex* used relatively few, noting that the composer as "master of harmonic and instrumental expression" could "well afford to base his opera-sized score on a limited number of fundamental, pregnant themes.... [The] result is a superbly unified, atmosphere-sustaining music which links and intensifies the line of dramatic action."[4] In another review for the *Pasadena Star News* (September 30, 1939) of the same film, he observed that "there are not many themes serving as symbols for individuals and situations," advising readers not to try "to differentiate too much between a melody typifying either Elizabeth or England and her court" and that "It is not so important that one recognizes the theme of the power-mad or the tender Essex." Nonetheless, he claims that "[I]n melodic contour the Korngold theme-melodies are plainly distinguishable, and for that very reason, the composer has been able to do much with them to reflect rising and waning affection, mounting pathos and intensified suspense." Indeed, Ussher seems to have treated this score with particular attention, writing a further detailed review in his column "Film Music and Its Makers" for *The Hollywood Spectator* (October 14, 1939) in which he declared that "Korngold has written eight film scores. This one, running at 65 minutes, almost as long as *Salome* by Strauss, strikes me as singular." It is clear that

---

[4] Bruno David Ussher, "Cinemusic and its Meanings" (1939), Erich Wolfgang Korngold Collection, Music Division, Library of Congress, Washington, DC (hereafter LOC), Box H Folder 27.

132 KORNGOLD IN AMERICA

Ussher appreciated the composer's ability to not only compose dramatically appropriate thematic material but also to adapt it to suit its situation, though his description of *Elizabeth and Essex* as using fewer themes than *Juarez* is somewhat difficult to justify—albeit remembering that what may be regarded as a separate theme for one critic may be regarded as a variant of the same theme for another. At any rate, Ussher's criticism suggests that Korngold's dramatic technique in film moved far beyond the caricature of film leitmotiv that Adorno and Eisler so mercilessly attacked in their infamous publication of the mid-1940s.[5]

I have previously explored the thematic structures of *The Adventures of Robin Hood* in some detail.[6] Here, though, I want to take a broader approach that looks across Korngold's film scores to draw some conclusions about his thematic technique. First, I want to explore his approach to characterization—the ways in which his themes signify clearly and quickly—and to suggest that film scoring offered Korngold various opportunities to deploy his dramatic gifts in ways that were arguably distinct from the world of opera, where the need to signify efficiently was somewhat less important. I then want to highlight some of the myriad ways in which he transformed thematic material for musico-dramatic purposes. As part of this, I will look in a little more detail at two examples of themes that undergo significant transformation: "Love and Ring" from *The Private Lives of Elizabeth and Essex* and "Julia" from *Another Dawn*. In addition, I want to draw attention to some of the non-thematic material that can be found in Korngold's film scores, by which I mean music that carries no obvious associative function with characters, objects, or locales but nonetheless retains an important dramatic role within the narrative. Korngold's film scoring is known for its showcase deployment of associative themes—the technique that aligns it most obviously with his own operatic practice—but it also relied on these rather more medium-specific techniques. Lastly, I examine the way in which Korngold used thematic and non-thematic material alike to support aspects of the continuity editing practices of Classical Hollywood. This is a clear way in which opera and film as dramatic genres can be distinguished and, taken with the differences in dramatic technique, suggests that the rather simplified equivalence between opera and film seized upon by many commentators overlooks many of the specific challenges and opportunities that film offered the composer.

---

[5] Hanns Eisler and Theodor Adorno, *Composing for the Films* (London: Athlone Press, 1994).

[6] Ben Winters, *Erich Wolfgang Korngold's* The Adventures of Robin Hood: *A Film Score Guide* (Lanham, MD: Scarecrow Press, 2007).

Characterization

Korngold's background as an opera composer is undoubtedly of relevance to his career in film, but the nature of the relationship between the two media in his output is fraught with difficulties, especially when thinking in terms of film analysis. Should the analyst treat one of Korngold's films as an opera text, and expect the score to work in similar ways? There are good reasons why treating film as akin to opera might actually limit our appreciation of the role of music in film, especially in its engagement with other recorded sound, a point I will return to in the next chapter. Moreover, the methodologies and concerns of the opera analyst may not be entirely suited to film. The discourse surrounding the application to film of analytical techniques associated with opera and Wagnerian music drama, in particular, is both rich and complex; and whether it is appropriate to use such theoretical terminology as "leitmotif" in discussing Hollywood film scores is moot. To do so arguably requires a proper appreciation of the enormous cultural baggage that the term brings. Others have explored that issue in a general sense in a way that needs no rehearsing here;[7] however, the question is worth acknowledging because it touches upon the fundamental issue of what Hollywood offered Korngold as a creative artist. It was not simply a chance to rehash a developed post-Wagnerian operatic technique, but an opportunity to develop a new dramatic language that although informed by his operatic and theatrical experience did not replicate it.

A full exploration of the relationship between Korngold's dramatic technique in opera and film, and wider operatic dramatic techniques, is one that is outside my scope here.[8] Suffice it to say that the films for which Korngold was writing music do not lend themselves to the kinds of musical canvases

---

[7] See Peter Franklin, "Underscoring Drama—Picturing Wagner," in *Wagner and Cinema*, ed. Jeongwon Joe and Sander L. Gilman (Bloomington: Indiana University Press, 2010), 46–64. Much of Franklin's recent work stresses cinematic aspects of Wagnerian and post-Wagnerian opera, and in that way he approaches this question from the other side, revealing incipient mass-culture elements in artworks some appear to treat uncritically as instances of "high art." I would maintain, though, that it is easier and more instructive to see obvious filmic elements in opera than it is to find operatic technique in film scores.

[8] Perhaps the most compelling connections between the film scores and the operas lie with those moments of on-stage performance and framing, which are found in all the operas with the exception of *Das Wunder der Heliane*. See, for example, Amanda Hsieh's discussion of the self-contained Commedia dell'arte performances in *Die tote Stadt*, which she argues provides an opportunity for Korngold to explore his assimilated Jewishness within the opera's larger Catholic framework. "Jewish Difference and Recovering 'Commedia': Erich W. Korngold's 'Die tote Stadt' in Post-First World War Austria," *Music & Letters* 103, no. 4 (November 2022): 685–707. These performative moments were also the basis of the comparison between opera and film in Robbert van der Lek's *Diegetic Music in Opera and Film: A Similarity between Two Genres Analysed in Works by Erich Wolfgang Korngold (1897–1957)* (Amsterdam: Rodopi, 1991). The somewhat fragmentary structure created by these scenes of phenomenal performance, though, would only be emphasized further in the film scores.

suited to Wagnerian leitmotivic structures, in which motives are combined and transformed in ways that are driven as much by musical relations as by narrative demands. Although there are numerous post-Wagnerian operas that bear closer comparison with film than Wagner's own, including Korngold's, I would suggest the kinds of thematic structures Korngold had used in his own operas are, in fact, only loosely connected with those found in the film scores. That, of course, is not to denigrate Korngold's cinematic technique, or deny the sophistication of his film scores—or, indeed, to laud Wagnerian art which, as Peter Franklin has argued, is as equally open to the same kinds of artistic skepticism often directed at mass-entertainment film.[9] It is, however, to acknowledge that film with its intermittent musical cues may work in different ways to theatrical genres, and that for all that Korngold film scores practice the same kinds of "accumulative association" that Matthew Bribitzer-Stull identifies in Wagnerian music drama—whereby "[in] each re-statement of theme there exists the possibility that added perspective will color the emotional associations we have with it"—they are often shaped as much by the scenic design of the narratives they accompany and called upon to do other signifying work that is just as important.[10]

Although Bribitzer-Stull has argued for retaining in film criticism the term "leitmotif" when used with precision, and despite the fact that his three-fold definition of leitmotif allows him to include certain film examples, he both acknowledges that the leitmotif is part of a larger grouping that might be termed "associative themes" and admits numerous critical and practical interpretations of the term.[11] It would seem prudent, then, to treat Korngold's film-score structures as ones involving "associative themes" rather than necessarily to assume the presence of leitmotifs. For example, not all Korngold's film themes develop; nor are they necessarily associated with emotions in the way that Bribitzer-Stull argues that leitmotifs must.[12] The use of associative themes do, it is true, help Korngold structure certain musical cues, and some themes are treated to multiple transformations that have narrative significance, or have strong emotional connections, but to label Korngold's themes as leitmotifs would be to invoke a tradition that is not necessarily appropriate without frequent qualification. In any case, the dramatic structures of Korngold's operas and the ways in which they use repeating thematic material are not, in themselves, entirely consistent.

[9] Franklin, "Underscoring Drama."
[10] Matthew Bribitzer-Stull, *Understanding the Leitmotif: From Wagner to Hollywood Film Music* (Cambridge: Cambridge University Press, 2015), 4.
[11] Ibid., 7.
[12] Ibid., 119.

Example 4.1 "Glück gibt Mut" from Scene 2 of *Der Ring des Polykrates*.

Korngold's approach to opera was undoubtedly one forged in the post-Wagnerian Viennese atmosphere dominated by Richard Strauss, and the younger composer's love for Strauss's *Elektra*—with its leitmotivic technique—is well documented by Luzi's memoirs.[13] Yet, Korngold in his youth was also inspired by Dukas's *Ariane et Barbe-Bleu*, which took Vienna by storm in 1908 and is indicative of a French tradition that maintained a complex relationship with Wagnerism and emphasized the centrality of the voice in a way that later Wagnerian music dramas and their leitmotivic structures seemed to disavow. An opera like Korngold's early one-act *Der Ring des Polkyrates* deploys networks of themes that operate across the work, and that bear loose associations with characters and emotions or concepts, yet *Polykrates* does not necessarily rely on thematic transformation and combination for its structure. Undoubtedly, that is not to deny that complex motivic treatments exist: the motif associated with Laura and her past relationship with the interloper Peter Vogel, for instance, undergoes a striking number of transformations of tempo, harmony, mode, and texture, and is subject to diminution and development. Moreover, a large number of short themes or motifs return periodically throughout the opera's ten scenes for dramatic effect. However, the structure of the opera is not dependent on these kinds of motivic relationships or developments. In particular, there are stretches that are devoted to identifiable extended melodies, such as "Jetzt hab' ich groß dich und männlich gesehen," which dominates the lengthy Scene 7, or "Erst ist Eines zu erledigen" from Scene 8. These extended melodies are fundamentally confined to the local level of the scene. An extended melody like "Glück gibt Mut" from Scene 2 (Example 4.1) is admittedly briefly recalled in Scenes 4 and 8, and returns in Scene 10 to conclude the opera, yet it functions as a recalled melody rather than a motif that is woven throughout the opera's structure.

That approach is even more evident with Korngold's fifth and last opera, *Die Kathrin*. Although it contains a number of repeating associative themes—including ones for Kathrin, herself, and for Malignac, the villain—it is very much dominated by melodic set pieces in which large stretches of thematic

---

[13] Luzi Korngold, *Erich Wolfgang Korngold: Ein Lebensbild* (Vienna: Elisabeth Lafite Verlag, 1967), 28.

136 KORNGOLD IN AMERICA

material are confined to a single scene. Thus, Francois's "Ich bin ein Lieder sänger" is heard only in Act I Scene 2 although the initial melody is treated to development and variation within this scene.[14] Similarly, the characteristic music that starts Act I Scene 2 is heard nowhere else in the opera. This must then be contrasted with the dense motivic structures of Korngold's third and most famous opera, *Die tote Stadt*. Although *Die tote Stadt* admittedly also has its famous set pieces (such as Pierrot's Lied) that are largely confined to a single place within the opera, it is the combination and development of a bewildering number of associative themes (which are often short enough to be easily labelled motifs) that constitutes the bulk of its structure. Many of these motifs return periodically throughout the opera's three acts, tying it together in ways that are totally different from the more localized structures of *Die Kathrin*. The film scores, then, do not necessarily represent one particular deployment of Korngold's operatic technique, since this was itself varied according to operatic subject.

A more significant difference between the operas and film scores lies in the nature of the thematic material. Aside from a few highly characterized themes in the operas, from which one can deduce an element of character identity or motivation,[15] much of the repeated thematic content seems semantically neutral: what matters is the growing association between motif and narrative. There is often very little intrinsic to the musical nature of motif that connects it with the concept, character, or emotion with which it becomes associated. That is assuredly not the case in the films, where the nature of a character's musical theme is closely tied to some aspect of their identity—something it needs to convey quickly and efficiently to an audience. Most films featured between ten and twenty identifiable themes or motifs, and although Korngold subjected this material to thematic transformation and variation that could be extensive, their associative function remains essentially clear to the analyst, and arguably to the watching audience. This can be contrasted with Korngold's approach to the use of recurring material in his operas, which are certainly much looser in terms of clear signifying connections. Thus, with a few exceptions—such as the hair or Bruges motifs in *Die tote Stadt*, the Ruler's theme in *Das Wunder der Heliane*, or the hate motif in *Violanta*—recurring thematic material in the operas is far more resistant to naming.

---

[14] It shares its profile (an ascent to a climactic melodic major seventh) with Francois's "Wo ist mein Heim, mein Haus" in Act III, but the two melodies are decidedly different.

[15] The antagonist characters of Peter Vogel in *Der Ring des Polykrates* and the Ruler in *Das Wunder der Heliane* are two such examples where the nature of the character is signaled symbolically by the motif. Similarly, the martial theme for Simone Trovai in *Violanta* signals his identity as a captain of the Venetian republic. Most operatic motifs, though, appear to tell us little about the characters with whom they are associated.

Naming any associative themes in opera or film is, of course, fraught with difficulties, not least because the act of naming has a kind of illocutionary force that may collapse interpretive ambiguities into one inflexible label.[16] If the film scores signify more clearly than Korngold's operatic structures, that is not to say that themes are always easily named in the film scores, or that they connect to characters, emotions, or locales unambiguously without offering interpretive freedom: indeed, themes may double both for individuals and locations associated with them (such as the theme in *Between Two Worlds* that signifies both the place and idea of heaven and the character of the Examiner, who is its representative). Nor is it the case, as I hinted above in commenting on Ussher's distinction between *Juarez* and *Elizabeth and Essex*, that all themes are easily separated and thus counted: in some cases, there is ambiguity about whether themes are distinct or merely variants of each other. This is particularly the case in a film like *Devotion*, where Emily Brontë's thematic material, with its bold opening fifth, is subject to a number of variants, some of which are associated with the geographical locations of the moors and Wuthering Heights: whether they constitute separate themes, though, or are better interpreted as extensions of Emily's persona is an indication of the interpretive richness that Korngold's score lends this film. Likewise, it is much more difficult to identify or to name themes in the melodrama *Of Human Bondage* than in a historical epic like *Anthony Adverse*. This is arguably because the narrative is so focused on Philip Carey (Paul Henreid) and Mildred Rogers (Eleanor Parker) that other characters, such as Athelny (Edmund Gwenn)—the patient who Philip befriends and with whose daughter, Sally (Janis Paige), he eventually finds happiness—do not seem to warrant their own music.[17] Despite the complexities, however, it is far easier to arrive at compelling interpretive explanations for the thematic associations of the film scores than for operas. Perhaps only the themes of Korngold's last score for Warners, *Deception*, of which there are very few indeed, offer the kind of resistance to signification that was rather more typical of his earlier operatic practice.

Aside from their use in opening titles, film themes associated with characters are generally introduced with, or around the time of, their first onscreen appearance, though dialogue mentioning them may also warrant an initial musical

---

[16] Peter Franklin, for instance, reveals the problems in Heather Laing's naming of themes in *Now Voyager*. See *Seeing Through Music: Gender and Modernism in Classic Hollywood Film Scores* (New York: Oxford University Press, 2011), 6.

[17] Indeed, the score is dominated by Philip's "limping" theme (which represents his clubbed foot), Mildred's short glittering theme (often played on celesta), and a fateful theme that is associated with the bondage she represents for Philip. These three themes are augmented with several others, including a seduction theme for Mildred, a theme associated with Philip's medical career, one for Philip's rival Harry (Patric Knowles), and a hopeful theme at the end of the film after Mildred's death. That being said, two female characters (Nora and Sally) receive themes that are instantly recognizable, and though Sally's is melodically and harmonically rather unsophisticated, Nora's theme remains one of the most musically memorable parts of the score.

Example 4.2 Thematic introductions (a) Anthony's theme in *Anthony Adverse*, cue 2A (b) subsidiary theme for Arabella Bishop in *Captain Blood*, cue 24.

reference.[18] The initial presentation of Anthony's theme in *Anthony Adverse* is even connected with his conception. In cue 2A, after their romantic liaison, Denis asks Maria why she is frightened and trembling (with matching beating heart rhythm in the music): as Anthony's theme is heard, Maria (Anita Louise) asks him "Can't you guess?" (Example 4.2a). Occasionally, though, the revelation of a character's musical identity is delayed: Nora's theme in *Of Human Bondage* is not heard until the middle of the film, despite the fact that her character is introduced at the narrative's beginning in Paris. Although the opening of the score went through a number of changes, with initial Korngold Parisian music replaced with an arrangement of the folk song "Aupres de ma Blonde" and Max Steiner's "A La Paris," it seems from the manuscript sources that Nora's theme never accompanied the first appearance of the character. On other occasions, the course of the narrative results in the late appearances of thematic material: a subsidiary theme for Arabella Bishop (Olivia de Havilland) in the swashbuckler *Captain Blood* is not heard until the character spends time in England (Example 4.2b); upon her return to Port Royal, Jamaica, at the end of the film, Arabella retains this thematic material alongside her primary theme. A Korngold film score thus allows characters to develop musically in ways that reflect narrative changes.

The length of these associative themes can vary markedly. Some characters seem to warrant extended melodies: thus, the theme for Nora (Alexis Smith) in

---

[18] Such is the case with themes for Emily and Charlotte in *Devotion* or the Queen in *The Sea Hawk*.

Example 4.3 Randy's theme in *Kings Row* (cue 7B).

Of Human Bondage is presented initially in cue 4A in its complete form, a passage of music lasting around four minutes; similarly, Randy (Ann Sheridan) in *Kings Row* is associated with a diatonic theme that in its most complete form consists of a sixteen-bar structure with two essentially repeating eight-bar phrases, the first of which ends in an imperfect cadence in the manner of a classical period structure (see Example 4.3).[19] Nor is this kind of extended melodic theme restricted to female characters. The Rev. William "Bunny" Duke (Dennis King) in *Between*

---

[19] The "sisters" theme in *Devotion* can likewise form a complete paragraph of music, as can Christine's theme in *Deception*, while Dona Maria's theme in *The Sea Hawk* consists of two extended melodies that can be separated and treated to their own thematic transformations.

Example 4.4 The *Albatross* in *The Sea Hawk* (cue 2A).

Example 4.5 Fragmentary themes (a) Wolf Larson in *The Sea Wolf*, cue 1A; (b) Fenella in *Escape Me Never*, cue 2A; (c) Dr Gordon in *Kings Row*, cue 2A; (d) Mildred Rogers in *Of Human Bondage*, cue 2B.

Two Worlds receives a melody that is somewhat open ended and amenable to extension in a way that Randy's theme in being harmonically closed and rather more periodic is less liable to warrant—though that does not prevent Korngold varying Randy's theme for dramatic effect. Other themes can be presented in melodically extended versions, yet can also be reduced to smaller motivic cells more suited to thematic transformation and variation. The theme for Thorpe's ship, the *Albatross*, in *The Sea Hawk* is a good example of this (Example 4.4) since it is often reduced to its opening three notes.[20] Other associative themes, though, are perhaps more fundamentally fragmentary or motivic in character: Larson's theme in *The Sea Wolf* consists of three falling fourths (Example 4.5a); Fenella's theme in *Escape Me Never* incorporates an oscillating-thirds motif with tritone harmony, and though it can be found extended it is usually presented in this short form (Example 4.5b); Dr. Gordon's in *Kings Row* is simply a rising pattern of minor triads (Example 4.5c); and Mildred in *Of Human Bondage* is characterized mainly by a distinctive four-chord motif (Example 4.5d) that is sometimes preceded by a celesta arpeggio or anacrusis—though, like Fenella's theme in *Escape Me Never*, it also may have a lengthy extension.

When looking across the film scores, it is also possible to detect commonalities of approach in Korngold's themes, such that common musical characteristics

---

[20] The appearance of the first three notes of the *Albatross* theme in cue 9C was a later addition and was probably made on the Scoring Stage, since it was added in Korngold's own hand to the Hugo Friedhofer-orchestrated full score at Reh. Figs. 11 and 12.

Example 4.6 Antagonistic themes (a) Sir Guy of Gisbourne in *Robin Hood*, cue 1C; (b) King James in *Captain Blood*, cue 3; (c) Faith in *Anthony Adverse*, cue 8.

Example 4.7 Gesturally similar themes (a) Cooky in *The Sea Wolf*, cue 8C; (b) Lingley in *Between Two Worlds*, cue 6B; (c) Pete Musick in *Between Two Worlds*, cue 4C.

would appear to clarify character identities and relationships all the more efficiently. It is here, perhaps, where Korngold's ability to characterize quickly in a way that is distinct from his operatic technique is most clearly demonstrated. The chief antagonists in films, for example, are often associated with melodic major sevenths, minor ninths, or tritones. Example 4.6 shows the themes for Sir Guy (Basil Rathbone) in *Robin Hood*, King James (Vernon Steele) in *Captain Blood*, and Faith (Gale Sondergaard) in *Anthony Adverse*, which share these characteristics.[21] Likewise, a comparison of a theme associated with the irredeemably nasty Cooky (Barry Fitzgerald) in *The Sea Wolf* and part of the theme for the uncaring capitalist Lingley (George Coulouris) in *Between Two Worlds* reveals themes that are undoubtedly cut from the same cloth—though Lingley admittedly also shares something with a portion of the theme for Pete Musick (George Tobias), an entirely sympathetic character from the same film (see Example 4.7). Descending chromatics, drawing upon their role in Korngold's opera *Die tote Stadt* to signify death, are also deployed throughout the film scores to represent something threatening. The fate motif in *Anthony Adverse*, for instance, is accompanied by a descending chromatic, and similar "death motifs" are heard in *The Sea Hawk*, *Between Two Worlds*, and *Deception*.

---

[21] Don Luis's theme sometimes involves a major seventh; at other times, it uses a minor seventh.

142 KORNGOLD IN AMERICA

Love themes can be characterized by melodies with relatively large intervallic leaps, though as this is also a general feature of Korngold's melodic writing, it is not necessarily a reliable way to identify the function of such music. Indeed, while the theme that appears to characterize Maria's love for Denis in *Anthony Adverse*, the two love themes from *Another Dawn*, and love themes from *The Adventures of Robin Hood*, *Captain Blood*, or *Kings Row* broadly fit this profile, other love themes are characterized more by their narrow ranges. Anthony's love for Angela (Olivia de Havilland) in *Anthony Adverse* is marked by more stepwise motion, as is the love theme from *Elizabeth and Essex*—though it does admittedly open out intervalically in its second half. The gentle love theme from *Devotion* is likewise marked by a hesitant ascending profile that is far less overt than other love themes, and thus appropriate for both the unreciprocated love that Emily (Ida Lupino) has for Nicholls (Paul Henreid) and the "quiet" emotion that Charlotte distinguishes from her "schoolgirl hysteria." Similarly, differentiating a love theme from a theme used for a female character that is the focus for the male protagonist's love is not always straightforward. Elise (Kaaren Verne) in *Kings Row*, for instance, is given a chromatic swooping theme that seems straight out of Korngold's Viennese past, but that might equally serve as a love theme between her and Parris Mitchell (Robert Cummings). The themes for obviously heroic (male) characters, by contrast, are often some of the most easily identifiable— whether it be the fanfare themes for Geoffrey Thorpe in *The Sea Hawk*, Peter Blood in *Captain Blood*, Denny Roark in *Another Dawn*, or Robin Hood, all of whom are played by Errol Flynn. The theme associated with Philip Carey's medical career in *Of Human Bondage*—optimistic-sounding music that hints at a future free of the burden of Mildred Rogers—is similarly fanfare-like.

Main characters tend to be signaled by strong opening fourths or fifths: Essex's theme in *The Private Lives of Elizabeth and Essex* is characterized by a falling fourth in dotted rhythm, while Parris in *Kings Row* is represented by a strong opening rising fifth. This gesture also identifies Emily's main theme in *Devotion*, which is further indication that this is a female character whom Korngold endows with considerable narrative agency. Likewise, royal characters are frequently marked by themes whose openings feature bold intervallic leaps that when combined with brass instrumentation can result in regal-sounding music. Elizabeth I of England, for example, can be found in two Korngold scores. In *The Sea Hawk* she is played by Flora Robson and characterized by a theme that in being shaped by a falling fourth and rising sixth is in some respects similar to the fanfare-like triadic opening to the theme used for the film's main protagonist, Geoffrey Thorpe.[22] In *The Private Lives of Elizabeth and Essex*, Bette Davis's

---

[22] Indeed, if the opening three pitch classes of the two themes (in C major, C-B-G for the Queen and E-D-G for Thorpe) are played simultaneously, they harmonize each other in thirds and then proceed to an octave. Although Korngold did not combine them like this, the close harmonic

Example 4.8 Gemma's theme in *Escape Me Never* (cue 3B).

Elizabeth I is likewise associated with thematic material that expresses her identity as England's sovereign and shares that regal ceremonial quality. Thus, the opening of the film introduces a brassy heraldic theme consisting of a rising fourth and fifth followed by stepwise descent that offers a public image of the Queen's power. That said, the character is also associated with other thematic material that speaks of her private identity as a suffering woman in love with a man (Essex) whose lust for power threatens her position: the theme connected with the Queen's sorrow consists of a similar rising fifth and fourth followed by stepwise descent, but here the string and wind orchestration signifies "sadness" more clearly than the theme's intervallic content, which in reminding us of the confident power theme neatly encapsulates the tensions that underpin her situation. There are other film protagonists, too, whose themes in avoiding large opening intervals might appear less overtly confident. Anthony's theme in *Anthony Adverse* is an example of this (Example 4.2a), though as it serves him from conception throughout a large part of his adult life, it is required to possess a certain flexibility befitting his stage in life. Its hesitant, stepwise opening is nonetheless worlds away from Essex's bold theme in *The Private Lives of Elizabeth and Essex*. Similarly, the stepwise theme for Tom Canty (Billy Mauch), the pauper in *The Prince and the Pauper* contrasts with the fanfare-like confident theme for the real Edward Tudor (Bobby Mauch), and in so doing signals quite clearly their differing origins and social status.

In terms of themes for his female characters, Korngold sometimes uses diatonicism to signify innocence and also a kind of moral purity in a way that is typical of the contemporary view of "virtuous" women in film: this is particularly apparent in Randy's kind-hearted reliability in *Kings Row* (Example 4.3), in Sally's characterization in *Of Human Bondage*, or even in the music for *Escape Me Never*'s Gemma, who despite being forced to steal and impersonate is portrayed as a deeply moral character (Example 4.8).[23] Clearly, her sequential diatonic theme contrasts with Fenella's tritone-harmony theme from the same film (Example 4.5b): Fenella (Eleanor Parker) is hardly a villain, but she is (to some

---

relationship perhaps helps us to hear the two characters as linked in motivation and identity. Both themes are also varied timbrally depending on their use in ceremonial/public or private contexts.

[23] The opening of Gemma's theme shares something with Francois's "Ich bin ein Lieder sänger" from *Die Kathrin*.

degree, at least) an antagonist character who disrupts the expected romantic pairing of Gemma and Sebastian. But this connection between diatonicism and virtue is not a simple equation that can be applied uncritically. Ann (Eleanor Parker) in *Between Two Worlds* is associated with the type of sinewy chromaticism that we might expect to accompany a more worldly character, whereas the main theme for Julia (Kay Francis) in *Another Dawn* ostensibly hints at little of the passion underlining her character.[24] The apparent uncomplicated diatonic innocence of some characters is, however, more obviously contrasted with those whose musical identity hints at something more complex. Here the musical themes associated with the mentally ill characters of Cassie Tower (Betty Field) and Louise Gordon (Nancy Coleman) in *Kings Row* are striking. In using fragmentary, repetitious themes that are harmonically unstable, Korngold is necessarily drawing on contemporary tropes of mental illness that would appear rather unkind to us today. Nonetheless, they signify quickly that something is out of place with these characters, though whether that makes Korngold and us somehow complicit in their violent treatment by figures of male patriarchal authority is a disturbing question.

Korngold's thematic material can also signal other kinds of otherness particularly clearly. The music for the character of Neleta (Steffi Duna) in *Anthony Adverse*—a native of the unnamed African country in which Anthony (Fredric March) engages in the slave trade—is the most obvious example of this: it is repetitious, chromatic, and melodically decorated, and as such seems to signify the quintessence of the exotic. Perhaps revealingly, and troubling given Neleta's racial identity, it is similar to music Korngold wrote for Thorpe's monkey in *The Sea Hawk* in being essentially static decoration,[25] yet in its saxophone instrumentation it signifies alluring and dangerous exoticism rather than comic relief (Example 4.9). Indeed, comic or flippant characters, too, can warrant particularly distinctive themes when they are deemed worthy of musical representation. Into this category we can place *Devotion*'s Mons. Heger, Miss Branwell, and Branwell Brontë (when drunk) and also *The Constant Nymph*'s Charles Creighton, who is represented by a wonderfully mock-pompous theme (Example 4.10). Similarly, the theme for the schoolgirls in *Escape Me Never* is light-hearted Korngold at his best, and explains why this music was later reused in his theatrical comedy *Die stumme Serenade*.[26] A sober character like Brother Francois in *Anthony Adverse* is also given an ecclesiastically serious theme, though given that themes for other

---

[24] Admittedly, Julia's introduction (a camera shot focusing on her legs) is set to a second saxophone theme that in its chromaticism and instrumentation more obviously signals "desire." Moreover, her simple diatonic theme is in fact subjected to extensive variation (of which more below).

[25] As revealed in Chapter 3, the theme was derived from incidental music written for the Hans Müller play *Der Vampir*.

[26] Act II Marsch und Revolution.

Example 4.9 (a) Neleta's theme in *Anthony Adverse*, cue 32 (b) the monkey in *The Sea Hawk*, cue 2A.

Example 4.10 Charles Creighton's theme in *The Constant Nymph* (cue 4B).

clerical characters (Father Andrew in *The Prince and the Pauper* and Father Xavier in *Anthony Adverse*) are rather different from this, it seems Korngold did not take a one-size-fits-all approach to representing the clergy.

Perhaps the kind of theme that needs to signal most clearly and quickly, though, is one referencing a location. In Korngold's operatic output, a strong sense of geographical place is only really evident in *Violanta* and *Die tote Stadt*: *Violanta*'s Venetian locale is signaled partly through instrumentation (the use of the mandolin) but also through invoking the Barcarolle song-form; Bruges in *Die tote Stadt* is signaled merely by a certain medievalism in Korngold's use of organum-like fourths alongside its bell sonorities.[27] Locations are much more overtly signaled in the film scores, though, owing to the often much larger geographical spread of their narratives. Thus, in *The Sea Hawk* the Spanish theme, which also doubles for Don Alvarez (Claude Rains), contains a distinctive melodic ornament that signals its otherness in contrast to the England of Thorpe and the Queen.[28] The Venetian theme written for the opening of *Escape Me Never* (Example 4.11b) uses the mandolin and parallel fourths, while Port Royal's Jamaican identity in *Captain Blood* is signaled as much by Korngold's parallel fifths/fourths music and percussion accompaniment as by its palm-tree townscape (Example 4.11c). Themes for Tortuga in *Captain Blood*, the Dolomites in *Escape Me Never*, Havana in *Anthony Adverse*, or Panama in *The Sea Hawk* are similarly distinctive.

---

[27] The mountain landscape of Switzerland of Act III of *Die Kathrin* is admittedly hinted at instrumentally by the presence of bells and accordion, and the use of pastoral-sounding oboe.

[28] This kind of ornamentation has long been associated with musical depictions of otherness. See, for example, Leo Treitler, "The Politics of Reception: Tailoring the Present as Fulfilment of a Desired Past," *Journal of the Royal Musical Association* 116, no. 2 (1991): 280–298.

Example 4.11 (a) Spanish theme's ornament in *The Sea Hawk*, cue 2A (b) Venetian theme in *Escape Me Never*, cue 1A (c) Port Royal in *Captain Blood*, cue 7.

Clearly, then, there are certain commonalities in themes that assist film- and music-literate audiences in making judgments about characters' identities and motivations, and about narrative settings. Yet, despite some obvious similarities across his film output, Korngold's approach to devising thematic material was hardly formulaic. Van Weyden (Alexander Knox) in *The Sea Wolf*, for instance, is notionally a hero, yet his theme contains a tritone that in other films is commonly found in the music for antagonists. Similarly, Leach (John Garfield) is the hero of the film, yet his theme contains a rising major seventh more appropriate to an archetypal villain; indeed, it is closest to that of Mrs Clivedon-Banks (Isobel Elsom) from *Between Two Worlds*—admittedly hardly a villain, but certainly far from a sympathetic character. The theme for Prior (Garfield again) in *Between Two Worlds* also features a prominent rising major seventh and minor ninth in a way that hints at the demons underpinning his personality, though its early acerbic presentation is softened on its final appearance as a result of the motherly attention of Mrs. Midget (Sara Allgood).[29] These themes can be seen in Example 4.12. Likewise, the scheming Prince John (Claude Rains) in *Robin Hood* is associated with the kind of fanfare one would expect to be associated with a typical hero, though his royal status may have persuaded Korngold to use something suitably regal;[30] he had, in any case, a more stereotypical villain to score in that film in the figure of Sir Guy. To some degree, though, the individual characteristics of a theme are secondary to the overall stylistic sound of a score, and it is within that context that Korngold's character themes signify most clearly. The fact that Korngold occasionally felt able to reuse thematic material across films, for instance, points to the fact that such signifying potential depended very much on context. The primary ways in which this occurs is in the transformation of thematic material through various forms of variation and development.

---

[29] A rising minor seventh is also the signature of Arabella's theme in *Captain Blood*.
[30] The theme for Prince John shares a great deal with the theme for Henry VIII in *The Prince and the Pauper*.

Example 4.12 Themes for (a) Van Weyden in *The Sea Wolf*, cue 11B; (b) Leach in *The Sea Wolf*, cue 1C; (c) Mrs Clivedon-Banks in *Between Two Worlds*, cue 5D; (d) Prior in *Between Two Worlds*, cue 3A.

Thematic Transformations

In their dismissive characterization of Hollywood film-scoring practices, Eisler and Adorno seized upon the use of leitmotif, suggesting it reflected a lack of compositional ability ("[the composer] can quote where he would otherwise have to invent"[31]) or functioned merely as duplication for that which is already visible onscreen. Yet, this is demonstrably false for many composers writing Hollywood film scores in the 1940s, and even were the criticism a valid one, close examination of Korngold's use of associative themes refutes the claim. Relatively few themes are presented only in one guise, and although Korngold certainly generates large stretches of music using this material, it is accomplished largely through various forms of transformation, development, and extension rather than "mere" repetition. The *Albatross* theme in *The Sea Hawk*, for instance, in signifying Thorpe's ship is wonderfully flexible (see Example 4.4): most obviously it can stand for the ship itself, or act as a musical symbol for Thorpe and his men, but it can also generate music material through what in symphonic contexts might be considered "developmental" procedures. As noted above, it can be reduced to its first three notes and repeated, but the ending can also be varied to allow it to modulate and to be repeated or fragmented, as happens in Reel 3. In cue 4A, Korngold repeats and varies its harmony, melody, and instrumentation (Example 4.13) in order to both cover a large span of film and characterize the physical space of the ship's decks over which Thorpe wanders as his men speculate about his romantic interest in Dona Maria (Brenda Marshall).

Indeed, it is the way that Korngold transforms thematic material wherein an important part of his dramatic technique in film resides.[32] Relatively simple transformations or variants of themes in the film scores encompass such things as changes of tempo or rhythm, mode, instrumentation, or texture, alongside

---

[31] Eisler and Adorno, *Composing for the Films*, 4.
[32] Korngold's operatic experience certainly prepared him well for this in that he was well used to transforming or varying thematic material in response to changes in narrative situation.

Example 4.13 *Albatross* theme varied in cue 4A of *The Sea Hawk* (with simplified texture).

thematic truncation. These kinds of transformation are pervasive in Korngold's film scores, and though they can be simple or complex they are nonetheless effective in clarifying aspects of narrative or character identity in addition to fulfilling more obviously musical functions in the construction of cues. A simple change of tempo or rhythm, for instance, can insert a complete theme into a small temporal gap, and is particularly useful when thematic material is closely tied to a character's physicality.[33] When Gemma (Ida Lupino) is introduced in cue 1E of *Escape Me Never*, having been caught stealing in the McLean family house, she is dragged struggling into the scene by her captors. We hear what later transpires to be a faster, rhythmically diminished version of her theme; as her progress into the room slows, however, it broadens and augments rhythmically in response to her movements. Throughout this cue, the rhythm and tempo of Gemma's theme are in constant flux: the character herself is seemingly in danger of jumping out of the window at any moment, and her music appears to underwrite and

---

[33] In cue No. 12 of *Another Dawn*, for instance, a theme associated with unrequited love, and particularly John's love for Julia, is heard at Reh. Fig. 3 at a much faster tempo than usual, and with an altered ending.

contribute to this apparently dangerous unpredictability, something that is reinforced by colorful tales of her background (stories we are perhaps not entirely sure we are supposed to take seriously). In quieter more reflective moments, however, a more rhythmically stable version of her theme is heard that reflects the quiet stillness that underpins her identity as a devoted mother and hopeless romantic (Example 4.8).

Transformations of a theme's mode (typically from major to minor) are often used to signal changes of fortune or character mood. A simple example can be heard in cue 7B of *Between Two Worlds* when the characters of the Rev. William "Bunny" Duke and Pete Musick reflect sadly on their evaporating hopes for the future, having realized that their ship is not taking them to America but instead to the afterlife. Bunny's theme is recast in F sharp minor, albeit with equivocal A♯s, as if to suggest the vicar's uncertain and conflicted frame of mind. The version we hear of Pete's theme, however, is more obviously tragic, and cast in D minor: it reflects his anger at having his chance of happiness with his wife and new baby snatched away by the air raid that has deprived them of their lives. Example 4.14 shows these two themes in their minor guise. Similarly, Dona Maria's grief and worry over the fate of her lover, Geoffrey Thorpe, who has been captured and condemned to the life of a galley slave prompts a minor mode version of her two-part theme in cue 10D of *The Sea Hawk*. More advanced thematic changes include harmonic "corruptions" beyond a simple change of mode, the combination of themes, and the ways in which themes evolve or are developed. The harmonic changes to Anthony's theme in cue 34-B of *Anthony Adverse*, for instance, reveals the effect on his character of his time as a slave

Example 4.14 Minor variants of (a) Bunny and (b) Pete in *Between Two Worlds* (cue 7B).

150   KORNGOLD IN AMERICA

trader in Africa: it is recast initially in D♭ minor before Brother Francois's urging causes it to firstly cadence in D♭ major before it pivots into E major at mention of Anthony's wife, Angela.

Associative themes often come with distinctive orchestration that speaks of character identity (such as the brass fanfares associated with heroic characters), and a shift in instrumentation can also signal a change of narrative situation: Thorpe's theme in *The Sea Hawk*, for instance, is heard in strings rather than brass during his love scenes with Dona Maria or in his interaction with Elizabeth I at the film's conclusion; while Fenella's theme in *Escape Me Never* is rendered in simplified form in wedding bells as Sebastian marries Gemma—a subtle indication of her jealousy and continued presence in their marriage. The most frequently applied thematic transformation, however, involves fragmentation or truncation, which allows Korngold to reference characters quickly when they appear onscreen or are mentioned in dialogue. In the scene in *The Sea Hawk* in which Thorpe entertains his Spanish guests to dinner aboard the *Albatross*, rapid cross cutting between Thorpe and Dona Maria prompts truncated versions of their themes before a toast to Queen Elizabeth demands a corresponding musical fragment: this then elides with the Queen's first onscreen appearance as the scene shifts to England and the music seamlessly links the two narrative spaces. Other themes, however, seem to warrant more frequent and systematic truncation. Fanfare themes such as those for Robin Hood or Geoffrey Thorpe are frequently reduced to a kind of "head motif" that signals the character's presence or influence at a distance.[34] Prior's theme in *Between Two Worlds* can often be heard in its shortened form, featuring just its first four notes, and repeated at different octaves. That said, themes can also be extended in a variety of ways. One of Emily's themes in *Devotion* gains an extension in the packing montage scene (cue 3A), in which she is shown preparing her brother's things ready for his journey to London.

Frequently, transformations are applied simultaneously.[35] In *Another Dawn*, for instance, several transformations are applied to Denny Roark's fanfare during the scene in which Roark and his men fight Acahaban's forces in the desert. When all hope seems lost, Denny's optimistic theme, which marks him out as a typical Korngold hero, is presented in B minor in strings rather than brass and at a slower tempo (Example 4.15a). The battle is subsequently won, however, thanks to the sacrifice of Wilkins (Herbert Mundin), and once the battle is over, Denny reviews

---

[34] See Winters, *Korngold's* The Adventures of Robin Hood, 119–120.

[35] One of the best-known transformations of a Korngold theme is found in *The Sea Hawk*, as detailed by Royal S Brown. What Brown calls the "romantic theme" is transformed into a "gloomy dirge" as Thorpe and his men row back to the *Albatross* having seemingly only narrowly escaped the Spanish. Royal S Brown, *Overtones and Undertones: Reading Film Music* (Berkeley: University of California Press, 1994), 102. This is Reh. Fig. 4 in cue 9C, and it takes two bars of the theme, lengthening it and treating it to sequential repetition.

Example 4.15 Thematic transformations (a) Roark's theme in *Another Dawn*, cue 23; (b) Dona Maria's theme in *The Sea Hawk*, cue 7B; (c) Piccolo's theme in *Escape Me Never*, cue 11C.

the cost of victory in lives. An even slower, more maudlin version of his theme is heard (in B♭ minor) to reflect the character's mood. Similar types of thematic variant can be heard in *The Sea Hawk* where the first part of Dona Maria's theme undergoes a transformation of both tempo and mode when she rushes to Dover to prevent Thorpe setting sail, knowing that he is headed into a trap set by Don Alvarez and Lord Wolfingham (Example 4.15b). The theme is recast in D minor *agitato* and is both truncated and subjected to sequential repetition. Similarly, the theme for Piccolo, Gemma's infant son in *Escape Me Never* is initially simply recast in the minor when Gemma takes him to the hospital in cue 11B.[36] The following cue 11C (Example 4.15c), after Piccolo's death, then presents it in E♭ minor whereupon it is treated to extension and obsessive grief-stricken development, including an eventual climactic rhythmic diminution and fragmentation.

Unlike the contrapuntal motivic webs sometimes found in *Die tote Stadt* or *Das Wunder der Heliane*, the vertical combination of themes occurs relatively rarely in Korngold's film scores, which generally demanded greater narrative clarity than such layering might allow. It does, however, take place on several occasions in *Anthony Adverse*.[37] Cue 2A accompanies the intertitle telling of the

---

[36] Piccolo's theme shares its oscillating upward major second with the music associated with Kathrin's young son in *Die Kathrin*.

[37] Even when it does, this is not an example of what is sometimes known as "thematic complex" because the combination itself does not function as a separate associative theme. As Bribitzer-Stull argues, "it is difficult, in the limited time span of the average film score, to establish a number of distinct leitmotifs and then combine them into a new associative entity." *Understanding the Leitmotif*, 288.

152 KORNGOLD IN AMERICA

progression of Maria and Denis's love over footage of Don Luis (Claude Rains) at the baths: it combines a variant of Don Luis's theme in bass register with a fragment of the love theme in violins.[38] Similarly, in cue 36 from Reel 10,[39] which takes place in Africa during Anthony's time as a slave trader, Korngold presents the rain theme associated with Anthony's growing sense of self-disgust in the upper voice with that of his mother Maria in an inner voice, while the camera focuses on the Madonna carving that once belonged to her—see Example 4.16. Here, the rhythm of the rain theme requires adjustment to accommodate the simultaneous presentation of Maria's theme. Likewise, *The Prince and the Pauper*—whose narrative premise relies on the confusion of identities of Prince Edward and Tom Canty—allows Korngold to combine simultaneously elements of the themes of Edward and Tom to characterize the dual identity of beggar boy Tom, who nonetheless carries the clothes and responsibilities of the Prince.[40] Occasional examples of vertical combination aside, the sequential presentation of themes in quick succession is far more often encountered in Korngold's film scores. This often happens alongside some form of thematic truncation, as with the conclusion of the dinner scene in *The Sea Hawk* (cue 3E), mentioned above, where we hear in quick succession fragments of themes for Thorpe, Dona Maria, and the Queen.

Perhaps the most complex types of thematic transformation involve instances of thematic evolution—where character developments result in apparently fundamental and permanent changes to their associated music. The distinctive alternating tritone that characterizes Louis's troubled theme in *The Sea Wolf* transforms after his death into the gentler and more peaceful perfect fourth of the harmonica song (cue 6C), which is in a very real sense the character's epitaph. Likewise, Robin's theme in *The Adventures of Robin Hood* transforms at the end of the film (11E) once he has been restored to the nobility as Baron of Locksley, Earl of Sherwood and Nottingham. The intervallic connection his theme shared with the "Jollity" theme, which characterizes his activities with his

---

[38] The presence of the love theme was a later addition; it does not feature in Korngold's short score manuscript for the cue. One wonders, indeed, whether the intertitle itself was a later addition. Korngold may already have written Don Luis's theme into the cue to match the image, but added a fragment of Denis and Maria's love theme to better match the content of the intertitle.

[39] By implication, 10F, though it is not labeled as such in the manuscript sources.

[40] The end of *Between Two Worlds* also contains an isolated example of vertical combination of sorts in cue 12E where in triumph at Henry and Ann's return to life, the Heaven theme in violins is combined with Ann's chromatic theme in horns. By "slotting" Ann's theme into the space of the sustained note of the Heaven theme, there is little need for adjustment to make the two themes work contrapuntally. Other examples of vertical thematic combination can be found in cue 9 of *Another Dawn*, which returns us to Dikut after a period of the narrative takes place onboard an ocean liner and in England. Dikut's railway-station theme, which signals the sonic space of the scene, is combined contrapuntally with the unrequited love theme that indicates the arrival of John and his new bride Julia into this world. The unrequited love theme subsequently fragments and morphs into Julia's theme.

Example 4.16 Combination of rain theme (top stave) with Maria's theme (middle stave) in cue 36 of *Anthony Adverse*.

band of Merry Men, is abandoned and a variant heard first in the love scene (8B) is adopted. Robin's theme is also allied to music associated with King Richard (Ian Hunter), as if to accomplish his severing from his outlaw life and readoption by the crown. Likewise, the love theme between Robin and Marian (Olivia de Havilland) abandons the same disjunct quaver movement that was common to "Jollity," Robin's theme, and the love theme, and instead embraces aspects of the King's own musical character. As such, Robin's love for Marian and for his country leave behind the youthful exuberance of life as an outlaw. The character has "grown up," and the final statement of his musical theme reflects this.[41]

Two Case Studies

The thematic structures that Korngold employed, and the ways in which he uses them for narrative purposes, are, then, rather unlike the rather simplistic, one-dimensional portrayal of "leitmotivic" film scoring suggested by Eisler and Adorno; and the treatment of numerous themes in Korngold scores reveal what appear to be considered musical choices that support or shape our experience of the narrative. Many of the examples I have mentioned above could be studied in greater detail, including the complexities of the themes for Emily and Charlotte in *Devotion*: Emily has as many as five themes, all of which share a common rising fifth interval, while Charlotte's pentatonic theme is varied, fragmented, and developed in narratively significant ways. Here, though, I want to examine more fully just two examples: the "Love and Ring" theme from *The Private Lives of Elizabeth and Essex*, and Julia's theme from *Another Dawn*. Both are subject to an extensive number of changes, and yet neither receive the kind of critical attention typically paid to better-known or more overtly stated thematic material.

---

[41] For a discussion of these thematic evolutions, see Winters, *Korngold's* The Adventures of Robin Hood, 121–123.

154   KORNGOLD IN AMERICA

As a symbol of the continued loyalty of Queen Elizabeth I to the Earl of Essex, the "Love and Ring" theme from *The Private Lives of Elizabeth and Essex* is certainly recognizable enough on each of its many occurrences, yet it nonetheless undergoes important changes that chart vacillating aspects of the couple's relationship. The theme itself is a simple one, but at first it resists clear signification. It is prefigured at the end of cue 5D, the love scene where Elizabeth and Essex talk of the complexity of their feelings for each other, and we first hear its characteristic opening falling minor seventh and distinctive rhythmic signature—see Example 4.17a. More disguised prefiguring statements of it are then heard at Reh. Fig. 9 in cue 6A, as Elizabeth talks of those enemies at court who would trick Essex into disaster, before a full statement of the theme is heard clearly at Reh. Fig. 14 in D♭ major in a tender moment as Elizabeth asks Essex to be careful and to promise her not to accept a post away from home. A passionate variant is heard at the beginning of cue 7A as Elizabeth responds angrily to Essex's acceptance of the role of military leader in Ireland, which breaks his promise to her; however, it arguably receives its archetypal statement in strings in cue 7B (marked *Andante con sentimento molto*) where Elizabeth and Essex are reconciled and Elizabeth gives him the ring that could save his life if ever they should become enemies—Example 4.17b. The theme at this point thus becomes associated with the physical object of the ring itself. A highly disguised version in vibraphone, harp, and cello pizzicato is heard in 7D (Example 4.17c) as Cecil (Henry Daniell) threatens his co-conspirator Penelope (Olivia de Havilland): notably the theme's falling minor seventh becomes a major seventh. Further regular statements are heard in 8A and in extended form in 10A as Essex and Elizabeth are reunited in their final love scene; however, it receives a prominent change of mode in 10B (Example 4.17d) and is presented in sequential fragmentation in response to Essex's perception of his betrayal, culminating in the breaking of his sword in protest. In 11B its distinctive falling seventh equivocates between a major and minor seventh as Elizabeth, having waited for the condemned Essex to send her the ring, realizes that Cecil's arrival carries no word from her lover (Example 4.17e). The same equivocation is heard in 11C in anticipation of the pair's final meeting, at which we hear a penultimate statement that restores its original form (12A). Its final presentation is in cue 12B at Reh. Fig. 9 as Essex approaches the block; however, it is now reduced from the rich string textures heard in cue 7B or 12A to a single flute line, answered by a violin solo over a superimposed D minor and D diminished seventh chord—a faint memory of a tragic love, as Essex kisses the ring prior to his execution.

"Love and Ring" is, in essence, a simple theme that is identified mostly by a distinctive melodic interval: a falling seventh. The defining characteristics of the theme for Julia Ashton (Kay Francis) in *Another Dawn* are perhaps more obviously rhythmic or gestural: the theme undergoes significant melodic and

Example 4.17 "Love and Ring" in *The Private Lives of Elizabeth and Essex* (a) cue 5D (b) cue 7B (c) cue 7D (d) cue 10B (e) cue 11B.

harmonic changes (corruptions from an archetype, even) in response to her narrative situation, yet it remains identifiable throughout. Julia is a character whom Col. John Wister (Ian Hunter), the commander of a military outpost in the fictional colony of Dikut, meets and with whom he falls in love while on holiday in England. The basic form of her theme, as it is introduced in cue 4 when we meet the character on an ocean liner, consists of a sentence structure to which Korngold sometimes appends a bar of parallel-triad celesta decoration (or extends using another sentence structure). Example 4.18 shows its basic, normative form, minus the celesta decoration and the repetitions. Although

Example 4.18 Julia's theme in *Another Dawn* (cue 4).

John knows Julia is still very much attached to her dead lover, the pilot Duncan Hitchens, he nonetheless proposes marriage and brings her back with him to Dikut, where she soon falls in love with Denny Roark, Wister's second in command. The love triangle that results is eventually resolved at the conclusion of the film as John sacrifices himself to allow Denny and Julia to be together. As such, Julia might be seen a character with little agency of her own, whose identity is tied closely to the desires of her male pursuers. Indeed, her theme is one that is subject to almost constant variation—whether reset in triple time (in cue 8, as John proposes marriage), or blended with the rhythmic accompaniment of the Bedouin love song (cue 14). It is the harmonic and melodic changes, however, that are arguably most telling.

In cue 9, the first phrase of the theme is treated to a melodic change when Julia is left standing at Dikut station as John departs to fetch their luggage (Example 4.19a).[42] Cue 12, "The Ride Out," continues this fragmentation and melodic disruption of her theme—perhaps in recognition that her show of wifely devotion to John as he prepares to ride out into the desert on a mission is somewhat artificial and awkward (Example 4.19b). A slightly different harmonic change occurs in cue 22A, as the theme is fragmented in response to Julia's mounting concern for Denny who she learns is under attack by Achaban's forces (Example 4.19c). This harmonic change continues in the following cue 22B, initially with a chromatically rising parallel sevenths accompaniment (Example 4.19d). In cue 25, the theme is changed in yet another way as the melody shifts further from its original version (Example 4.20a), though the first bar did not survive an edit. John (seemingly deaf to the changes in her music and blind to the real reasons behind her concern for the injured Denny) asks "why so pensive?" Later in the cue, Julia's theme returns to near harmonic and melodic normality as John quizzes her about her apparent unhappiness and she puts on a (musical) act to convince him otherwise; however, its triple meter is a continuing sign of the fluidity of her thematic identity—and the "warped" version

---

[42] This has been transcribed from the film as the piano-conductor score is incorrect at this point. Since a bar needed to be cut, this was likely rewritten on the Scoring Stage.

Example 4.19 Julia's theme in *Another Dawn* varied in (a) cue 9; (b) cue 12; (c) cue 22A; (d) cue 22B.

returns at Reh. Fig. 10. After Denny and Julia admit their feelings for each other, Julia's theme is again changed harmonically (cue 26) in the same way as in cue 25 before the falling motif of the theme is combined in the next cue with the theme for the sandstorm (a rising and falling figure)—Example 4.20b; the theme is then heard in another triple-time variant as Denny tells Julia of Ireland where they dream of being happy together, the last time in the film that Julia's theme is heard (Example 4.20c). The theme, then, is varied according to the narrative situation in which Julia finds herself—and the character might be interpreted not as someone whose identity is passively shaped by others but as a woman capable of adjusting her own musical voice to her advantage. These are not simple

Example 4.20 Julia's theme in *Another Dawn* varied in (a) cue 25; (b) cue 27; (c) triple time, cue 27.

changes of mode or tempo, either, but relatively complex changes of thematic character, perhaps even harmonic and melodic corruptions of an archetype that are motivated by the events of the narrative.

Non-Thematic Scoring and Continuity Editing

It is tempting to assume that musical material involving repeating associative themes constitutes the only important part of Korngold's film scores. Yet, the stretches of non-thematic music heard in these films are also of significance, particularly for the atmospheric qualities that help to construct a convincing and distinctive audiovisual film world for the viewer. In some cases, these non-thematic stretches of music encompass Korngold's much-dreaded action scenes, of which there are many—particularly in the swashbucklers—though often "action music" could incorporate thematic material, as with the duel in *Robin Hood* (11C) or with Mildred's explosive rage in *Of Human Bondage* (10C).[43] In any case, one suspects Korngold's antagonism toward such scenes is predicated on the fact that sound effects are frequently in danger of drowning out what often has to be quite dense and sophisticated music—indeed, Korngold had initially refused to score *The Adventures of Robin Hood* on the grounds that he was not a musical illustrator for a ninety percent action picture.[44]

Certainly, Korngold's music can play a valuable role in underscoring the energy of an action scene, or its underlying emotion, and to do so without making use of associative thematic material. Rhythm is particularly important in battle scenes, even if its carefully considered structures are sometimes in direct competition with recorded sound, and Korngold often uses repetition, harmonic sequence, and fragmentation to generate a large musical canvas. The fight scene (7B) in *The Sea Wolf*, for instance (Example 4.21a), or the battle music in *Another Dawn* (cue 21), relies on such procedures, as do the duel scenes in *The Sea Hawk*; and although one occasionally feels that Korngold was trying to cover a lot ground as efficiently as possible, they are undeniably effective cues at underscoring the tempo and rhythm of the action.[45] Similarly, the cue written to underscore the Queen's outburst of fury in *Elizabeth and Essex* (3D), in which she smashes the mirrors in the palace, is effective in releasing the energy that has accumulated in the previous scene, in which Penelope artfully sings a satirical song designed to ridicule the Queen's age. Elizabeth interrupts the song by smashing the mirror into which she has been gazing, but her anger is initially rendered as unscored dialogue: only the second mirror smash prompts

---

[43] Sometimes, these cues can even be built entirely from a varied fragment of thematic material, as with cue 8E in *The Sea Hawk* in which Thorpe and his men battle with the Spanish in the Panamanian jungle. The material is generated from Thorpe's head motif, and was also used in Reel 2 during the sea battle between the *Albatross* and the *Santa Eullàlia del Monte*. The propulsive qualities of its new syncopated rhythm are key to the scene's drama, however.

[44] For the text of Korngold's letter to Wallis, see Winters, *Korngold's* The Adventures of Robin Hood, 77–78.

[45] The Knife Fight in *Robin Hood* (10A) is another example, though its prominent falling fourth may be related to Robin's thematic material. Other non-thematic action scenes include large parts of the music for Cooky's encounter with the shark in *The Sea Wolf* (cue 8C).

Example 4.21 Non-thematic music (a) fight in the *Sea Wolf*, cue 7B; (b) Elizabeth I smashes mirrors in *The Private Lives of Elizabeth and Essex*, cue 3D; (c) dinner music in *The Sea Hawk*, cue 3E; and (d) the Island of Virgen Magra in *Captain Blood*, cue 27.

the entrance of music. This part of the cue is built on a typical Korngold harmonic sequence, with this and the subsequent mirror smash aligned with a half-diminished seventh chord followed by a skittish hexatonic string descent that amplifies and extends the sound of falling glass (Example 4.21b). It is a remarkably satisfying moment in which the music amplifies the inherent emotion, action, and sound of the scene without recourse to the score's extensive thematic content.[46]

Less action-heavy cues that nonetheless avoid thematic references include large parts of the golf game in *Another Dawn* (as discussed in Chapter 3) or the

---

[46] The Queen's sorrow theme is subsequently heard part-way through this cue, after her anger subsides.

KORNGOLD, THE HOLLYWOOD DRAMATIST   161

domestic dinner music heard aboard the *Albatross* in *The Sea Hawk* (near the beginning of cue 3E), which perfectly captures the initial congenial atmosphere of a dinner party before tensions rise in response to undiplomatic conversational slips and the discovery of Thorpe's looting of Spanish treasures (Example 4.21c). Nonetheless, the music is melodically and texturally quite complex. Cue 27 of *Captain Blood*, however, is an example of a simple non-thematic cue that, like the globe scene in *The Sea Hawk*, is largely about the strangeness of its harmony: its string chords outline a series of magical, distantly related triads to introduce the island of Virgen Magra, where Blood and Levasseur will fight to the death, as a place of mystery (Example 4.21d).

As an extended example of non-thematic writing, though, the escape scene in *The Sea Hawk* (cue 11E) is particularly instructive: owing to its lack of dialogue, it is a noteworthy example of the power of Korngold's music to carry the drama and to create tension. Thorpe and his men have been chained to the oars of a Spanish "galleass" as slaves, but, having learned of the Spanish Armada and treachery in the English court, they have resolved to warn an unsuspecting England. After stealing a knife, they have waited for nightfall and for the timekeeper to fall asleep before attempting to free themselves. The scene contrasts sudden movement with moments of stasis as they pretend to sleep. Indeed, there are seven distinct types of shot in the sequence, many of which are seen several times: (1) busy (but quiet) activity as Thorpe and his men work with the knife to remove the staples holding their chains to the deck, (2) the sleeping timekeeper, (3) men pulling on the chains to free the staples and moments when the staple suddenly gives way, (4) the guards as they patrol the deck above, (5) Thorpe and his men pretending to sleep or stopping in their activity, (6) the knife being thrown from one side of the galleass to the other, and (7) the men passing the now freed chain through guide rings or the loops attached to their belts.[47] It is striking just how carefully Korngold matched characters' physical movements (and the cinematography and editing) with his music, which contrasts static held chords with various levels of musical activity.[48] It is a section of music that Korngold would never have written in an opera, since it relies on precise visual editing, but it is arguably one of his most effective creations for film. Table 4.1 shows the musical gestures Korngold uses for all these physical actions. Moreover, Example 4.22 shows how precisely Korngold matches changes of shot (and thus of narrative space) with a musical event—in this case, in a section when activity is halted and Thorpe looks nervously to the darkened doorway leading to the guards on the upper deck. The held half-diminished seventh chord is heard in

---

[47]   Thus, the scene required the preparation of detailed cue sheets (as discussed in Chapter 3).

[48]   Synchronization was aided during recording, of course, by well-placed punches, as discussed in Chapter 3. These were spaced at 15-frame intervals (or 96 bpm), and enabled Korngold to work out how long to hold a fermata before aligning the continuation of music with the change of shot.

Table 4.1 Matching musical and physical gesture in *The Sea Hawk* escape scene (Cue 11E)

Physical Gesture	Image	Musical gesture
Knife activity to remove staple		
Sleeping timekeeper		
Pulling on chain		
Guards patrolling on deck above		

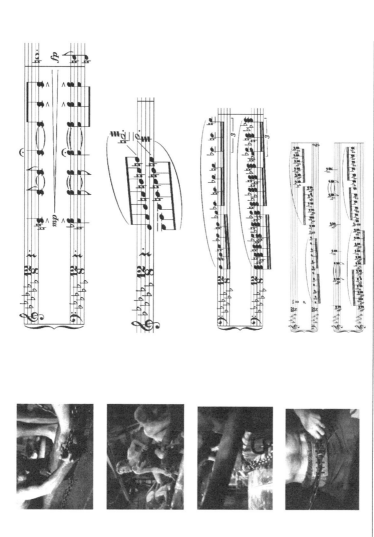

Staple coming loose

Passing knife by throwing it across gangway

Passing chain

Passing chain ctd.

Example 4.22 Matching shots in *The Sea Hawk* (cue 11E).

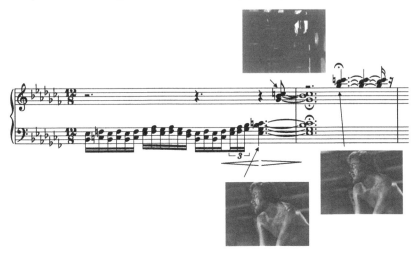

three different octaves to correspond with Thorpe's worried look, his point-of-view shot of the guards' shadows, and the return shot of Thorpe, before the activity of escape begins again—points of synchronization that are made possible by Korngold's deployment of punches, as discussed in Chapter 3. Music thus helps articulate the physical relationship between two different (albeit related) spaces in the narrative world. There is no thematic material here at all, and the absence of Thorpe's theme is itself narratively significant in reflecting his status in working alongside his men to win their freedom. Only once his status as leader is re-established through dialogue ("Now men, you know what to do") does his thematic material return to the score.

As with other Classical Hollywood composers, Korngold's film-scoring technique periodically makes use of "stingers" to draw attention to narrative events of significance. This is an important function of music in film and in their brevity such stingers are usually non-thematic. Thus, in cue 7A of *The Sea Hawk*, the significance of the news delivered to Don Alvarez by his spy, Samuel Kroner (Francis McDonald), about Captain Lopez sailing to Panama before Dona Maria's lover, Geoffrey Thorpe, prompts a subtle F augmented with added fourth chord sforzando stinger as the camera cuts to Maria's surprised reaction.[49] Dona Maria, however, must maintain her equilibrium at the news. She continues her game of chess with Don Alvarez—only later do we learn later of her emotional turmoil—and thus the music returns to the previous variant of her theme, heard on bass clarinet. Two important stingers with mystical implications can be

---

[49] Scored for muted trumpet, vibraphone, harp, celesta, four solo violins, and pizzicato strings.

found in *Between Two Worlds* and *The Sea Wolf*, though both the Fm maj7 "glass-breaking" chord of *Between Two Worlds*, and the B♭maj7 heard in *The Sea Wolf* have such important narrative roles to play that they might almost be considered thematic. Certainly, the glass-breaking chord has a strong associative function; both, at any rate, will be discussed in the following chapter. A more conventional half-diminished seventh sforzando stinger can be found in cue 21 of *Another Dawn* to signal the death of Wilkins (it actually precedes the shot of Wilkins's body, but was perhaps timed to match Roark's look of concern). Similarly, in *The Sea Hawk* (cue 8C), the narrative significance of Thorpe's name being known to Spanish forces in Panama ("under protest, Captain Thorpe") is underlined with an E♭ augmented chord stinger.

In addition to using non-thematic stingers, Korngold was also adept at creating atmospheric textures that, as with the mirror smashing in *Elizabeth and Essex*, can be thought of as special effects that amplify or replace recorded sound. In *Between Two Worlds*, for instance, Prior's "magic show" sees him set fire to the money that Lingley had earlier forced on Henry (cue 6D).[50] Korngold provides a suitably quicksilver repeating figure in flute over held Novachord, vibraphone, and string chords to suggest the flickering flames (Example 4.23a). The continuation of this music as the camera cuts away to show us the interested reactions of Prior's fellow passengers persuades us that the money continues to burn. Similarly, in *Another Dawn*, Korngold scores the morse-code communication scenes with hesitant but regular major seconds in xylophone that work with not only the pitched sound of the morse code, but also the telegraph operator's hesitant translation. Indeed, the second of the three scenes featuring this music involves the operator simply reading out a translated message; the music provides a re-creation of the hesitancy of the initial decoding, and functions alone as an iconic symbol (Example 4.3b). At other times, however, Korngold's music creates a longer-lasting atmospheric effect: the fog scenes in *The Sea Wolf* (cues 1C and 9D–see Example 4.23c) are a potent example of this: despite its appearance in two separate cues, this music is not really thematic in the way that, for example, the Port Royal theme in *Captain Blood* points to a specific location. Instead, these cues seem to be designed to suggest the oppressive mystery of the environment through a slow, sinewy marimba line, and to act as an atmospheric sound bed over which other thematic material can be layered: thus, the former cue features Leach's theme, and the latter incorporates Larson's. The music Korngold provided for the flood scene in *The Green Pastures* (cue 3), and which was subsequently reused in altered form in *The Sea Hawk* (cue 2E), is yet another example (Example 4.24d). In

---

[50] Prior uses a conductor's baton as his magic wand, a further indication of how much music is implicated in the strange world of this metaphysical ocean voyage.

Example 4.23 Atmospheric music (a) fire music in *Between Two Worlds*, cue 6D (b) morse code in *Another Dawn*, cue 22A (c) fog in *The Sea Wolf*, cue 1C (d) the flood in *The Green Pastures*, cue 3.

the former its sequential repeated cascading quintuplet demisemiquavers and surging chromatic bass figures are related to biblical rainfall;[51] in the latter it is used to underscore the nautical scene in which the *Albatross* approaches the disabled Spanish galleass prior to boarding.

One of the most important distinctions from Korngold's operatic practice, though, is the way in which his music in film is required to support and clarify aspects of Classical Hollywood continuity editing. Often, the role of music in

---

[51] Similar surging bass figures were first used in *Captain Blood* in the scene at the end of the film when grappling hooks are again used to draw two ships together.

Classical Hollywood is simply to smooth over changes of shot and thus to help stitch together separate pieces of film into a perceived continuity. On occasion, though, music can be used specifically to highlight difference. When the narrative shifts location, for example, Korngold's music can sometimes effect a change almost instantaneously in a way that is not possible in opera, where scene-shifting often requires long transitional passages of music to cover the mechanisms of stage machinery. Although such transitional passages to cover journeys can also be used in film (the map scene in *The Sea Hawk* is an obvious example in demonstrating Thorpe's sea voyage to Panama), the narrative can just as easily shift location in under a second.[52] Thus, in *Devotion* as the narrative jumps from a scene of Emily on the Yorkshire moors to Brussels, where the sisters have been sent to complete their education, Korngold's music shifts rapidly in tone to reflect the more-or-less instantaneous change in location. Moreover, this more condensed characteristic of film narrative—and music's role in supporting it—is also apparent in examples of parallel editing, in which the audience must be aware that consecutive shots happen in different narrative spaces and that the narrative "cross-cuts" between them. Thus, in the *Sea Hawk* escape scene referenced in Table 4.1, cross-cutting between above- and below-deck spaces is matched with a precise change in the music to signal that all is quiet above deck while below furious activity is taking place. Admittedly, there is not much chance of an audience confusing the spaces above and below decks; however, on occasion music seems absolutely essential to a clear understanding of the narrative. In the attack on the treasure caravan in *The Adventures of Robin Hood*, for example, the parallel editing of the scene relies on exactly synchronized changes in music to suggest, on the one hand, the space of Robin and his Merry Men lying in wait and, on the other, Sir Guy and his party approaching the site of the ambush (cue 4C). Here, Korngold makes use of thematic material but in very different ways from that found in opera. The perceived contrast in narrative space that is essential to understanding the narrative relies almost entirely on the musical contrast between Sir Guy's theme and that of the Merry Men, since the visual background of Sherwood Forest remains largely consistent throughout. Similarly, as the advance guard are attacked by the Merry Men, but Sir Guy's party carry on in ignorance of the trouble ahead, Korngold's music is essential to clarifying the physical distance that separates the groupings. The sudden appearance of Sir Guy's stately theme and disappearance of the scurrying semiquavers thus clarifies a relationship not made overtly clear in the images (Example 4.24). Eventually, as the two narrative spaces collapse into one (as Sir Guy's second section of guards with the treasure

---

[52] Although the scene can alter in 1/24th of a second, it was customary to signal large changes in narrative location with a gradual fade through black.

Example 4.24 Cross-cutting between the ambush site and Sir Guy's party in *The Adventures of Robin Hood* (cue 4C).

wagon enters the ambush site) the music aids the connection.[53] This, then, is a fundamentally filmic use of music that has no precedent in Korngold's operatic output, for the simple fact that it is very difficult to portray two different but parallel narrative spaces in opera and to cross-cut between them.

***

This chapter has provided only a snapshot of Korngold's film scoring techniques. Although it would be folly to deny there are continuities with operatic practices—particularly in the ways in which thematic material could be varied and extended both to create large stretches of musical material and, particularly, to aid dramatic explication—it is also the case that there are substantial differences occasioned by the very specific demands of film. These differences include film's need for many more character themes that signify quickly, alongside the demand for music to underscore often prolonged periods of action; however, as mentioned above, the differences also include the ways in which music may support the editing practices of Classical Hollywood cinema, and (even more obviously) the requirement to fit predetermined lengths of film. This last point has not been labored in any great detail, but it is a fundamental compositional difference between the two genres and one that should not be underestimated. It frequently results in completely different compositional priorities, and Korngold took specific pains to ensure that his music was precisely synchronized with onscreen events in a way that was neither desirable nor possible with opera. This resulted in some finely controlled small forms and larger structures alike, including the

[53] Similar parallel editing can be found earlier in *Robin Hood* to distinguish the forest space occupied by Robin and Will Scarlett from that of Sir Guy and his men who are arresting Much the Miller's son.

sword duels found in the Errol Flynn swashbucklers, *Captain Blood*, *The Prince and the Pauper*, *The Adventures of Robin Hood*, and *The Sea Hawk*. Surprisingly, Korngold never wrote ballet—apart from the one he provided for the film *Escape Me Never*—but the instinct to match human movement with musical gesture was amply catered for by his Hollywood output in a way that the opera scenarios he set never did.[54]

The duel in *Robin Hood*, for instance, is particularly instructive in this regard, and consulting Korngold's handwritten cue sheet reveals much about his approach.[55] As the transcription in Table 4.2 reveals, Korngold breaks the scene into twenty-five significant onscreen events, recording the duration between each. He then brackets events together to forge the structure of the cue: an introduction of fourteen seconds followed by three main sections of approximately twenty-six, twenty-two (further split into two sections of ten and twelve seconds) and sixty-four seconds, then concluding with three more subsections of 16.5, 2, and 9.5 seconds.[56]

It is striking how closely the finished musical cue aligns with this planned structure, which is derived from Korngold's viewing of the scene and his appreciation of its structure and pacing. The opening (up until Reh. Fig. 3) is characterized by Sir Guy's angular rising-sevenths theme and is gesturally introductory, acting as dominant preparation for Korngold's first main section (I): a paragraph of music rooted in A minor that continues Sir Guy's angular theme but elides it more obviously with Robin's distinctive fanfare motif. It ends with an E♭ augmented chord with fermata to match the temporary cessation of the duel after Sir Guy drops his sword. Korngold's second section (II) then resumes the duel in C minor and, after another sustained E♭ augmented chord (with added ninth) to match the locking of swords, its second subsection begins at Reh. Fig. 13, once again resuming the duel in C minor—this time with Robin on the floor trapped by a candelabra. The third section (III, Reh. Fig.16) begins after Robin is back on his feet and has retrieved his sword, and Korngold scores this with a version of Sir Guy's theme harmonized with pairs of chords (E–C♯m; F–Dm7; G♭–E♭aug$^{(\text{add }9)}$) under a chromatic ascent (G♯–A–B♭–B). For all its fragmentary beginnings, though, this C major/minor third section constitutes the bulk of the duel, and Korngold does not break down the sixty-four-second

---

[54] That said, some of the description of action in the published score to *Das Wunder der Heliane* reads almost like a screenplay, such is its specificity. Here, for instance, is the description at the start of Act II, scene iii: "Von einer Wache geleitet, tritt der Schwertrichter ein. Uralt, schloweißes Haar, fast durchsichtig, doch von hoher, kaum gebeugter Gestalt; er ist blind." ("Led by a guard, the Sword Judge enters. Ancient, snow-white hair, almost transparent, but tall and scarcely stooped; he is blind.") Yet, no more than a loose synchronization with music is implied.

[55] The cue sheet is reproduced in Winters, *Korngold's* The Adventures of Robin Hood, 84.

[56] Korngold is only approximate in adding together the individual timing of shots (since this is before the time he utilized timing punches). In any case, comparison of the manuscript sources and final film reveals minor edits that clearly happened after the sequence was composed.

170 KORNGOLD IN AMERICA

Table 4.2 Transcribed cue sheet information for 11C in *The Adventures of Robin Hood*[a]

Event, as noted by Korngold[b]	Section and section timing (with corresponding rehearsal numbers in score)	Timing of individual events
Guy	14 [seconds]	8 [seconds]
Flynn stairs (jumping)		6
Sword (fight)	I 26 [Reh. Fig. 3]	3 ½
Dialogue		6
Fight		5 ½
Guy falling		2
Flynn jumping		1+1
Suspension		7
Fight	II 10 [Reh. Fig. 10]	6 ½
Stop	12 [Reh. Fig. 13]	1 ½
Rush		2
Kandle [sic] [?] hits floor		2 1/3
Guy sword		2 1/3
Stop		1
Dialogue		3 1/3
Flynn up		3
Fight (slower)	III 64 [Reh. Fig. 16]	
Stop	16 ½ [Reh. Fig. 35]	7
Dagger	2	2 ½
Last [?]	9 ½	7
Push and Kill		2
Falling		2+3
Guy		½
Flynn		2
Guy		2

[a]The timings in this table are transcribed from the cue sheet, and do not match the final film.
[b]Some elements of Korngold's description of events are illegible.

sequence in his cue sheet any further. In itself, this is significant: what concerns the composer in designing this cue are moments of visual stasis or dialogue, and there are many fewer of these in this sixty-four-second section. In addition, any pauses in action in this section of the duel are only seen in long-shot or in Sol Polito's striking shadow cinematography. Korngold thus felt able to stress musical continuity in this long unbroken third section (Reh. Figs. 16 to 35), which contains the primary thematic material of the duel (Robin's theme elided with Sir Guy's). Only toward the end of the section does he again match closely the visual rhythm of the duel (Reh. Fig. 32, where two fermatas align with the momentary stillness of the two combatants). The end of this third part of the duel is signaled on the cue sheet by the next moment of visual interest: the point where Robin and Sir Guy are locked together ("Stop"). This is indicated musically by a significant textural change at Reh. Fig. 35: a high G trill and surging G#m7 and G7 chords repeated at three different octaves that is practically a quotation from Strauss's *Salome*.[57] Sir Guy then attempts to use his dagger, a dastardly ruse that Robin parries before dispatching him: his fatal stab is aligned precisely with a B♭ minor chord (♭vii in the prevailing C tonality), after which Sir Guy's body falls over the staircase, matched by *precipitando* chromatic descent ("Falling"). The cue ends with a delayed, punctuating C minor chord synchronized with a shot of Sir Guy's dead body.

Korngold's approach to composing music for this duel, then, was to create a precisely synchronized audiovisual ballet in which pauses in the action are often matched with corresponding moments of stasis in the music, and where space is allowed for significant dialogue. It is, however, an approach that in incorporating an extended period of musical continuity in the middle of the cue also avoids being overly didactic in its technique of audiovisual synchronization. Nonetheless, Korngold's film-scoring technique in this sort of scene is clearly motivated by the movement apparent in the image, and the desire to synchronize it with musical gesture. Moreover, it emphasizes one of the fundamental differences between film and opera, which as a live performance genre simply does not allow close synchronization of this kind. Indeed, a further difference between the two genres wherein the importance of synchronization can also be demonstrated lies with the necessity to score the opening and closing titles of films. Although there are some overlaps with concepts of operatic overtures, preludes and interludes, Korngold in any case did not use these consistently in his operatic output. Of the operas, only *Violanta* opens with an extended *Vorspiel* before the curtain rises that, in introducing thematic material for the characters of Violanta and Alfonso, might be compared productively with a film's opening titles—and even then only with a certain model of title sequence that presented an identifiable secondary theme.[58] As such, the opening titles of the film scores required Korngold to explore suitable forms of miniature overture that are more extensive than the much briefer introductions that were often heard in contemporary opera. Frank Lehman has made a sophisticated study of these opening titles as autonomous pieces that provide opportunities for "compositional precision, immediacy, and

---

[57] See Reh. Fig. 148+9 in *Salome*, where surging chords of Dm7⁹ and C#m are heard under a C# tremolo.

[58] Although *Violanta*'s mysterious *Vorspiel* introduces thematic material, it is far less declamatory in tone than Korngold's film titles, which are always brisk in tempo and loud in volume. The other operas contain much shorter introductions of fourteen bars (*Polykrates*), eight bars (*Die tote Stadt*), five bars (*Heliane*), and eight bars (*Kathrin*) before the curtain rises.

economy."[59] He makes a compelling case for the enormous variety of these somewhat self-contained cues, and traces changes to Korngold's preferred formal design, with *The Sea Hawk* the last to include a strongly differentiated main theme and subsidiary theme (of a type that might bear comparison with *Violanta*'s opening *Vorspiel*).[60] The later main titles, Lehman suggests, tend to be "more intricate, more unpredictable, and more internally sectional than earlier titles"[61]; thus, the large-scale tonal and formal complexity of some of the earlier scores' opening titles is channeled in the later films into the inventiveness of a single theme. Even with those earlier examples, such as *Captain Blood*, Lehman pointedly and quite correctly rejects the suggestions of quasi-sonata structures, instead identifying the titles' intrinsically filmic qualities of "expedience, malleability, impatience, and formal idiosyncrasy."[62] As such, he highlights the different demands and expectations of film music in even these most supposedly "autonomous" of cues.

I say "supposedly" since even in opening credits, Korngold was working with a defined cue length and a set image track. Although the main title sequences of early films such as *Captain Blood, Anthony Adverse*, and *The Prince and the Pauper* pay little attention to the visual impact of the credits, from *The Private Lives of Elizabeth and Essex* onward Korngold often chose to synchronize significant title cards with his music.[63] This is particularly the case with the appearance of his own name, which is precisely aligned with the return of the heraldic main theme in *Elizabeth and Essex*, the main theme in *The Sea Hawk*, and Wolf Larson's theme in *The Sea Wolf*.[64] Likewise, ensuring the appearance of the film's title is highlighted musically and synchronized with a significant musical theme dictates the length of any introductory section: thus, Philip's theme arrives with the film's title in *Of Human Bondage*, and precise punch markings in the manuscript indicate that this was very much a planned synchronization point. Korngold even made notes in his short score of where his own name appears, and that of the film's producer, Henry Blanke, though these do not match the

---

[59] Frank Lehman, "Form und thematische Struktur in Vorspannmusiken Erich Wolfgang Korngolds," in *Musik im Vorspann*, ed. Guido Heldt, Tarek Krohn, Peter Moormann, and Willem Strank (Munich: Edition Text-Kritik, 2020), 10.

[60] A case might also be made for *The Sea Wolf* as having a secondary contrasting theme (Leach's theme), though it is understandable why Lehman does not distinguish this clearly from Wolf Larson's falling fourths theme.

[61] Lehman, "Form und thematische Struktur," 21.

[62] Ibid., 39.

[63] Nonetheless, some films eschew this kind of title synchronization, such as *The Constant Nymph* and *Deception*.

[64] Admittedly, the 1947 re-release of *The Sea Wolf*, which cut Hal B. Wallis's credit from the titles and reordered the title cards, changed the synchronization of Korngold's music in most of this title sequence; however, the strong musical synchronization with Korngold's name was retained. In *The Sea Hawk*, the second theme appears along with Wallis's name, which is possibly an indication of his importance to Korngold.

version accessible today, suggesting that the credits sequence in *Of Human Bondage* may have changed at a late stage.[65] As with *The Sea Hawk*, Korngold's name would originally have aligned with a more gesturally significant moment in the music. In other words, even Korngold's compositional decisions in these main titles were not always quite as "autonomous" as Lehman might assume, and some of those idiosyncrasies he identifies in phrase lengths may be the result of a desire to synchronize with significant visual moments.

In addition to the precise synchronization demands of film, though—a factor that distinguishes film music and its compositional processes from opera in ways that are often glossed over—music in film may be required to work with prominent elements of sound design. Although such integration is often assumed to be far less important to Classical Hollywood cinema than later traditions, nonetheless it is another way in which Korngold's film scores differ from their operatic predecessors, where such alignments with on-stage sounding events are much rarer.[66] The next chapter will explore further some of the ways in which Korngold's music accomplishes this, and its implications for our understanding of music's narrative source in film.

---

[65] The title sequence uses an onscreen book to suggest the film's literary origins (it is based on William Somerset Maugham's 1915 novel of the same name), and evidently an extra "page" was inserted. That said, the film is still not available in 2024 on modern home entertainment formats, and the edit I have access to is a broadcast version for Turner Classic Movies.

[66] Peter Franklin has drawn my attention to the stage directions at the end of the second scene in Act I of Wagner's *Die Walküre*, which state that Hunding's drawing back of the bolt that secures the bedroom door should be heard ("man hört ihn von innen den Riegel schliessen"). Yet, although the stage directions of an opera like Korngold's *Das Wunder der Heliane* contains screenplay-like levels of descriptive detail about actions, lighting, and stage design, aside from one mention of thunder, it contains nothing about "non-musical" sounds.

5
Korngold, Materiality, and Worldbuilding

Film is a medium that sits uneasily at times in relation to older dramatic forms that include music, such as opera or stage melodrama. In one sense, film is self-consciously realistic—one might even say "materialist"—in its evocation of a visceral reality to which audiences often feel a profound connection. In another way, however, in appearing to follow traditions of musical drama such as opera that call into question that realist aesthetic, it might appear to simultaneously disavow that very materiality. Such a tension was clearly felt when grappling with the possibilities of synchronized recorded sound by early filmmakers, for whom music's role was not readily apparent—unless it issued from a source within the portrayed screen world. Moreover, it is a tension that has continued to exercise film theorists, and one that has resulted in a variety of terms drawn from narrative theory to describe music's supposed narrative source (diegetic, nondiegetic, metadiegetic, intradiegetic, transdiegetic, focalization, and so on), along with the necessary qualifications (fantastical gaps, diegetic swaps) to adequately account for audience experience.[1] Much of my work on film has been centered on challenging these accounts of music's narrative source so that they better reflect my experiences as a film viewer, and questioning in particular the underlying assumption that characters in film worlds are deaf to the music that surrounds them.[2] Although we might assume that Korngold's approach to scoring films might inherit the "metaphysical" attitude to orchestral

[1] See Robynn Stilwell, "The Fantastical Gap Between Diegetic and Nondiegetic," in *Beyond the Soundtrack: Representing Music in Cinema*, ed. Daniel Goldmark, Laurence Kramer, and Richard Leppert (Berkeley: University of California Press, 2007), 184–202, and Guido Heldt, *Music and Levels of Narration in Film: Steps Across the Border* (Bristol: Intellect, 2013). For an operatic perspective, see Carolyn Abbate, *Unsung Voices: Opera and Musical Narrative in the Nineteenth Century* (Princeton, NJ: Princeton University Press, 1991). This urge to compartmentalize music in a space separated from the rest of a film's sound, though, arguably taps into much older metaphysical discourses that, although challenged in other spheres, continue to exercise a certain influence over both opera and film. See, for instance, Nicholas Till, "A New Glimmer of Light: Opera, Metaphysics and Mimesis," in *The Legacy of Opera: Reading Music Theatre as Experience and Performance*, ed. Dominic Symonds and Pamela Karantonis (Amsterdam: Rodopi, 2013), 39–64; and Gary Tomlinson, *Metaphysical Song: An Essay on Opera* (Princeton, NJ: Princeton University Press, 1999).

[2] Ben Winters, *Music, Performance, and the Realities of Film: Shared Concert Experiences in Screen Fiction* (New York: Routledge, 2014). See also my earlier articles "Musical Wallpaper: Towards an Appreciation of Non-narrating Music in Film," *Music, Sound, and the Moving Image* 6, no. 1 (Spring 2012): 39–54; and "The Non-diegetic Fallacy: Film, Music, and Narrative Space," *Music & Letters* 91, no. 2 (May 2010): 224–244.

Korngold in America. Ben Winters, Oxford University Press. © Oxford University Press 2025.
DOI: 10.1093/9780197684818.003.0006

voice typical of post-Wagnerian operatic culture, wherein the "noumenal" orchestra is assumed to be inaudible to the characters, a case can be made nonetheless for music's apparent materiality in the filmic worlds we witness. Indeed, Korngold's scores often work harmoniously with other elements of recorded sound commonly assumed to be materially present in the world of the characters in a way that might be thought surprising for films made in the late 1930s and early 1940s: sound and music seem not to be poles at opposite ends of a spectrum, devoted to fundamentally different narrative functions, but rather appear to work together in a number of ways that anticipate aspects of what Danijela Kulezic-Wilson termed the "integrated soundtrack" in the context of contemporary filmmaking.[3] Kulezic-Wilson's use of the term, however, appears to be in the service of a perspective that seems unashamedly modernist in its rejection of the Hollywood product. Indeed, she states openly that: "The main objective of Hollywood film is to tell a story in a straightforward manner, avoiding anything that might prevent the pleasure of passive comprehension, and this agenda accounts for a consistently unadventurous use of music."[4] While her description of Hollywood's desire for narrative clarity is unproblematic (though I would question the implied criticism contained within it) I cannot agree that the adventurousness or otherwise of the music—however that is measured or defined—is necessarily the result.

In this chapter, then, I want to show how the way in which Korngold scored film creates situations in which ambiguities about the narrative source of music arise on a regular basis. This is not something that I claim is confined to Korngold's scores. Although I do not have the space here to demonstrate it, I would propose that it is, in fact, relatively common to numerous scores of Classical Hollywood cinema, and other composers working within the Hollywood studio system were alive to similar possibilities.[5] Similarly, some of the decisions that characterize the sonic design of these films were clearly outside of Korngold's control. As a result, I am reluctant to suggest that this approach to interrogating his film scores necessarily reveals an aspect of Korngold's personal compositional identity or development, in ways I discussed in the previous two chapters. Nonetheless, I suspect Korngold, having maintained a long career in opera and other forms of musical drama, was particularly sensitive to such opportunities, and it is striking how easily his scores yield to such an approach. Having demonstrated the extent to which Korngold's music can be thought of as a material, even a "sounding,"

---

[3] Danijela Kulezic-Wilson, *Sound Design Is the New Score: Theory, Aesthetics and Erotics of the Integrated Soundtrack* (New York: Oxford University Press, 2020).

[4] Ibid., 65–66.

[5] David Cooper, for instance, comments on Bernard Herrmann's tendency to write music that sometimes takes on the role of sound effects or that otherwise calls into question a strict division between the two. See *Bernard Herrmann's* Vertigo: *A Film Score Handbook* (Westport, CT: Greenwood Press, 2001), 68–70.

176   KORNGOLD IN AMERICA

presence in the worlds of his characters, I then want to explore the implications of this approach for the ways in which Korngold's scores can be interrogated in terms of the modern onscreen subjectivities they might appear to illuminate. In other words, in regarding music as somehow fundamental to the environment of the worlds we see onscreen, rather than merely part of the film's presentation of those worlds, I see a newfound significance for the score's ability to contribute to critical spaces where gender, disability, and race might be brought into sharper focus. In so doing, though, I am not claiming that this is where their value as films *solely* resides, that their ability to reflect and critique the conditions of modernity encountered in everyday life somehow elevates them above other Hollywood films of the period. Instead, and perhaps more in line with the value that Richard Rushton ascribes to film, I want to think of these scores and the films of which they are a part as creating narratively engaging, self-contained worlds wherein complex characters are convincingly portrayed.[6]

Film's Materiality

There are many examples in Korngold's films where score and sounds could be said to interact, or where what we would now term "sound design" plays a prominent part in the film's soundworld (even though the films Korngold scored predate by several decades the emergence of the concept of "sound design" to describe the deliberate composition of a film's audio elements). The sonic environment of a film like *The Sea Wolf*, for instance, is distinguished as much by the sound of creaking ropes on deck, the whistling of wind, and low-frequency groaning of wood in the ship's galley as by its quasi-expressionist music score.[7] Yet, these elements of soundtrack are not always easily separated. In cue 5B, for instance, it is almost impossible to divorce the recorded sound of a marlinspike thrown by Leach (John Garfield) at Wolf Larsen (Edward G. Robinson) hitting the deckhouse from the brief full orchestral chord (G7 with added sharpened 4th) that accompanies it: originally, Korngold wrote surrounding music, but large parts of this scene were lost when the film was re-released in 1947 in an eighty-seven-minute edit, which for many years was the only version available on home-entertainment formats. In this eighty-seven-minute version of the film, only this isolated moment of music/sound fusion remains in this scene.[8] Perhaps

---

[6] Richard Rushton, *The Reality of Film: Theories of Filmic Reality* (Manchester: Manchester University Press, 2011).

[7] The groaning is particularly noticeable when Larson asks Van Weyden to read to him from Milton's *Paradise Lost*.

[8] The chord is scored for strings, harp, side drum, marimba, timpani, tuba, trombones, trumpets, horns, bassoons, bass clarinet, clarinets, cor anglais, oboes, and flutes. Side drum is particularly prominent. The synchronization of the chord with the strike was made possible by two preparatory

significantly, too, the initial meeting between Van Weyden and Ruth Brewster on board the paddle steamer *Martinez* originally introduced Ruth's theme, but this cue (1D) was cut and the brooding fog horns of the *Martinez* and the vessel it collides with allowed instead to shape the soundscape and to hint of the impending disaster.[9] As Ruth (Ida Lupino) breaks away from the policemen attempting to arrest her, Korngold's score returns in a saturated soundscape featuring more insistent foghorn blasts entirely appropriate to the chaos of a disaster at sea: the foghorn combines with scurrying strings and major-second horn writing to create an almost Charles Ives–like texture that culminates with the collision. As the vessel sinks, the sounds of screaming women and gushing water are blended with a typical Korngold approach to action: cascading strings and ascending chromatic harmonic sequences. Admittedly, as we saw in previous chapters, decisions about cuts to the score are unlikely to have been made by the composer, and the changes to cue 1D reveal the extent to which the film's sound world is sometimes ascribable to a variety of creative personas and decisions. Nonetheless, there can also be little doubt that Korngold sometimes chose deliberately to incorporate recorded sound seamlessly into his scores. One particularly clear example of this can be found in *The Sea Hawk*, where the timekeeper's drum strokes in the galleass *Santa Eullàlia del Monte* are allowed to dictate the meter and tempo of the score (see Figure 5.1). The drum strokes continue to shape the music even as the camera shows the slaves chained to their oars—though the whip cracks of their masters create an implied metrical dissonance.[10] Audiovisually, this momentary alignment of image, sound, and music is, I would suggest, enormously powerful. A similar effect is created at the climax of *The Private Lives of Elizabeth and Essex* as Essex marches to his death. He is accompanied by a minor variant of his march theme, but this is amplified by onscreen drummers whose music is written into the score. Likewise, in *Of Human Bondage*, Korngold notates the sound of Athelney's clock striking eight in his manuscript short score for cue 8B (Figure 5.2).[11]

---

punches spaced at 16 frames giving Korngold two preparatory flashes at 90 bpm. The recently released hundred-minute cut of the film, however, reveals a quite different build-up, and one that accords with the manuscript sources. Indeed, the eighty-seven-minute cut does not merely trim scenes, it recuts dialogue such that Ruth's earlier lines cover the closeup of Leach at the point at which he decides to throw the marlinspike. Given the independence of sound and picture, it seems curious that the musical "stinger" was left in place when the film was re-edited. The restored version was released on Blu Ray by Warner Archive Collection, and the story of its restoration can be found in Leonard Maltin, "*The Sea Wolf*: Longer and Better!," https://leonardmaltin.com/the-sea-wolf-lon ger-and-better/ (accessed March 28, 2024).

[9] 1D was cut in both versions of the film.

[10] Once we hear dialogue between Tuttle and his fellow slaves, the drum strokes are quietly audible in the background, though they have separated from the music's meter.

[11] A similar thing happens with Caryl's watch in *Escape Me Never*. Its implied minute-repeater chimes are notated at the end of cue 3D.

Figure 5.1 The timekeeper in *The Sea Hawk*.

Other instances where Korngold duplicates or replaces implied sounding phenomena in his music include the hooves of Emily Brontë's ghostly rider in cue 3F of *Devotion*, which are rendered in pounding marimba. Emily, who has acknowledged to her unrequited love, the local curate Arthur Nicholls, that she's both "seen and heard" ghosts, describes her dream: "and then suddenly I hear a sound that terrifies me" (the marimba starts), "the beating of a horse's hooves coming nearer and nearer." The prominent use of the marimba here was a conscious decision by Korngold made late in the day, clearly designed as an iconic sign that would suggest the percussive nature of a horse's hooves. As a result, he revised Friedhofer's full-score orchestration for the second half of the cue.[12] Nicholls dismisses her "strange fancies," at which point they both hear "real" horses' hooves. Ghostly hooves are one thing we might expect to be represented musically, but the sonic representation of wind can also be found in Korngold's music. It is perhaps most obvious in *Another Dawn*, where parallel seventh chords move up and down along with harp glissandi in imitation of the sandstorm we see and hear; but it is also found in *Devotion*, where the subtle recorded sound of the wind at the beginning of cue 3F is replaced by the surging of

---

[12] The revised orchestration is marked "Retake No. 16 Reel IV [III]." It adds the marimba solo and a new solo for vibraphone (the E minor chords that end the cue), all of which is in Korngold's hand.

KORNGOLD, MATERIALITY, AND WORLDBUILDING 179

Figure 5.2 Notating the clock in *Of Human Bondage*, cue 8B. Box 11 Folder 4, Erich Wolfgang Korngold Collection, Music Division, Library of Congress, Washington, DC, Courtesy of the Korngold Family Estate.

third-less triads in the orchestra (G–C♯–C–F♯). Music can even render materially present something much more abstract, such as numeracy. In *Anthony Adverse*, Maria tells her lover Denis of her plan to light candles to signal to him: one candle if she can go with him, two if she cannot, and three if she is in trouble (cue 2A). As she mentions each number, we hear the corresponding number of notes on the glockenspiel.

At other times, a Korngold score plays a more obviously material role in constructing the physicality of the world we see onscreen. An example of this has already been explored in Chapter 4 in connection with clarifying the cross-cutting between different narrative spaces seen in cue 4C of *The Adventures of Robin Hood*. Rather than think of the role of Korngold's score purely in terms of clarifying an aspect of continuity editing for the audience—helping us to understand that the forest space containing Sir Guy and his men is not the same forest space containing Robin Hood and his followers—we might instead think of the score as a material sound in the film's environment that is shaped by the characters' presence. In swapping between these locations in this sequence, we therefore also hear the corresponding music that characterizes the materiality of those spaces. A slightly different kind of example again is found in *The Sea Hawk*, wherein the signaling hail from Thorpe's ship the *Albatross* to the galleass *Santa Eullàlia del Monte* bearing the Spanish Ambassador is accompanied by a muted trumpet fanfare that is answered by a slightly different woodwind echo in clarinets (Example 5.1).[13] When no reply is received, Thorpe asks Preston to repeat the hail, resulting in a fanfare sounding a semitone higher. Both pairs of fanfares are followed by a triangle roll, as if to suggest forms of domestic signaling in which a bell pull rings a service bell in a distant room. Even without the triangle roll, though, the echo effect created by the change of sonorities between hard present (albeit muted) brass and softer more distant woodwind, coupled with the change in harmony, implies something about the physical separation of the two ships. It is an orchestral effect that Korngold would have been familiar with from Mahler's Symphony No. 1—where horn fanfares in the fourth movement are repeated in clarinets marked *Echoton* (echo tone).[14] Likewise, in *The Private Lives of Elizabeth Essex*, the opening scene in which a triumphant Earl of Essex returns to England and parades through the streets of London uses the score's orchestration to suggest the physical distance between Essex's men and the watching crowd. As such, it implies that the music exists in the physical space of the film, played by unseen marching soldiers in time with those who are shown beating drums, and with which Korngold's score synchronizes perfectly. Thus, when the camera focuses on the watching Penelope (Olivia de Havilland),

---

[13] The progression of quasi-parallel triads—C, B♭, B—is straight out of Act II of Richard Strauss's *Der Rosenkavalier* as Octavian arrives bearing the silver rose. See *Der Rosenkavalier*, Act II, Reh. Fig. 15.

[14] In the first movement, muted brass fanfares are marked *In der Ferne* (in the distance) or *In weiter Enternung* while clarinet fanfares have no such marking. Nonetheless the difference in tonal qualities creates a kind of implied theatrical space.

Example 5.1 The first signaling hail in *The Sea Hawk* (cue 2A).

the orchestration is adjusted to suggest a receding sound source: trumpets give way to softer horns and strings. When the shot changes to show the marching men, the trumpets return. This is also a typical response of Korngold to onscreen drummers, in that he takes the opportunity to augment any implied music and elide it completely with the sound of his score. No other instrumentalists are seen until Essex has dismounted, and we see palace guards announce his arrival by raising trumpets. By now, though, there is absolutely no distinction between the brassy heraldic music we have heard during Essex's approach and any fanfares issuing from the trumpeters we see. A similar situation can also be found in *Another Dawn*, which with its scenes of military procession with only the merest suggestion of buglers in the image allowed Korngold to write a Mahlerian military march for cues 12 and 19 that incorporated trumpet fanfares in its musical logic.[15] The latter cue, though, is mostly "heard" from inside the room in which Julia gazes out at the departing Denny Roark and, as such, is mostly played by softer strings as if to emphasize her physical distance from its apparent source.

Indeed, outside of those Warner Bros. films largely or exclusively about musicians—*The Constant Nymph*, *Escape Me Never*, *Deception*, *Between Two Worlds*—several films presented Korngold with the opportunity to score scenes in which onscreen musicians are playing. Crucially, though—and as with Essex's march in *The Private Lives of Elizabeth and Essex* or the military marches of *Another Dwan*—he often chose to do so in a way that integrates almost seamlessly with the rest of his score: in other words, even if the instrumentalists were not onscreen, the musical "moment" would not stand out self-consciously from the rest of the score as a moment of narrative "source music." The effect, then, is to emphasize the fundamentally *integrated* nature of the film's soundtrack and to suggest film worlds that do not appear to support a strict division between the sounding material world of sound effects, performed music, and dialogue, on

---

[15] The writing would not have been out of place in the military setting of the first act of Korngold's fifth opera, *Die Kathrin*.

182 KORNGOLD IN AMERICA

the one hand, and the implied noumenal world of score, on the other. Often, any onscreen "visual" music is augmented by the orchestra in a way that calls into question the distinction between what is seen and heard. The technique is used at numerous points in *The Adventures of Robin Hood*. These include: the opening announcement scene ("news has come from Austria"), where the tonic-dominant timpani strokes heard at the close of cue 1A over the title cards elides seamlessly with the first image of mounted drummers playing; the banquet scene (cue 1E), in which the orchestral music that accompanies a prefatory title card, and clearly designed by Korngold to sound archaic, is subsequently associated with the static instrumentalists we subsequently see in the foreground;[16] and throughout the archery tournament in Reel 6 where onscreen trumpeters raise their instruments and are seen to be performing in synchronization with the brass fanfares heard in the full orchestral score. As a technique, it is used most prominently at the climax of the film in connection with the ceremonial music heard in the coronation procession, where onscreen trumpeters are presented as the source of the fanfares heard in cue 10E. Indeed, this approach—having already been used in the coronation scene of *The Prince and the Pauper*—was subsequently adopted for similar ceremonial scenes featuring trumpeters in both *The Private Lives of Elizabeth Essex* and *The Sea Hawk*. The augmentation of onscreen musical performance is not confined to these obvious moments of historical pageantry, however.

A particularly clear example of the technique can be found in the hunting scene of *The Private Lives of Elizabeth and Essex* (cue 4D). Arriving after the poignant moment in which Queen Elizabeth realizes she will have to inform Margaret Radcliffe of the death of her lover Sir Peter Finchley, the sequence begins with a jubilant ascending trumpet and trombone fanfare in B♭ major as we see a falconer and mounted men, while others move through the frame carrying the carcasses of slain animals. Only as the camera pans left and moves forward into the scene to reveal a man clearly playing a hunting horn (Figure 5.3) do we hear horns take over the fanfare, now ironically somewhat less fanfare-like in character. Punctuated by F7 and C7 chords and thus alternating E♭ and E♮ chromaticisms, it opens out into a full melodic statement reminiscent of the horn writing of Richard Strauss. Something similar happens in the later battle scene (cue 8B), which incorporates the onscreen trumpeters into the musical logic of the cue. These trumpet parts point to the relish with which Korngold seized upon such opportunities to stitch music into the narrative worlds of the films he scored.[17]

---

[16] On this "English Air" theme from cue 1E, see Ben Winters, *Erich Wolfgang Korngold's* The Adventures of Robin Hood: *A Film Score Guide* (Lanham, MD: Scarecrow Press, 2007), 127–128.

[17] These extra parts were a late addition: the parts do not exist in the full score, and have been added in red pencil to a copy of the piano-conductor score. See Erich Wolfgang Korngold Collection, Music Division, Library of Congress, Washington, DC (hereafter, LOC), Box 52 Folder 4.

Figure 5.3 Hunting horn in *The Private Lives of Elizabeth and Essex*.

The apparent materiality of the score in inhabiting a film's narrative space is also often reflected in the dialogue, and in characters' injunctions to "listen." Evidently, "listen" is sometimes uttered merely as an attention grabber at the beginning of a statement (in the same way as "look"). On many occasions, though, it prompts the character at whom it is directed to adopt a pose and to stop talking in order to better concentrate on a particular sound—often the sound of music.[18] The narrative reasons for these demands vary from the casual to the profound, but their implications for the material qualities of the music experienced in a film are significant. Such dialogue reminds us of the presence of sound and encourages the kind of interpretation I have suggested is particularly suited to Korngold's approach to film scoring: one in which musical listening is itself of peculiar importance. In *Another Dawn*, an act of musical listening even prompts Denny Roark and Julia to engage in a casual conversation about musical aesthetics:

Roark: "Listen."
Julia: "What is it?"

---

[18] A notable and oft-remarked precedent for this occurs in Steiner's score for *King Kong* (dir. Merian C. Cooper/Ernest B. Schoedsack, 1933) in the scene wherein the boat approaches Skull Island: Driscoll exhorts others to "Listen!" It is appropriate to many of the scenes I explore in what follows that the narrative source of music in this scene is similarly ambiguous.

R: "Bedouin music."

J: "Strange and wistful, isn't it?"

R: "I've heard that love song a thousand times, and each time it sounds like the first."

J: "Somehow, it seems to go with the desert, and the night . . . sort of a . . . a melodic will-o-the-wisp that dares your emotions to follow it."

R: "That's it! that's it exactly. It's what I've always felt and never been able to put into words."

No musicians are onscreen, but the stylistic distinctiveness of Korngold's "Tango" composition also prompts us to "listen." The score then continues with a presentation of Julia's theme while the tango rhythm persists, in a way that calls into question any comfortable distinction between what is "heard" and "unheard" by the characters. Similarly, in *The Sea Wolf*, the initial love scene between Leach and Ruth (cue 6C) is accompanied by an unseen character playing a harmonica: "Listen," Leach urges. "That's the kid. Whenever he's sad, he plays that harmonica. Makes up the songs. He's good ain't he? I guess he's playing that one for Louis." The thematic material for the song—subsequently reused in the Third String Quartet (of which more in Chapter 6)—relates directly to material connected with Dr. Louis Prescott, who by this point in the film has committed suicide by leaping from the ship's mast. In a very real sense, then, Leach's identification and association of the mournful music with Louis is significant, because it suggests at least the possibility of the materiality of earlier music: that we admit the possibility that some aspect of the score is heard by characters. Such an explanation (though clearly not the only logical one) nonetheless accounts for both Leach's identification of the melody and his ability to make quite obscure thematic connections. Louis's music is one of the most sublimated parts of the score, and to apparently connect it with the harmonica song requires what might be thought of as a display of Leach's advanced listening skills.

Wolf Larsen's headaches and visual disturbances in the same film also extend to a kind of aural hallucination that points to a similar conceptual mystery. At the beginning of cue 9B, Larsen stops suddenly, and we hear a high B♭maj7 stinger. "What's that noise?" he asks (answered by a low G♯maj7 chord). "What noise?" Van Weyden replies. "Didn't you hear the sound of ship's siren off in the distance?" Larsen queries. The music continues with thematic material associated with Larsen's headaches to suggest it is a symptom of his condition, but for us in the watching audience who also hear a "noise" (if not the siren that Larson describes) it might also suggest the material presence of the score in the world of the film. Indeed, *The Sea Wolf* is typical of a number of films scored by Korngold that feature characters who, as dreamers or sufferers of physical or mental trauma, seem to have the ability to hear things that others do not, or might be interpreted as having the ability to affect the music in the score that surrounds them. In other words, they could be said to engage with the music that might have been thought to define their subjectivity in a supersensible nondiegetic realm. Yet, I do not propose interpreting these characters as having access to a musical space unavailable to others—as mystics able to cross Robynn Stilwell's "fantastical gap."[19] Instead, I want to think of them as characters "unusually attuned" to sounding phenomena that may exist in their physical film worlds, and to suggest that they thus call into question assumptions we may hold about the narrative source of music in film—assumptions that may be unduly shaped by an implicitly modernist perspective that has labeled the products of Classical Hollywood as "conventional" or "unadventurous."

The main character in *The Constant Nymph*, Tessa Sanger (Joan Fontaine), for instance, suffers from a heart condition—one that is scored by Korngold with a hesitant heartbeat rhythm and high-pitched violin harmonics.[20] As an apparent consequence of her physical frailty and its material manifestation, though, Tessa seems unusually attuned to the material qualities of sound, and the injunction to "listen" is heard a number of times in the film's dialogue in connection with her. The film concerns the relationship between a composer, Lewis Dodd (Charles Boyer), and his muse, Tessa, and charts the difficulties Dodd faces in realizing his conception of a symphonic poem, in addition to reconciling his attraction for the much younger Tessa with his marriage to her cousin, Florence (Alexis Smith). At the climax of the film, Tessa listens to Dodd's symphonic poem *Tomorrow* over the radio. In so doing, she imagines a nostalgic reunion between herself and her would-be lover in a Swiss Alpine landscape. Although it is signaled as a memory, dream, or vision, it is not instantly clear whether the music we hear is a continuation of the symphonic poem we know is being performed in "Regent's Hall," or is functioning as supposedly "unheard" score. Indeed, it functions far more obviously as score to accompany the dialogue between Lewis and Tessa than as a performed concert work; however, once the main melody begins in strings, Tessa evidently hears it; she looks around in a panic and tells Lewis: "that song of death frightens me." Here, then, the typical functions of source music and scoring are conflated. Tessa (in her vision) clearly hears music in a way that we might explain "conventionally" by suggesting that she is still listening to the

---

[19] Stilwell, "The Fantastical Gap Between Diegetic and Nondiegetic."

[20] This striking orchestral effect was changed during the scoring process. Tessa's weak heart was originally simply expressed in cue 4A immediately after the death of Sanger as a hesitant irregular rhythm on a single pitch (F3). A similar approach was also used in: cue 5A, when she is told about Lewis's engagement to Florence; in 7B, when Tessa runs to Lewis's studio; in 8A; and in 10A, when Tessa has her near-fatal collapse. At some point on the Scoring Stage, however, Korngold added to the rest of these cues the high string harmonic he had used in 5A, perhaps reasoning that it was more likely to be heard than the irregular or syncopated rhythm sometimes used.

186   KORNGOLD IN AMERICA

radio, yet it also functions in an entirely standard fashion within the conventions of 1940s Hollywood film to underscore their scene together.

Tessa is both a muse to Lewis and his musical conscience; and, throughout the film, she has been portrayed as someone with advanced musical gifts and keen hearing. When Lewis announces himself by whistling, Tessa recognizes the significance of the sound and exclaims: "Father, Listen! It's Lewis."[21] When Lewis has written a two-piano modernist version of his work, full of motoric energy, Tessa expresses her disappointment at its dissonance. Her sister Paula (Joyce Reynolds) agrees, noting "there's no melodic line . . . it's very modern" and then in exasperation exhorts her to "listen to it." Tessa replies: "I am, and he's forgotten his heart again." The following morning, she castigates Lewis for the work in a way that I have previously explored as indicative of the film's rather overblown romantic excess.[22] In attempting to defend himself, though, Lewis's straightforward demonstration of melodic material and injunction ("the melody is here . . . listen") is rebuffed by Tessa's reply: "I did listen last night. Eight measly little bars and then off you go; you sound like a railway engine." Taking her criticisms to heart, he allows her to help him rediscover his original plan for the work. After she demonstrates a version on the piano, he sits down and plays an expanded version of the piece. "That's it, Lewis!" Tessa cries, whereupon music erupts from the unseen orchestra. Tessa looks up and her eyes dart back and forth, as if she both hears it and luxuriates in its sound. There is an ambiguity in her movements that at least suggests the possibility that she can hear what the score supplies. Ostensibly, it is the sign of her supernatural musicianship—a quality that in the context of other characters like Wolf Larsen might be linked to her physical frailty. Lewis, though, also appears to be "listening" to it: when Tessa looks at him, his eyes also turn upward, and there are subtle movements of his head and hands that suggest he is engaged in a form of musical activity. Although other films by Korngold have dramatized the act of composition—something I will return to in Chapter 6—this moment is significant in that it appears to be shared by both characters. The film seems to suggest, then, that they both hear what we, the audience, hear—that characters and audience partake in a form of shared subjectivity. The connection between Tessa and music—whether the sound of performed music in the space in which it is played or over the radio, or indeed as score—is, in fact, so close that at the end of the film Tessa collapses to the symphonic poem's closing gestures. When Lewis returns from the concert hall, he sees her body lying on a sofa; upon "hearing" the descending motif from the symphonic poem in flute, he takes her in his arms, whereupon a version of

---

[21] Significantly the draft of the script in Korngold's possession talked of the sound of a train whistle at this point. Korngold evidently adapted this to make Lewis provide his own whistle. LOC, Box 44 Folder 1.

[22] Winters, *Music, Performance, and the Realities of Film*, 98.

the symphonic poem's main motif is heard in parallel chords. It seems to be an attempt to resuscitate her using the generative motif of the music. The music replies an octave below, reflecting back to him: Tessa, though, is dead.

Characters throughout other films also appear to interact directly with the material presence of Korngold's score. Sometimes, this may be something as simple as appearing to whistle along with a pre-existing musical texture. In *Of Human Bondage*, the former artist and sensitive soul Philip Carey whistles along with the score as he waits for Mildred Rogers outside the café in which she works (cue 2C "The Alley"). Significantly, he is whistling a variant of Mildred's own theme. Likewise, in cue 5A of *Escape Me Never* both Gemma and Sebastian are heard and seen whistling along with Sebastian's flirting theme in the score: Sebastian is a composer, while Gemma is both a singer and his inspiration. In *Anthony Adverse*, Angela sings a portion of one of her own themes while riding in a carriage with Anthony—a theme that is also played by the band celebrating her father's lottery win. Although we might explain this "logically" by suggesting that the theme is well known in the world of Anthony and Angela (and thus also known by the band), we have already heard it introduced in the score earlier in the scene. It thus seems as though the characters' familiarity with its thematic material is the plausible result of hearing it along with the audience. In *Deception*, the thematic material of Hollenius's Cello Concerto is certainly known by the characters in the narrative, but Christine's behavior as she anxiously waits for her husband, the cellist Karel Novak, to return from his rehearsal with Hollenius suggests she is actively engaging with the score in that moment. As Christine paces her apartment in silence, having turned off the radio, the score begins with preparatory triplet tied gestures and a repeated bass clarinet motif that appear to call Christine to the piano, prompting her to join in (cue 7B). She duly obliges and picks out the main theme of the Concerto in C minor, which likewise begins with a tied triplet rhythm. The score accompanies her, adding the concerto's descending chromatic line. This engagement with score is not a one-way street, either. Earlier in *Deception*, Christine's playing of Beethoven's "Appassionata" Sonata at her own wedding reception seeds the sonic space around her with Beethoven's music. The score continues to bear its trace long after she has stopped playing. Thus, in cue 4A, the opening ascending arpeggios of the Beethoven are heard in celli bass either side of a descending chromatic line, before Korngold quotes more recognizably the sonata's opening four bars (albeit in C♯ minor rather than F minor and with changes to the harmony). Likewise, when Parris Mitchell plays the opening of Beethoven's "Pathétique" Sonata in *Kings Row*, the score continues on with four more bars of Beethoven-inspired sequential material—again suggesting a seeding of musical space by the main character.[23]

---

[23] An extension to Randy's theme heard in cue 8E of *Kings Row* also contains a distinctive dotted rhythm that might be thought of as related to this Beethoven extract.

188   KORNGOLD IN AMERICA

The question of who can hear music, though, is of peculiarly profound importance to Korngold's score for *Between Two Worlds*, which was based on a 1923 Sutton Vane play called *Outward Bound* that had previously been filmed under that title by Warners in 1930. Whereas the play features a young couple who have committed suicide owing to the shame of an extra-marital pregnancy, the plot of *Between Two Worlds* concerns a concert pianist named Henry Bergner (Paul Henreid). Having been exiled from Austria because of the war and suffering from depression as a result, he attempts to gas himself. Henry's wife Ann (Eleanor Parker) refuses to leave his side, and they find themselves on the same strange voyage as a group of passengers killed during an air raid. On board ship, Henry finds that his musical skills—lost as a result of his depression— are mysteriously returned to him, and having realized that he and his wife are dead, they both recover their desire to live again, having witnessed their fellow passengers being weighed in the balance by a clergyman Examiner (Sydney Greenstreet) and sent on to their respective afterlives. Significantly, the profession of the main character is entirely the invention of the screenplay, which also introduces a character not found in the original play or the earlier film version intriguingly named Pete Musick (George Tobias). The script, by Daniel Fuchs, was developed between July and November 1943 following some initial work by Alvah Bessie and Charles Beiden in June and early July, and while early drafts make little mention of music (following in the footsteps of the original play and the first version of the film), it seems that more musical references were incorporated as the script developed. The draft dated September 22 includes the use of a spinning phonograph record as part of the transition between Henry's flat where he and Ann have gassed themselves and the space on board ship; however, the moment where Benjamin (Gilbert Emery) decides to leave his ambitious social-climbing wife still makes no mention of music: "My dear. I've thought and thought these last few hours. It wouldn't do. That love I had—it's gone long ago. It, too, is dead. You must understand."[24] As the script developed, however, musical contemplation became a key part of the process through which Benjamin makes a decision about this future. By October 1, the dialogue read: "My dear, I've thought and thought. I believe it all started with the music we heard in the lounge. (turning to Henry) Your music . . . Yes, it took me back. . . twenty years . . . (back to Mrs Clivedon-Banks) No. It wouldn't do. That love I had—it's gone, it's vanished. You must understand."[25] Given that Korngold was involved in the film prior to the filming in October 1943 of scenes involving Henry playing the piano, it is perfectly possible that his involvement with the

---

[24] Warner Bros. Archives (hereafter WBA), "BETWEEN TWO WORLDS" STORY— TEMPORARY SCRIPT 9/22/43, O-21, 2139.
[25] WBA, "BETWEEN TWO WORLDS" STORY- FINAL SCRIPT 10/1/43, O-21, 2139.

KORNGOLD, MATERIALITY, AND WORLDBUILDING   189

film, or at least the prominence afforded his music, prompted these changes to the script.

The strange space between the two worlds of life and afterlife, here represented as an ocean, is one that is filled with music and musicalized sound, a material blurring that challenges conventional assumptions we may have held about music's unheard narrative source for the characters. In particular, Henry's performances at the piano and their relationship with the score are positively mysterious. His first try out of the piano (cue 2A), in which he plays a version of the music heard on the gramophone in his flat before the couple's attempted suicide, seeds the space around him just as Christine was later to do with her piano playing in *Deception*. Finishing on a D6 chord, Henry lifts his hands from the keyboard, at which point the unseen orchestra sustain the chord for him (cue 2B). As he turns to Ann, the orchestra now take over the melody he had performed, maintaining the scene's musical content, while he tells her that this is what they'd wanted: "a world with room for music, for love." The orchestra swells as if prompting Henry to take over, and he duly obliges, the musical elision with the next solo piano cue (2C) happening seamlessly. Thus, the piano and the unseen orchestra seem to be working in tandem. This piano cue, which we continue to hear as we are taken into another space where other characters converse, was in fact written to be performed by two pianists—an indication of a supernatural mystery, perhaps, wherein Henry not only regains the steady use of his hands but is also able to perform feats of physical impossibility. This piano music, which prompts Benjamin to reminisce about the past and encourages Maxine (Faye Emerson) to break up with Prior ("it's a nice sentimental number," she says) then disappears as Lingley (George Coulouris) enters the scene. The piano music is replaced by orchestral score carrying Lingley's menacing theme, but it soon returns. In so doing, it is the piano—and not the orchestra—that debuts Maxine's theme as she introduces herself to Lingley. In retrospect, we might hear this as Henry authoring Maxine's theme (Example 5.2a), seeding the space of the score with its thematic content. In any case, it reveals the close correspondence between the obvious materiality of Henry's piano playing in the space of the ship and the less obvious materiality of the score—two worlds that become increasingly difficult to tell apart as the narrative progresses. When the Examiner's launch approaches the ship, each announcing ring of its bell is followed by an orchestral halo of high strings, as if the very air resonates orchestrally. This happens on four occasions. An obviously material sound (the bell) creates ripples in the surrounding score (Example 5.2b).

At the climax of the narrative, with the fates of the other characters decided, Henry and Ann are left alone with the steward, Scrubby (Edmund Gwenn)—since the role of suicides like them is to ferry other souls across to the afterlife. Scrubby's appeal to the Examiner to "do something" about them,

Example 5.2 *Between Two Worlds* (a) Maxine's theme, cue 10A (b) second bell, cue 8B (c) glass-breaking chord, cue 12A.

however, suggests a happy ending may be in store. As Henry ponders the fate to which he has doomed both Ann and himself, a distinctive F minor chord with added major seventh is heard in the score (Example 5.2c).[26] Henry stops talking. "Ann ... what's that?' "What Henry?' "That noise [the chord stinger is heard again] ... the sound of glass breaking. Don't you hear it?" Ann hears nothing, but we do, and it prompts several questions in the audience: What exactly does Henry hear? Is it glass breaking, as he claims, or is he hearing the same thing as us—a musical chord with percussive xylophone emphasis standing in for a commonly encountered sound? Does rendering the sound

---

[26] This is scored for three flutes, one clarinet, piano, xylophone, vibraphone, two harps, Novachord, celesta, and three muted solo violins playing harmonics.

as music make it simultaneously more mysterious and Ann's incredulity more believable, perhaps? It is certainly a conceptual mystery, and Henry returns to playing the piano. As Ann approaches him, he stops on an E half-diminished seventh chord. "Don't stop, dear. You must try not to think," she coaxes. The orchestra enters with an encouraging melodically prolonged version of the same chord in high strings, celesta and Novachord, an insertion into the musical logic of Henry's playing that seemingly prompts him to continue: again, it seems, material and (supposedly) immaterial sound work together seamlessly, and the music of the unseen orchestra appears to be something he registers and to which he responds. He duly obliges but cannot complete the phrase. Instead of the expected A major chord that would finish the phrase, he hits the same Fm maj7 chord on the piano, which triggers an echo in the score (cue 12B overlapped with cue 12C). Henry stops. "That noise, Ann." The chord repeats. "Listen! I'm sure I hear glass shattering. Don't you hear it?" The chord dies away, and Ann replies: "No dear, there's no sound, nothing." The chord is sounded again five more times, as Henry says he must have been wrong, but it then becomes increasingly insistent as the narrative drives toward its conclusion and Henry finds his way back to life. The chord is, of course, the "sound" of glass breaking in the real world—which, in allowing the gas to escape, will ultimately revive both Henry and Ann.

The extent to which characters hear and engage with the score, and the narrative status of Korngold's music, is thus fundamental to *Between Two Worlds*. Whatever answers we find plausible, the narrative's unusual premise undoubtedly belies the film's naturalistic look and self-consciously implicates music in its conceptual mystery. Even the transition back to the real world is made via a spinning gramophone record, whose Weimar-influenced jazz recording (arranged by Leo Arnaud) seems the real-world source of the saxophone sonorities sometimes heard on board ship and whose thematic material had been replicated in Henry's own performances. The space of the ship is one, then, where distinctions between audible phenomena and the apparently super-sensible world of musical score naturally break down, and where music is afforded power to shape destinies and subjectivities. Nonetheless, the question "who can hear this music?" remains satisfyingly difficult to answer.[27]

---

[27] Given the prominent role of music in challenging the film's implicit metaphysics, it is hermeneutically rather satisfying that Korngold's score alludes prominently to the richness of Richard Strauss's tone poem *Also Sprach Zarathustra*—particularly the chromatic infill of the "Von dem Freuden und Leidenschaften" (Of Joys and Passions) section—which intertextually invokes Nietzsche's thinking about materialism. The composer's scoring strategies might also encourage us to recognize affinities with the early twentieth-century thinking of Paul Bekker in his conception of music as a material of the air. See Thomas Patteson, *Instruments for New Music: Sound, Technology, and Modernism* (Berkeley: University of California Press, 2016), 37.

192 KORNGOLD IN AMERICA

Even in Korngold's final film project, *Magic Fire*, which the composer undertook for Republic Pictures in 1954 largely as a favor to director William Dieterle, Wagner's composition of the prelude to *Tristan und Isolde* is depicted as an act involving apparently super-sensible listening. As Mathilde Wesendonk (Valentina Cortese) tells Wagner (Alan Badel) to "drink this, Maestro" and he wonders "is this some sort of potion?" a solo cello intones the opening of the prelude. The scene then shifts, and Wagner accompanies the unseen cello on the piano before stopping to write down its first phrase. In other words, the composition seems to be a matter of Wagner "hearing" something mysterious and numinous (entirely appropriate to the Schopenhaurian aesthetics of *Tristan*, it must be said). Wagner plays the next phrase, and again stops to notate it. Having played the third phrase, he continues on at the piano as we see Mathilde reading his letter, again with a solo cello line taking the melody and Wagner's piano playing accompanying it. As we cut back to Wagner apparently improvising on the piano, his eyes looking up, the cello drops out. Then, as he stops, the orchestra take over, cutting bars 25–44 in the process. At the move to the more unstable diminished seventh chord halfway through bar 48, Wagner's eyes flick upward in the classic pose of one listening, and as the music becomes ever more charged, he rises to his feet, wringing his hands in apparent frustration. At the sforzando of bar 52, Wagner grabs his head in anguish, then paces around the room moving to the open French windows to gaze at Mathilde before rushing to manuscript paper to write out the title *Tristan and Isolde* (*sic*, a mixture of Germanic names and an English conjunction). As the prelude becomes ever more passionate (bars 64ff.) he frantically starts to write, banging his fist and looking up (as if the orchestra are moving too fast for him to take dictation). The spell is finally broken by the arrival of his wife, Mina. It is, of course, a highly romanticized idea of composition, but one that crucially bears comparison with the earlier films for Warner Bros. that prompt questions about the material "source" of music.

Whether marked out as different because of some mental or physical trauma, then, or merely on account of their innate musicianship, many of the characters we encounter in Korngold's films are scored in such a way that they appear to challenge what may be assumed to be the conventional nondiegetic model of music's source in Classical Hollywood cinema. Some of these situations were no doubt amplified by the choices Korngold made in scoring, while other aspects of the interpretations I have offered above were clearly influenced by decisions outside his control. No matter the extent to which the composer shaped these opportunities, it is clear that Hollywood offered Korngold a chance to explore the relationship between musical materiality and drama and to do so in a way that in relying on the incorporation of recorded sounding phenomena was more-or-less peculiar to the medium of film.

Modern Onscreen Subjectivities

Many writers—either laboring under the sort of unacknowledged modernist anxiety I spoke of in the Introduction or genuinely convinced of the value of modernism as a legitimizing discourse of artistic value—have sought to demonstrate the ways in which Classical Hollywood cinema can be thought of as "modernist." The genre of melodrama, for example, has often been linked to modernism, with Lea Jacobs noting that since the 1970s scholars have pointed to its heightened stylization of visual and musical elements alike as suitable for "evoking social and psychological conflicts that cannot be directly expressed."[28] Similarly, Miriam Hansen, in proposing that mass-produced and mass-consumed products could mediate the experience of modernity, argues for the ability of some Classical Hollywood cinema to challenge "prevailing social and sexual arrangements and [advance] new possibilities of social identity and cultural styles."[29] In so doing, she labels them instances of "vernacular modernism."[30] This maximalist approach to a definition of modernism that can include mass-culture Hollywood films, though, still involves an othering of part of the repertoire: it is simply more narrowly and more precisely defined.

Veronica Pravadelli, for example, highlights melodrama of the early 1930s, and *films noir* and women's films of the 1940s, as engaged with socially progressive ideas that are associated with both modernity and opportunities for women. Moreover, she suggests they utilized narrative techniques that are associated more with "spectacle." As a result, the label "Classical Hollywood" is redefined to apply to films of the mid-late 1930s that are marked by a narrative classicism that she pairs with a reactionary attitude to gender. Thus, the emancipated woman seen in films of the late 1920s and early 1930s gives way to narratives in which couple formation and marriage were the goal, and where narrative causality reigned supreme over what Tom Gunning identified as an avant-garde cinema of attractions.[31] In other words, in the context of Hollywood film, Pravadelli redefines the "mass culture" against which true modernist art of value defines itself as these narratively classical films of the late 1930s. Such an argument is significant because Korngold's first foray into films occurred at precisely the time Pravadelli identifies a shift from films focused on the New Woman of modernity

---

[28] Lea Jacobs, "John Stahl: Melodrama, Modernism, and the Problem of Naïve Taste," *Modernism/Modernity* 19, no. 2 (April 2012): 304.

[29] Miriam Bratu Hansen, "The Mass Production of the Senses: Classical Cinema as Vernacular Modernism," *Modernism/Modernity* 6, no. 2 (April 1999): 68.

[30] Ibid., 65.

[31] Veronica Pravadelli, *Classic Hollywood: Lifestyles and Film Styles of American Cinema 1930–1960*, trans. Michael Theodore Meadows (Urbana: University of Illinois Press, 2015), 22. Tom Gunning, "The Cinema of Attraction: Early Film, Its Spectator and the Avant-Garde," *Wide Angle* 8, nos. 3/4 (1986): 63–70.

194   KORNGOLD IN AMERICA

to ones with male leads and to child/adolescent stars. She suggests that this shift is particularly apparent in the rise of the adventure film and costume drama, both of which emphasized male agency. Indeed, it is striking that many of the films for which Korngold provided a score were in genres that Pravadelli associates specifically with narrative classicism and a temporary regression in US gender politics: historical costume drama, biopic, and adventure films.

Pravadelli further argues "the emergence of subjectivity as a process, rather than a fact or given, is visible only in the cinema produced during the war and subsequent years,"[32] and connects that with a re-emergence of the spectacular, and a renewal of those qualities highlighted by Gunning. Although she draws on compelling visual evidence found in *films noir* such as use of out-of-focus shots, dissolves, and image doubling to suggest that "a subjective and embodied vision emerges in 1940s narratives. . . . [that] makes a corporealized self visible,"[33] Pravadelli notably does not consider the role music plays in mediating an audience experience of subjectivity: that a corporealized self might be *audible* through musical means in many of the films otherwise considered "classical" and lacking in the kinds of visual spectacle she associates with this mode of filmmaking. Indeed, the attitude to music's materiality that I have suggested is apparent in many of Korngold's film scores might encourage us to see ways in which characters and audiences alike might, through engagement with the materiality of musical score, practice that very process of exploring character subjectivity in ways that Pravadelli finds lacking in late 1930s cinema.

As Richard Rushton points out, though, Gunning's "cinema of attractions" is simply another means of dividing films of value (allied with modernism) from those deemed less worthy of critical attention.[34] And Pravadelli's distinction between a "classical" cinema associated with gender regression and a later visually spectacular mode that "makes a corporealized self visible" can be understood in similar terms. There is a danger, then, that in attempting to identify films that, through their scores, accomplish the very thing that Pravadelli otherwise finds lacking in their narratives, the result speaks to the same impulse: a modernist anxiety that encourages the valuing of some films only at the expense of identifying "an other" to be denigrated. What, I wonder, might happen were we to inquire after the potential for Korngold's film scores to explore critically questions of gender, disability, and race—as marked by a corporealized subjectivity—yet attempt to do so without seeking to ascribe value to these films (or to denigrate them) for having (or lacking) those characteristics; and without crediting (or castigating) the composer over and above his collaborators when a

---

[32]   Pravadelli, *Classic Hollywood*, 74.
[33]   Ibid., 80.
[34]   Rushton, *The Reality of Film*, 25–26.

film has or does not have those characteristics? After all, as I have acknowledged already, many of the decisions that affect the ways in which Korngold scored films—or in which the sound was eventually mixed—lay outside the composer's hands. Crediting the composer for the "progressive" gender politics of a film would be problematic because of the difficulties of separating the composer's own views on such questions from the filmmaking process—or, indeed, from any act of musical interpretation. For instance, although Korngold's operas are striking for their strong female characters, and can be interpreted as challenging contemporary gender politics, it would be folly to suggest that such interpretive possibilities provide any proof of intention on behalf of the composer.[35]

In any case, at first glance, the films that welcomed Korngold's early forays into scoring might indeed seem to exemplify the very gender-regressive turn that Pravadelli identifies in the mid- to late 1930s. Arabella Bishop (Olivia de Havilland), for instance, though undoubtedly portrayed as a spirited and independent woman who defies her slave-trading uncle in the first part of *Captain Blood*, is ultimately reduced to Blood's love interest—a woman to be rescued from the clutches of Levasseur and one who at her moment of romantic confusion looks to an older man for advice: "Oh, help me Lord Willoughby," she pleads; "I see your point, my child, but that's something you must decide for yourself. Life can be infernally complex," he responds patronizingly. Her music, too, can be read in terms of standard connoters of femininity found in 1930s and 1940s Hollywood scoring: she tends to be surrounded by a high halo of strings, and her thematic material undergoes relatively little change or development. Although she is given a secondary theme after her trip to England, her main theme is often heard in combination with one of two love themes, and any variation or development in her musical voice is largely confined to urgent repetitions of the opening rising seventh and an occasional re-harmonization.

Yet, although adventure films and biopics may not provide the most obvious opportunities for progressive treatment of women, it is possible nonetheless that through a consideration of the score and its implied material interactions with character, we can find ways in which music is able to explore subjectivity in a manner that is not apparent visually. In so doing, even if Pravadelli is correct about a decline of the spectacular and dominance of the narrative mode in the 1930s, this might be balanced by a renewed role for music: in other words,

---

[35] The characters of Violanta in *Violanta* and Marietta in *Die tote Stadt*, for example, can be read/heard as examples of the modern woman who, to some extent, challenges contemporary gender politics. I have explored this in "Strangling Blondes: Nineteenth-Century Femininity and Korngold's *Die tote Stadt*," *Cambridge Opera Journal* 23, nos. 1–2 (March–July 2011): 51–82; and in "Korngold's *Violanta*: Venice, Carnival, and the Masking of Identities," in *Music, Modern Culture, and the Critical Ear*, ed. Nicholas Attfield and Ben Winters (Abingdon: Routledge, 2018), 51–74. Admittedly, as with much opera wherein female characters feature prominently, their portrayals are rarely unproblematic from today's perspective.

the visual "spectacle" that is so frequently connected with film's revolutionary and avant-garde possibilities might find audible expression in the score even as it temporarily declined in the visual sphere to be replaced with a renewed interest in narrative causality. For the avoidance of doubt, I advance this line of thought not to claim this is what we should value in film music—that these "regressively" classical films are somehow "saved" by their "progressive" scores—but instead to undercut the thrust of modernist arguments about film that work through exclusion and hierarchy, often at the expense of overlooking interesting elements. One of the most intriguing possibilities for this in a Korngold score can be found in 1939's *Juarez*—ostensibly an historical costume drama focused on men—and a character who not only seems to see things that others miss, but who might also be read as having the ability to interact with and shape the music that surrounds her. Played by Bette Davis, Carlota is the wife of the Austrian Archduke Maximilian (Brian Aherne), who is duped by Napoleon III (Claude Rains) into taking the crown of Mexico. She is portrayed throughout the film as someone with gifts of foresight. Upon the royal couple's arrival in Mexico, Maximilian says he feels surrounded by mystery and hidden meanings, but believes that Carlota has a comprehension that lets her see into the heart of things. Moreover, when it is discovered that Napoleon has betrayed them, and Carlota sets off to confront him, she lays claim to a mystical power typical of a romanticized idea of distance: "our thoughts will bridge the distance between us," she tells her husband: "open your soul to me, and I shall be with you." These statements are accompanied by the Spanish-Mexican song "La Paloma"—the quasi-folk tune that Carlota had described in her romanticized naivety earlier in the film as the loveliest melody she knew, having encouraged her husband to "Listen . . . listen, Maxl!"

When translating the lyrics of "La Paloma,"[36] Carlota had mused how terrible it must be to be separated from one's love, and the importance of the song for her abilities to bridge distances is at this moment established in a way that is reminiscent of one of Robert Schumann's 1833 letters to Clara Wieck, which proposed a similarly mystical union over a great distance through the simultaneous playing of the music of Chopin.[37] It is perhaps unsurprising, then, given the Schumann connection, that Carlota's apparently mystical abilities are in retrospect associated with mental illness—the trope of the mad woman who nonetheless sees

---

[36] "If to your window should come a dove, treat it tenderly for it is I. Tell it of your love, my life's enchantment. Crown it with flowers, for it is I."

[37] July 13, 1833. "Since there is no chain of sparks to draw us together or even remind us of one other [*sic*], I have a mystical proposal. Tomorrow at exactly 11 o'clock, I'll play the adagio from Chopin's *Variations* and will think intently, indeed exclusively, of you. Now the request is that you do the same so that we can see each other and meet in spirit." Eva Wissweiler, ed., *The Complete Correspondence of Clara and Robert Schumann*, vol. 1, trans. Hidegard Fritsch and Ronald L Crawford (New York: Peter Lang, 1994), 5.

beyond the here and now is, after all, a pervasive one; and upon confronting Napoleon, Carlota's mind becomes unhinged. Yet, significantly, Carlota's subjectivity also seems capable of warping the music that surrounds her.[38] At the end of the film, as Maximilian is awaiting execution at the hands of Benito Juarez's Mexican nationalists, he requests to hear "La Paloma" sung outside his prison cell. The music is then portrayed as crossing the ocean to reach Carlota in Europe, in fulfilment of her parting promise of a mystical union of minds; however, once it arrives, we hear it apparently warped by the presence of her damaged subjectivity—both harmonically and temporally. This moment, I suggest, is an example of a kind of musical "spectacle" that makes audible the corporealized self. A suggestion of the rhythm of the song is heard in a quasi-octatonic progression in celesta and electric organ, which leads to a mutated octatonic version of the song's first phrase on electric organ with sharpened fourth and lowered seventh scale degrees (Example 5.3).[39] Seemingly called to the window by this obsessively repeated phrase, Carlota appears to re-establish both the un-warped "La Paloma" in F major and briefly her own sanity via a transformational harp scale akin to Ravel's "La Belle et La Bête" from *Ma Mère l'Oye* only to cry out in anguish with the apparent knowledge of events happening thousands of miles away. In an early draft of the film's screenplay, this ability of Carlota to hear "La Paloma" from across the ocean was even made explicit: "CLOSEUP CARLOTA Her face expressionless, her eyes staring straight ahead. Like one who has heard a faint sound, she turns her head very slightly, and the music begins to grow in clarity. Intelligence, comprehension and finally joy show on her face. The music grows clear and true, with even a suggestion of the voice of the singer in far-off Queretaro."[40]

Although much of this conception changed in the way that Korngold scored the scene, the idea that Carlota hears music was clearly in play long before the composer began work. Nevertheless, I suggest what causes Carlota's cry of anguish is not necessarily some mystical gift to see events in Mexico, but perhaps the belated recognition that "La Paloma" is no mere pleasing melody to be appropriated with colonialist naivety. Rather, it had always represented the forces of Mexican nationalism to which Carlota and her husband were previously blind and that have led to the couple's ruin. In hearing and shaping the physical sound of the score, Carlota arguably gains a newfound understanding

---

[38] In the scene with Prince Metternich, the harmonies of her love theme (now more familiar to us through its inclusion in Korngold's Violin Concerto) are altered; once Metternich leaves her, however, the theme is immediately restored, suggesting her physical presence alone has the power to reshape the music. This cue is missing from the extant manuscript sources.

[39] This is cue 16B (also labeled cue 69). The first two bars are $Oct_{0,1}$ and the third bar is $Oct_{1,2}$. The melody uses $Oct_{0,1}$.

[40] WBA, "JUAREZ" STORY—SCREENPLAY 6/2/38, 2813.

198 KORNGOLD IN AMERICA

Example 5.3 Warped octatonic version of "La Paloma" in *Juarez* (cue 16B).

of her own damaged subjectivity, the political situation, and its relationship with the song.

Other Korngold films, because of their plotlines, invite similar kinds of critical engagement. *Kings Row*, for instance, is an historical melodrama set at the turn of the twentieth century.[41] Based on Henry Bellamann's novel of the same name, it deals with such hallmarks of modernity as psychiatry, the stigma of mental health, unnecessary medical procedures, fraud, suicide, and disability.[42] Visually, with the expressionistic style of Director of Photography James Wong Howe's shadowy cinematography, it would be a relatively easy task to align *Kings Row* with those discourses of value espoused by those who seek a maximalist definition of modernism in order to include certain instances of Hollywood cinema. Narratively, too, it articulates and explores many anxieties of modernity, supported by a Korngold score that helps distinguish the old world of Madame von Eln—whose passing Colonel Skeffington laments as indicative of the loss of "gentleness and dignity"—from the troubled world of a new generation, of characters like Cassandra Tower, Drake McHugh, Louise Gordon, Randy Monaghan, and even Dr. Tower. Indeed, although Dr. Tower (Claude Rains) counsels the main character, Parris Mitchell (Robert Cummings), on

---

[41] For John Mercer and Martin Shingler, this is specifically a "family melodrama." See *Melodrama: Genre, Style and Sensibility* (New York: Columbia University Press, 2013), 121.

[42] As Neil Lerner points out, the novel also explored incestuous sexual abuse (between Dr. Tower and Cassie) and mercy killings, while its themes of homosexuality are, as Lerner hints, sublimated in the relationship between Parris and Drake. See "The Caverns of the Human Mind Are Full of Strange Shadows: Disability Representation, Henry Bellamann, and Korngold's Musical Subtexts in the Score for *Kings Row*," in *Korngold and His World*, ed. Daniel Goldmark and Kevin C. Karnes (Princeton, NJ: Princeton University Press, 2019), 131–166.

Example 5.4 Louise Gordon's theme in *Kings Row* (cue 3B).

the discomforts of man—arguing that "psychic man" was more comfortable in the thirteenth century than he is now in this "modern, complicated world," where "man breaks down under the strain, the bewilderment, disappointment and disillusionment; gets lost, goes crazy, commits suicide"—ultimately he kills his own daughter (and himself) seemingly to save Parris's medical career. Korngold's music for the mentally ill Cassie Tower, for the nefarious and crazed doctor turned butcher Dr. Gordon, and for his psychologically disturbed daughter, Louise (Example 5.4), is all nervous repetition and quasi-modernist fragmentation.[43] In this regard, Korngold might be said to recognize and enact what Joseph Straus has identified as fundamental alignments between musical modernism and disability. Straus articulates the ways in which musical modernism and culturally stigmatized disabilities are both defined in relationship to a regulating, normative standard that requires an explanatory story. As such, he argues that "the sorts of qualities that make music distinctively modern—forms made of discrete blocks, stratified textures, immobile harmonies, radical simplification of materials, juxtaposition of seemingly incommensurable elements, extremes of internal complexity and self-reference—can be understood as representations of disabled bodies," and, as a consequence, he finds value in the ways in which music can aestheticize "disability into new forms of beauty."[44]

Undoubtedly, Korngold uses many of these techniques in connection with the characters of *Kings Row* to draw attention to the disabilities on display. Louise Gordon's mental illness, triggered by knowledge of her sadistic surgeon father, is audible through her repetitive blocks of chromatic material long before we learn of her illness (Example 5.4); similarly, Cassie's supposed inherited mental condition is likewise marked musically by its nervous repetitions; while Dr. Gordon's sadism is reflected in a restricted musical palette of rising minor

---

[43] Peter Franklin reads Korngold's ever-more-fragmented score as a commentary on the "past history of the symphony, perhaps even of 'music' as a constructional conceit or formalist proposition whose ideological import was always concealed from view." Peter Franklin, *Seeing through Music: Gender and Modernism in Hollywood Film Scores* (New York: Oxford University Press, 2011), 112.

[44] Joseph N. Straus, *Broken Beauty: Musical Modernism and the Representation of Disability* (New York: Oxford University Press, 2018), 3.

200 KORNGOLD IN AMERICA

triads that can only repeat. Admittedly, the narrative of *Kings Row* practices the kind of medical model of disability that requires it to be normalized through cure or institutionalization. Parris grapples with these alternatives when trying to treat Louise, whose institutionalization in an insane asylum will keep safe her terrible secret: that Drake's legs were amputated unnecessarily. Having informed Louise that she should tell her secret to anyone who will listen—and having told his best friend Drake (Ronald Reagan) the same, thus also "curing" him of his "mental scars"—the aesthetic style of modernism is replaced by the diatonic forces of Parris's fanfare theme wedded to the words of William Ernest Henley's "Invictus" ("I am the master of my fate: I am the captain of my soul"). The score, in ending with a choral rendition of Parris's theme, is thus ostensibly complicit in "othering" the characteristics of musical modernism as non-normative in the same way it appears to treat mental illness: as something to be overcome.

That said, the treatment of Drake's musical theme suggests something more interesting in the score's relationship with physical disability. Drake's theme (Example 5.5a) is essentially composed of an initial descent and upward rise, but it is subject to fragmentations (musical "amputations," if you will) and repetitions long before his accident. His anger at Louise's inability to stand up to her father, for instance, results in an obsessive repetition of the opening of a minor version of his theme (cue 3D), and in the scenes in which Drake loses his fortune as a result of bank fraud, this opening is treated to sequential repetition, imitative counterpoint, and rhythmic augmentation (cue 8D). However, even before his financial misfortune, in the scenes with Randy in which their romance starts to blossom as Drake contemplates a real-estate deal, the opening of his theme is presented in a strangely static and repetitious manner (Example 5.5b). Although this has none of the chromatic harmony that signals "mental illness" in the other characters of the film, it might be thought nonetheless to be a some-what curious, and immobile, treatment of Drake's thematic material that appears to foreshadow his impending physical transformation. Moreover, Drake's moment of realization in cue 9H that his legs have been amputated ("Randy! Where's the rest of me?") is perhaps given new meaning by the material perspec-tive I have outlined in this chapter. As such, Drake's outburst might be read as much as a belated response to his truncated musical theme as it is to his dimin-ished physicality. Like those other characters in Korngold films who are marked as dreamers or sufferers of physical or mental trauma, and who thus seem to have the ability to hear things that others do not, Drake perhaps finally hears what the score has been heralding throughout—the threat to his sense of self and his need to undergo a number of misfortunes before he can discover his true character. Ultimately, Drake's "heroic" overcoming of his "mental scars" at the film's con-clusion creates a further change in his musical material, one that appears to be born hesitantly from his theme's characteristic falling fourths. It initially loses the

KORNGOLD, MATERIALITY, AND WORLDBUILDING   201

Example 5.5 Drake's theme in *Kings Row* (a) melody from cue 3B (b) truncated repetitions of in cue 7D (c) birth of Drake's new theme in cue 13B (d) Drake's new "mobile" theme in cue 13B.

distinctive ornamental turn and instead explores a celebratory ascending shape (Example 5.5c); "Where did Gordon think I lived? In my legs? Did he think those things were Drake McHugh?" Even though he remains a double amputee, Drake regains his mobility, resolving to leave the bed to which he has been bound in order to face the world with a newfound confidence. The music then explores the upward sequential potential of his thematic material (Example 5.5d), re-embracing the original distinctive ornamental turn of the first part and the rising shape of the second part, but giving it a modulatory harmonic agency that seems to suggest newfound and "mobile" possibilities for the character.

Drake McHugh's disability, however, represents only the most recent chapter in Korngold's artistic experience with traumatic limb loss, one that has its roots in the 1920s with his involvement with the one-armed pianist, Paul Wittgenstein. Indeed, the two Korngold works that were commissioned by Wittgenstein can also be regarded as sites for provocative engagement with modernity through the enabling lens of disability. In the Concerto in C sharp and, particularly, the lesser-known Op. 23 Suite for Piano and Strings, Wittgenstein's disability and the composer's creative response to its restrictions are placed center stage. The Suite rehearses many of the qualities that Joseph Straus associates with modernist musical culture: remarkably, it features a movement entitled "Groteske" (Grotesque) that is curiously mechanistic—another trope of disability that brings to mind the prostheses that gave so many amputees the ability to continue working, but for which Wittgenstein never found the need.[45] Moreover, the Groteske follows a Waltz that is curiously off-kilter, with halting minor-ninth missteps (at first in piano), again seemingly dramatizing a body that does not quite fit social conventions and, as such, chiming with Straus's observations about the treatment of dance forms in modernist music—particularly the waltz.[46] Here, though, the approach is arguably inspired directly by Wittgenstein's traumatic disability rather than indicating "genuine" modernism. At any rate, the personal vulnerability of Wittgenstein's disability feels more on show in this Suite than in the heroic fireworks of the Concerto—a work that in its triumphal "overcoming" seems in thrall to the medical approach to disability often on show in *Kings Row*. The first movement of the Suite, though, begins with an extended thirty-one-bar piano solo while the strings' first entrance is in unison, as if drawing attention to the narrowness of the texture. This starkness is relatively unusual for Korngold,[47] all the more so when it is compared with the textural richness of the earlier Piano Quintet. Taken together with the Groteske and Waltz, it all adds to the impression that the suite in some sense dramatizes Wittgenstein's disability in ways that were only hinted at by the concerto. As such, then, *Kings Row* is

---

[45] Herbert Strutz's review of the first performance on October 21, 1930 referred to this movement as "spukhaft" or "spooky," articulating the uncomfortable feelings about the body it may have elicited, while Hedwig Kanner simply heard demonic humor. See Herbert Strutz, "Schluß der Wiener Konzertseit 1930/31," *Freie Stimmen*, June 16, 1931; Hedwig Kanner, "Konzerte," *Der Morgen*, October 27, 1930.

[46] Straus, *Broken Beauty*, 21–22.

[47] It is, however, something that is more common in later works such as the opening movements of the Third String Quartet and the Symphony.

merely a continuation of an artistic engagement with questions of disability that Korngold had already tackled in his pre-Hollywood concert works.

From the point of view of gender politics, *Kings Row* might also be perceived, in some senses at least, as "progressive." Randy (Ann Sheridan) can be read as a strong woman who initially refuses Drake McHugh's half-serious offer of marriage and later displays the necessary business acumen to rebuild his fortune and self-esteem after his series of misfortunes. Nonetheless, her musical theme is perhaps rather lacking in the agency her character displays, at least for large parts of the film. Like Arabella's theme in *Captain Blood* it appears instead to be a standard connoter of beauty—a rather harmonically "naïve" melody that circles back on itself (see Example 4.3) and that changes little in character from her introduction as a child (cue 1F) to her depiction as an adult (cue 7A onward). Admittedly, Randy does receive a significant "comic" variation in cue 7E, as her romance with Drake blossoms, but it is noticeable that the music associated with Drake and Parris is heard in many more guises. In the latter part of the film, Randy is also more often accompanied with a subsidiary theme that is associated with her love for Drake. It is introduced in cue 8E and acts as a coda to a standard presentation of her theme (Example 5.6a): indeed, from this point on, it seems to largely take over from her own theme, as if she is now only constituted musically in relation to Drake. That said, however, the next cue (9A) returns briefly to her original thematic material, albeit with a significant melodic and harmonic variation, which perhaps suggests that her own musical voice survives intact. A similar variant is heard once more in cue 9H (Example 5.6b) as Randy grapples with the reality of Drake's accident before a last full statement of her theme is heard in cue 10A. This is perhaps a significant moment wherein we might suggest that the character interacts with the material sound of the score. In response to Drake's understandable pessimism at his situation, she tells him "you're alive and I love you," whereupon he turns away from her; however, as her theme returns in its original form in the orchestra, she hesitates and, appearing to draw confidence from hearing her own musical identity (and with a knowing flicker of an eyebrow), tells him: "I'm going to tell you something and I want you to listen until I've finished. Then you can talk if you want to, but I want my say first."[48] Although at first glance, then, Randy is scored in a way that promises little musical agency, there are moments nonetheless where Korngold appears to recognize the inherent strengths of the character. She is no mere appendage to Drake, and her musical treatment in allowing for a certain amount of thematic variation acknowledges her capacity to change, with the last statement of her theme in 10C even suggesting a potential for development (Example 5.6c). At any rate, she is given more musical attention than is afforded the mentally ill characters of the

---

[48] A further small variant is heard in 10C as she greets Parris from his return from Vienna.

Example 5.6 (a) Randy's subsidiary theme in *Kings Row*, cue 8E (b) Randy's theme in cue 9H (c) Randy's theme in cue 10C.

narrative, whose musical material remains largely static and repetitious. Louise's theme (Example 5.4) as introduced in 3B, for instance, is essentially the same in 8A, 9F, 9G, 10E, 11A, 12B, and 12D with only changes in rhythm and tempo to match the physical activity of the character.

In the same way, we might examine *Devotion*—a film that, in being focused on two sisters who are respected artists and acclaimed as geniuses by a figure of male authority (Sydney Greenstreet as Thackeray), could be said to challenge at least some prevailing attitudes to women in the 1940s. Although most of the narrative intrigue of the film concerns a historically spurious love triangle with the curate Arthur Nicholls (Paul Henreid)[49] and, at the end of the film, a grieving Charlotte discovers that literary success is not what she had dreamed and confesses at her sister's grave that she has "found the meaning" with Nicholls, the film at least gives the women a certain agency in the narrative.[50] It even passes (just) the famed Bechdel test in that at one point the sisters converse about the publication of their poems, and the work Ann and Charlotte completed while working as governesses. Furthermore, despite the fact that the sisters' relationship with their brother Branwell (Arthur Kennedy) and Nicholls seems to define them in the narrative, the musical treatment of these two women nevertheless lends them the kinds of thematic independence more often associated with male characters in Korngold's films. Emily, for example, is associated with a large amount of thematic material: two principal themes, linked by a rising perfect fifth, are subject to processes of fragmentation, variation, and development throughout the film in a way that is simply not the case to the same extent for Nicholls.[51] In the scene in which Branwell dies (cue 9D), her theme also opens out in new ways in solo violin as she exhorts him to "please try . . . for me, Branwell, please try"; her brother's imminent death seems to prompt changes in her musical identity as her familial responsibilities change. Similarly, Charlotte's theme is frequently fragmented and undergoes some striking variation and development in Reels 6 and 7, where her romance with Mons. Heger occurs, and as her literary success takes her to London (most notably in the montage scene, cue 9D, and in cue 10C). Significantly, too, both women's themes are introduced long before they are seen onscreen. When their Aunt, Miss Branwell, refers to them in the village, and in her conversation with Lady Thornton (Dame May Whitty) in cue 1B, we hear in the former case Emily's "moors" theme and, in the latter, Charlotte's theme in flute ("Miss Charlotte writes a clear, bold hand"). As such, their thematic material has an independence from their physical presence onscreen—something that cannot be said for Nicholls, whose theme is first introduced only when he appears (despite him being mentioned in dialogue) and is rarely present when he is offscreen.[52] Along with the "sisters" theme, which is likewise

---

[49] See Lucasta Miller, *The Brontë Myth* (London: Vintage, 2002), 117.

[50] A somewhat more progressive stance might be found in the figure of Angela from *Anthony Adverse*, who ultimately choses her singing career over marriage to Anthony, and leaves him to raise their son as a single parent. Korngold chooses Angela's theme to end the film.

[51] We hear a slight variant of his theme in London (10D).

[52] Only once in 10D, when Thackeray and Charlotte arrive outside his London home, do we hear Nicholls's theme when he is not onscreen.

subject to variation, the score is dominated by the musical material associated with the film's women.

Korngold thus appeared to be offered multiple opportunities to explore modern gender politics and depictions of disability in his music even in those films Pravadelli might argue are distinguished by their narrative classicism and socially regressive plots. Yet, to what extent those reflect conscious decisions on the composer's part as an artist critically engaged with social and political concerns and worthy of "praise" is a question that, once we are free of modernist anxiety, becomes less important. As such, assessing his contributions to the problematic 1936 film *The Green Pastures*—which uses an entirely black cast to tell Bible stories—becomes less about attempting to demonstrate his credentials as a politically engaged artist with a commitment to civil liberties. Undoubtedly, the film, which was based on the Pulitzer Prize–winning play by Marc Connelly, was, as Judith Weisenfeld notes, "a lightning rod for discussions of African American religion … on the American political and social scene."[53] The play had attracted both praise and censure from the US black community, in part because Connelly presented only one view of a diverse religious practice; there was little doubt, though, that it was of significance. The black press, however, lambasted the film's production, concerned about the indiscretions of actor Rex Ingram and convinced that the film would not reflect well on black Americans. Reviews of the completed film were mixed. As Weisenfeld argues, *The Green Pastures'* presentation emphasized the artificial "fable" quality of the story by presenting it in the context of an infantilizing Sunday School class, and God is presented with powers of neither omnipotence nor omniscience. As such, Weisenfeld suggests, the film erroneously "renders black theology parochial, limited, and childish,"[54] and demonstrates the apparent fears of white society of black urban culture in seeming to suggest that black Americans could "remain truer to accepted moral standards … when contained in rural environments."[55]

As with the play, *The Green Pastures* made use of spirituals arranged by Hall Johnson and sung by the Hall Johnson Choir, a factor that Weisenfeld suggests was "one of the most important legitimating markers of the work as culturally African American," even as she notes that Johnson later repudiated the film.[56] Similarly, the music was the only aspect praised in an otherwise scathing review by Roi Ottley.[57] The film, though, is undeniably problematic, and there are uncomfortable aspects to the ways in which Warner Bros. treated the actors and

---

[53] Judith Weisenfeld, *Hollywood Be Thy Name: African American Religion in American Film, 1929–1949* (Berkeley: University of California Press, 2007), 53.

[54] Ibid., 77.

[55] Ibid., 79.

[56] Ibid., 61, 85–86.

[57] Ibid., 83.

singers, who are referred to repeatedly in studio correspondence, specifically, as "colored." In other words, their racial identity is referenced even though it is of no significance to the subject of the communication. Korngold's uncredited role undertaken in April 1936 was perhaps small enough, in any case, to absolve him from association with its uncomfortable depictions of black culture, and he was asked to contribute by Hal Wallis the day after he finished work on *Anthony Adverse*. In that sense, this was an assignment rather than a film project to which Korngold signed up willingly. Yet, according to Luzi Korngold's biography of her husband, he opposed the restrictions imposed on people of color by Warner Bros. in preventing their access to "the Green Room," the fine-dining restaurant attached to the studio's Commissary, and consequently joining Johnson and Rex Ingram in the main restaurant in an act of solidarity.[58] Luzi also suggests that Korngold had so fallen in love with the story that he did not require any payment for the six cues he provided for the film, a story that Brendan Carroll repeats and augments by suggesting that Korngold also did not ask for onscreen credit for his contribution fearing it would divert attention away from Johnson;[59] however, this may simply be because he was still on salary for *Anthony Adverse* at the time he undertook the work. The score's recording completion date is listed in the archives as April 19, 1936, and Korngold was certainly on salary at Warners until May 9.[60] The agreement he had signed for *Anthony Adverse* is missing from the archives, and it may be that it clarified the situation with regard to the screen credit he could expect for contributions to other film projects provided while under salary. At any rate, there is no reason to doubt Korngold's liberal sensibilities, especially with his apparently later adherence to the causes that HICCASP supported, including civil liberties and the abolition of racial segregation (see Introduction). Yet, this does mean that his participation in the film rescues it from its problematic status, or indeed that his involvement somehow compromises his own position on the question of civil liberties.

In addition to the problematic nature of the film's racial politics for black American communities, *The Green Pastures* was also controversial in foreign markets, earning a number of bans (including briefly in the United Kingdom and more widely in territories that forbade impersonation of the deity on film); other countries or territories banned it specifically because it depicted a black God.[61] In that sense, then, it is undoubtedly a film that engaged (albeit

---

[58] Luzi Korngold, *Erich Wolfgang Korngold: Ein Lebensbild* (Vienna: Elizabeth Lafite Verlag, 1967), 74.

[59] Brendan Carroll, *The Last Prodigy: A Biography of Erich Wolfgang Korngold* (Portland, OR: Amadeus Press, 1997), 261.

[60] He had started the beginning of his "12-week guarantee" for *Anthony Adverse* on February 16 (at $833.34 per week), though a contract terminated note in the payroll is not dated until May 9.

[61] Weisenfeld, *Hollywood Be Thy Name*, 84.

controversially and not uncomplicatedly) with contemporary social issues of profound significance. Many of the other films to which Korngold contributed also had strong political overtones of contemporary resonance, which is perhaps hardly surprising given the strongly anti-Nazi stance of Warner Bros. in these years. *Juarez*, for instance, was seen by contemporary critics as a "powerful document for democracy"[62]; and even an apparently simplistic adventure film such as *The Adventures of Robin Hood* can be interpreted as commenting upon contemporary national and international politics, with the Viennese character of Korngold's music playing an important role in such readings.[63]

***

In commenting on the ways in which such "ordinary" Hollywood fare can be read as socially engaged—or as illuminating modern subjectivities and contemporary concerns—via Korngold's musical contributions, I have deliberately sought to avoid appearing to ascribe added value to these films over and above any of Korngold's other film scores, or those of his contemporaries. These are undoubtedly viable ways to read these films within the contexts of their production, but therein does not lie their sole value as artistic products nor a reason to esteem them over other contemporary Hollywood fare. Likewise, the way in which Korngold's scores can be integrated with the sounding phenomena of these screen worlds does not elevate them in my view to a position that is fundamentally separated from other Hollywood products of the time. In much the same way that we might question the value-laden discourses of modernism in musicology that seem to value music only for its ability to instruct us about our proper relationship with the power structures of society, so might we question whether this potential for Korngold's music to make us reflect on the ways in which character subjectivity is negotiated through musical means, or to ponder the material nature of musical score in filmworlds, is serving a perspective that values film not for itself but instead only for the ways in which it represents and serves reality. In so doing, we may overlook much of interest. Just as I am uncomfortable, then, trying to find ways in which Korngold might be counted among an "elevated" group of twentieth-century modernists, so I am wary of trying to demonstrate too closely the methods by which the films he scored might be admitted to a pantheon of cinematic art whose self-reflexivity rises above the assumed illusionistic manipulation of "ordinary" Classical Hollywood narrative.

---

[62] See, for instance, Donald Ogden Stewart and Meyer Levin's articles on the Hollywood and New York premieres of the film in *The Hollywood Tribune*, April 28, 1939.

[63] I have explored various possible readings of this film in Winters, *Erich Wolfgang Korngold's* The Adventures of Robin Hood and in my chapter "Swearing an Oath: Korngold, Film and the Sound of Resistance?," in *The Impact of Nazism on Twentieth-Century Music*, ed. Erik Levi (Vienna: Böhlau Verlag, 2014), 61–76.

Rather, I see enormous value in what might be thought of as decidedly ordinary films, including their scores, and although films like *Juarez* or *Kings Row* can be interrogated in ways that might appear to "legitimize" them according to the discourse of the "modernity thesis," I do not seek to denigrate scores by Korngold (or, indeed, by others) that, in comparison, might be regarded as less amenable to such perspectives.

Where, then, does this chapter leave Korngold's role in music history? If I do not claim him and the films to which he contributed for some pantheon of artistic value—but instead draw attention to the ways in which these films in their very ordinariness can nonetheless create rewarding artistic experiences—how does this help resolve Korngold's position in music history, about which I spoke in the Introduction? One possible solution to this intractable historiographical problem may lie in the fact that both his later film scores and his final concert works help to bring into productive dialogue what might be thought of as two fundamentally different realms: Hollywood and contemporary concert culture. It is to these later film scores, then, with their self-consciously "musical" narratives, that I next turn.

6

Korngold between Two Worlds

Hollywood and the Concert Hall

—"Listen ... your music"
—"Yours, too"

(Escape Me Never)

I suggested in Chapter 5 that Korngold's film scores frequently called into question apparently clear divisions between music thought to be sourced in the world of the narrative and music commonly held to exist outside of that world and to be accessible only to a watching audience. I stressed the frequency with which characters exhort each other to "listen" and the other ways in which Korngold's scoring choices seem to suggest an ambiguous musical space to which characters might have access: a music that has a materiality in their environment and contributes to the sense of a recognizable and unique film world. In so doing, I was continuing an argument I began in an earlier book, *Music, Performance, and the Realities of Film*, where I stressed music's role in the participative aspect of film experience: one that is shared not only among a film's spectators but also with its characters.[1] I argued there that theoretical explanations of music's narrative source that rely overly on a realist aesthetic might seem to deny aspects of our film experiences, notably the strong emotional connections we may feel with characters through a shared musical experience, positing instead that we might embrace a non-realist (or, more appropriately, a film-realist) response to the question "who can hear this music?" If many aspects of Korngold's scores warrant this approach—whether it be the fanfares of *The Private Lives of Elizabeth and Essex*, the warped music of Carlota in *Juarez*, or the strange space of *Between Two Worlds*—or, at least, encourage us to revisit this question, it is equally the case that some of Korngold's scores also prompt us to posit further questions about the relationship between film and concert-hall experiences.[2] In their focus on composers and the composition of concert-hall items for performance, *The Constant Nymph*, *Escape Me Never*, and *Deception* all seem to stress

---

[1] *Music, Performance, and the Realities of Film: Shared Concert Experiences in Screen Fiction* (New York: Routledge, 2014).

[2] I also explored this functional equivalence of film and concert-hall experiences in ibid., 119–146, 158–170.

Korngold in America. Ben Winters, Oxford University Press. © Oxford University Press 2025.
DOI: 10.1093/9780197684818.003.0007

the functional equivalence that exists between underscoring and concert repertoire, something I touched on in Chapter 5 when discussing the performance of *Tomorrow* in *The Constant Nymph*. In so doing, these three films not only add to the notion of a shared musical space that offers a critique of traditional understandings of Hollywood scoring practices but also offer Korngold a way back to the concert hall, and a chance seemingly to remold the world of Western art-music in Hollywood's image. As such they reveal a newfound significance for Hollywood in Korngold's career and point, potentially, to its wider importance for twentieth-century music historiography.

In this chapter, then, I want to explore these three composer-centered films and their emphasis on creating a shared musical space when representing the creative act of composition. In prompting questions in a watching audience about the relationship between film scoring and concert music, these films can challenge the standardized distinctions between narrative sources for music in film-music theory: the diegetic/nondiegetic pairing. This is something that Korngold did throughout his film-scoring career, as I remarked upon in Chapter 5 in connection with the materiality of his music and the choices he made to augment recorded sound with music; but it becomes increasingly the case that the films he opted to score and the decisions he made about how to score them could be said to make significant contributions to this ongoing theoretical discourse. Moreover, they also have the capacity to contribute to contemporaneous debates about the obtrusiveness or audibility of music in film. As such, in blurring distinctions between film scoring and concert works, I argue that they not only offered Korngold a navigable route back to the concert hall but also precipitated an aesthetic alignment between film and concert-hall culture. Furthermore, in examining the treatment of film-score material in the works he composed, I show how the spectator's film experiences are able to inform their engagement with a concert work.

Korngold's post-Hollywood works, by placing film-score material front and center in a sustained and committed manner, thus bring Hollywood film culture and music of the concert hall together in provocative ways that call into question comfortable assumptions we may hold about the place and value of mass culture, actively partaking in a reframing of concert-hall culture in a way that is in dialogue with, rather than in opposition to, mass culture. Korngold's commitment to this process has perhaps not been sufficiently recognized before, and it is where his position as an artist thoroughly immersed in questions surrounding artistic value is most significant. As a result, we may look upon Korngold's time in Hollywood not as a retreat from artistic relevancy into the safe nostalgic world of commercial entertainment, but as a transforming period that enabled him to reframe the terms of his art in ways that are consistent with his own artistic identity.

212 KORNGOLD IN AMERICA

Three Composer-Centered Films

Given their narrative concerns with composers, it is perhaps unsurprising that Korngold's involvement with these three Warner Bros. films (*The Constant Nymph*, *Escape Me Never*, and *Deception*) was far more extensive than previous projects, and that he was keen to contribute to them.[3] As mentioned in Chapter 5, *The Constant Nymph* is centered around the composer Lewis Dodd, and his relationship with the family of his mentor, Albert Sanger (Montagu Love), as Dodd seeks to discover his true compositional voice. Korngold engaged with the film at a much earlier stage in production than was typical. A letter from the composer to Hal Wallis of March 1941 mentions him having read a script,[4] and he also saw a later copy of the "2nd revised final" script dated August 27, 1941, a copy of which resides in the Korngold Collection at the Library of Congress. This copy, which producer Henry Blanke marked on the front "For Mr Korngold who will pick it up," is full of the composer's annotations.[5] On the cover Korngold made a list of all the "playback" scenes the script suggests, and within he underlines virtually any mention of music. Elsewhere he crosses out, corrects, or underlines and questions dialogue, or writes "scoring" in the margin. One small bit of dialogue apparently added by Korngold even made it into the finished film (in bold):

LEWIS: What would you make of it?
SANGER: A symphonic poem—anything you want ...

Became in the final film:

LEWIS: What would I make of it?
SANGER: **A love scene in an opera**—A symphonic poem—what you will ...[6]

---

[3] Evidently, his feelings about composer films may have changed, since Luzi reports in connection with his much later work on *Magic Fire* that Korngold was initially reluctant, that "he didn't want to hear anything more about film and much less from a musician film" (er wollte vom Film überhaupt nichts mehr hören und noch viel weniger von einem Musikerfilm). Luzi Korngold, *Erich Wolfgang Korngold: Ein Lebensbild* (Vienna: Elizabeth Lafite Verlag, 1967), 96.

[4] Letter of March 10 reproduced in Winters, *Music, Performance, and the Realities of Film*, 64. Yet, even though the film—which had been in development since 1940—was once again in production, it was almost a year before the composer started on the prescoring work (January 1942) and over a year until he started scoring the picture.

[5] Erich Wolfgang Korngold Collection, Library of Congress (hereafter LOC), Box 44 Folder 1.

[6] Alternatively, this may simply be an instance of Korngold correcting his own copy of the script: the dialogue throughout was to change extensively, and the end of the treatment had not yet been decided (it states, "There follows, at Mr Wallis's request for budget purposes, a brief outline of the finish of the picture – as discussed with Messrs. Wallis and Blanke. To be written").

Significantly, too, the script mentions the composer by name. Scene 11 notes "At that moment, music (arranged: Korngold) is heard from Sanger's piano upstairs." Korngold's involvement in proceedings, then, was confirmed at least as early as August 1941, at a much earlier stage in the film's development than was typical for the composer. By February 19, 1942, with Korngold's prescoring work done, Henry Blanke could send a memo to Jack Sullivan that gives an indication of the extent to which Korngold's cooperation was required before filming:

> As per our telephone conversation, you will get [together] with Korngold at 2 o'clock and he will tell you all about the spotting of the music, preparation of actors for same, and how it is to be done. All this Korngold knows since he has had several meetings with [director Edmund] Goulding and me, and it is very important for you to know so that you can follow this up throughout the entire picture so that there will be no confusion of mistakes possible.
>
> You also must know that if we have as a cover set for Tuesday SANGER'S ROOM, Montague [sic] Love should know how to finger the piano and should come in now to learn it.
>
> Furthermore, if you intend to shoot the song on Thursday, [Charles] Boyer must know the conducting and be able to speak the first six lines to the playback of the music. [Joan] Fontaine must also study the mouthing of the song.
>
> All these things will take a lot of time and it may be wiser for you, after you learn from Korngold how many difficulties are attached to this, to postpone the song to a later time—both Korngold and I consider this to be much better.
>
> Kindly get with Korngold and after you are through with him, let me know that you understand everything perfectly because this a responsibility that belongs in your department and you should be fully informed about it and be able to follow it through on your own.[7]

Production reports indicate that rehearsals took place in late February, while filming of the musical scenes, involving playback of Korngold's music, occurred in late March. Work on the score in April (including the trailers) then appears to have followed Korngold's normal pattern. On May 12, 1942, a memo to Jack Warner from McCord reported "Forbstein advises that he expects to finish the scoring by next Tuesday or Wednesday, in which case we should be able to preview by the following Monday."[8] Scoring work seems to have been completed by the end of May.[9] On June 22, Victor Blau wrote to Forbstein having seen the cue sheet to remind him of an earlier correspondence:

---

[7] Warner Bros. Archives (hereafter WBA), "THE CONSTANT NYMPH"—MEMO & CORRESPONDENCE 8/8/41–7/28/43 2 of 2.

[8] Ibid.

[9] The copyright cue sheet for the film (production no. 996–1006) lists the final recording date as June 17, 1942.

214   KORNGOLD IN AMERICA

> Sometime in March I read in the trade papers that Korngold was doing a symphonic poem called "TOMORROW" FOR "THE CONSTANT NYMPH." At that time I wrote you [March 11 letter] and asked that you send me some piano copies of this work in order that we may examine it as to publication value.[10]

The "symphonic poem" was published as Korngold's Op. 33 by the Warner Bros. publishing firm Witmark in 1943, and this may indeed have been what Blau's memo concerned. Further correspondence between Blau and Forbstein in late 1942 and early 1943, though, worried about *Tomorrow*'s text, which had been taken directly from Margaret Kennedy and Basil Dean's play.[11] By this time, release of the film had been delayed by almost a year,[12] and it was not until April 1943 that Korngold's father, Julius, could write to the studio expressing admiration for the finished product.[13]

Korngold was thus heavily invested in the project in a way that was distinct from earlier films. Moreover, and perhaps as a result of his input, the film appears to explore a number of aesthetic issues of interest to the composer. Indeed, Lewis Dodd's relationship with musical modernism might be said to shadow aspects of Korngold's own aesthetic outlook, albeit vastly simplified and caricatured—something that would also happen later with *Deception*.[14] Dodd, it seems, struggles with his desire to compose in a modernist fashion—here represented by the word "dissonance"—and yet it is a style that his audiences unequivocally reject. Ironically, the only character who seems to like the "inauthentically" modernist Dodd is his wife, Florence—who we are meant to see as the

---

[10]   WBA, 996–1006A "THE CONSTANT NYMPH," 1121A.

[11]   In Act I scene 1 of the play, as they are rehearsing Lewis's "little charade" for the children to act on Sanger's birthday, *Breakfast with the Borgias*, Lewis sings, "Unsay that doom, oh faithful heart! What's life to me, if she depart? When thou art dead, the birds will stop their singing, When thou art cold no sun will ever rise. No more, no more the joyful day's upspringing Shall bless these eyes. When thou art in thy grave, the flowers blowing Shall hang their heads and sicken in the grove, Beauty will fade and wither at they going, My only love." Tessa sings in reply "Ah, say not so! Another love will cheer thee, The sun will rise as bright to-morrow morn, The birds will sing, though I no longer near thee Must lie forlorn. When I am in my grave, the flowers blowing Shall make thee garlands twenty times as sweet, Beauty will live though I must sleep, unknowing, Beneath thy feet." Margaret Kennedy and Basil Dean, *The Constant Nymph: A Play in Three Acts* (London: Samuel French, 1930), 20–21. In the novel, *Breakfast with the Borgias* is described as "a one-act opera," but no text is mentioned: Margaret Kennedy, *The Constant Nymph* (London: William Heinemann, 1924), 41. On January 6, Blau stated: "Since Korngold was the one who originally claimed that 'WHEN THOU ART DEAD' was an old 17th Century song, I would appreciate your securing from him the source of his information."

[12]   Supposedly for its lack of relevance to the war. See Matthew Kennedy, *Edmund Goulding's Dark Victory: Hollywood's Genius Bad Boy* (Madison: University of Wisconsin Press, 2004), 215.

[13]   WBA, "THE CONSTANT NYMPH" Story—memos and correspondence 8/8/41–7/28/43 2 of 2

[14]   Alternatively, one might see the figure of Albert Sanger (Montagu Love), who encourages Dodd to develop his lyrical gifts as a Korngold representative. After all, his study has a poster of Korngold's *Die tote Stadt* visible. (I am grateful to Donald Greig for pointing this out to me.)

barrier between the romantic leads, Lewis and Tessa, but who ultimately comes across rather sympathetically. Florence's enthusiasm for the two-piano version of Dodd's composition (cue number 30), which she describes as "exciting" is dismissed by Tessa, who rather pompously implies that some would pretend to like the "very loud, very defiant and very aggressive" piece even if they did not understand it. Lewis is castigated by Tessa for failing to develop his melodic line, and only succeeds once he returns to a more heartfelt style of music, one of which he had "become ashamed" and hidden under "a lot of mathematics."

Korngold's own relationship with modernism—or at least those styles of modernism that became the dominant type in music histories of the twentieth century, namely Schoenbergian dodecaphony and Stravinskian neoclassicism—was certainly conflicted. One only has to look at the composer's *Vier kleine Karikaturen*, op. 19, which had been written in 1926, to appreciate the situation. The four "caricatures" parody the leading modernists of the day (in order Schoenberg, Stravinsky, Bartók, and Hindemith), and while they might simply be appreciated as witty, there is nonetheless a barbed component to the humor.[15] By the time of *The Constant Nymph*, though, he was on friendly enough terms with Arnold Schoenberg and Igor Stravinsky in their shared Californian exile, and was even eventually on good terms with Adorno.[16] The arch modernist critic sent Korngold a copy of his newly published *Philosophy of New Music* in 1953 signing it "with friendliest regards" ("mit den freudlichsten Empfehlungen"),[17] a form of greeting he used in letters to his sociologist colleague and friend René König.[18] In Chapter 5 I explored the way in which *Kings Row* might appear to "other" the characteristics of musical modernism as nonnormative, and for *The Constant Nymph* Korngold writes music designed to be perceived as unattractively modern and dissonant—though ironically it ends up being rather interesting, with a compelling motoric content. Despite the rather simplistic dialogue that surrounds it, in which a needlessly aggressive defense of melody is mounted and modernist music is ridiculed, what matters here I would suggest is not the style of the music per se, but rather the message the film delivers about the "authenticity" of compositional voice, an argument that is curiously persuasive.

---

[15] The pieces were first published in *Musikleben* Heft 1 (November 1931). See Winters, "Korngold's *Violanta*: Venice, Carnival, and the Masking of Identities," in *Music, Modern Culture, and the Critical Ear*, ed. Nicholas Attfield and Ben Winters (Abingdon: Routledge, 2018), 66.

[16] Although Korngold was never targeted by Adorno in the same way as Rachmaninov or Richard Strauss, possibly because he was not considered of high enough profile, nonetheless it would seem that he is partly the target of Eisler and Adorno's *Composing for the Films*.

[17] Arne Stollberg, ed., *Erich Wolfgang Korngold: Wunderkind der Moderne oder letzter Romantiker?* (Munich: Edition Text + Kritik, 2008), 8–9.

[18] René König, *Briefwechsel*, Vol. 1, ed. Mario and Oliver König (Opladen: Leske + Budrich, 2000). Adorno and König disagreed professionally, but were on friendly terms. See Stefan Müller-Doohm, *Adorno: A Biography* (Cambridge: Polity Press, 2005), 338–339.

The film's narrative begins with Dodd reflecting on the failure of his symphony to win over the London critics. Dodd assumes it is because he is a modernist (and is so identified by the paper) and because his music contains "uncomfortable dissonances" and "tonal mechanics"; yet, Dodd is lambasted by fellow composer Albert Sanger not because he tries to be a modernist but because he denies his true musical identity in the hope of obtaining success.[19] His "nice, sugar candy" that he writes for the children, Sanger identifies as his "real" compositional voice. "That is me?" Dodd asks incredulously. "That is you," Sanger replies. Dodd is assuredly not Korngold, but despite the somewhat simplified aesthetics on display in the Hollywood dialogue, there is nonetheless arguably something relevant in Dodd's eventual embracing of a musical style of which he—undoubtedly conditioned by the critical frame of modernism—was otherwise dismissive. Korngold's music in the form of the tone poem *Tomorrow* represents that derided musical style, albeit in a way that is perhaps slightly exaggerated. Yet, it was close enough to Korngold's own compositional voice for him to accept publication of *Tomorrow* as a separable concert item and assign it an opus number. In other words, no matter the extent to which Korngold's aesthetics shaped the story and dialogue, it is difficult to ignore the potential parallels between the fictional and real composer. Rather than offering us a simplistic anti-modernist manifesto, what *The Constant Nymph* may highlight for us—for all its melodramatic excess—is the importance of an aesthetics of music that recognizes and accepts what we might term (not unproblematically, I admit) an "authentic" compositional voice, no matter how fashionable or otherwise that voice may be.

In addition to this aesthetic message about the value of compositional voice, the responses of Tessa to the performance of *Tomorrow* we see in the film—and her imagined engagement with its content, which I mentioned in Chapter 5— also speaks of important hermeneutic responses to music. These responses, although popular in the Viennese environment of Korngold's youth in the form of Kretzschmar's *Guides to the Concert Hall*, were increasingly under attack from a modernist aesthetic viewpoint.[20] What Korngold offers us with *Tomorrow*, though, is a richly meaningful concert work that is fully integrated with its film-score origins and whose ability to prompt interpretive (one might say "escapist") reverie of the type that Rushton advocates is actively demonstrated for watching cinematic audiences: this is music that conjures authentic and believable worlds.[21] Tessa's fantasy as she listens to Dodd's music (and which the film

---

[19] In the 1928 British film of the same name, directed by Adrian Brunel, Lewis (Ivor Novello) is the famed composer of the "Symphony in Three Keys," though his piece performed at the London concert is his new Symphony No. 2 in D minor. Very little is said about music in this version.

[20] Heinrich Kretzschmar, *Führer durch den Kozertsaal*, 3 vols. (Leipzig: Liebeskind, 1887–1890).

[21] Richard Rushton, *The Reality of Film: Theories of Filmic Reality* (Manchester: Manchester University Press, 2011).

dramatizes for us) might even be said to act as an analogue for Hollywood cinema itself and its relationship with orchestral music: Korngold's performed concert work and film score thus function interchangeably as soundtrack to these kinds of romantic scenes. As such, the film might seem to suggest to a watching audience, then, that cinematic responses might be entirely appropriate, in turn, in the concert hall; that the symphonic discourse of the concert hall might be valued alongside the products of Hollywood for its ability to create compelling worlds into which listening audiences might find solace. This is something that we can also ascribe retrospectively to Korngold's 1919 symphonic overture *Sursum Corda*, portions of which were used as part of the score for *The Adventures of Robin Hood*.[22] In this instance, *Robin Hood*'s heroic narrative provides a hermeneutic lens through which to hear the overture. Although Korngold had originally supplied a program for the work in an attempt to explain it for listeners, the film that appeared some twenty years later arguably does this job in a more direct way. This bringing together of cinematic and non-cinematic musical experiences is something that was also explored in Korngold's penultimate film for Warner Bros., *Escape Me Never*.

Escape Me Never, like *The Constant Nymph*, was centered on the composition of a musical work—the ballet *Primavera*. As with *Tomorrow*, *Primavera* would also be shown in performance (albeit only in rehearsal), and would thus require prescoring.[23] Like *The Constant Nymph*, the creative processes in play were considered appropriate for narrative exploration, and at various points composer Sebastian Dubrok (Errol Flynn) asks both his true love Gemma (Ida Lupino) and his future lover Fenella (Eleanor Parker) to listen to his whistling as he demonstrates the thematic material of the ballet and its connections with the two women. Rather as with the scene in *The Constant Nymph* discussed in Chapter 5, the quasi-mystical act of composition is shown in these films as one involving characters seemingly listening to the sound of the orchestral score, having seeded the initial idea into the film's soundworld. When Sebastian whistles the melody—a theme that had previously been intended for a song for Gemma but which is repurposed in that moment for the ballet inspired by Fenella—Fenella remarks, "Oh yes, it must be terribly exciting to do things like that, be able to create something out of the air . . . I never could." As with *The Constant Nymph*, the orchestra carry on the musical logic after a short gap (cue 6C), and the implication is that Sebastian magically listens to that which is already "in the air," namely orchestral underscore.

---

[22] For details, see Ben Winters, *Erich Wolfgang Korngold's* The Adventures of Robin Hood: *A Film Score Guide* (Lanham, MD: Scarecrow Press, 2007), 97–102.

[23] Producer Henry Blanke had written to Forbstein on September 26, 1945, informing him of the production's start date (October 15) and in noting that the film would be shot "more or less in continuity," and observed that "this is for your and Korngold's information."

218   KORNGOLD IN AMERICA

At the climax of *Escape Me Never*, though, the score also offers us something with the potential to contribute to contemporary critical responses regarding the aesthetics of Hollywood film music, at least as characterized in the newspaper criticism of the time. Gemma and Sebastian are reunited on the steps to the gallery of the concert hall at which the ballet is to receive its premiere. The music starts (cue 12E), and we may well identify it as the beginning of the ballet's overture ("they're going to start," Gemma pleads, "let me go"),[24] but we have very little indication that this music is somehow narratively distinct from score. Perhaps the only clue is that Jack Warner had asked in his cutting notes after the first preview for the volume level of music in this scene to be raised.[25] However, after the initial gesture, the music continues with material (marked "solenne" or solemn) never previously associated with the ballet, as Sebastian apologizes to Gemma and expresses sympathy over the loss of her baby, Piccolo. With its calmness and simple phrases, it works perfectly to underscore Sebastian's heartfelt statements. A solo violin then enters with the main theme of the ballet. This music, then, is apparently performed within the narrative, and yet its function is *utterly indistinguishable* from score: indeed, one could argue that it is far *more* suited to the role of underscoring dialogue than as the overture to a ballet. And thus, when Gemma announces to Sebastian "listen . . . your music" and he replies "yours, too . . . I could never have written it without you" they are clearly hearing the melody in the score. We never see any musicians, and the continuing music elides seamlessly with the ending of the film, completely abandoning its identity as the beginning of a performed ballet. This alignment of positions between the characters and watching audience is, I would suggest, enormously powerful, and it touches on wider questions of relevance to concert culture. Thus, this blurring of identities between music that is to be listened to as accompaniment to an on-stage ballet—something that although not the presumed autonomous music of the concert hall nonetheless approaches it—and music that is to accompany and shape the narrative space of a film's characters suggests that Korngold's music here might be read as questioning assumptions about "structuralist" or modernist attitudes to concert listening. As such, it appears to suggest that the reverie-like listening experiences that we might deem appropriate in a Hollywood film can also be actively embraced in the concert hall or opera house rather than shame-facedly disavowed. Simultaneously, though, it also draws attention to contemporary film aesthetics, wherein the noticeability of music in film prompted a good deal of debate.

---

[24] Korngold's short score for this cue is labeled "recommendation Overture," but this is likely connected with a proposed version of the film that would contain extra "theatrical" music suitable for a lavish premiere.

[25] Dated April 12, 1946, WBA, "ESCAPE ME NEVER" STORY-MEMOS & CORRESPONDENCE 1 OF 3 1/3/46–7/12/46, 1885B.

The idea that music should not be consciously noticed was, in fact, such a common aesthetic position that Warner Bros. composer Adolph Deutsch commented in 1946 that "'Unobtrusive' is the gold standard for a dramatic score."[26] The view was certainly advocated by *New York Times* film critic Bosley Crowther, whose article of June 21, 1945, argued, "the best test of a musical score of a film is whether the average person is conscious of it. If he's not, then it has merit. If he is—if the incidental music or atmospheric music, as it is called, comes sharply and persistently to attention—then there's something wrong with the score." For Crowther, music should remain hidden. This might be expected of a film critic for whom music was not an area of obvious expertise. Yet composer Paul Bowles, who wrote a regular column on film for the journal *Modern Music*, advocated something similar, saying, "Film-music should not be heard. The spectator should only be conscious of its presence," while Ernest Irving noted in typically snobbish fashion that "Its appeal must be eighty per cent subconscious because it has to operate on a large body of people of whom at least eighty per cent are non-musical."[27] Even Bruno David Ussher went as far as to claim in June 1938 that it was a mark of quality when music was heard but not "noticed," praising Max Steiner for practicing the "art of suggestion."[28] Ussher, though, had elsewhere criticized the idea that music should not be noticed—as indeed had Adorno and Eisler's 1947 *Composing for the Films*[29]—and his newspaper articles constantly returned to this question. Ussher was a musicologist trained by Arnold Schering and Hugo Riemann, and a frequent contributor to *The Hollywood Spectator* and *Los Angeles Daily News*, where he continually attacked what he saw as the fallacy that good film music ought to go unnoticed, noting in 1938 that this was "nonsense" and a superstition that belonged to "the dark ages of Hollywood."[30] The following year he again suggested it was "one of the deadliest stupidities preserved among Hollywood's snap slogans."[31] Ussher's own position was not without its nuances, however. As he wrote in his weekly column for the *Los Angeles Daily News* on August 10, 1938, "Film music *should* be noticed, though, of course, it should not prove disturbing."[32] This nuanced

---

[26] Adolph Deutsch, "Three Strangers," *Hollywood Quarterly* 1, no. 2 (January 1946): 216. Similarly, Alfred Hitchcock, in comparing music and editing, noted that "just as the ideal cutting is the kind you don't notice *as* cutting, so with music." Stephen Watts, "Alfred Hitchcock on Music in Films," *Cinema Quarterly* 2, no. 2 (Winter 1933–1934): 83.

[27] Paul Bowles, "On the Film Front," *Modern Music* 18 (1940–1941): 60; Ernest Irving, "Music in Films," *Music & Letters* 24, no. 4 (October 1943): 227.

[28] "Music in Current Pictures," *Hollywood Spectator*, June 18, 1938. Reproduced in Bruno David Ussher, *Music in the Films, 1937–1941*, ed. G. D. Hamann (Hollywood: Filming Today Press, 2011), 67.

[29] Hanns Eisler and Theodor Adorno, *Composing for the Films* (London: Athlone Press, 1994).

[30] "Music," *Los Angeles Daily News*, August 10, 1938. Reproduced in Ussher, *Music in the Films*, 74.

[31] "Sounding Board," *Los Angeles Daily News*, December 7, 1939. Reproduced in Ussher, *Music in the Films*, 137.

[32] Reproduced in Ussher, *Music in the Films*, 74.

220 KORNGOLD IN AMERICA

idea of "disturbing" music, it seems, encompassed a number of deficiencies, including music that was too soft (and thus was able to rouse one's curiosity), the quotation of familiar music, and—most significantly—poor placement of music. Ussher, as a critic, commented on numerous scores of Korngold, mentioning for instance that in *The Adventures of Robin Hood* Korngold had provided "more than a background score in the conventional sense of the word, and again the music, not withstanding outer richness and true eloquence, is never obtrusive."[33] Yet it seems he had no opportunity to publish a review of *Escape Me Never* and thus did not have the chance to recognize, in the score's blurring of roles between underscore and performed music within the narrative, the ability of the film to contribute to the debate that exercised him so much—that it, like *The Constant Nymph*, not only calls into question comfortable divisions between the kind of film music considered appropriate for romanticized reveries and hermeneutic imaginings and the kinds of "autonomous" music that one encounters in the concert hall, but also challenges the aesthetics of what should be "heard" and "unheard" and what it means for music in film to be unobtrusive.

It would be tempting, again, to see *Escape Me Never*'s reflexive score, and the way in which it speaks to contemporary debates about the audibility of film music, as a route to elevating the film and its score above other Hollywood products of the time. As I have emphasized throughout this book, though, I see that temptation as something to be actively resisted. What *Escape Me Never* reveals to me is not a special case that deserves to be considered alongside proclaimed modernist examples of cinematic art that draw attention self-reflexively to the artificiality of film-scoring conventions or otherwise reveal the artifice of cinema. Instead, I want to emphasize that those reflexive aspects associated with modernist art can also be found in Hollywood films otherwise assumed to be narratively "ordinary" or "conventional" precisely as a way to dilute the legitimizing discourse of exclusion that modernism practices. *Escape Me Never* and *The Constant Nymph* are two such examples; *Deception*, Korngold's last film for Warner Bros., is a third.

Set in present-day New York, *Deception* tells the story of a gifted pianist, Christine Radcliffe (Bette Davis), who has been involved romantically with a Svengali figure, the acclaimed composer Hollenius (Claude Rains), only to discover that her former lover, the cellist Karel Novak (Paul Henreid), whom she believed dead, has survived the war and has arrived in America to resume his concert career. Christine and Karel marry, but Christine keeps her previous

---

[33] "Music in Current Pictures," *Hollywood Spectator* 13, no. 3 (May 7, 1938). Reproduced and sent to Korngold in 1939 by the *Hollywood Spectator*. LOC, Box H Folder 27. Ussher was not always totally complimentary. He criticized, for instance, the too-obvious placement of harp glissandi in *The Private Lives of Elizabeth and Essex* of which he was "too aware." See Bruno David Ussher, "Film Music and Its Makers," *Hollywood Spectator* 14, no. 13 (October 14, 1939): 11.

relationship with Hollenius from her husband out of fear of his jealousy. When Hollenius asks Karel to perform his new cello concerto, however, Christine struggles to keep her secret, and when Hollenius threatens to tell Karel the truth, she murders him on the night of the concerto's performance. The film ends with Christine confessing all to Karel, and the two facing an uncertain future. As with *Escape Me Never*, Korngold was involved in *Deception* long before scoring work was undertaken, and even before he had agreed (in writing) to author the cello concerto that features so prominently in its narrative, let alone compose the score.[34] He was also fully involved in the musical choices that would feature in the film, which include the Haydn D-major Cello Concerto performed by Karel in the opening scenes.[35] Yet, it was the centrality of his own cello concerto to the project that is significant for Korngold's career trajectory. In the same way that *Tomorrow* from *The Constant Nymph* was published as Korngold's Op. 33, so the concerto appeared as Korngold's Op. 37. Brendan Carroll has claimed that Korngold subsequently "expanded" the Cello Concerto for publication after the film's completion, and this is the typical way in which this process is described.[36] As such, use of this word might imply a rescuing of film-score material and an elevation involving a "purely autonomous" musical process. Yet, evidence suggests that the composition of the concerto may have been conceived more-or-less in its entirety alongside the film's production—that its origins as a concerto are tied more closely to the processes associated with film than Carroll would have us believe. Indeed, we might wonder whether this underplaying of the film's role in the published concerto reflects a desire to separate these two spheres of Korngold's career more distinctly than the evidence supports, in ways that deny their fundamental interrelatedness.

[34] Initial ideas for the film included using approximately two minutes from the finale of Saint-Saëns's Cello Concerto No. 1 in A minor, and, as a result, there is correspondence about trying to clear both this item (quoted at $1,000) and the Haydn D-major Cello Concerto, which had been recently "discovered" and published in an edition with a cadenza by François-August Gevaert. A letter of May 2, 1946, to Helen Schoen of the Copyright and Clearance Division in New York reports, "I [presumably Joe McLaughlin] had just been talking with Eric [*sic*] Korngold who is writing the music for DECEPTION and both he and Leo Forbstein feel that the price quoted for the use of the [Haydn] CONCERTO IN D MAJOR is a bit high." A follow-up letter of May 7, 1946, reports that "Leo and Korngold were 'weeping' so much about the price." WBA, 1417A DECEPTION 1126A.

[35] Other items recorded as prescoring included Christine's performance of the opening of Beethoven's "Appassionata" Sonata, Op. 57, and arrangements for cello and piano of Schubert's A-flat Impromptu D935 (transposed to G major), a three-bar extract from the Adagio from J. S. Bach's C major Toccata, Adagio and Fugue BWV564; Chopin's E-flat Nocturne, Op. 9 No. 2; and an original piece by Korngold now known as the *Romance-Impromptu*. Of these cello and piano pieces, only the Schubert and Bach were used, however, as recordings from the record library to which Hollenius listens. A set of undated music notes reveals the prominent role the Music Department would need to play in the film (WBA, "DECEPTION" MUSIC 1053). At this point, Bette Davis's character Christine is still known as Stella, as she was in the early drafts of the film's script. She did not become "Christine" until April 27, 1946, so the music notes most likely predate this point.

[36] Brendan Carroll suggests it was expanded into an eleven-minute work from the six minutes we hear in the film. *The Last Prodigy: A Biography of Erich Wolfgang Korngold* (Portland, OR: Amadeus Press, 1997), 326.

222 KORNGOLD IN AMERICA

Certainly, the full-score manuscript of the concerto, orchestrated by Simon Bucharoff, contains the concerto extract we hear in the rehearsal scene, and which is skipped over in the concert performance at the end of the film, in its "correct" place. This would appear to indicate that the overall structure of the work was clear during work on the film rather than being conceptualized as separate cues that were later stitched together as part of an expansion process. In addition, more of the published concerto survives in the manuscript materials at Warner Bros. Archives and the Library of Congress than appears in the film: bars of the concerto that feature in the published concerto, but are not heard in the film, are nonetheless extant in these sources.[37] Importantly, too, the Bucharoff score seems incomplete. The *Allegro moderato* section (Reh. Fig. 39 in the published version) is preceded by pasted-in pages, and the four bars following the cadenza have been pasted over to match what is heard in the film: a piano-conductor score, however, shows these bars were present, and they subsequently appear in the published concerto. This suggests that the published concerto more closely matches sources produced contemporaneously with the film than the version actually heard in *Deception*.

Admittedly, substantial differences still exist between this Bucharoff score and the published Op. 37. One of the most obvious, at first glance, is the very opening of the concerto, which is a bar longer in the published version than the performed version we hear in concert at the end of the film. Yet, even that longer version existed prior to filming, as the Korngold manuscript visible in the film and sitting on Hollenius's piano reveals (Figure 6.1). Indeed, this manuscript appears to be Korngold's original short score that has subsequently been adapted as a prop (the addition, in Korngold's hand of "Cello Concerto" and "Alex Hollenius, op. 6" has clearly been added later).[38] This extended version of the concerto's opening is even "performed" by Hollenius on the piano for Karel. It would seem plausible, then, that the concerto was conceived more or less as a complete work prior to filming and simply split up for filmic presentation rather than a fragmented work that was subsequently expanded for publication. Nonetheless, Bucharoff's orchestration differs from Korngold's published version, which suggests at the very least that Korngold revised Bucharoff's orchestration prior to publication. It is even possible that the composer prepared his own orchestrated version prior to filming, which then formed the basis of the concerto. Such a scenario is certainly suggested by what is obviously a real score of the concerto shown in the film on

---

[37] For instance, seven bars between Reh. Figs. 10 and 12 in the published version that are not heard in the film are nonetheless present in the copyist's short score held in Box 5 Folder 2 of the Korngold Collection. That said, multiple versions of the concerto are implied in the film. The "ending" of the concerto played by Hollenius on the piano (Cue 4C) differs from the ending heard as performed in the concert at the end of the film, and the published version.

[38] This cue is missing from the short score held in LOC, Box 5 Folder 2.

Figure 6.1 Korngold's short-score manuscript in *Deception*.

Einar Nilson's stand during the performance, a manuscript source that is seemingly no longer extant. Magically, the score's pages turn rapidly, and unaided, to suggest a musical edit. This "prop" score is certainly different from Bucharoff's full score held in Warner Bros. Archives, and which contains the usual musical shorthand indications to save on copying.[39] It is also a different source to the manuscript that formed the basis for the published version of the concerto, and which is held in the Korngold Collection.[40] A comparison of this prop score, were it ever located, with the final published version of the concerto could reveal further evidence to corroborate the theory that Korngold composed a more complete cello concerto and then worked out how to incorporate elements of it into the rehearsal scene and concert performance scenes in the film. If so, it would seem to indicate that he merely revised it for publication as Op. 37 rather than undertaking the "expansion" usually claimed. Indeed, that desire to disconnect as far as possible the process of composing the post-Hollywood concert works

---

[39] The prop score includes the word "Fugato," an indication that does not exist in the published concerto. The scenes in Carnegie Hall featuring the concerto were shot on Stage 2 at Warner's Burbank Studios in August 1946.

[40] LOC, Box 28 Folder 1. This is written on manuscript paper bearing the legend "PROPERTY OF SELZNICK INTERNATIONAL PICTURES, INC. AND/OR PIONEER PICTURES, INC.—No. 126-B—1M—4-37—K-I Co."

224 KORNGOLD IN AMERICA

from the production practices associated with the films—even with a concert work that has palpably undeniable filmic origins—might reflect an unconscious desire to emphasize the autonomy of concert-hall composition. An "expansion" that happened in a post-Hollywood sphere, rather than a "revision" of something that was essentially complete, suggests an "elevation" or, at least, a more complex "purely musical" process that normalized or legitimized a Hollywood product.[41] Examining the sources, though, has painted a more complex picture than such a statement would suggest.

Deception, then, was a film that was self-consciously about music and musicians, and even more than with *The Constant Nymph* and *Escape Me Never* required Korngold to re-engage with his experiences as a composer for the concert hall—a process he had already begun by starting a Third String Quartet, the sketches for which he had bound and presented to Luzi as a gift for Christmas 1944.[42] Indeed, it is also significant that there is much less scoring present in *Deception*, with Korngold's attention much more obviously on the onscreen performance items. As with *The Constant Nymph* and *Escape Me Never*, though, *Deception* also blurs lines between score and performed concert item in ways that reflect on the connections between Hollywood scoring practices and concert-hall culture. This was clearly on the composer's mind at the time. In a newspaper interview to promote *Deception*, Korngold had apparently stated:

> "Although I wrote very little music for 'Deception' I think it's more important than all the movie music I've ever written. For the picture I wrote an original cello concerto which is heard for seven minutes. I consider this score a bridge from movie to concert music" ... "Every number in an important production can be played in a concert," he declared. "Fine symphonic scores for motion pictures cannot help but influence mass acceptance of finer music."[43]

The concerto is presented primarily in the narrative as witnessed "performance"—in other words, we see many more musicians onscreen performing than in either *The Constant Nymph* or *Escape Me Never*—but nonetheless it too functions in ways that can also be considered unmistakably "filmic."

---

[41] Robbert van der Lek even concludes his study of the re-use of film-score material in the concert works by referring to it as "rehabilitation music." See "Concert Music as Reused Film Music: E.-W. Korngold's Self-Arrangements," trans. Mick Swithinbank, *Acta Musicologica* 66, fasc. 2 (July–December 1994): 102.

[42] LOC, Box 13 Folder 7. The bound sketches bear the inscription "Für Lucherl, Weihnachten 1944."

[43] Hy Hollinger, "'Deception' Score Turning Point in Composer's Career," *The New York Morning Telegraph*, October 23, 1946.

Korngold weaves parts of the concerto into the score, of course.[44] However, it also "underscores" Christine's entrance to the concert hall after her murder of Hollenius. She takes her seat (exchanging a glance with Karel as he performs) to a moment of structural importance in the concerto, namely its G-major second subject, which is also entirely appropriate as a love theme for the pair. Moreover, this is music that also carries intertextual connections with the promise of future happiness represented by the "Heaven" theme from *Between Two Worlds*, several bars of which it shares.

When compared with *The Constant Nymph* and *Escape Me Never*, however, *Deception* is noteworthy in also using the music of others to demonstrate this fundamental blurring of roles between performed concert music and film scoring. Of particular significance was the choice made for scene 17, in which Karel and Christine are reunited backstage after Karel's performance of the Haydn D-major Concerto. As I explored in *Music, Performance, and the Realities of Film*, this used an "unseen" performance of the opening Schubert's Symphony No. 8 "arranged" by Korngold. This is quite simply one of the most effective pieces of scoring in the film, with Karel and Christine's actions seemingly dictated as much by the inherent drama and narrative contained in Schubert's music as in the script.[45] Unfortunately, no manuscript materials or cue timing sheets for this cue survive, nor does any communication relating to its selection and arrangement, though given Korngold's involvement with the musical choices throughout pre-production, it seems inconceivable that he would not have played a prominent role in the preparation of the extract. The arrangement is, at least, credited to him on the film's copyright cue sheet. Here, as with the extracts from Beethoven's Symphony No. 7 and the "Egmont" Overture heard later in the film, Korngold is actively demonstrating the ways in which his scoring practices—and those of others working in the industry—are at least partially rooted in concert-hall repertoire. The music practices of "silent" cinema[46] had done something similar, of course, and it is sometimes easy to forget that a film like *Deception* is only separated by twenty years from those days in which approaches to scoring

---

[44] The scene in which Christine picks out notes from the Concerto on the piano to accompany the unseen orchestra also blurs the concerto's dual role as concert item and score in similar ways to those found in *The Constant Nymph* or *Escape Me Never*. Likewise, the scene in which the Concerto is rehearsed plays on the intertextual connection with another Bette Davis character. The camera shows us a medium shot of Christine while we hear music (heard at Reh. Fig. 27 in the published concerto) associated with the Queen's sorrow from *The Private Lives of Elizabeth and Essex*, a film in which Bette Davis played the Queen. In that sense, we have "performed" music simultaneously occupying the role of underscoring Christine's emotions via a complex intertextual connection with another Korngold-scored film.

[45] Winters, *Music, Performance, and the Realities of Film*, 161–163.

[46] Gillian B. Anderson has long argued that the term "mute" cinema is far more appropriate. See "The Shock of the Old: The Restoration, Reconstruction, or Creation of 'Mute'-Film Accompaniments," in *The Routledge Companion to Screen Music and Sound*, ed. Ronald Sadoff, Miguel Mera, and Ben Winters (New York: Routledge, 2017), 201.

films in large metropolitan centers used classical favorites in just the way that *Deception* does. Moreover, as I have demonstrated elsewhere, Korngold's film scores were not the only contemporary films of this period to draw attention to the ongoing and fertile connections between Hollywood film narrative and classical concert or operatic culture. Indeed, something similar happens in Billy Wilder's 1944 film *Double Indemnity*, where another performance of Schubert's Symphony No. 8 is used to underscore a key scene.[47] Nonetheless, the functional equivalence in the music created or arranged for these three films for Warner Bros. reveals that Korngold's thoughts had already turned back toward his concert-hall and stage career. Added to this, the approaching end of the war in Europe and—in particular—the death of his music critic father in September 1945 created the conditions in which this transition to the last phase of his compositional career could take place. What is striking, though, is the sense of continuity between his film-scoring career and these final works for the concert hall.

A Return to the Concert Hall

If *The Constant Nymph* and the last two Warner Bros. films were showing increasing evidence of the close relationship between concert-hall culture and film scoring, this was also the case with the concert works Korngold was writing. The new string quartet made use of film themes in three out of its four movements, with only the opening *Allegro moderato* lacking any identifiable film content. Indeed, this opening movement might have been written in Korngold's Viennese youth, such is its initial modernist sparseness. Its chromaticism, though, is also very much in line with *Deception*'s cello concerto that would follow in 1946, as is the spiky music of the scherzo, which carries on the lineage of the *Groteske* of the Op. 23 Suite of 1928–1930. The Trio of the Scherzo, however, is entirely different. After a nine-bar transition, the harmonic world shifts suddenly to diatonic E major, and Korngold presents us with a version of Bunny's theme from *Between Two Worlds*, the score of which he had written largely between December 1943 and March 1944. Bunny (the nickname of the Rev. William Duke) is a kindly figure, but importantly is someone who yearns for a new start: indeed, the section of the score this extract from the Third String Quartet most clearly resembles is Bunny's speech to the others at dinner (cue 4C) where he speaks about wanting "to go out into the world at last . . . get away from books and dust. So, you see, everything about this trip

---

[47] Winters, *Music, Performance, and the Realities of Film*, 165–170. Certainly, too, the ability of Wagner's music to underscore cinematic drama is demonstrated in Korngold's final film project, *Magic Fire*. See my article "*Magic Fire*: A Wagner Film with a Difference," *The Wagner Journal* 15, no. 3 (November 2021): 11–22.

is adventure. It's all so exciting. In reality, it's a brand new beginning for me." The music is, admittedly, metrically transformed in its new string-quartet guise, but harmonically it is practically identical (albeit with some slightly different chromatic voice leading) with the same temporary tonicization of a chromatic mediant before returning to the original tonic. It remains entirely identifiable as film-score material with no attempt made to hide its origins or to transform it whatsoever; indeed, it is stylistically rather distinct from the scherzo material that surrounds it. As a result, this might be seen as an announcement by Korngold of his "new beginning": as a deliberate attempt to reconcile the two parts of his career.

The third and fourth movements are even more dependent on film-score content. The third is built around material from *The Sea Wolf* (1941), namely cue 6C, which is described in the film's cue lists as a "Love Scene." It is the scene in which Ruth (Ida Lupino) and Leach (John Garfield) listen to the offscreen "song" played on the harmonica by an unseen character in memory of Louis, the ship's surgeon who (tormented by Larson) had killed himself. Cue 6C includes the description "like a sad folk song" and the description "like a folk song" is reproduced in the published Quartet, which transposes the melody from B♭ minor to E♭ minor. Again, the material is instantly recognizable, though Korngold has made a couple of rhythmic and metrical changes. He misses out some of the repetitions of 6C, and at Reh. Fig. 43 in the Quartet incorporates thematic material associated with Leach heard later in the same cue, before combining the two thematic areas contrapuntally at Reh. Fig. 47 in ways that do not happen in the film. At Reh. Fig. 54, Korngold introduces Ruth's theme, which is also heard towards the end of 6C, before returning to the opening material. That the movement is based entirely on music from *The Sea Wolf*, though and, largely on one particular cue, is patently obvious to anyone who knows the film. Whereas the third movement drew the entirety of its thematic material from *The Sea Wolf*, the finale took a number of themes from *Devotion*, the Brontë biopic on which Korngold had worked from 1942 to 1943. The finale's opening gesture (recapitulated in varied form at Reh. Fig. 80) is related to the theme associated in the film with the house that inspires Emily's novel *Wuthering Heights*. Unlike the *Sea Wolf* references, though, its origins are rather difficult to detect. The jaunty F-major viola theme at Reh. Fig. 67, in contrast, is instantly recognizable despite a markedly different kind of instrumentation as Miss Branwell's theme (heard prominently in cue 1B of *Devotion* on the oboe and in cue 3D on celesta with glissandi violin harmonics and pizzicato). Likewise, the theme heard at Reh. Fig. 76 (again first on the viola) is a version of Charlotte Brontë's pentatonic theme (see Example 3.13c). As such, it is almost impossible not to recall the atmosphere of *Devotion*'s nineteenth-century narrative when listening to the movement.

228   KORNGOLD IN AMERICA

The pattern established by the Third String Quartet of reusing film themes, sometimes varied slightly, but nearly always entirely recognizable in their new contexts, was one Korngold was to repeat in all his subsequent concert music. Even his final stage work, *Die stumme Serenade*, makes limited use of film-score material: two numbers present Mons. Heger's theme from *Devotion* (originally intended for *Another Dawn*—see Example 3.1) followed by the schoolgirl music from *Escape Me Never* (heard in cue 1D). Table 6.1 lists Korngold's post-1944 output of published music and the films from which they drew material. The material's origins would have been obvious to any listener familiar with Korngold's film scores, and yet previous commentators—perhaps embarrassed about these mass-culture links—have been rather keen to disavow such connections. In the same way that his comments about the Cello Concerto emphasize its distinctiveness from *Deception*, Carroll suggests somewhat defensively in connection with the third movement of the Symphony that "Korngold's use of these themes is entirely different [from their use in the films], however, and they are transformed into a cohesive symphonic whole."[48] Likewise, in his 2000 preface to the Eulenberg score of the Symphony, Helmut Pöllmann is at even greater pains to distance the work from its filmic associations. He plays down the connections (identifying only the *Elizabeth and Essex* theme in the *Adagio* and the *Kings Row* theme in the finale) and then patently explains them away as of little relevance to their new context:

> Although the matter is sometimes presented differently, this fact does not imply any reference to the films in question. Furthermore, it is in most cases merely a question of the basic shape of a musical subject, which is then treated in a completely new way in a completely different context.[49]

This is, in part, to support a narrative where the films are merely a necessary evil for Pöllmann—that Korngold "did not freely choose this activity at all but was forced into it by the pressures of his life in exile."[50] Given that Korngold contributed to nine out of the twenty films he was involved with before the *Anschluss* even occurred, this seems somewhat disingenuous. Yet, it is undeniably an indication of the cultural suspicion with which many commentators have viewed the film scores.

Reading these concert works in a way that ignores the filmic origin of their material, though, seems an exercise in intertextual futility. I have

---

[48]   Carroll, *The Last Prodigy*, 347–348.

[49]   Helmut Pöllmann, trans. David Jenkinson, "Preface," in *Korngold, Symphony in F Sharp*, Edition Eulenburg No. 8048 (London: Ernst Eulenburg, Ltd, 2000), vi.

[50]   Ibid., iv. I detail other instances of this kind of rhetoric about Korngold's re-use of film themes in *Music, Performance, and the Realities of Film*, 129–130.

Table 6.1 Korngold's published output and its principal filmic connections, 1937–1953

Year	Work	Film
1932–1937	*Die Kathrin*, Op. 28	-
1937	*Narrenlieder*, Op. 29	"O Mistress Mine": *The Private Lives of Elizabeth and Essex* (Penelope's song [postdates])
1941	*Passover Psalm*, Op. 30	Opening: *The Sea Wolf*, cue 11D Reh. Fig. 19: *The Prince and the Pauper* (Tom's theme)
1937–1941	*Vier Shakespeare-Lieder*, Op. 31	-
1941	*Prayer*, Op. 32	-
1942	*Tomorrow*, Op. 33	*The Constant Nymph*
1944–1945	String Quartet No. 3, Op. 34	2nd movement: *Between Two Worlds* (Bunny's theme) 3rd movement: *The Sea Wolf* (Harmonica song, Leach's theme, Ruth's theme) 4th movement: *Devotion* (Miss Branwell's theme, Charlotte's theme)
1945	Violin Concerto, Op. 35	1st movement: *Another Dawn* (love theme), *Juarez* (love theme) 2nd movement: *Anthony Adverse* (love theme) 3rd movement: *The Prince and the Pauper* (Edward's theme, continuation)
1946–1950	*Die stumme Serenade*, Op. 36ª	No. 18 "Auftritt der Richter" and No. 26 "Marsch und Revolution": *Devotion* (Mons. Heger's theme), *Escape Me Never* (Schoolgirls)
1946	Cello Concerto, Op. 37	*Deception*
1948	Fünf Lieder, Op. 38	"Glückwünsch": *Devotion* ("sisters" theme) "Der Kranke": *Juarez* (cue 3A) "Alt-spanisch": *The Sea Hawk* (Dona Maria's song)
1947–1948	Symphonic Serenade, Op. 39	3rd movement (first at Reh. Fig. 71): *Anthony Adverse* (Brother Francois's theme) 4th movement (first at Reh. Fig. 95): *Captain Blood* (love theme)

(continued)

230 KORNGOLD IN AMERICA

Table 6.1 Continued

Year	Work	Film
1947–1952	Symphony in F sharp, Op. 40[b]	2nd movement (Reh. Fig. 48): *Juarez* (cue 44—cut from film)[c] 3rd movement: *The Private Lives of Elizabeth and Essex* (Essex's theme); *Captain Blood* (Blood's theme) *Anthony Adverse* (Rain theme) 4th movement: *Kings Row* (Grandmother's theme)
1953	*Sonnett für Wien,* Op. 41	*Escape Me Never* (Primavera theme)
1953	Theme and Variations for Orchestra, Op. 42	*The Adventures of Robin Hood* (variation of "March of the Merry Men" heard in cue 10E)

[a] I have only included the most obvious connections in this table. There are other allusions to film-score material, though, including Reh. Fig. 7 in No. 25 "Schönste Nacht," which alludes strongly to a phrase in the opening titles of *The Private Lives of Elizabeth and Essex* (cue 1A, Reh. Fig. 3), though it is recast as a waltz.

[b] Other strong allusions to film-score material include: the beginning of the Trio from the Second Movement, which appears to allude to cue 11B in *Deception*, where Christine confesses to Karel (a moment that Peter Franklin suggests is "explicit quotation" in *Reclaiming Late-Romantic Music: Singing Devils and Distant Sounds* [Berkeley and Los Angeles: University of California Press, 2014], 124); Reh. Fig. 93-2 in the *Adagio*, which appears to reference briefly the fog ostinato from *The Sea Wolf*; or, indeed, Reh. Fig. 95-3, which seems to invoke a motif from *Captain Blood* and *The Sea Hawk* associated with despair.

[c] This was first identified by van der Lek. See "Concert Music as Reused Film Music," 99. Consulting Korngold's short score for cue no. 44/10C (LOC, Box 8 Folder 4) confirms this. The initial part of the cue was designed to accompany Captain Lopez riding (presumably to Maximilian and Carlota with the news that Uradi had turned against Juarez), but that scene itself was cut, likely as part of the large-scale cuts made in April 1939. The theme heard in the Symphony, however, is marked "molto moderato" and likely covered the scene following. There were cuts (both of music in surviving scenes, and of entire scenes) in this section of the film, though, so it is difficult to reconstruct the original purpose of this music.

previously suggested how we might read the Symphony through its filmic associations, commenting on its invocation of the conflict narratives of the Errol Flynn swashbucklers from which it draws some of its material,[51] despite the composer's own conflicted attitudes to such questions. Thus, Korngold claimed that the Symphony was a work of "pure, absolute music with no program whatsoever," yet simultaneously set out possible connections with the horrors of the war years in the first movement, and with the sufferings of the victims in the third.[52] Similarly, Peter Franklin has pointed to the ways in

[51] Winters, *Music, Performance, and the Realities of Film*, 131–133.
[52] Ibid., 129.

which the Symphony's references to film scores offers us "tantalizing herme-neutic challenges, precisely because they seem so deliberate and so nearly and strikingly coherent."[53] As a consequence, he reads the *Adagio* as participating in a complex gendered discourse that points to the flaws in the composite pa-triarchal heroes found in many of the films that Korngold scored.[54] It would seem patently absurd to attempt to deny the narrative connections such re-use of material implies—an act born of modernist anxiety, perhaps. And although Korngold, himself, was arguably complicit in this compulsion to sever the link between his film scores and concert works, the nature of what his music ac-tually does seems undeniable. Stated boldly, it brings the concert hall and the movie theatre together in provocative ways that challenges the hegemony of modernist discourse. Yet, I do not want to succumb to that same modernist anxiety of which I have spoken in previous chapters by claiming that this is the only reason to value them—that the worth of these works lies only in the way in which Korngold might be said to radically challenge the content of a con-cert genre like the symphony or string quartet.[55] Instead, I want to suggest that these concert works reveal the ways in which Korngold was true to his own artistic path, one that he followed all the way to Hollywood and back. As such, just as Lewis Dodd is shown his true compositional voice in *The Constant Nymph*, even as he recognizes the danger it poses to his critical reputation, so might the process of writing Korngold's post-Hollywood concert works dem-onstrate to the composer the validity of his chosen compositional path—one that combined works for the opera house and concert hall with music for film. That Korngold continued to wrestle with the implications of this path in his written statements concerning the content of the Symphony is surely an indi-cation of the strength of prevailing views of mass culture (and, potentially, a reflection of the critical position he inherited from his father). Yet, ultimately, as I will argue in Chapter 7, Korngold found an acceptance of the truth of his own compositional voice and was able to articulate it in robust terms that de-serve to be taken seriously.

This "new" approach to composing concert works was also a logical extension of the recycling practices that Korngold had used at Warner Bros., as discussed in Chapter 3. The example of the Cello Concerto not only set a precedent for con-necting film-score material and a concert-hall work but itself also contains the-matic material from previous films: after all, the concerto presents the Queen's sorrow theme from *The Private Lives of Elizabeth and Essex* and incorporated part of the Heaven theme from *Between Two Worlds*. As such, it demonstrated

---

[53] Franklin, *Reclaiming Late-Romantic Music*, 123.

[54] Ibid., 122–127.

[55] Admittedly, I have previously claimed this in my chapter "Korngold's *Violanta*," 69, and am thus guilty of that very same modernist anxiety.

232 KORNGOLD IN AMERICA

how Korngold could repurpose film themes successfully within works destined for the concert hall. Yet, in addition to this kind of compositional recycling—which might be thought analogous to Hollywood's habit of reusing sets, props, and costumes—Korngold also had a history of repurposing material long before his move to America. Often, as noted in Chapter 3, he would create songs in a number of versions, or incorporate instrumental versions of songs in his chamber output.[56] Notable examples include: an arrangement of the song "Was Du mir bist" (from Op. 22) as the fourth movement of the Op. 23 Suite for piano left hand and strings; the use of the song "Schneeglöckchen" as the basis for a movement of the Violin Sonata, Op. 6; and the use of *Vier Lieder des Abschieds* as the basis for a set of variations that form the Adagio of the Piano Quintet.[57] The practice is, in fact, so pervasive in Korngold's late output of works for the concert hall that it re-emerges as a distinct creative signature and, moreover, one that crosses the otherwise distinct realms of the concert hall/opera house and movie theatre. Other composers have admittedly dabbled in something similar, and some like Bernard Herrmann have also pursued this course more assiduously.[58] As David Cooper has detailed, for instance, there is a certain overlap in compositional material between Herrmann's opera *Wuthering Heights* (1943–1951) and his score to *The Ghost and Mrs Muir* (1947).[59] Perhaps the best-known case is Vaughan Williams's *Sinfonia Antartica*, and Daniel Grimley details the ways in which *Sinfonia Antartica* may have developed in parallel with the film score with which it shares much of its material, *Scott of the Antarctic* (1948).[60] But, with the exception of various concert suites from film scores and a song cycle that reuses material from the short film *The Vision of William Blake*, this is an isolated example of cinematic reuse in Vaughan Williams's concert-hall output. Moreover, unlike Vaughan Williams's Symphony, or indeed Miklós Rózsa's *Spellbound Concerto*, both of which carry the name of the film score whose material they share, most of the reuses of Korngold's film-score material can be found in concert works that have no such obvious "named" connections with film

---

[56] An example of the process going the other way was the use of the opening violin ascent heard in the Intermezzo of the String Sextet (1914) to open the unpublished song "Die Gansleber im Haus Duschnitz," which Brendan Carroll notes was written in honor of a goose-liver paté enjoyed at the house of a family friend in 1919. See Carroll, *The Last Prodigy*, 133.

[57] This movement is largely drawn from "Mond, so gehst du wieder auf," though "Sterbelied" also makes an appearance played by the cello at the end of the fifth variation.

[58] William Wrobel details Herrmann's self-borrowings across multiple musical spheres (radio, television, feature film, and the concert hall) in "Self-Borrowing in the Music of Bernard Herrmann," *The Journal of Film Music* 1, nos. 2–3 (Fall–Winter 2003): 249–271. He shows how, for instance, Herrmann's *Sinfonietta for Strings* (1935) provided material for five cues in *Psycho* (dir. Alfred Hitchcock, 1960). I am grateful to the book's anonymous reviewer for reminding me of this.

[59] David Cooper, *Bernard Herrmann's* The Ghost and Mrs Muir: *A Film Score Guide* (Lanham, MD: Scarecrow Press, 2005).

[60] Daniel M. Grimley, "Music, Ice, and the 'Geometry of Fear': The Landscapes of Vaughan Williams's *Sinfonia Antartica*," *The Musical Quarterly* 91, nos. 1–2 (Spring–Summer 2008): 116–150.

projects.[61] As a result, the reconceptualization and juxtaposition of film-music material apparent in works like the Symphony, the Third String Quartet, and the Violin Concerto is, I would suggest, fundamentally different.[62]

***

Taken together, the films discussed in this chapter alongside the direction Korngold took with his new concert works suggest a reconciling of two areas of musical culture that modernism has, in some senses, sought (unsuccessfully) to keep far apart: the techniques of mass culture film and the genres and language of the concert hall and, to a lesser extent perhaps, the opera house and its ballet culture. Indeed, Korngold was to continue to explore this dialogue between these two worlds in his last film project, *Magic Fire*, a film that actively dramatized the potential for opera and concert music alike to serve as score. For instance, in a romantic scene between Wagner (Alan Badel) and his new young wife, Cosima (Rita Gam), set at the composer's villa Tribschen on the shore of Lake Lucerne, we glimpse a figure in the window crossing the frame as the couple embrace. Cosima spots him and announces: "It's Father." This important moment in which the arrival of Franz Liszt (Carlos Thompson) threatens Wagnerian domestic bliss is aligned by Korngold with a moment of intensification and interruption in the *Siegfried Idyll* that Korngold uses to accompany the scene—see Example 6.1. As Liszt raps on the door, the rhythm is echoed in the wind triplets we hear. In other words, Korngold astutely recognizes the potential for a piece of Wagnerian concert music (admittedly one derived from his music drama *Siegfried*) to function perfectly as a piece of Classical Hollywood scoring.

Undoubtedly, Korngold is not revealing anything about Wagner that modernist critics such as Adorno, who looked on Wagner's music dramas with some suspicion for precisely these proto-cinematic qualities, had not already highlighted.[63] In that sense, he is not resolving the tension that exists between modernism and mass culture; but what his music does consistently in both the film scores and the post-Hollywood concert works is to unselfconsciously dramatize this tension, to enact it in a way that challenges and even transcends the exclusionary

---

[61] Copland, admittedly, drew upon his score for *Something Wild* (dir. Jack Garfein, 1961) when composing his *Music for a Great City* in an example that might provide the closest example to Korngold's practice. Perhaps as we might expect, though, Copland claimed that "No attempt has been made . . . to follow the cinematic action of *Something Wild.*" See *Aaron Copland. A Reader: Selected Writings, 1923–1972*, edited with an introduction by Richard Kostelanetz (New York: Routledge, 2004), 277. Again, I am grateful to the book's anonymous reviewer for drawing my attention to this Copland example.

[62] Rózsa also arranged concert suites from his film scores. In general, however, he kept the two aspects of his "double life" separate. Indeed, this seems to have been important to him; he commented that "I spent the winters in Hollywood and the summers in Italy . . . for my non-cinematographic music I need the geographical change . . . I have never written any film music [in Italy] and can keep the two halves of my Double Life separate." *Double Life: The Autobiography of Miklós Rózsa* (Tunbridge Wells: The Baton Press, 1984), 191.

[63] T. W. Adorno, *In Search of Wagner*, trans. Rodney Livingstone (London: NLB, 1981).

234 KORNGOLD IN AMERICA

Example 6.1 Wagner's *Siegfried Idyll* in *Magic Fire.*

discourse on which modernism relies. The evidence of the music seems to indicate that it matters not for Korngold whether something is destined for the commercial sphere of Hollywood or the imagined rarefied world of the concert hall or opera house: in reality, of course, these distinctions are overdrawn precisely in order to serve the ideological project of modernism. Despite what he sometimes said in print, which reveals Korngold was not immune to the modernist anxiety of which I have spoken, his music appears to admit no such anxiety and freely brings these areas of cultural discourse into productive dialogue. Although commentators like Leon Botstein might characterize Korngold's post-Hollywood music as essentially nostalgic—a quality that Botstein suggests Korngold shared both with Vienna and Hollywood alike ("self-deception, misplaced nostalgia and a taste for obscuring reality and therefore the truth")—he is essentially correct in identifying the spirit of optimism that emerges from Korngold's film scores.[64] Though he notes that in the 1930s and 1940s such "seemingly naïve and simplistic hopes were radical assertions," and therefore might seem to apologize for them, it is this optimistic ambition of Korngold's music that I turn to in the last chapter in the process of reflecting on the legacy of his cinematic output.[65]

---

[64] Leon Botstein, "Before and After Auschwitz: Korngold and the Art and Politics of the Twentieth Century," in *Korngold and His World*, ed. Daniel Goldmark and Kevin C. Karnes (Princeton: Princeton University Press, 2018), 290.

[65] Ibid., 302.

7

Korngold's Hollywood Legacy

The Purer Realm of Phantasy

I, myself, do not believe in the mistaken thesis that art should mirror its time. The horrors of the Napoleonic war years are hardly recognizable in the compositions of Schubert or Beethoven; the beginning of the industrial-mechanical age, which surely had its roots in the invention of the steam driven locomotive, is mirrored in no way in the poetic works of Chopin, and still less in the music dramas of Richard Wagner, derived as they are from German legend. No, I am much more inclined to believe the opposite: the genuine artist creates at a distance from his own time, even for a time beyond. The true creative artist does not wish to re-create for his fellow man the headlines screaming of atom bombs, murder, and sensationalism found in the daily paper. Rather for his fellow men, he will know how to take and uplift him into the purer realm of phantasy.[1]

In October 1955, Korngold was asked to write an introduction, from which the above quotation is taken, to Ulric Devaré's book *Faith in Music*. First published in 1958, the year after the composer's death, it stands as a self-penned epitaph that not only outlines Korngold's positive aesthetics of music but also might be read as articulating the disappointment he felt in the latter years of his career, when his new concert works were not the unqualified success for which he had hoped. Significantly, it was also written not long after the release of Korngold's final film assignment, *Magic Fire*, a biopic of Richard Wagner for Republic Pictures for which he had arranged the music, and that had promised to open new doors. The film had been directed by Korngold's old friend William Dieterle, and although it might be seen as a backwards step for the composer—a return to the kind of work that had brought him initially to Hollywood at the behest of Max Reinhardt in connection with *A Midsummer Night's Dream*—filming the picture on location in Europe allowed him to be present in Vienna at the first performance of his new Symphony in F Sharp in October 1954. Moreover, the filming of staged performances of Wagner's music dramas took place in German theatres and with German singers, providing Korngold with valuable opportunities to

---

[1] Erich Korngold, "Faith in Music," in *Korngold and His World*, ed. Daniel Goldmark and Kevin C. Karnes (Princeton, NJ: Princeton University Press, 2019), 258.

Korngold in America. Ben Winters, Oxford University Press. © Oxford University Press 2025.
DOI: 10.1093/9780197684818.003.0008

236   KORNGOLD IN AMERICA

reforge connections with European theatrical institutions.[2] Rudolf Hartmann, artistic director of the Bavarian State Opera, supervised the film's opera scenes and subsequently mounted a full production of Korngold's *Die tote Stadt* in 1955 with tenor Hans Hopf—who had also worked on *Magic Fire*—taking the central role of Paul. The film likewise allowed Korngold to forge a strong working relationship with Alois Melichar, who conducted most of the score owing to the composer's poor health, and who then conducted a broadcast performance of Korngold's Symphony in Graz in April 1955.[3]

Despite the recent opportunities afforded by his work on *Magic Fire* to resurrect connections with European institutions and performers, though, Korngold's sense of disappointment in contemporary music culture as expressed in October 1955 is palpable. Moreover, the idea of a post-war critical failure of Korngold's music is firmly entrenched in much of the existing literature. In the late 1990s, Andreas Giger could talk of the composer "falling into oblivion" after World War II, while Bryan Gilliam suggested that "Korngold was outdated in a progressive postwar world of concert music . . . [he] returned [to Austria] an anachronism."[4] Similarly, Brendan Carroll once wrote that "post-war Europe did not welcome the returning composer. The artistic environment was at odds with Korngold's philosophy, and the new musical trends were incompatible with his melodic, tonal style."[5] Such views are perhaps rather sweeping and might seem to perpetuate a somewhat simplistic idea of Hollywood as a sanctuary for an outmoded and long-abandoned romanticism that was no longer welcome in the rarefied world of the concert hall, so much so that when Korngold attempted to resurrect a "serious" career—to "return" from the cultural abyss Hollywood represented—it further tarnished his already questionable art credentials with the sheen of mass culture.

Undoubtedly, that perceived separation between "high art" and mass culture existed among the contemporary critical establishment, and it would be naïve to claim that Korngold's association with popular culture did not have detrimental effects on his post-war concert career. Indeed, Bryan Gilliam has argued that the

---

[2] Filming took place in Munich's Bavaria Studios beginning in August 1954 and on location at such venues as the Festspielhaus and the Markgräfliches Opernhaus, in Bayreuth, at the Großes Haus of the Hessisches Staatstheater Wiesbaden, and the Schlosstheater in Schwetzingen. See Ben Winters, "*Magic Fire*: A Wagner Film with a Difference," *The Wagner Journal* 15, no. 3 (November 2021): 11–22.

[3] Brendan Carroll, *The Last Prodigy: A Biography of Erich Wolfgang Korngold* (Portland, OR: Amadeus Press, 1997), 355.

[4] Andreas Giger, "A Matter of Principle: The Consequences for Korngold's Career," *The Journal of Musicology* 16, no. 4 (Autumn 1998): 546. Bryan Gilliam, "A Viennese Opera Composer in Hollywood: Korngold's Double Exile in America," in *Driven into Paradise: The Musical Migration from Nazi Germany to the United States*, ed. Reinhold Brinkmann and Christoph Wolff (Berkeley: University of California Press, 1999), 228.

[5] Brendan Carroll, *Erich Wolfgang Korngold: His life and Works 1897–1957* (Paisley: Wilfion Books, 1984), 13.

composer's migration into mass culture in the 1930s was far more damaging to his inclusion in the modernist narrative of music history than his retention of a tonal vocabulary.[6] Moreover, by the late 1940s it was not only Hollywood that tarnished Korngold's high-art aspirations—especially in America. He had spent time in the 1930s as an arranger and adaptor of Viennese operetta, and new English versions of *Die Fledermaus* (as *Rosalinda*) and *La belle Hélène* (as *Helen Goes to Troy*) were prepared for the American stage. Given that his new comic work *Die stumme Serenade* was also reported in 1947 to be in preparation for a Broadway production,[7] the composer must surely have been associated more in the United States with Broadway and Hollywood than Carnegie Hall or the Met. Such an alliance might have damaged the willingness of conductors or orchestral administrators to risk programming his new works. In American newspapers, after all, proclaiming something encountered in the concert hall as "movie music" was a damning critique. In reviewing Heitor Villa-Lobos's concert with the New York Philharmonic, for example, Ross Parmenter referred to the *Chôros No. 6* as "disjointed and over-inflated, with only occasional touches of wit to save it from sounding like movie music."[8] Such opinions even extended retrospectively: in a review of a performance of Mahler's Second Symphony at Carnegie Hall, for instance, Howard Taubman suggested that: "the sad truth is that it is difficult for a listener today . . . to make much of this symphony. There is enormous skill in the piece. Mahler knew how to make an orchestra sound; he knew how to make it dramatic. He had lots of musical ideas, but he was fond of overextending them. He ended by sounding, at least to some of us today, like a brilliantly resourceful writer of movie music."[9] Taubman also suggested that Strauss's *Ein Heldenleben* sounded in parts "if one dares to say so in public meeting . . . [like] super-elegant movie music,"[10] and there are numerous more references on this order in contemporary East Coast reviews.[11] These attitudes were also present on the other side of the Atlantic: a 1962 article in *The Times* commented that "one would hardly set out to consider seriously [Hollywood composers'] claims

---

[6] Gilliam, "Korngold's Double Exile in America," 223.

[7] Adapted by Denes Agay. See Louis Calta, "Musical Is Added to Schubert Agenda: Production of 'Silent Serenade' Is Planned for Its Winter Opening on Broadway," *New York Times*, September 16, 1947. The production does not seem to have occurred, however.

[8] Ross Parmenter, "Orchestra Led by Villa-Lobos: Brazilian Conducts Three of His Own Compositions in Philharmonic Concert," *New York Times*, March 29, 1957.

[9] Howard Taubman, "Ormandy Conducts Philadelphians in Mahler Work at Carnegie Hall," *New York Times*, February 25, 1953. Ironically, it could be argued that Korngold's film scores, which are often Mahlerian in language and tone, helped set the standard for what was considered the archetypal "movie music."

[10] Howard Taubman, "Renardy Soloist in Lalo Symphony: Violinist in First Appearance With Philharmonic—Berlioz and Strauss on Program," *New York Times*, October 20, 1950.

[11] Harold C. Schonberg, for instance, damns with faint praise in labeling film composers "skilful technicians who are almost as much psychologists as composers." "Records: Background Music for Films," *New York Times*, July 14, 1957.

238   KORNGOLD IN AMERICA

as creative musicians" and, in discussing film music in the concert hall, reported that some films used to feature a "tabloid "concerto" . . . which subsequently obtains some sort of shadowy light-musical currency . . . Erich Wolfgang Korngold, an ex-juvenile prodigy and one of Hollywood's most prolific film composers of the 1940s, was even, it is recorded, so delighted with the tabloid cello concerto he wrote for *Deception* that he later wrote in the missing sections to make a full-length work which enjoyed a modest success in the American concert repertoire."[12] Despite the errors (Korngold was hardly prolific in this arena when compared with Max Steiner), the disapproval for this kind of practice is plain. Composers like Steiner, Franz Waxman, and Miklós Rózsa are derided in the article as "capable craftsmen, merely, with at best an ear for a good tune or a striking orchestral sound."[13] James Wierzbicki has suggested that confusion about the Hollywood origins of Gershwin's *Second Rhapsody* had a detrimental effect on its reception history,[14] and Korngold might have found it difficult to persuade orchestras and conductors with short memories that his new orchestral works were not merely the product of a capable film composer, with all the negative associations that label carried in the 1950s.

I do not wish to deny, then, the separation between the products of high art and mass culture that existed in the critical discourse of the 1940s and 1950s. That said, I believe the post-war critical failure of Korngold's music has been somewhat overstated. And although it might have been emphasized by some commentators precisely in order to argue more convincingly for a "renaissance" of interest in the composer's music in the 1970s, the effect is to lend that modernist rejection of his style more credence and legitimacy than it may have occupied at the time. There is evidence, after all, of a warmer response to Korngold's later concert works—both from within some parts of the critical fraternity, and if their reports are to be believed, from contemporary audiences—that should not be ignored simply because it does not fit the received historiographical orthodoxy about modernism. In this chapter, then, I want to explore some of the more positive reception history of Korngold's post-Hollywood works as a partial corrective to the myth of a post-war critical failure, a myth that helps to reinscribe entrenched ideological positions about the value of Korngold's music that may not stand up to scrutiny. I then want to return to the role of Hollywood in Korngold's career and address the place of both Korngold and Hollywood in twentieth-century music history. As such, the optimism that Korngold recognized in his music, and highlighted in his introduction to *Faith in Music*, emerges as his legacy.

---

[12] "Music that Must Serve as a Background for Film," *The Times*, May 1, 1962.
[13] Ibid.
[14] James Wierzbicki, "The Hollywood Career of Gershwin's *Second Rhapsody*," *Journal of the American Musicological Society* 60, no. 1 (Spring 2007): 133–186.

KORNGOLD'S HOLLYWOOD LEGACY   239

Korngold Reception

There is evidently some validity to the idea of a post-war critical failure of Korngold's works, at least in historiographical terms. Nothing of Korngold's orchestral music (from before or after the war), for example, is mentioned in contemporary studies—such as Hans Renner's 1952 concert guide, or Homer Ulrich's 1952 book *Symphonic Music*[15]—and by the time that volume 7 of *Musik in Geschichte und Gegenwart* was published in 1958, the composer's last works were dismissed by Wilhelm Pfannkuch as having lost the "undeniable individuality of [his] earlier output."[16] Similarly, the last work listed in the 1954 Grove dictionary article on the composer is Korngold's 1927 opera, *Das Wunder der Heliane*,[17] while Karl Robert Brachtel's 1957 obituary in *Musica* notes that the instrumental music had disappeared entirely from the repertory.[18] A study of the performance history and contemporary European and US newspaper reviews of the new works and opera revivals, however, reveals a much less decisive view of the composer's reputation. While many of the positive reviews might be traced to supporters or friends of Korngold (Joseph Marx or Marcel Prawy, for instance), these viewpoints were nonetheless in contemporary circulation, and while Korngold may never have won over the modernist critics, the notion of a wholesale critical rejection in the 1940s and 1950s is something of an overstatement that places undue emphasis on the attitudes of voices with strong modernist leanings. A more balanced view can be gained by examining in more detail the initial reception of three of the new orchestral works: the Violin Concerto, the Symphonic Serenade, and the Symphony.

The Violin Concerto is, of course, forever tainted by Irving Kolodin's entertaining quip that it is "more corn than gold,"[19]— a quotation that Korngold's biographers are as fond of repeating as his detractors—yet initial critical responses were not entirely negative, despite some prominent damning comments. The work was premiered by Jascha Heifetz and the St Louis Symphony Orchestra under Vladimir Golschmann in St Louis on February 15, 1947, and was greeted enthusiastically by the local press: Korngold noted in a letter that they had described "the most enthusiastic ovation in the history of the hall" and prophesied "a lifespan like that of Mendelssohn's concerto."[20] Reaction

---

[15] Hans Renner, *Reclams Konzertführer: Orchestermusik* (Stüttgart: Reclam-Verlag, 1952); Homer Ulrich, *Symphonic Music* (New York: Columbia University Press, 1952).

[16] Wilhelm Pfannkuch, "Korngold, Julius Leopold," in *Musik in Geschichte und Gegenwart*, vol. 7, "Jensen-Kyrie," ed. Friedrich Blume (Basel: Bärenreiter, 1958), 1630–1631.

[17] H. C. Coles, "Korngold, Erich (Wolfgang)," *Grove's Dictionary of Music and Musicians*, 5th ed., ed. Eric Blom, vol. IV: H–K (Macmillan, 1954), 825.

[18] Karl Robert Brachtel, "In Memoriam Erich Wolfgang Korngold," *Musica* 12 (February 1958): 104–105.

[19] Quoted in Carroll, *The Last Prodigy*, 330.

[20] Letter to Josef Reitler, quoted in ibid., 330.

240 KORNGOLD IN AMERICA

further afield was rather less effusive, but by no means negative; a review for the *Christian Science Monitor* noted that the first movement contained "true nobility of expression," the second movement "a logic of charm which cannot be denied," while the third movement was said to be "in the tradition of the violin concerto from Beethoven to the present, built on the architectural plans of the grand style." The review concludes that "with a more individual second movement the concerto would, one ventures, remain in welcome fellowship with allied works in this form. As to the orchestration, it is the work of a master."[21] Korngold was, in fact, so delighted with the St Louis premiere and its reception, and so worried about the forthcoming New York performance, that he wrote to Josef Reitler, an old colleague of his father but by then a professor at Hunter College in New York, to ask him to "Please do what you can. If the knowledge of this success reaches the music world (violinists, directors, and audience) before the New York critics vent their snobbish, atonal anger on it, the violin concerto may be a decisive turning point for me, a comeback!"[22]

Korngold was perhaps right to be concerned, since Kolodin's comments are in response to the New York performance on March 27, 1947, again with Heifetz as the soloist. *The New York Times*'s music critic Olin Downes evidently agreed with Kolodin and not only decried it as "a Hollywood concerto" but also concluded that "the facility of the writing is matched by the mediocrity of the ideas."[23] Yet, the concerto survived the onslaught to be given in Chicago the following month, and Claudia Cassidy's review for the *Chicago Daily Tribune* was, in contrast, not unkind. She described Korngold's trick of wrapping the audience "in a luxurious cocoon of voluptuous tone, drenched in the hues and textures of night," but noted that in lesser hands than Heifetz it might turn cloying; nevertheless, she concluded that "whatever you think of the content and style of the concerto, there is no denying its skill or its ability . . . to hold an audience enthralled."[24] Heifetz later performed the concerto with the Los Angeles Philharmonic under Alfred Wallenstein and though Raymond Kendall's review opined that the concerto was "almost totally lacking in any real inventiveness or development," he also pointed out, significantly, that "the disillusioning fact is that very many persons in the audience woke up and enjoyed this portion of the concert in contrast to their earlier boredom."[25] Other reviews of this performance were similarly

---

[21] E. R. C., "Korngold's Violin Concerto," *Christian Science Monitor*, February 21, 1947.

[22] Quoted in Carroll, *The Last Prodigy*, 330.

[23] Olin Downes, "Heifetz Features Work by Korngold," *New York Times*, March 28, 1947.

[24] Claudia Cassidy, "On the Aisle: Heifetz Meets Bach on His Own Ground and Works a Little Magic with Korngold," *Chicago Daily Tribune*, April 4, 1947.

[25] 'Music by Raymond Kendall," *Mirror* (Los Angeles) with handwritten date of August 1, 1953. Clipping found in Box H Folder 4 of the Korngold Collection (Library of Congress), hereafter LOC. The rest of the program consisted of: Haydn's Overture to *Armida*; Sibelius, Symphony No. 7; Mozart, Violin Concerto No. 5; and Richard Strauss, *Don Juan*.

ambivalent, Albert Goldberg noting that "it is obviously genial music that displays the solo instrument in a consistently grateful parade of melodies and effects, and that backs it up with an orchestration that is always alive with color and movement. The slow movement is a particularly attractive evocation of poetic mood, and it was pleasant to hear music that makes no particular strivings for profundity and that remains so well within its definite purpose and limits."[26]

The concerto was, admittedly, less well received in Europe, though it was considered worthy enough to be given its European premiere in the last concert of the first Viennese International Music Festival on June 30, 1947, under Otto Klemperer, with Bronislaw Gimpel as soloist and the Vienna Symphony Orchestra.[27] This apparent endorsement of a Korngold work hides a story though, as Peter Hayworth relates: "Meanwhile, Klemperer had turned against Korngold's glib attempt to resuscitate the rhetoric of the romantic concerto and demanded that it be removed from the program. That was a concession the festival's director, Egon Seefehlner, could not make; in an American-occupied city it would have been politically embarrassing to withdraw a work by a former Austrian who was both a Jew and an American citizen."[28] Helmut A. Fiechtner evidently shared Klemperer's opinion, dismissing the work in the July 12 edition of *Die Furche* as "inconceivably empty and styleless,"[29] while *Melos* called the work "frankly disappointing."[30] And yet Heifetz, for one, kept faith with the concerto and went on to record it in January 1953, one of his greatest recorded performances.[31]

Although the Violin Concerto received mixed reviews in both Europe and America, it nevertheless hints at Korngold's ability to attract high-profile performances, even after more than a decade in the apparent wilderness of Hollywood, and to be popular with audiences and some critics, if not those with an entrenched modernist position. The Symphonic Serenade, too, received an

---

[26] Albert Goldberg, "Artistry of Heifetz Hits Peak in Concert." Margaret Harford's review "Heifetz Treats Large Crowd To 2 Concerto Performances" (dated by hand August 1, 1953) was less complementary, noting that the work was "conventionally romantic . . . whose melodies sounded extremely ordinary." Both are clippings of unknown source found in LOC, Box H Folder 4. Goldberg was a critic of the *Los Angeles Times* known particularly for his interest in exiled composers. See Barbara Zeisl Schoenberg, "The Reception of Austrian Composers in Los Angeles: 1934–1950," *Modern Austrian Literature* 20, nos. 3–4 (1987): 135–144.

[27] See Friedrich C. Heller and Peter Revers, *Das Wiener Konzerthaus: Geschichte und Bedeutng 1913–1983* (Vienna: Im Selbstverlag das Wiener Konzerthausgesellschaft, 1983), 162–163, and Erwin Barta, *Das Wiener Konzerthaus zwischen 1945 und 1961: eine Vereinsgeschichtliche und Musikwirtschaftliche Studie* (Tutzing: Hans Schneider, 2001).

[28] Peter Hayworth, *Otto Klemperer: His Life and Times*, vol. 2 (Cambridge: Cambridge University Press, 1996), 164.

[29] Quoted in ibid.

[30] "Melos bericht: Das Internationale Musikfest in Wien," *Melos* 14 (November 1947): 386–387.

[31] The *New York Times* review of the recording noted that "The Korngold work is a middle-European, sentimental, not particularly distinguished work. Heifetz plays it as if it were." "Capsule Reviews: Sonatas by Mendelssohn Among New Releases," *New York Times*, May 23, 1954.

242   KORNGOLD IN AMERICA

auspicious start. At one time it looked as though the work would follow the pattern established by the Third String Quartet and the Cello Concerto in receiving a Los Angeles premiere, this time under fellow film composer Franz Waxman. It evidently attracted a higher profile, though, when Wilhelm Furtwängler, at the height of his powers and notoriety, performed it with the Vienna Philharmonic on January 15, 1950. Although Carroll has suggested that Furtwängler may have been keen to conduct the work in part because of Korngold's Jewishness, which may have helped in his de-Nazification process,[32] the conductor's reputation had been cleared sufficiently for him to resume his duties with the Vienna and Berlin Philharmonics for several years already. While Furtwängler's reputation in the United States would never recover,[33] it seems unlikely that Korngold's Jewishness would persuade him to conduct a work in Vienna about which he was in any doubt. Indeed as Sam Shirakawa has pointed out, the rate at which Furtwängler was giving first performances of contemporary works "was no different from most other conductors entering the late summer of their middle years; it was slowing down markedly."[34] While another contemporary work premiered by Furtwängler a few months later was to prove much more successful (Strauss's *Vier letzte Lieder* on May 22), the composer-conductor seems to have been genuinely impressed by the Symphonic Serenade, if Luzi Korngold's letter to her mother-in-law of January 17, 1950, is anything to go by: "Furtwängler . . . never stopped repeating how much joy he had derived from conducting this charming and masterly piece."[35]

Joseph Marx's review of the Symphonic Serenade for the *Wiener Zeitung* was similarly complimentary. After speaking of Korngold's exceptional talent, and summarizing his career—including describing his film music as "compelling" and noting that he returned from Hollywood a matured artist—Marx proceeds to describe the work fully, praising the first movement, in particular, for its Viennese charm. He concludes by labeling the piece "extremely pleasing."[36] Marx's attitude toward Korngold is perhaps unsurprising given his innate conservatism. As a composer himself, and a friend of Korngold dating back to his time as principal of the Vienna Academy of Music and Performing Arts, their relationship was warm if somewhat formal.[37] Korngold maintained correspondence with Marx from California, and there are several letters that indicate

---

[32] Carroll, *The Last Prodigy*, 337.
[33] See Curt Riess, *Wilhelm Furtwängler: A Biography*, trans. Margaret Goldsmith (London: Frederick Muller, 1955).
[34] Sam H. Shirakawa, *The Devil's Music Master: The Controversial Life and Career of Wilhelm Furtwängler* (New York: Oxford University Press, 1992), 349.
[35] Luzi Korngold, *Erich Wolfgang Korngold: Ein Lebensbild von Luzi Korngold* (Vienna: Elisabeth Lafite, 1967), 93. Quoted and translated in Carroll, *The Last Prodigy*, 342.
[36] "Bunte Musikwelt Von Joseph Marx," *Wiener Zeitung*, January 22, 1950.
[37] See Luzi Korngold, *Erich Wolfgang Korngold*, 36.

KORNGOLD'S HOLLYWOOD LEGACY   243

Marx sent Erich his own compositions.[38] While Marx, as a personal friend of Korngold, might be expected to provide critical support, Hans Rutz's review for the *Neue Zeitschrift für Musik* is similarly positive:

> In contrast to that other post-war Korngold work, the Violin Concerto (which received its first Viennese performance in 1947), the new Serenade demonstrates significantly more of the composer's obvious change of heart. One notices, particularly in the outer movements—which do not lack an architecturally-constructed development—an admirable effort to create music of an absolute character, which is self-sufficient and wants to avoid those dramatic or solely illustrative gestures so characteristic of Korngold's other works ... The style adheres to a middle line between a received tradition and something that reaches towards harmonic modernity. Korngold could not have wished for anyone better than Furtwängler and the Vienna Philharmonic, who delivered him a deserved success.[39]

While Rutz was a supporter of Gottfried van Einem—a figure also often attacked as a musical conservative—and therefore perhaps more likely to respond favorably to Korngold's musical aesthetics, these critical reactions are evidence that positive viewpoints were not entirely in abeyance. An American premiere of the Symphonic Serenade followed in December 1953, given by William Steinberg in Pittsburgh,[40] after a planned first performance by Eugene Ormandy and the Philadelphia Orchestra the previous year was cancelled at the last minute.[41] That the Symphonic Serenade was attracting such high-profile conductors and positive reviews (no matter the identity of the reviewers) suggests that these years were not quite as barren for Korngold as might be imagined.

A more complicated picture is suggested by the early reception history of Korngold's Symphony. The Symphony's premiere was undertaken by Harald Byrns and the Vienna Symphony Orchestra on October 17, 1954, in a public

---

[38] The letter of April 4, 1951 (833/32-4 in the Austrian National Library; hereafter ONB), discusses three quartets that Marx had sent Korngold, while that of September 10, 1952 (833/32-5), indicates that the "classical" (the "Quartetto in modo classico" of 1940/1941) was Korngold's favorite.

[39] Hans Rutz, "E.W. Korngold: Symphonische Serenade," *Neue Zeitschrift für Musik* 111 (March 1950): 164–165. My translation.

[40] Luzi Korngold, *Erich Wolfgang Korngold*, 96.

[41] The *Philadelphia Inquirer* advertised the concert as taking place on December 19 at 2.30 pm and December 20 at 8.30 pm, as part of Ormandy's annual "Viennese Program" (December 14, 1952). A review of the concert on December 20, however, reported that "An almost last-minute substitution of the Schubert 'Unfinished' Symphony for the originally announced American premiere of Erich Korngold's Symphonic Serenade for String Orchestra, kept the concert completely classical in character. Perhaps omission of the contemporary work was no major musical loss." Linton Martin, "Orchestra Gives Viennese Program," *Philadelphia Inquirer*, December 20, 1952. There is also a letter from Korngold to Joseph Marx dated December 12, 1952, referring to the forthcoming premiere under Ormandy (see 833/32-6 in ONB).

244 KORNGOLD IN AMERICA

concert at the studios of Austrian Radio,[42] and while Luzi Korngold noted the satisfactory reviews,[43] most have intimated that the performance was a disaster. Carroll, for instance, talks of "reasonable" reviews, yet gives the impression of a deeply depressed composer who, unhappy with the performance, begged for the broadcast to be cancelled and for whom the only chance of a success now depended on a successful American performance.[44] Certainly, Korngold wrote to his publisher Willy Strecker, bemoaning the second-rate conductor, and in a letter to Heinrich Kralik implied that though the concert was a success, the radio broadcast was a disaster.[45] The work's apparent misfire also seems to have prompted Hans Redlich to make his 1968 pronouncement that "[Korngold's] attempt to stage a come-back as a serious symphonist failed."[46] Yet, a glance at the contemporary press reveals a somewhat different picture: far from the critical indifference we might expect from Carroll's account, or Redlich's blanket statement of fact, the initial Austrian reviews were surprisingly positive. Helmut Fiechtner's review for *Musica*, for instance, talks of the Symphony making amends for the recent production of Korngold's fifth opera, *Die Kathrin*. He describes the work as containing echoes of Richard Strauss, Mahler, and Bruckner, and goes on to claim that it "impresses through its serious language and the masterfully accomplished instrumentation."[47] In his review for the journal *Melos*, that bastion of the avant-garde, he repeats the praise for the work's instrumentation and acknowledges that, in the first movement in particular, Korngold had assimilated some of the elements of the modern musical language.[48] Perhaps he was thinking of the opening, in which the clarinet melody uses all but two of the twelve chromatic pitch classes.

As with his review of the Symphonic Serenade four years previously, Joseph Marx's review for the *Wiener Zeitung* was also positively glowing, though it reveals Marx's tacit acknowledgment of the separation that was perceived between mass culture and "high art." Labeling the Symphony a first-rate work, and with a full description of the movements, he states that the biggest and best

---

[42] Luzi Korngold, *Erich Wolfgang Korngold*, 96. The performance was later broadcast on Austrian radio on the morning of Sunday November 28. The concert and intended broadcast date were announced in *Radio Österreich: Zeitschrift des Österreichischen Rundfunks*, October 16, 1954, 10; for the broadcasting listing, see *Radio Österreich*, November 28, 1954, 12. This appears to contradict Luzi's memory that the Symphony was due to be broadcast the next day, despite Erich's objections. See Luzi Korngold, *Erich Wolfgang Korngold*, 97.

[43] Luzi Korngold, *Erich Wolfgang Korngold*, 97.

[44] Carroll, *The Last Prodigy*, 354–355.

[45] See the letter to Strecker of October 26, 1954 (1283/11-12) and to Kralik of November 30 (1283/12-6) in ONB.

[46] This was in a review of Luzi's book. "A Phenomenon Forgotten," *The Musical Times* 109, no. 1499 (January 1968): 41–42.

[47] Helmut A. Fiechtner, "Saisonbeginn in Wien," *Musica* (December 1954): 540.

[48] Helmut A. Fiechtner, "Korngold-Uraufführung in Wien," *Melos* 21, no. 12 (December 1954): 359–360.

surprise was the highly gifted composer himself, who had successfully avoided importing the dangerous elements of American popular culture into his serious musical works. Placing Korngold in the tradition of the great symphonists, he notes that "each bar is carefully worked through; every outward effect-gesture is rejected." Marx concludes effusively: "we greet this valuable, exemplarily-designed work and its creator with utmost warmth and sincerity."[49] Moreover, *Die Presse*'s review reveals just what a success the Symphony seemed to have been with the public, noting that the "extremely lively applause means not only a unanimous approval for the new works, but it is also an expression of a joyful renewal of acquaintance and sympathy for an artist to whom Vienna owes countless hours of musical pleasure."[50]

Evidently, there is little in these reviews to suggest why Redlich labeled Korngold's comeback as a serious symphonist "a failure." The question remains, though, why did the Symphony—and, by extension, the other works—not receive more performances? Helmut Pöllmann offers us the initially attractive but rather simplistic explanation that when Korngold wrote the Symphony "times were hard for this genre,"[51] that "this Symphony is part of the history of the genre in an age which appeared to have lost all ability to appreciate it."[52] In other words, it was Korngold's choice of genre that was the problem. Yet, while the 1950s were certainly not the heyday of the Germanic symphony,[53] traditionally structured tonal symphonies by Prokofiev, Shostakovich, and Vaughan Williams were nonetheless attracting numerous performances and critical acclaim—and that is to name only the most prominent symphonists of what Arnold Whittall describes as a "mid-century moderate mainstream, [characterized by an acknowledgment of] the forms and textures of the tonal past, as well as many of its compositional procedures."[54] Korngold's Symphony, one might feel, would belong perfectly in this category, and might be capable of attracting similar levels of performance.

The Symphony, like the vast majority of the other post-war works, was not written to commission, however, and Korngold himself had to actively seek

---

[49] "Orchester- und Klaviermusik von Joseph Marx," *Wiener Zeitung*, October 24, 1954.

[50] "Korngold-Uraufführung in Wien: Fis-dur Symphonie und Lieder im Sendesaal des Rundfunks," *Die Presse*, October 19, 1954.

[51] See Helmut Pöllmann's preface to the Eulenberg study score of the work No. 8048 (Mainz: Ernst Eulenburg & Co GmbH, 2000), iii.

[52] Ibid., vii.

[53] See Karen Painter, *Symphonic Aspirations: German Music and Politics, 1900–1945* (Cambridge, MA: Harvard University Press, 2007), 4.

[54] Arnold Whittall, "Individualism and Accessibility: The Moderate Mainstream, 1945–1975," in *The Cambridge History of Twentieth Century Music*, ed. Nicholas Cook and Anthony Pople (Cambridge: Cambridge University Press, 2004), 370. Other symphonies of the moderate mainstream roughly contemporary with Korngold's include Shostakovich's 10th, Prokofiev's 7th, Vaughan Williams's 8th, Furtwängler's 2nd and 3rd symphonies, and Robert Simpson's 1st.

246 KORNGOLD IN AMERICA

out performance opportunities. His initial aim upon completing it had been to secure a premiere with Golschmann and the St Louis Symphony Orchestra, who had premiered the Violin Concerto with Heifetz so successfully in 1947. Golschmann, who admired the Symphony enormously, programmed it for the 1954–1955 season, but was beaten to the first performance by the aforementioned Harald Byrns.[55] Nevertheless, it looked as though Golschmann would at least give the work its American premiere. As is revealed, though, in letters in the Korngold Collection at the Library of Congress, communication problems, issues surrounding the orchestral parts, and orchestral politics all played their part in conspiring against the performance. In a 1955 letter, Golschmann writes to Korngold:

> You may remember how much I insisted upon getting the orchestra parts early in our 1954–55 season as I knew that if I would not play it *early*, [sic]—later I was certain of nothing. Unfortunately you could not send me the parts in time and I wrote you a long letter in which I told you that I would perform your Symphony when I would see a possibility of doing so but that for the time being it was the right thing for me to tell you that you could offer the American premiere to whoever you could think of who would be worth this great privilege and honor. From your last letter I understand that my letter did not reach you and I feel so, so distressed ... When I will see you, soon I hope,—I'll tell you of the situation I am facing ... I can say,—*confidentially*—that our executive Board and also the Musical Committee are *new ones*. That for this coming season I have been asked to greatly reduce the number of "modern works" ... [and] to play almost week after week exclusively the past "favorites." Do know that I am heartbroken and that my hope is that your Symphony will soon be heard in America—no one is wishing you for this new work more success than I do.[56]

A 1961 letter from Luzi Korngold to Associated Music Publishers President Leonard Feist, however, recalls that this may have been partly Korngold's own fault—that he deliberately delayed sending the parts because he did not want the first US performance to take place while he was still in Europe.[57] Golschmann never did conduct the work, and Korngold turned instead to his old friend Bruno Walter.[58] Like Golschmann, Walter admired the work greatly, but considered it

---

[55] Jessica Duchen also refers to abandoned performances at the Musikverein and in Pittsburgh under William Steinberg in *Erich Wolfgang Korngold* (London: Phaidon, 1996), 215, but cannot recall from where this information came (email correspondence 3/26/08).

[56] LOC, Box G Folder 21, dated August 27, 1955, Paris.

[57] LOC, Box 93 Folder 12, dated December 15, 1961.

[58] Walter had initially chosen not to listen to a recording of the Symphony when the composer visited him in September 1955 (due to the stuffiness of the room), but later sent a letter of apology, offering to listen to the work at the composer's convenience. Unpublished letter of September 12, 1955

KORNGOLD'S HOLLYWOOD LEGACY   247

too difficult to consider learning himself. Instead, he offered to write to other conductors—such as Fritz Reiner, Charles Munch, and Dimitri Mitropoulos— urging them to take up the work: "Yesterday I had the opportunity to hear a recording of a symphony by Erich Wolfgang Korngold," he writes. "It was a profound impression for here was an important work of original thematic substance, of a rare emotional power in a masterly symphonic form. The instrumentation is also that of a master.[59] Here is, without any doubt, a new symphonic work with the potentialities of a genuine great success."[60]

All rejected the opportunity, apart from Mitropoulos, who responded with enthusiasm, apparently writing to the composer to assure him of his willingness to program the work.[61] Yet, as with Golschmann and the St Louis Symphony, Mitropoulos's position with the New York Philharmonic was far from secure in the mid-1950s: he faced both opposition from within the orchestra and a mauling in the press, who were critical of the Philharmonic's program choices.[62] This negative criticism culminated in Howard Taubman's damning attack in the *New York Times* in which he accused the orchestra of Euro-centric programming, orchestral mismanagement, and declining standards, and for which Mitropoulos, as Taubman put it, bore "the heaviest responsibility."[63] Mitropoulos's last full season as musical director in 1955–1956, therefore, was not a happy one, and was perhaps not the time to be introducing a new work that, although American by definition, might be interpreted as, at best, clinging to an Old World sensibility or, at worst, film music.[64] Mitropoulos eventually went on record in 1959

(BWP 1.307), referred to in Erik Ryding and Rebecca Pechefsky, *Bruno Walter: A World Elsewhere* (New Haven, CT: Yale University Press, 2001), 361.

[59] Walter to Mitropoulos, quoted in Carroll, *The Last Prodigy*, 357–358. Carroll does not mention the date, but he does note that "Korngold was writing to [Mitropoulos] as late as April 1957 to ask what plans he had concerning the work and offering him the score," which suggests that Walter's letter to Mitropoulos (and Mitropoulos's positive comments about the work) probably date from 1955–1956.

[60] Walter to Charles Munch May 26, 1956. Unpublished letter (BWP 1.307) reproduced in part in Ryding and Pechefsky, *Bruno Walter*, 362.

[61] See Luzi's letter to Alma Mahler, reproduced in part in Carroll, *The Last Prodigy*, 358. The reasons why Reiner and Munch rejected the work are unknown. Had Wilhelm Furtwängler not died in November 1954, it is possible of course that he might have taken on the Symphony, given his reported admiration for the Symphonic Serenade.

[62] The *New York Herald Tribune* asked on November 11, 1955, "How do they make their program selections? By composer's initials, tonalities, or just by flipping a coin?" See William R. Trotter, *Priest of Music: The Life of Dimitri Mitropoulos* (Portland, OR: Amadeus Press, 1995), 403.

[63] Howard Taubman, "The Philharmonic—What's Wrong With It and Why," *New York Times*, April 29, 1956.

[64] See Trotter, *Priest of Music*, especially 410–413. Nevertheless, in the following season (shared with Leonard Bernstein), Mitropoulos certainly introduced his fair share of new works (some thirty performances of "new or neglected works" in twenty-three concerts), and his position was not terminated until November 20, 1957, six weeks into the new season and just nine days before Korngold's death. It suggests a conductor that, although under severe pressure, was still in a position to advocate for new works. The reasons why he did not program the Korngold are unrecorded, but it is possible that his fractious relationship with Bruno Walter may have been a factor.

248   KORNGOLD IN AMERICA

to claim of the piece that "all my life I have searched for the perfect modern work. In this symphony I have found it. I shall perform it next season."[65] Unfortunately, Mitropoulos died the following year, and the Symphony remained unperformed in America until January 1977.[66] It seems then that Korngold, for all his friendship with musical émigrés on the West Coast of America, lacked enough personal contacts in the major East Coast centers or in Europe to ensure a high-profile performance, one that might launch the Symphony into the repertoire.[67] That the admirers of the work were either too old (Walter) or in a difficult position with their respective orchestras (Golschmann and Mitropoulos) merely added to the problem.

Korngold's publishers, Schott, probably did little to help. Andreas Giger has written of Korngold's standing with Schott in the 1920s and 1930s, noting the refusal of the Strecker brothers (who ran the concern) to accept *Die Kathrin* for publication, fearing an antisemitic backlash.[68] By the 1950s, Schott were the embodiment of the musical avant-garde, and, as Luzi Korngold makes clear, a self-professed romantic like Korngold could not rely on the support of his publishers to help him revive his concert career: "Upon seeing Ludwig and Willy Strecker in Mainz again, the old and—how should I say it—mutual sympathy and goodwill was quickly restored. That Erich, once a favored child of Schott, now found no support from this publisher in the re-establishment of his works, we found, depressingly, to be a sign of the times. But even this fact could do nothing to alter the true devotion for the Strecker brothers in Erich's heart."[69]

An indication of this lack of support can perhaps be gleaned by a cursory glance through the back pages of *Melos*, Schott's house journal. There are numerous advertisements for the music of Schott's composers, illustrated with effusive quotations from newspaper reviews; Korngold, however, is notable by his absence.[70] In the matter of the Symphony, specifically, Carroll has also brought

---

[65] Quoted in Nicolas Slominsky's liner notes for the 1972 Munich Philharmonic/Rudolf Kempe recording. RCA Gold Seal GL42919.

[66] The American premiere was given by the Milwaukee Symphony Orchestra under Kenneth Schermerhorn on January 28, 1977. The rest of the program consisted of Mozart's overture to *Die Entführung aus dem Serail* and Prokofiev's Violin Concerto No. 2. See Troy O. Dixon, "The American Premiere of Korngold's *Symphony in F-Sharp*." Available at: https://korngold-society.org/site/wp-content/uploads/2022/01/US_Premiere_EWK_op40_rev.pdf (accessed May 9, 2024).

[67] Indeed, as he had remarked in a February 20, 1947, letter to Josef Reitler, "I seem to be helpless and neglected here, I have no manager, no agent, not even a publisher in America. (All I can do is to send a copy to Schott in London who will print the work. But they obviously have no influence in New York)." Quoted in Carroll, *The Last Prodigy*, 330.

[68] Giger, "A Matter of Principle," 559.

[69] Luzi Korngold, *Erich Wolfgang Korngold*, 95.

[70] In the May/June 1947 issue, for example, Schott advertised the works of Ottmar Gerster, composer of *Enoch Arden* and *Die Hexe von Passau*, as part of a special fiftieth birthday celebration: Korngold's fiftieth birthday was in May 1947, yet no corresponding advert appeared. Similarly, the July 1947 issue of *Melos* saw Schott advertising new string quartets by Degen, Fortner, Gerster, Hindemith, Maler, and Pepping on page 268; Korngold's Third String Quartet, first performed in 1946 in Los Angeles, was not mentioned. The June/July 1948 issue also featured a large Schott

my attention to the absence of a proper engraving of the work: orchestras wanting to perform this particularly difficult work would only have a Xerox of the copyist's manuscript to work from. When consulting the score as late as 1971, he was presented with a "barely legible and shabby loose bound copy," and a proper engraving was only made by Schott in 1977.[71]

As we have already seen, Golschmann too had difficulty obtaining the parts of the Symphony and was seemingly reliant on Korngold sending them; indeed problems with orchestral parts or scores seem to have been a feature of these years, and certainly caused the cancellation of a planned Berlin performance of *Die stumme Serenade* in 1953—albeit with a different publisher, Weinberger.[72] Similarly, the abandonment of the 1953 American premiere of the Symphonic Serenade, by Eugene Ormandy and the Philadelphia Orchestra, could conceivably have been due to problems in obtaining the parts: Schott, after all, had no representative in the United States. Korngold certainly wrote to Ormandy in February 1952 to bemoan the last-minute cancellation of his *Much Ado About Nothing* suite, for the want of "a few dollars." He notes that he had tried everything possible to facilitate the performance, sanctioning cuts and the doubling of wind parts in the harmonium, and had even cabled the publishers (twice) to insist that the hire fee be waived. Unfortunately, as the composer reluctantly acknowledged, the publisher could not countenance taking less money for his music than for another composer's.[73] Nevertheless, had Korngold been able to place the Symphony and these other post-war orchestral works with a more supportive publisher, who could make the most of the positive early reviews to promote the works and provide legible scores and parts when needed, more performances might indeed have been forthcoming.

It seems likely, then, that the reason for the failure of the Symphony and the other post-war works to establish themselves in the repertoire probably had less to do with their initial critical reception, or any opposition to Korngold's aesthetic language, and more to do with the unwillingness of orchestras and conductors to risk programming works tainted with the brush of mass culture, a situation compounded by the relative inactivity of Schott in promoting the music.[74] In any case, we can nuance the idea of a critical rejection of the Symphony and the

---

advert detailing Wolfgang Fortner's *Sinfonie* (1947) complete with press comments labelling it "Ein ungewöhnlicher Erfolg" (an unusual success) (p. 200).

[71] Personal email correspondence, August 15, 2007.

[72] See the August 4, 1953, letter from Victor Clement. LOC, Box G Folder 8.

[73] Korngold to Eugene Ormandy, February 12, 1952, letter 1283/13-4 in ONB.

[74] Given that the Symphony was also dedicated to Franklin D. Roosevelt and contained a barely disguised allusion to the George M. Cohan patriotic song "Over There" (Reh. Figs. 122 and 147-3 in the finale), it may also have trodden on some toes in a Europe with an ambivalent attitude toward the influx of American popular culture: the American occupation had, after all, only recently ended in Germany, and four-power occupation was still in place in Austria at the time of the Symphony's premiere.

250 KORNGOLD IN AMERICA

other post-war works, and challenge some of the underlying assumptions. The real picture is potentially far more complex than the simplistic suggestion that Korngold's supposedly anachronistic tonal language was to blame, and suggests a world wherein problems with conductors, orchestra committees, publishers, and prevailing attitudes toward mass culture, all placed within a volatile cultural-political climate, played their part in denying the Symphony and the other works places in the orchestral repertoire. Moreover, the flip side to this historiographical tendency to emphasize a post-war critical failure is to stress a Korngold "renaissance," inspired (ironically enough) by the "rediscovery" of the film scores in the recordings of Charles Gerhardt in 1972. Yet, interest in the composer's works had not entirely disappeared after Korngold's death. *Die tote Stadt*, for instance, received a 1967 production in Vienna and Ghent, *Der Ring des Polykrates* was produced in Vienna in 1964, and *Das Wunder der Heliane* was seen in Ghent in 1970.[75] Indeed, the idea that Korngold had been forgotten was denied as early as 1977 with Harold Schonberg citing not only the recent 1975 New York production of *Die tote Stadt* but also the reruns of the films on television as supporting evidence. There are grounds, then, for questioning the extent of the "renaissance" and whether it represents anything more than an ambivalent fluctuating response to Korngold's works and his mass culture credentials. Arguably, the same modernist ambivalence that characterized Korngold reception in the 1950s persisted in certain quarters into the twenty-first century. When *Das Wunder der Heliane* received its first UK performance in 2007, critical press reaction in the United Kingdom did not greet it with the unqualified positivity that the renaissance narrative might suggest. Some of the more vitriolic comments included those made by Rupert Christianson of the *Daily Telegraph*, who labeled it "opera's biggest load of codswallop,"[76] and *The Spectator*'s Michael Tanner, who described the evening remarkably as one of "disgust and revulsion."[77]

Evidently, writing composer biography—especially of the more hagiographic variety—often requires simplified narratives. What interests me more than the accuracy (or otherwise) of the "rejection and renaissance" narrative, though, is the purpose it serves. The idea of critical rejection by one's own contemporaries and later acceptance by a future generation is certainly one that appealed not only to the composer's biographers but also to Korngold himself. Indeed, biographers

---

[75] See Helmut Pöllmann, *Erich Wolfgang Korngold: Aspekte seines Schaffens* (Mainz: Schott, 1998), 36–37. In addition, Bel Canto Opera put on a production of *Violanta* in 1975. See "Music," *New York Times*, January 5, 1975, sec. D.

[76] Rupert Christiansen, "Das Wunder der Heliane: Opera's Biggest Load of Codswallop Rises from the Grave," *Daily Telegraph*, November 24, 2007. Neil Fisher's review for *The Times* (November 23, 2007) was, however, more complimentary.

[77] Michael Tanner, "Good Humour, Bad Taste: L'Elisir d'amore; Das Wunder der Heliane," *The Spectator*, November 28, 2007.

KORNGOLD'S HOLLYWOOD LEGACY 251

can be forgiven for not interrogating this myth too closely when it was one that he actively propagated. Smarting from the decline of his fame from as early as the mid-1920s, and realizing that his post-war career, in being affected by prominent modernist critics with an overwhelmingly negative view of mass culture, would never reach these heights again, Korngold might thus have recognized an affinity with great romantic figures. Beethoven and Schubert, for example, were somewhat inaccurately thought (particularly after Wagner) to be unappreciated in their time.[78] As the 1945 book on Mahler by Korngold's contemporary Alfred Rosenzweig reveals, prevailing opinion in conservative Vienna stated that "as with the two great masters Schubert and Bruckner, it has always been the case that no composer gained success in Vienna during his lifetime, but only found recognition once dead."[79] Similarly, Leon Botstein has argued that "The notion that [Mahler] was unfairly treated, misunderstood, and victimized is a historical distortion not dissimilar in its sources and currency from the familiar pseudo-historical assertions that shaped posthumous nineteenth-century legends about the lives and careers of Mozart and Schubert."[80] Whereas Korngold had certainly enjoyed more than his fair share of Viennese popularity in his youth—to the extent that he aroused Anton Webern's jealousy[81]—the gradual decline of his reputation from the 1920s onward might have encouraged him to play down any modest successes in the post-war period that did not reach the heights of his earlier works, and to claim that "beautiful music is only tolerated if the composer has been dead for fifty years."[82]

Whether or not Korngold deliberately colluded with attempts to downplay the modest success of his music, it is certainly this ideology of struggle and triumph over the contemporary world that Korngold devotees, from the composer's widow onward, seem to have seized upon to explain the composer's later works. Jessica Duchen, for example, notes that "If Korngold was out of step with his

---

[78] See Daniel Gregory Mason, *The Romantic Composers* (New York: Macmillan, 1906), 87–88, on Schubert. Also see K. M. Knittel's "Wagner, Deafness, and the Reception of Beethoven's Late Style," *Journal of the American Musicological Society* 51, no. 1 (Spring 1998): 49–82, and Hans Lenneberg, "The Myth of the Unappreciated Musical Genius," *The Musical Quarterly* 66, no. 2 (April 1980): 219–231. Knittel, for instance, writes that "vehement reactions (to the late Beethoven quartets) are rare, however, and the extent to which the late music was harshly viewed during the three decades following Beethoven's death has been greatly exaggerated" (52).

[79] Alfred Mathis-Rosenzweig, *Gustav Mahler: New Insights into His Life, Times and Work*, trans. Jeremy Barham (Aldershot: Ashgate, 2007), 51. Rosenzweig was born, like Korngold, in 1897, and he too was the inheritor of romantic myths: on page 118, for instance, he refers to Beethoven's "then little-understood piano sonatas and string quartets."

[80] Leon Botstein, "Whose Gustav Mahler? Reception, Interpretation, and History," in *Mahler and His World*, ed. Karen Painter (Princeton, NJ: Princeton University Press, 2002), 20.

[81] In a letter dated November 13, 1910, to Schoenberg, Webern wrote that "Publishers, performances—the boy has everything. I will become old before *that*." Quoted in Carroll, *The Last Prodigy*, 378.

[82] Ross Parmenter, "He's Fed Up With Music for Films," *New York Times*, October 27, 1946, 69.

252 KORNGOLD IN AMERICA

times, that is not his fault; if twentieth-century humanity has been scared of the heart-on-sleeve emotion in his music, that is not his fault either."[83] In order to account for the composer's less-than-prominent position in the post-war concert and operatic repertories, then, it has become necessary in some quarters to entertain the idea of an almost wholesale critical rejection, a romantic myth that ignores many of the positive reviews in order to fit the story. Moreover, in maintaining this notion of a critical rejection rooted in Korngold's aesthetic style or prompted by a modernist suspicion of the nefarious influence of mass culture, it arguably obscures the ways in which Korngold's music actively brought into dialogue those twin poles of mass culture and high art that modernism relied upon, as the previous chapter demonstrated. A more nuanced account of his reception history reveals that Korngold's music continued to reach an audience, and asks provocative questions about the value of musical art. How, then, might we assess Korngold's place in music history? And how might we reconcile Korngold's Hollywood activities with the rest of his output in a way that acknowledges the pervasiveness of modernist anxieties that have dominated much of the historiography and criticism of the mid-late twentieth century?

Reappraising Korngold

Even if Korngold's relationship with modernism was ambivalent in his formative years,[84] by the mid-1950s his introduction to *Faith in Music* appears to make clear his doubts about its artistic project. It is striking, indeed, that by appearing to advocate the avoidance of confronting the problems of the day a composer should so clearly and openly deny any connection whatsoever with what Adorno might claim to be the function and purpose of music in the twentieth century. For those Korngold scholars conditioned by the legitimizing discourse of modernism, it might even be thought embarrassing to admit that he could have genuinely believed in what he wrote. One response to the introduction to *Faith in Music* might, then, look upon Korngold's self-diagnosis with a certain amount of skepticism. Just as we might challenge the composer's view of Beethoven, Schubert, Chopin, and Wagner, so might Korngold's self-image be open to question. Such is the position I have often been tempted to take before, reasoning that Korngold was not well placed to recognize or control the ways in which his music might be interpreted or received, and was simply unaware

---

[83] Duchen, *Erich Wolfgang Korngold*, 9.

[84] Let us not forget, after all, that Korngold's music was performed by Schoenberg's Society for Private Musical Performances, and he was regularly involved in meetings of the International Society of Contemporary Music (ISCM). See Charles Youmans, "'You Must Return to Life': Notes on the Reception of *Das Wunder der Heliane* and *Jonny spielt auf*," in Goldmark and Karnes, *Korngold and His World*, 54.

of its ability to undertake the essential role of modernist art: to carry out a critical function with respect to the power structures of society. Yet, I suspect this kind of response is merely symptomatic of that anxiety concerning value, which I have referenced throughout this book, and which can be found persisting in much musicological writing of the last forty years. It is an anxiety in which the sometimes-unspoken legacy of Adorno and other modernist critics (simplified, no doubt, and filtered through other voices, and likely further complicated by issues of class snobbishness) has loomed large over the discourse of twentieth-century music, and where a split between modernism and mass culture remains remarkably pervasive in the study of Western classical music. Thus, for all that postmodernism promised in holding up repertoires of popular music as worthy of study, Korngold has remained problematic precisely because he challenges the clear lines of the "great divide" and because so many of his supporters so dearly wish him to gain access to that "respectability" from which his music, in challenging those clear lines, disbars him. As a consequence, attempts to include him within histories of Western classical music have not been entirely successful, and he remains a marginal figure in ways that ignore both his popularity in the 1920s, his apparent importance for film-scoring history, and his undoubted popular appeal today (allowing for the fact that this popularity is certainly not universal). Even without his move west to Hollywood, his aesthetics would likely always have been problematic in such contexts, but his work for Warner Bros. arguably makes it even more difficult to fit him in to ongoing and pervasive (if often unacknowledged) modernist models of music historiography, and thus to ascribe to him value as a composer whose music is worthy of study.

The most successful of recent attempts to reconcile Korngold with the telling of music history is undoubtedly Peter Franklin's efforts to incorporate Hollywood into a larger history of twentieth-century music and to rehabilitate modernism itself as a late flowering of romanticism. As a result, he has sought to show how the Hollywood film scores of Korngold and others might operate semi-autonomously from their films and, in turn, transform these films into discourses about music that reflect critically on contemporary debates, much as I have attempted in Chapter 6. Likewise, Christopher Chowrimootoo has performed a delicate balancing act to demonstrate how the concept of "middlebrow modernism" can ascribe value to the operas of Benjamin Britten and to show how composers, critics, and audiences can be "torn between seemingly conflicting commitments—on the one hand to uncompromising originality and radical autonomy, and on the other to musical pleasure and communication with a new mass audience."[85] Ultimately, although Chowrimootoo's project

---

[85] Christopher Chowrimootoo, *Middlebrow Modernism: Britten's Operas and the Great Divide* (Oakland: University of California Press, 2018), 3.

254   KORNGOLD IN AMERICA

is undeniably shaped by the contemporary reception of Britten's music, it does allow him to have his cake and eat it: to preserve Britten's (albeit conflicted) modernist respectability while acknowledging the musical pleasure his music engenders in mass audiences. It is tempting, indeed, to attempt something similar for Korngold while ignoring the composer's own unambiguous statement about the matter in 1955.

Talk of having one's cake and eating it, though, might also draw our attention to the significance of an audio recording made at Ray Heindorf's birthday party in 1951, at which Korngold played the piano for Heindorf's guests.[86] The surviving recording opens with "Pierrot's Lied" from *Die tote Stadt* but despite the obvious enthusiasm from the audience it soon transitions into Korngold performing themes from film scores. Does this in fact demonstrate the truth of that essential equivalence between opera and film that I have been questioning throughout this book, at least in Korngold's eyes? Or rather, does it simply show Korngold as entertainer, selecting the most appropriate pieces of music for his fellow guests of movie insiders?[87] Those are two possible interpretations. Another response, though, might claim that it demonstrates Korngold's abiding affection for the film-score material he had created *alongside* his earlier operatic output. The piano performances are rendered in Korngold's most bravura orchestral style—and clearly played from memory. Moreover, they seem an indication that he was not ashamed of his own melodiousness, nor, as we saw in the previous chapter, was he content to keep his film-score material isolated from his non-Hollywood output. The party performance, in juxtaposing "Mein Sehnen, Mein Wähnen" from *Die tote Stadt* with "Love from Love" from *Escape Me Never*, points then to the possibility of seeing Korngold in a different light, historiographically. Rather than subscribing to the ways in which music historians have been tempted to position Korngold—as a compromised talent gone to waste in Hollywood, as a musical "has been" whose career did not fulfil the modernist promise he showed as a *Wunderkind*, or even as a "closet" modernist who engaged knowingly with Hollywood as a socially engaged artist and whose music can play on the same terms as other modernist music of the twentieth century (with some suitable allowances for what might be termed "modernist")—we might take the evidence of the party recording as corroborating evidence for Korngold's own statement in *Faith in Music* that "the genuine artist creates at a distance from his own time, even for a time beyond" and that he "will know how to take and uplift him into

[86] https://youtu.be/kOxMuSXgl2Y (accessed May 10, 2023). A version of this recording (minus Pierrot's Lied) was included in the DVD release of *The Adventures of Robin Hood* 65131.

[87] One cannot help but also think of the entertainment Adorno provided while sitting at Charlie Chaplin's piano after a dinner in 1947, an indication that even arch-modernists found it difficult to keep the worlds of high art and popular culture convincingly separated. See Theodor W. Adorno, *Letters to his Parents 1939–1951*, ed. Christoph Gödde and Henri Lonitz, trans. Wieland Hoban (Cambridge: Polity, 2006), 280.

the purer realms of phantasy." Korngold perhaps affirmed in the party recording his commitment to his music's ability to bring "pleasure and exultation, dedication and happiness."[88]

In addressing the separation between modernism and mass culture, Andreas Huyssen noted that "the nightmare of being devoured by mass culture through co-option, commodification, and the 'wrong' kind of success is the constant fear of the modernist artist, who tries to stake out his territory by fortifying the boundaries between genuine art and inauthentic mass culture."[89] This Korngold assuredly did not do. As such, he escapes Huyssen's accusation that at the root of this "nightmare" is fear of, and devaluing of, "the feminine." Instead, Korngold embraced virtually all forms of musical activity available to him—ranging from operas to popular operetta, musical theatre, and incidental music for plays in the theatrical world; from art song to popular song suitable for inclusion in the hit parade; and from orchestral works destined for the concert hall to orchestral scores for Hollywood film. Throughout his career he displayed a flexibility in terms of the styles he adopted and the audiences for which he wrote, such that the individual who composed the serious Op. 18 songs and *Das Wunder der Heliane* could also write a musical comedy like *Die stumme Serenade* without contradiction. Moreover, he was capable of adjusting his technique and art to suit the kind of compositional task required, whether it needed him to collaborate with others, to work with the latest technology, or to meet strict deadlines. That flexibility is likewise attested by a consistent attitude to musical re-use throughout his career. The recycling of concert works within film scores (*Sursum Corda* in *Robin Hood* or *Kaiserin Zita-Hymne* in *Elizabeth and Essex*, for example) is matched not only in his pre-Hollywood output by the reframing of songs as instrumental works ("Schneeglöckchen" as the basis of the finale in the Violin Sonata, Op. 6 or "Was Du mir bist" from the Op. 22 songs arranged as the Lied of the Op. 23 Suite for Piano Left Hand and strings) but also by the use of film-score material in concert works.[90] Few composers in the twentieth century have straddled these varied worlds so successfully. Indeed, one could argue that the Korngold "problem" arises from the ways in which he challenges comfortable critical pigeonholes and refuses to be labeled. It is, though, in his very adaptability and stylistic flexibility wherein his prominent position in twentieth-century musical culture most persuasively lies: in attempting to embrace both sides of a growing mass culture divide that characterizes the twentieth century, he provides a possible way out

---

[88] Korngold, "Faith in Music," 258.

[89] Andreas Huyssen, *After the Great Divide: Modernism, Mass Culture, Postmodernism* (London: Macmillan Press, 1980), 53.

[90] Another prominent example is the Adagio of the Piano Quintet, Op. 15, which drew its thematic material from "Mond, so gehst du wieder auf" and "Sterbelied" from the *Vier Lieder des Abschieds*, Op. 14.

of the critical tensions that modernism has created surrounding the value and purpose of art.

The new critical stance I am suggesting we adopt to view Korngold's output and significance may, in fact, align with recent perspectives that recognize the recent emergence of a "new sincerity" in art, where the cynicism and irony that characterized postmodernism are supplemented by a genuineness of response, and even a neoromantic emotionality. Indeed, such qualities have been associated with a "metamodernism" that moves beyond both modernism and postmodernism.[91] In the realm of popular culture, for instance, *The Simpsons* (1990–) has been heralded for its ability to both celebrate sentiment and quickly undercut it through irony, with Michael Farmer noting that the sitcom in its first decade was able to "embrace both straightforward human emotion and cock-eyed irony."[92] A perspective on Korngold that allows the genuine emotion his music elicits to stand alongside, and on an equal footing with, other qualities more amenable to interrogation as social critique may ultimately offer the most appropriate way forward for the composer. As such, we can take Korngold's comments in *Faith in Music* at face value, and see him as someone for whom the pleasure his music gave—and its ability to "uplift" the listener (to allow them to engage in artistic reverie, as Richard Rushton might characterize the value of cinema)—is of just as much value as any social function his music might have had as an artistic response to modernity.[93] Clearly, there are ways in which one could choose to emphasize this social function, particularly since his music was a key part of cinematic narratives that might legitimately be thought of as reflecting or critiquing questions of social relevance. But to do so at the cost of the value his music has to inculcate that sense of artistic reverie Rushton sees as inherent to the cinematic experience would be to artificially emphasize one relatively minor aspect of the composer's music while ignoring a larger part, and all because of a historiographical anxiety about the value of mass culture. Aside from challenging many of the myths surrounding the composer, the larger aim of this book, then, has been to attempt to rebalance our attention on the entirety of the composer's output; and to actively question the legitimizing power of modernist discourse in dictating the stories we tell about twentieth-century

---

[91] See Timotheus Vermeulen and Robin van den Akker, "Notes on Metamodernism," *Journal of Aesthetics and Culture* 2, no. 1 (2010), DOI: 10.3402/jac.v2i0.5677. The term has, admittedly, been used in quite different ways to describe contemporary literature and art history, on the one hand, and, on the other, to signal a fundamental shift in thinking. For example, Jason Ānanda Josephson Storm's book *Metamodernism: The Future of Theory* (Chicago: University of Chicago Press, 2022) offers a grand vision for an interdisciplinary reconstructive project for the human sciences that offers a commitment to "non-dogmatic, humble knowledge" (281).

[92] Michael Farmer, "'Cloaked In, Like, Fifteen Layers of Irony': The Metamodernist Sensibility of *Parks and Recreation*," *Studies in Popular Culture* 37, no. 2 (Spring 2015): 103.

[93] Richard Rushton, *The Reality of Film: Theories of Filmic Reality* (Manchester: Manchester University Press, 2011).

music, stories that I contend should include the activities of composers working in Hollywood alongside those writing for the concert hall. In that sense, I suggest Hollywood musical activity can be thought of as in dialogue with other practices encountered within the related realms of the concert hall and opera house, rather than in opposition. Although I have emphasized the differences between film-scoring and operatic practice throughout this book, I have done so precisely to counter the temptation for some to denigrate scoring practices by essentializing them, or to use opera as an uncomplicatedly high-art genre to which film scores should be thought to somehow aspire.[94]

For Korngold, the result is hopefully a more complete picture of his output that allows a more honest engagement with his style and his activities in Hollywood; that allows us to understand how he worked with others in the Music Department at Warners without worrying that the collaborative nature of these relationships, or the mechanically assisted processes that he used in producing his music, challenge his status as an artist. We may choose instead to value his music for its ability to create compelling Korngoldian worlds that are true to his own conception of music, and that cross and problematize comfortable historio-graphical boundaries between styles and genres and between categories such as "art" and "entertainment." Those Korngoldian worlds, which can "lift us into the purer realm of phantasy," may be encountered in the movie theatre, in the concert hall, or in the opera house, but their value as art might be tied more closely to the pleasure they provide than to their ability to reflect, or critically comment on, the conditions of twentieth-century modernity.

---

[94] In that sense, my target is not work like Peter Franklin's that shows how opera and film scores can be placed in productive dialogue.

Bibliography

"Capsule Reviews: Sonatas by Mendelssohn Among New Releases." *New York Times*, May 23, 1954.

"Electric Musical Instrument Imitates Orchestra Pieces." *Science News Letter*, February 25, 1939.

"Korngold-Uraufführung in Wien: Fis-dur Symphonie und Lieder im Sendesaal des Rundfunks." *Die Presse*, October 19, 1954.

"Melos bericht: Das Internationale Musikfest in Wien." *Melos* 14 (November 1947): 386–387.

"Music that Must Serve as a Background for Film." *The Times*, May 1, 1962: 15.

"Music." *New York Times*, January 5, 1975: 14.

"Today's Program at the Fair." *New York Times*, May 17, 1940: 14.

Abbate, Carolyn. *Unsung Voices: Opera and Musical Narrative in the Nineteenth Century*. Princeton, NJ: Princeton University Press, 1991.

Adorno, T. W. *In Search of Wagner*. Translated by Rodney Livingstone. London: NLB, 1981.

Adorno, T. W. *Letters to His Parents 1939–1951*. Edited by Christoph Gödde and Henri Lonitz. Translated by Wieland Hoban. Cambridge: Polity, 2006.

Anderson, Gillian B. "The Shock of the Old: The Restoration, Reconstruction, or Creation of 'Mute'-Film Accompaniments." In *The Routledge Companion to Screen Music and Sound*, edited by Ronald Sadoff, Miguel Mera, and Ben Winters, 201–212. New York: Routledge, 2017.

Barta, Erwin. *Das Wiener Konzerthaus zwischen 1945 und 1961: eine Vereinsgeschichtliche und Musikwirtschaftliche Studie*. Tutzing: Hans Schneider, 2001.

Behlmer, Rudy. *Inside Warner Bros. (1935–51)*. London: Weidenfeld and Nicolson, 1986.

Bingen, Steven. *Warner Bros: Hollywood's Ultimate Backlot*. Guildford, CT: Globe Pequot, 2018.

Blades, James. *Percussion Instruments and Their History*. Revised edition. Westport, CT: The Bold Strummer, 2005.

Botstein, Leon. "Before and After Auschwitz: Korngold and the Art and Politics of the Twentieth Century." In *Korngold and His World*, edited by Daniel Goldmark and Kevin C. Karnes, 263–313. Princeton, NJ: Princeton University Press, 2019.

Botstein, Leon. "The Enigmas of Richard Strauss: A Revisionist View." In *Richard Strauss and His World*, edited by Bryan Gilliam, 3–32. Princeton, NJ: Princeton University Press, 1992.

Botstein, Leon. "Whose Gustav Mahler? Reception, Interpretation, and History." In *Mahler and His World*, edited by Karen Painter, 1–54. Princeton, NJ: Princeton University Press, 2002.

Bowles, Paul. "On the Film Front." *Modern Music* 18 (1940–1941): 58–61.

Brachtel, Karl Robert. "In Memoriam Erich Wolfgang Korngold." *Musica* 12 (February 1958): 104–105.

Bribitzer-Stull, Matthew. *Understanding the Leitmotif: From Wagner to Hollywood Film Music*. Cambridge: Cambridge University Press, 2015.

Brown, Royal S. *Overtones and Undertones: Reading Film Music*. Berkeley: University of California Press, 1994.

Bubbeo, Daniel. *The Women of Warner Bros: The Lives and Careers of 15 Leading Ladies, with Filmographies for Each*. Jefferson, NC: McFarland, 2010.

Calta, Louis. "Musical Is Added to Schubert Agenda: Production of 'Silent Serenade' Is Planned for Its Winter Opening on Broadway." *New York Times*, September 16, 1947: 27.

Carroll, Brendan. *Erich Wolfgang Korngold: His Life and Works 1897–1957*. Paisley: Wilfion Books, 1984.

260 BIBLIOGRAPHY

Carroll, Brendan. *The Last Prodigy: A Biography of Erich Wolfgang Korngold*. Portland, OR: Amadeus Press, 1997.

Cassidy, Claudia. "On the Aisle: Heifetz Meets Bach on His Own Ground and Works a Little Magic with Korngold." *Chicago Daily Tribune*, April 4, 1947: 21.

Catalog of Copyright Entries: Musical Compositions, Part 3. Washington, DC: Library of Congress Copyright Office, 1943.

Cheng, William. "Opera *en abyme*: The Prodigious Ritual of Korngold's *Die tote Stadt*." *Cambridge Opera Journal* 22, no. 2 (July 2010): 115–146.

Chowrimootoo, Christopher. *Middlebrow Modernism: Britten's Operas and the Great Divide*. Oakland: University of California Press, 2018.

Christiansen, Rupert. "Das Wunder der Heliane: Opera's Biggest Load of Codswallop Rises from the Grave." *Daily Telegraph*, November 24, 2007.

Coles, H. C. "Korngold, Erich (Wolfgang)." In *Grove's Dictionary of Music and Musicians*, Volume 4: H–K, 5th edition, edited by Eric Blom, 825. London: Macmillan, 1954.

Cooke, Mervyn. *A History of Film Music*. Cambridge: Cambridge University Press, 2008.

Cooper, David. *Bernard Herrmann's* The Ghost and Mrs Muir: *A Film Score Guide*. Lanham, MD: Scarecrow Press, 2005.

Cooper, David. *Bernard Herrmann's* Vertigo: *A Film Score Handbook*. Westport, CT: Greenwood Press, 2001.

Danly, Linda, ed. *Hugo Friedhofer: The Best Years of His Life. A Hollywood Master of Music for the Movies*. Lanham, MD: Scarecrow Press, 2002.

Davidson, Jane, and Robert Faulkner. "Music in our Lives." In *The Complexity of Greatness: Beyond Talent or Practice*, edited by Scott Barry Kaufman, 367–389. New York: Oxford University Press, 2013.

Del Mar, Norman. *Richard Strauss: A Critical Commentary On His Life and Work*. 2nd edition, 3 volumes. Ithaca, NY: Cornell University Press, 1986.

Delehanty, Thornton. "A Score for 'Robin Hood.'" *The New York Times*, May 22, 1938: 154.

Dent, Edward. "Erich Korngold's New Sonata." *The Musical Standard*, January 31, 1914: 109.

Deutsch, Adolph. "Three Strangers." *Hollywood Quarterly* 1, no. 2 (January 1946): 214–223.

Dick, Bernard F. *Hal Wallis: Producer to the Stars*. Lexington: University Press of Kentucky, 2004.

Dixon, Troy O. "The American Premiere of Korngold's *Symphony in F-Sharp*." https://korng old-society.org/site/wp-content/uploads/2022/01/US_Premiere_EWK_op40_rev.pdf, accessed May 9, 2024.

Downes, Olin. "Heifetz Features Work by Korngold." *New York Times*, March 28, 1947: 27.

Duchen, Jessica. *Erich Wolfgang Korngold*. London: Phaidon, 1996.

E. R. C. "Korngold's Violin Concerto." *Christian Science Monitor*, February 21, 1947: 16.

Eisler, Hanns, and Theodor Adorno. *Composing for the Films*. London: Athlone Press, 1994.

Farmer, Michael. "'Cloaked In, Like, Fifteen Layers of Irony': The Metamodernist Sensibility of *Parks and Recreation*." *Studies in Popular Culture* 37, no. 2 (Spring 2015): 103–120.

Fiechtner, Helmut A. "Korngold-Uraufführung in Wien." *Melos* 21, no. 12 (December 1954): 359–360.

Fiechtner, Helmut A. "Saisonbeginn in Wien." *Musica* (December 1954): 540.

Franklin, Peter. "Deception's Great Music. A Cultural Analysis." In *Film Music 2, History, Theory, Practice*, edited by Claudia Gorbman and Warren B. Sherk, 27–41. Sherman Oaks, CA: The Film Music Society, 2004.

Franklin, Peter. *Reclaiming Late-Romantic Music: Singing Devils and Distant Sounds*. Berkeley and Los Angeles: University of California Press, 2014.

Franklin, Peter. *Seeing Through Music: Gender and Modernism in Classic Hollywood Film Scores*. New York: Oxford University Press, 2011.

Franklin, Peter. "Underscoring Drama—Picturing Wagner." In *Wagner and Cinema*, edited by Jeongwon Joe and Sander L. Gilman, 46–64. Bloomington: Indiana University Press, 2010.

BIBLIOGRAPHY 261

Fruchtman, Aaron. "Max Steiner's Jewish Identity and Score to *Symphony of Six Million.*" *Journal of Film Music* 9, nos. 1–2 (2016): 80–93.

Giger, Andreas. "A Matter of Principle: The Consequences for Korngold's Career." *The Journal of Musicology* 16, no. 4 (Autumn, 1998): 545–564.

Gilliam, Bryan. "A Viennese Opera Composer in Hollywood: Korngold's Double Exile in America." In *Driven into Paradise: The Musical Migration from Nazi Germany to the United States*, edited by Reinhold Brinkmann and Christoph Wolff, 223–242. Berkeley: University of California Press, 1999.

Goose, Benjamin. "Opera for Sale: Folksong, Sentimentality, and the Market." *Journal of the Royal Musical Association* 133, no. 2 (2008): 189–219.

Grimley, Daniel M. "Music, Ice, and the 'Geometry of Fear': The Landscapes of Vaughan Williams's *Sinfonia Antartica.*" *The Musical Quarterly* 91, nos. 1–2 (Spring–Summer 2008): 116–150.

Gunning, Tom. "The Cinema of Attraction: Early Film, Its Spectator and the Avant-Garde." *Wide Angle* 8, nos. 3–4 (1986): 63–70.

Haas, Michael. *Forbidden Music: The Jewish Composers Banned by the Nazis.* New Haven, CT: Yale University Press, 2014.

Halo, Jay L. *A Midsummer Night's Dream.* Manchester: Manchester University Press, 2003.

Hansen, Miriam Bratu. "The Mass Production of the Senses: Classical Cinema as Vernacular Modernism." *Modernism/Modernity* 6, no. 2 (April 1999): 59–77.

Harmetz, Aljean. *Round up the Usual Suspects: The Making of Casablanca—Bogart, Bergman and World War II.* London: Weidenfeld and Nicolson, 1993.

Hayworth, Peter. *Otto Klemperer: His Life and Times.* Volume 1. Cambridge: Cambridge University Press, 1996.

Heldt, Guido. *Music and Levels of Narration in Film: Steps Across the Border.* Bristol: Intellect, 2013.

Heller, Friedrich C., and Peter Revers. *Das Wiener Konzerthaus: Geschichte und Bedeutng 1913–1983.* Vienna: Im Selbstverlag das Wiener Konzerthausgesellschaft, 1983.

Hollingdale, R. J. "The Hero as Outsider." In *The Cambridge Companion to Nietzsche*, edited by Bernd Magnus and Kathleen Higgins, 71–89. Cambridge: Cambridge University Press, 1996.

Hollinger, Hy. "'Deception' Score Turning Point in Composer's Career." *The New York Morning Telegraph*, October 23, 1946.

Holmes, Thom. *Electronic and Experimental Music: Technology, Music, and Culture.* 5th edition. New York: Routledge, 2016.

Holston, Kim R. *Movie Roadshows: A History and Filmography of Reserved-Seat Limited Showings, 1911–1973.* Jefferson, NC: McFarland, 2013.

Horlacher, Gretchen. *Building Blocks: Repetition and Continuity in the Music of Stravinsky.* New York: Oxford University Press, 2011.

Hsieh, Amanda. "Jewish Difference and Recovering 'Commedia': Erich W. Korngold's 'Die tote Stadt' in Post-First World War Austria." *Music & Letters* 103, no. 4 (November 2022): 685–707.

Huyssen, Andreas. *After the Great Divide: Modernism, Mass Culture, Postmodernism.* London: Macmillan Press, 1980.

Irving, Ernest. "Music in Films." *Music & Letters* 24, no. 4 (October 1943): 223–235.

Jacobs, Lea. "John Stahl: Melodrama, Modernism, and the Problem of Naïve Taste." *Modernism/Modernity* 19, no. 2 (April 2012): 303–320.

Kalinak, Kathryn. *Settling the Score: Music and the Classical Hollywood Film.* Madison: University of Wisconsin Press, 1992.

Kanner, Hedwig. "Konzerte." *Der Morgen*, October 27, 1930: 4.

Kennaway, George. "Haydn's (?) Cello Concertos, 1860–1930: Editions, Performances, Reception." *Nineteenth-Century Review* 9, no. 2 (2012): 177–211.

262   BIBLIOGRAPHY

Kennedy, Margaret. *The Constant Nymph.* London: William Heinemann, 1924.

Kennedy, Margaret, and Basil Dean. *The Constant Nymph: A Play in Three Acts.* London: Samuel French, 1930.

Kennedy, Matthew. *Edmund Goulding's Dark Victory: Hollywood's Genius Bad Boy.* Madison: University of Wisconsin Press, 2004.

Knittel, K. M. "Wagner, Deafness, and the Reception of Beethoven's Late Style." *Journal of the American Musicological Society* 51, no. 1 (Spring 1998): 49–82.

König, René. *Briefwechsel.* Volume 1. Edited by Mario and Oliver König. Opladen: Leske + Budrich, 2000.

Korngold, Erich. "Faith in Music." In *Korngold and His World*, edited by Daniel Goldmark and Kevin C. Karnes, 255–259, introduced by Kevin C. Karnes. Princeton, NJ: Princeton University Press, 2019.

Korngold, Erich. "Some Experiences in Film Music." In *Korngold and His World*, edited by Daniel Goldmark, and Kevin C. Karnes, 247–252. Princeton, NJ: Princeton University Press, 2019.

Korngold, Erich. "Some Experiences in Film Music." In *Music and Dance in California*, edited by José Rodriguez, compiled by William J. Perlman, 137–139. Hollywood: Bureau of Musical Research, 1940.

Korngold, Luzi. *Erich Wolfgang Korngold: Ein Lebensbild.* Vienna: Elisabeth Lafite Verlag, 1967.

Kostelanetz, Richard, ed. *Aaron Copland. A Reader: Selected Writings, 1923–1972.* New York: Routledge, 2004.

Kretzschmar, Heinrich. *Führer durch den Kozertsaal.* 3 volumes. Leipzig: Liebeskind, 1887–1890.

Kulezic-Wilson, Danijela. *Sound Design Is the New Score: Theory, Aesthetics and Erotics of the Integrated Soundtrack.* New York: Oxford University Press, 2020.

Lack, Russell. *Twenty-Four Frames Under: A Buried History of Film Music.* London: Quartet Books, 1997.

Lehman, Frank. "Form und thematische Struktur in den Vorspannmusiken E. W. Kornoglds." In *Musik im Vorspann*, edited by Guido Heldt, Tarek Krohn, Peter Moormann, and Willem Strank, 11–52. FilmMusik 4. Munich: Richard Boorberg Verlag, 2020.

Lehman, Frank. *Hollywood Harmony: Musical Wonder and the Sound of Cinema.* New York: Oxford University Press, 2018.

Lehman, Frank. "Manufacturing the Epic Score: Hans Zimmer and the Sounds of Significance." In *Music in Epic Film: Listening to Spectacle*, edited by Stephen C. Meyer, 27–55. New York: Routledge, 2017.

Lenneberg, Hans. "The Myth of the Unappreciated Musical Genius." *The Musical Quarterly* 66, no. 2 (April 1980): 219–231.

Lerdahl, Fred. *Tonal Pitch Space.* New York: Oxford University Press, 2001.

Lerner, Neil. "'The Caverns of the Human Mind Are Full of Strange Shadows': Disability Representation, Henry Bellamann, and Korngold's Musical Subtexts in the Score for *Kings Row*." In *Korngold and His World*, edited by Daniel Goldmark and Kevin C. Karnes, 131–166. Princeton, NJ: Princeton University Press, 2019.

Lustig, Milton. *Music Editing for the Motion Pictures.* New York: Hastings House, 1980.

MacQueen, Scott. "Midsummer Dream, Midwinter Nightmare: Max Reinhardt and Shakespeare versus the Warner Bros." *The Moving Image: The Journal of the Association of Moving Image Archivists* 9, no. 2 (Fall 2009): 30–103.

Maltin, Leonard. "*The Sea Wolf*: Longer and Better!" https://leonardmaltin.com/the-sea-wolf-longer-and-better/, accessed March 28, 2024.

Martin, Linton. "Orchestra Gives Viennese Program." *Philadelphia Inquirer*, December 20, 1952: 18.

Marx, Joseph. "Bunte Musikwelt Von Joseph Marx." *Wiener Zeitung*, January 22, 1950: 4.

Marx, Joseph. "Orchester- und Klaviermusik von Joseph Marx." *Wiener Zeitung*, October 24, 1954: 3.

BIBLIOGRAPHY 263

Mason, Daniel Gregory. *The Romantic Composers.* New York: Macmillan, 1906.

Mathis-Rosenzweig, Alfred. *Gustav Mahler: New Insights into His Life, Times and Work.* Translated by Jeremy Barham. Aldershot: Ashgate, 2007.

Mercer, John, and Martin Shingler. *Melodrama: Genre, Style and Sensibility.* New York: Columbia University Press, 2013.

Miller, Lucasta. *The Brontë Myth.* London: Vintage, 2002.

Müller-Doohm, Stefan. *Adorno: A Biography.* Cambridge: Polity Press, 2005.

Neumeyer, David, and Nathan Platte. *Franz Waxman's Rebecca: A Film Score Guide.* Lanham, MD: Scarecrow Press, 2012.

Neumeyer, David. "The Resonances of Wagnerian Opera and Nineteenth-Century Melodrama in the Film Scores of Max Steiner." In *Wagner and Cinema*, edited by Jeongwon Joe and Sander L. Gilman, 111–130. Bloomington: Indiana University Press, 2010.

Painter, Karen. *Symphonic Aspirations: German Music and Politics, 1900–1945.* Cambridge, MA: Harvard University Press, 2007.

Palmer, Christopher. *The Composer in Hollywood.* London: Marion Boyars, 1990.

Parmenter, Ross. "He's Fed Up With Music for Films." *New York Times*, October 27, 1946: 69.

Parmenter, Ross. "Orchestra Led by Villa-Lobos: Brazilian Conducts Three of His Own Compositions in Philharmonic Concert." *New York Times*, March 29, 1957: 17.

Patteson, Thomas. *Instruments for New Music: Sound, Technology, and Modernism.* Berkeley: University of California Press, 2016.

Pfannkuch, Wilhelm. "Korngold, Julius Leopold." In *Musik in Geschicte und Gegenwart*, vol. 7 "Jensen-Kyrie," edited by Friedrich Blume, 1630–1631. Basel: Bärenreiter,1958.

Platte, Nathan. "Dream Analysis: Korngold, Mendelssohn, and Musical Adaptations in Warner Bros.' *A Midsummer Night's Dream* (1935)." *19th-Century Music* 34, no. 3 (Spring 2011): 211–236

Platte, Nathan. *Making Music in Selznick's Hollywood.* New York: Oxford University Press, 2018.

Platte, Nathan. "Max Steiner in the Studios, 1929–1939." In *The Routledge Companion to Screen Music and Sound*, edited by Ronald Sadoff, Miguel Mera, and Ben Winters, 257–269. New York: Routledge, 2017.

Pöllmann, Helmut. *Erich Wolfgang Korngold: Aspekte seines Schaffens.* Mainz: Schott, 1998.

Pöllmann, Helmut. "Preface." Translated by David Jenkinson. In *Korngold, Symphony in F Sharp*, Edition Eulenburg No. 8048, iii–viii. London: Ernst Eulenburg, Ltd, 2000.

Pravadelli, Veronica. *Classic Hollywood: Lifestyles and Film Styles of American Cinema 1930–1960.* Translated by Michael Theodore Meadows. Urbana: University of Illinois Press, 2015.

Putney, Bryant. "Wage Rates and Workers' Incomes." In *Editorial Research Reports 1938*, Volume 1. Washington, DC: CQ Press, 1938. http://library.cqpress.com/cqresearcher/cqr esrre1938012000, accessed May 18, 2020.

Redlich, Hans. "A Phenomenon Forgotten." *The Musical Times* 109, no. 1499 (January 1968): 41–42.

Renner, Hans. *Reclams Konzertführer: Orchestermusik.* Stüttgart: Reclam-Verlag, 1952.

Riess, Curt. *Wilhelm Furtwängler: A Biography.* Translated by Margaret Goldsmith. London: Frederick Muller, 1955.

Rózsa, Miklós. *Double Life: The Autobiography of Miklós Rózsa.* Tunbridge Wells: The Baton Press, 1984.

Rushton, Richard. *The Reality of Film: Theories of Filmic Reality.* Manchester: Manchester University Press, 2011.

Rutz, Hans. "E. W. Korngold: Symphonische Serenade." *Neue Zeitschrift für Musik* 111 (March 1950): 164–165.

Ryding, Erik, and Rebecca Pechefsky. *Bruno Walter: A World Elsewhere.* New Haven, CT: Yale University Press, 2001.

Schoenberg, Barbara Zeisl. "The Reception of Austrian Composers in Los Angeles: 1934–1950." *Modern Austrian Literature* 20, nos. 3–4 (1987): 135–144.

264 BIBLIOGRAPHY

Schonberg, Harold C. "Films—A New Dimension for Opera." *New York Times*, April 20, 1975: 133.

Schonberg, Harold C. "Records: Background Music for Films." *New York Times*, July 14, 1957: 88.

Schweinhardt, Peter, and Johannes C. Gall; Oliver Dahin, trans. "Composing for Film: Hanns Eisler's Lifelong Film Music Project." In *The Oxford Handbook of Film Music Studies*, edited by David Neumeyer, 131–187. New York: Oxford University Press, 2014.

Shirakawa, Sam H. *The Devil's Music Master: The Controversial Life and Career of Wilhelm Furtwängler*. New York: Oxford University Press, 1992.

Smith, Steven C. *Music by Max Steiner: The Epic Life of Hollywood's Most Influential Composer*. New York: Oxford University Press, 2020.

Stephens, E. J., and Marc Wanamaker. *Early Warner Bros. Studios*. Charleston, NC: Arcadia, 2010.

Stilwell, Robynn. "The Fantastical Gap Between Diegetic and Nondiegetic." In *Beyond the Soundtrack: Representing Music in Cinema*, edited by Daniel Goldmark, Laurence Kramer, and Richard Leppert, 184–202. Berkeley: University of California Press, 2007.

Stollberg, Arne, ed. *Erich Wolfgang Korngold: Wunderkind der Moderne oder letzter Romantiker?* Munich: Edition Text + Kritik, 2008.

Storm, Jason Ānanda Josephson. *Metamodernism: The Future of Theory*. Chicago: University of Chicago Press, 2022.

Straus, Joseph N. *Broken Beauty: Musical Modernism and the Representation of Disability*. New York: Oxford University Press, 2018.

Strutz, Herbert. "Schluß der Wiener Konzertseit 1930/31." *Freie Stimmen*, June 16, 1931: 2.

Tanner, Michael. "Good Humour, Bad Taste: L'Elisir d'amore; Das Wunder der Heliane." *The Spectator*. November 28, 2007.

Taruskin, Richard. *The Danger of Music and Other Anti-Utopian Essays*. Berkeley: University of California Press, 2008.

Taruskin, Richard. *The Oxford History of Western Music*, Volume 4: *The Early Twentieth Century*. New York: Oxford University Press, 2005.

Taubman, Howard. "Ormandy Conducts Philadelphians in Mahler Work at Carnegie Hall." *New York Times*, February 25, 1953: 23.

Taubman, Howard. "The Philharmonic—What's Wrong With It and Why." *New York Times*, April 29, 1956: 139.

Taubman, Howard. "Renardy Soloist in Lalo Symphony: Violinist in First Appearance with Philharmonic—Berlioz and Strauss on Program." *New York Times*, October 20, 1950: 32.

Thomas, Tony. *Music for the Movies*. 2nd edition. Los Angeles: Silman-James Press, 1997.

Till, Nicholas. "A New Glimmer of Light: Opera, Metaphysics and Mimesis." In *The Legacy of Opera: Reading Music Theatre as Experience and Performance*, edited by Dominic Symonds and Pamela Karantonis, 39–64. Amsterdam: Rodopi, 2013.

Tomlinson, Gary. *Metaphysical Song: An Essay on Opera*. Princeton, NJ: Princeton University Press, 1999.

Treitler, Leo. "The Politics of Reception: Tailoring the Present as Fulfilment of a Desired Past." *Journal of the Royal Musical Association* 116, no. 2 (1991): 280–298.

Trotter, William R. *Priest of Music: The Life of Dimitri Mitropoulos*. Portland, OR: Amadeus Press, 1995.

Ulrich, Homer. *Symphonic Music*. New York: Columbia University Press, 1952.

Ussher, Bruno David. "Film Music and Its Makers." *Hollywood Spectator* 14, no. 13 (October 14, 1939): 11–13.

Ussher, Bruno David. "Music in Current Pictures." *Hollywood Spectator* 13, no. 3 (May 7, 1938): 11–12.

Ussher, Bruno David. *Music in the Films, 1937–1941*. Edited by G. D. Hamann. Hollywood: Filming Today Press, 2011.

BIBLIOGRAPHY 265

van der Lek, Robbert. "Concert Music as Reused Film Music: E.-W. Korngold's Self-Arrangements." Translated by Mick Swithinbank. *Acta Musicologica* 66, fasc. 2 (July–December 1994): 78–112.

van der Lek, Robbert. *Diegetic Music in Opera and Film: A Similarity between Two Genres Analysed in Works by Erich Wolfgang Korngold (1897–1957).* Amsterdam: Rodopi, 1991.

Vaughan, Stephen. *Ronald Reagan in Hollywood: Movies and Politics.* Cambridge: Cambridge University Press, 1994.

Vermeulen, Timotheus, and Robin van den Akker. "Notes on Metamodernism." *Journal of Aesthetics and Culture* 2, no. 1 (2010). DOI: 10.3402/jac.v2i0.5677.

Wallis, Hal, and Charles Higham. *Starmaker: the Autobiography of Hal Wallis.* New York: Macmillan, 1980.

Walter, Michael. "Music of Seriousness and Commitment: The 1930s and Beyond." In *The Cambridge History of Twentieth-Century Music*, edited by Nicholas Cook and Anthony Pople, 286–306. Cambridge: Cambridge University Press, 2004.

Watts, Stephen. "Alfred Hitchcock on Music in Films." *Cinema Quarterly* 2, no. 2 (Winter 1933–1934): 80–83.

Weisenfeld, Judith. *Hollywood Be Thy Name: African American Religion in American Film, 1929–1949.* Berkeley: University of California Press, 2007.

White, Daniel. *The Music of* Harry Potter *and* The Lord of the Rings: *Sounds of Home in the Fantasy Franchise.* Abingdon: Routledge, 2024.

Whittall, Arnold. "Individualism and Accessibility: The Moderate Mainstream, 1945–1975." In *The Cambridge History of Twentieth Century Music*, edited by Nicholas Cook and Anthony Pople, 364–394. Cambridge: Cambridge University Press, 2004.

Wierzbicki, James. "The Hollywood Career of Gershwin's *Second Rhapsody*." *Journal of the American Musicological Society* 60, no. 1 (Spring 2007): 133–186.

Wierzbicki, James. *Film Music: A History.* Abingdon: Routledge, 2009.

Winters, Ben. "The Composer and the Studio: Korngold and Warner Bros." In *The Cambridge Companion to Film Music*, edited by Mervyn Cooke and Fiona Ford, 51–66. Cambridge: Cambridge University Press, 2016.

Winters, Ben. *Erich Wolfgang Korngold's* The Adventures of Robin Hood: *A Film Score Guide.* Lanham, MD: Scarecrow Press, 2007.

Winters, Ben. "Historical Sound-Film Presentation and the Closed-Curtain Roadshow Overture." In *The Oxford Handbook of Cinematic Listening*, edited by Carlo Cenciarelli, 139–155. New York: Oxford University Press, 2021.

Winters, Ben. "Influence." In *Richard Strauss in Context*, edited by Morten Kristiansen and Joseph E. Jones, 311–319. Cambridge: Cambridge University Press, 2020.

Winters, Ben. "Korngold's Merry Men: Music and Authorship in the Hollywood Studio System." DPhil dissertation, University of Oxford, 2006.

Winters, Ben. "Korngold's *Violanta*: Venice, Carnival, and the Masking of Identities." In *Music, Modern Culture, and the Critical Ear*, edited by Nicholas Attfield and Ben Winters, 51–74. Abingdon: Routledge, 2018.

Winters, Ben. "*Magic Fire*: A Wagner Film with a Difference." *The Wagner Journal* 15, no. 3 (November 2021): 11–22.

Winters, Ben. *Music, Performance, and the Realities of Film: Shared Concert Experiences in Screen Fiction.* New York: Routledge, 2014.

Winters, Ben. "Musical Wallpaper: Towards an Appreciation of Non-narrating Music in Film." *Music, Sound, and the Moving Image* 6, no. 1 (Spring 2012): 39–54.

Winters, Ben. "New Opportunities in Film: Korngold and Warner Bros." In *Korngold and His World*, edited by Daniel Goldmark and Kevin Karnes, 111–129. Princeton, NJ: Princeton University Press, 2019.

Winters, Ben. "The Non-diegetic Fallacy: Film, Music, and Narrative Space," *Music & Letters* 91, no. 2 (May 2010): 224–244.

266 BIBLIOGRAPHY

Winters, Ben. "Strangling Blondes: Nineteenth-Century Femininity and Korngold's *Die tote Stadt.*" *Cambridge Opera Journal* 23, nos. 1–2 (March–July 2011): 51–82.

Winters, Ben. "Swearing an Oath: Korngold, Film and the Sound of Resistance?" In *The Impact of Nazism on Twentieth-Century Music*, edited by Erik Levi, 61–76. Vienna: Böhlau Verlag, 2014.

Wissweiler, Eva, ed. *The Complete Correspondence of Clara and Robert Schumann.* Volume 1. Translated by Hidegard Fritsch and Ronald L Crawford. New York: Peter Lang, 1994.

Wrobel, William. "Self-Borrowing in the Music of Bernard Herrmann." *The Journal of Film Music* 1, nos. 2–3 (Fall–Winter 2003): 249–271.

Youmans, Charles. "'You Must Return to Life': Notes on the Reception of *Das Wunder der Heliane* and *Jonny spielt auf.*" In *Korngold and His World*, edited by Daniel Goldmark and Kevin C. Karnes, 37–65. Princeton, NJ: Princeton University Press, 2019.

Index

For the benefit of digital users, indexed terms that span two pages (e.g., 52–53) may, on occasion, appear on only one of those pages.

Tables and figures are indicated by an italic *t*, and *f* following the page numbers.

Adorno, Theodor W., 131–32, 147, 153, 215, 219–20, 233–34, 252–53, 254n.87
Adventures of Robin Hood, The, 24*t,* 29–31, 31n.32, 35–36, 37, 62–64, 69–70, 81–82, 84–87, 88n.16, 88–90, 91–92, 96–97, 99–101, 103n.49, 104–5, 110–11, 115–16, 117–24, 121*f,* 131–32, 140–41, 141*f,* 142, 146, 152–53, 159, 159n.45, 166–68, 168*f,* 169–72, 180–82, 207–8, 216–17, 219–20, 229*t,* 255–56
Alexander, Gerald, 21
Alleborn, Al, 27, 77–78
Aller, Eleanor, 115–16
Aller, Victor, 20–21
American Society of Composers, Authors, and Publishers (ASCAP), 64–66
Amy, George, 21, 41–42
Anderson, Gillian B., 225n.46
Another Dawn, 24*t,* 29n.23, 30–31, 35–36, 35n.44, 40, 44, 46–49, 53–54, 59, 60–61, 71–72, 103–4, 104*f,* 108–9, 111–12, 117–18, 123n.84, 142, 143–44, 148n.33, 150–51, 151*f,* 152n.40, 154–58, 156–58*f,* 159–61, 164–66, 166*f,* 178–82, 183–84, 229*t*
Anthony Adverse, 24*t,* 25–27, 29–31, 29n.23, 47, 49–50, 50n.91, 58–59, 85–87, 87n.14, 89n.19, 98–100, 103–4, 105*f,* 106–8, 137, 138*f,* 140–41, 141*f,* 142–43, 144–45, 145*f,* 149–50, 151–52, 153*f,* 172–73, 178–80, 187, 205n.50, 206–7, 229*t*
Arnaud, Leo, 32–35, 191
art, escapist function of, 10, 16, 216–17, 257
Arvey, Verna, 54–55

Bach, J.S., 84–85
  Toccata and Fugue in C major, BWV564, 221n.35
Bartók, Béla, 215
Bassermann, Albert, 77–78
Beelby, Malcolm, 78

Beethoven, Ludwig van, 85–86, 99–100, 235, 239–40, 250–51, 252–53
  "Appassionata" Sonata, Op. 57, 187, 221n.35
  Overture "Egmont", Op. 84, 225–26
  "Pathétique" Sonata, Op. 13, 187
  Symphony No. 7, Op. 92, 225–26
Beiden, Charles, 188–89
Bekker, Paul, 191n.27
Bellamann, Henry, 198–99
Berg, Alban; *Lulu,* 111n.62
Bessie, Alvah, 188–89
Between Two Worlds, 24*t,* 30–32, 74, 75, 85–86, 101–2, 110–11, 113–15, 117–18, 119*f,* 123–24, 137, 138–41, 141*f,* 143–44, 146, 147*f,* 149–50, 149*f,* 152n.40, 164–66, 166*f,* 188–91, 190*f,* 210–11, 224–25, 226–27, 229*t,* 231–33
Blanke, Henry, 27, 36–37, 38–39, 50, 56–57, 62–63, 66–67, 68–69, 76, 78, 172–73, 212, 213, 217n.23
Blau, Victor, 40–41, 99–100, 213, 214, 214n.11
Blumenstock, Mort, 70
Botstein, Leon, 6n.15, 233–34, 250–51
Bowles, Paul, 219–20
Boyer, Charles, 213
Brachtel, Karl Robert, 239
Bradford, James, 66–67
Bribitzer-Stull, Matthew, 133–34, 151n.37
Britten, Benjamin, 9, 253–54
Brown, Harry Joe, 41–42, 44
Brown, Royal S., 150n.35
Bruckner, Anton, 243–44, 250–51
Bryant, Joe E., 21
Bucharoff, Simon, 20–21, 20n.4, 29–30, 31–35, 33*t,* 53–54, 79–80, 102–3, 110n.61, 222–24
Buckner, Robert, 50, 51, 72–73, 85n.4
Byrns, Harald, 243–44, 245–46

Cagney, James, 39

Captain Blood, 12–13, 20–21, 24*t*, 27–28, 29n.23, 30–31, 32–35, 35n.44, 37, 41–42, 57–59, 87n.14, 88n.16, 96, 97–98, 100–1, 103–4, 106–8, 107*f*, 137–38, 138*f*, 140–41, 141*f*, 142, 145, 146*f*, 160*f*, 160–61, 165–66, 166n.51, 171–73, 195, 203–4, 229*t*

Carroll, Brendan, 7, 14, 63–64, 87n.15, 206–7, 220–21, 228, 232n.56, 236, 241–42, 243–44, 247n.59, 248–49

Casablanca, 41–42, 102–3

Cassidy, Claudia, 240–41

Centrone, Vito, 20–21, 20n.3

Chambers, Dudley, 67–68, 77–78

Charge of the Light Brigade, The, 32n.37

Chasin, George, 108

Cheng, William, 107n.53

Chopin, Fryderyk, 196–97, 235, 252–53
Nocturne in E flat major, Op. 9 No. 2, 221n.35

Chowrimootoo, Christopher, 9, 10, 253–54

Christianson, Rupert, 249–50

chromatic mediant chord progressions, 118–25, 124–25*f*, 226–27

Churain, Jaro B., 20–21, 29, 31–32, 33*t*, 85–86, 87–88

Classical Hollywood film, 83–84, 128–29, 168–69, 173, 174–75, 184–85, 193–94, 208–9

Classical Hollywood film score, 11, 17–18, 128–29, 132, 147, 164–65, 166–69, 173, 175–76, 184–85, 192, 195, 210–11, 233

click track, 11–12, 11n.30, 13–14, 93–96, 95*f*.
See also Korngold, Erich Wolfgang, use of synchronization technology

Connelly, Marc, 206

Constant Nymph, The, 18–19, 24*t*, 27, 30–31, 40–41, 71, 73, 75, 87n.15, 110–11, 113–15, 117–18, 119*f*, 144–45, 145*f*, 172n.63, 185–87, 210–11, 212–17, 228–31, 229*t*

continuity editing, 132, 166–69, 180–81

Cooper, David, 97n.25, 175n.5, 231–33

Copland, Aaron; *Music for a Great City*, 233n.61

copyright, 53–54, 56–57, 60n.21, 64–66, 69–70, 76–77, 79–80, 213n.9

Crime School, 102–3

Crowther, Bosley, 219–20

cue identification systems, 28–29, 29n.23

cue timing sheets, 11–14, 11n.30, 27–28, 86–87, 90–91, 91*f*, 93–96, 161n.47, 169, 170*t*, 225–26

Curtiz, Michael, 50, 62–63, 67n.44, 68–69

Cutter, Murray, 32–35

Damiani, Leo, 20–21

Danton, 59–61

Davidson, Jane, 6–7, 21n.6

Davis, Bette, 67n.44, 195–96, 221n.35

Dawson, Ralph, 44

Deception, 18–19, 24*t*, 27, 29n.23, 31–32, 78–80, 81–82, 88n.16, 99–100, 103–4, 110–11, 113–16, 137, 139n.19, 140–41, 172n.63, 187, 189, 210–11, 214–15, 220–26, 223*f*, 229*t*, 236–38

de Havilland, Oliva, 24*t* n.e, 58–59, 67–68, 73

de Novara, Medea, 66–67

Del Cioppo, Eugene, 20–21

Dent, Edward, 2–3

Deutsch, Adolph, 20–21, 53–54, 64–65, 80–81, 112–13, 219–20

Devotion, 24*t*, 24*t* n.e, 29–35, 50–51, 72–73, 74, 86–87, 103–4, 104*f*, 105*f*, 108–9, 110–12, 113–15, 117–18, 125–28, 127*f*, 128*f*, 137, 138n.18, 139n.19, 142, 144–45, 150, 153, 166–68, 178–80, 205–6, 227, 229*t*

diatonicism, 118–20, 123–24, 126–28, 138–40, 143–44, 199–200, 226–27

Dieterle, William, 39, 40n.56, 60–61, 66n.41, 192, 235–36

disability (in film and music), 17–18, 175–76, 198–203, 206

ditto printing, 21, 102–3

Don Juan, 120n.81

Double Indemnity, 225–26

Downes, Olin, 240–41

Dubin, Al, 47, 48n.83, 48–49

Dubin, Joe, 29–30, 32n.36

Duchen, Jessica, 7, 12–13, 15–16, 246n.55, 251–52

Dukas, Paul; *Ariane et Barbe-Bleu*, 135

Dvořák, Antonin; Symphony No. 9 "From the New World," 112–13

Eggett, Charles, 20–21, 88n.16

Eisler, Hanns, 112–13, 131–32, 147, 153, 219–20

Ellfeldt, Bill, 20–21

Emmanuel, Manuel, 20–21

Escape Me Never, 18–19, 24*t*, 27, 29n.23, 30–31, 32–35, 41n.63, 49–50, 75, 78–80, 81–82, 92–93, 92–94*f*, 108–9, 110–11, 126n.94, 137–38, 140*f*, 143*f*, 143–45, 146*f*, 147–49, 150–51, 151*f*, 168–69, 177n.11, 187, 210–11, 217–18, 220–21, 228, 229*t*
"Love for Love," 49–50, 77–78, 108, 254–55

Fabares, Nanette, 67–68

Fall, Leo; *Rosen aus Florida*, 62–63, 100–1

Farmer, Michael, 256–57

INDEX   269

Faulkner, Robert, 6–7, 21n.6
Feist, Leonard, 246–47
Fiechtner, Helmut A., 241, 243–44
Findlay, Hal, 20–21, 28n.22
Flynn, Errol, 46, 60–61, 67n.44, 68–69, 142, 168–69, 228–31
Fontaine, Joan, 213
Forbstein, Leo, 20–22, 22n.11, 25–27, 26n.13, 29–30, 32–35, 36–37, 39, 40–41, 47, 47n.80, 48, 50n.91, 57, 61–62, 66–67, 70, 72, 74, 76, 79–81, 85n.4, 97–98, 99–100, 213, 214, 221n.34
Forrest, Dave, 21, 39
Fortner, Wolfgang, 248–49n.70
Franchetti, Aldo, 29n.23, 49–50, 58–59, 98–99
Franklin, Peter, 7–8, 116n.75, 133n.7, 137n.16, 173n.66, 199n.43, 228–31, 230t n.b, 253–54, 257n.94
Friedhofer, Hugo, 16–17, 20–21, 20n.4, 25–27, 29–35, 31nn.32–33, 33t, 47, 53–54, 70, 80, 87–88, 93–96, 111–12, 178–80
Friedman, Izzy, 21, 31–32
Fruchtman, Aaron, 81n.100
Fuchs, Daniel, 188–89
full score manuscripts (of Korngold films), 29n.23, 29–30, 30n.28, 31–32, 35n.39, 35–36, 49–50, 74–75, 87n.15, 88–93, 102–3, 104–5, 106t, 115n.71, 115–16, 116n.72, 140n.20, 178–80, 182n.17, 222–24
Furtwängler, Wilhelm, 241–42, 243, 247n.61

Garfield, John, 85–86
gender (in film), 17–18, 175–76, 193–96, 203–6
Gerhardt, Charles, 249–50
Gershwin, George; Second Rhapsody, 236–38
Gerster, Ottmar, 248–49n.70
Ghost and Mrs Muir, The, 231–33
Gibbons, Jimmie, 66–67
Giger, Andreas, 236, 248
Gilliam, Bryan, 5–6, 7–8, 14, 236–38
Give Us This Night, 23, 24t, 48–49, 57–59, 58n.17, 97n.26, 97–98
Goettman, Jay, 78–79
Goldberg, Albert, 240–41
Golschmann, Vladimir, 239–40, 245–48, 249
Gone With The Wind, 102–3
Goulding, Edmund, 213
Green Pastures, The, 24t, 29n.23, 49–50, 50n.91, 58–59, 102–3, 165–66, 166f, 206–8
Greenstreet, Sydney, 126–28
Grier, Art, 20–21
Grimley, Daniel, 231–33
Grofé, Ferde, 112–13

Groves, George, 39, 44
Gunning, Tom, 193–95

Haas, Michael, 11–12, 14–15
Hammerstein II, Oscar, 48–49
Hammond, Laurens, 112–13
Handel, G. F., 84–85
Hansen, Miriam, 193
Harford, Margaret, 241n.26
harmonic planing. See parallel voice-leading
Hartmann, Rudolf, 235–36
Haydn, Joseph, 97n.27
    Cello Concerto in D, Hob. VIIb: 2, 79–80, 220–21, 225–26
Hayworth, Peter, 241
Hearts Divided, 24t, 29n.23, 49–50, 58–59
Heifetz, Jascha, 239–41
Heindorf, Ray, 20–21, 29–30, 32–35, 32n.35, 56, 70, 79–80, 113–15, 254–55
Henreid, Paul, 74
Herrmann, Bernard, 97n.25, 175n.5, 231–33
    Sinfonietta for Strings, 232n.58
    Wuthering Heights, 231–33
hexatonic collection, 123–25, 159–60
Higgins, Ed., 21, 28n.22
Hindemith, Paul, 215
historiography of music, 2, 7–8, 16, 18–19, 210–11, 238, 252–53, 254–55
Hitchcock, Alfred, 219n.26
Hollingdale, R. J., 21–22
Hollywood, entertainment values of, 8–9, 11–12, 175–76, 194–96, 198–99, 208–9. See also mass culture, value of
Hollywood Independent Citizens Committee of the Arts, Sciences and Professions (HICCASP), 15–16, 16n.49, 206–7
Hollywood studio system, 16–17, 21–22, 83–84
Holston, Kim R., 31–32n.34
Honold, Elisabeth, 101–2
Hopf, Hans, 235–36
Howe, James Wong, 198–99
Hsieh, Amanda, 7–8, 107n.53, 107n.55, 133n.8
Huhn, Bruno, 40–41
Huyssen, Andreas, 11–12, 13–14, 252–53, 255–56

Ingram, Rex, 206–7
Irving, Ernest, 219–20

Jackman, Fred, 38–39
Jacob, Heinrich Edward, 15–16
Jacobs, Lea, 193
Johnson, Hall, 49–50, 206–7

270 INDEX

Juarez, 24*t*, 29–32, 40n.56, 46–47, 47n.77,
66–67, 87n.15, 88–91, 89*f*, 99–101, 102–3,
120n.82, 131–32, 137, 195–98, 198*f*, 207–9,
210–11, 229*t*
"La Paloma," 195–98
Juárez y Maximiliano, 66–67. *See also Mad
Empress, The*

Kalinak, Kathryn, 12–13, 42, 116–17
Kaun, Bernard, 29–30, 32–35, 49–50
Keighley, William, 61–63
Kendall, Raymond, 240–41
Kennedy, Margaret, 71, 75, 214
Kiepura, Jan, 48–49, 57–58, 57n.13
King Kong, 183n.18
Kings Row, 24*t*, 30–31, 32–35, 40–41, 46–47,
47n.79, 70–71, 81–82, 88n.16, 90n.20,
99–100, 110–11, 113–15, 117–18, 120n.81,
137–40, 139*f*, 140*f*, 142–44, 187, 198–204,
199–204*f*, 208–9, 215, 228, 229*t*
Kisco, Chas, 78
Klemperer, Otto, 241
Knittel, K. M., 250n.76
Koehler, Ted, 49–50
Koenig, Bill, 39, 57
Kolodin, Irving, 239–41
König, René, 215
Korngold, Erich Wolfgang
career of, 4, 7–8, 11, 210–11, 235–36, 250–
51, 254–55
charitable donations of, 54n.3, 70, 80–81
compositional identity of, 17–18, 84–85,
128–29, 175–76, 216–17, 228–31, 255–56
compositional technique of, 6–8, 17–19, 88–
96, 130–31, 132, 164–65, 171–72, 255–56
contracts of, 14–15, 16–17, 25–27, 53–82
fanfares in music of, 96–97, 98–99, 103n.49,
115–26, 142–43, 146, 150–51, 169–71,
180–82, 199–200, 210–11
financial recompense of, 54–55, 56, 57–60,
59n.19, 61, 62–64, 66–71, 72–73, 76, 78–
79, 80–82, 207n.60
fondness for keyboard percussion of, 111–12
harmonic characteristics in music of, 46n.73,
84–85, 106–8, 116–29
as humorist, 108–10
Jewish identity of, 7–8, 106–8,
133n.8, 241–42
and modernism, 2–4, 7, 8–9, 198–200,
202–3, 208–9, 214–15, 218, 226–27, 252–
53, 254–55
myths about, 10–18, 19, 23–25, 37–38, 40, 44,
51–52, 53–54, 60–61, 81–82, 84–85, 86–87,
88, 93–96, 238, 250–52, 256–57

non-thematic material in film music of, 130–
31, 132, 159–66, 160*f*
operetta arrangements of, 1–2, 6–7, 23,
49n.89, 55–56, 62–63, 66, 71–72, 96–97,
100–1, 108–9, 236–38
as orchestrator, 29–30, 35n.42, 110–
12, 178–80
pencil annotations of, 28–29, 35–36, 88–90,
92–93, 98–99, 108–9, 110–11, 182n.17
piano-conductor scores of, 35–36, 91–92,
156n.42, 182n.17
place in music history of, 2, 7–8, 18–19, 208–
9, 236–38, 251–57
political engagement of, 6n.15, 15–16, 16n.49
reception history of, 15–16, 18–19, 238–52
recycling practices of, 17–18, 84–85, 96–106,
128–29, 146, 231–33, 255–56
relationship with Schott, 15–16, 248–50
scholarship about, 4–9, 10–11
short score manuscripts of, 20–52, 33*t*,
58n.17, 74–75, 85–86, 87–90, 89*f*,
91–93, 92–95*f*, 96, 98–99, 104–5, 114–15*f*,
116n.72, 152n.38, 179*f*, 218n.24, 222–24,
222n.38, 223*f*, 230*t* n.e
sketches of, 85–86, 92–93, 92*f*, 99–100,
120n.82
stylistic eclecticism of, 84–85, 106–10, 116–
17, 128–29, 255–56
synchronization practices of, 11–14,
16–17, 85–86, 88–90, 92–93, 161–64, 168–
73, 180–81
thematicism in music of, 130–58, 198–99,
200–2, 203–6
timbral characteristics in music of, 84–85,
110–16, 128–29
use of bell sonorities, 110–11, 145, 150, 180–
81, 189
use of mickey-mousing, 109–10. *See
also* Korngold, Erich Wolfgang,
synchronization practices of
use of multi-track recording techniques,
115–16
use of stingers, 164–65, 176–77n.8, 184–
85, 189–91
use of synchronization technology,
11–14, 87n.12, 88–96, 161–64, 161n.48,
176–77n.8
working methods of, 23–25, 84–85, 86–
87, 255–56
Korngold, Erich Wolfgang, works of
"Angedenken," 100–1
Cello Concerto, Op. 37, 115–16, 220–25,
226–27, 228, 229*t*, 231–33, 241–42
"Das Mädchen," 68–69n.50, 101–2

Das Wunder der Heliane, Op. 20, 1–2, 4–5, 6–7, 57n.13, 101–2, 106–9, 110–12, 117n.78, 124–25, 133n.8, 136, 136n.15, 169n.54, 171n.58, 173n.66, 239, 249–50, 255–56
Der Ring des Polykrates, Op. 7, 1–2, 108–9, 135f, 135, 136n.15, 171n.58, 249–50
Der Sturm, 100–1
Der Vampir, 101–2, 107n.54, 144n.25
"Die Gansleber im Haus Duschnitz," 232n.56
Die Kathrin, Op. 28, 1–2, 15–16, 96–97, 104n.51, 106–8, 110–12, 117n.78, 123n.84, 135–36, 143n.23, 145n.27, 151n.36, 171n.58, 181n.15, 229t, 243–44, 248
Die stumme Serenade, Op. 36, 108–9, 144–45, 228, 229t, 236–38, 249, 255–56
Die tote Stadt, Op. 12, 1–3, 4n.6, 49n.87, 66, 106–9, 110–12, 117n.78, 118n.79, 124n.90, 125n.93, 125–28, 133n.8, 135–36, 140–41, 145, 171n.58, 195n.35, 214n.14, 249–50, 254–55
Drei Gesänge, Op. 18, 255–56
Drei Lieder, Op. 22, 100–1, 231–33, 255–56
Fünf Lieder, Op. 38, 101n.43, 101–2, 229t
Helen Goes to Troy, 236–38
Kaiserin Zita-Hymne, 100–1, 255–56
Much Ado About Nothing, Op. 11, 249
Narrenlieder, Op. 29, 229t
"Österreichischer Soltatenabschied," 100n.40
Passover Psalm, Op. 30, 54n.3, 229t
Piano Concerto in C Sharp, Op. 17, 123n.84, 202–3
Piano Quintet, Op. 15, 100–1, 202–3, 231–33, 255n.90
Piano Sonata No. 2, Op. 2, 117n.78
Piano Sonata No. 3, Op. 25, 124n.90
Prayer, Op. 32, 229t
Romance-Impromptu, 221n.35
Rosalinda, 71–72, 236–38
Schauspiel-Ouvertüre, Op. 4, 123n.84
"Schneeglöckchen," 100–1, 231–33, 255–56
Sechs Einfache Lieder, Op. 9, 101–2
Sextet for Strings, Op. 10, 126n.94, 232n.56
Sinfonietta, Op. 5, 108–9, 124n.90
Sonnett für Wien, Op. 41, 229t
String Quartet No. 3, Op. 34, 7–8, 184, 202n.47, 224, 226–28, 229t, 231–33, 241–42
Suite for Piano Quartet, Op. 23, 100–1, 202–3, 226–27, 231–33, 255–56
Sursum Corda, Op. 13, 62–63, 69–70, 100–1, 216–17, 255–56
Symphonic Serenade, Op. 39, 229t, 241–43, 249
Symphony in F Sharp, Op. 40, 15–16, 202n.47, 228–33, 229t, 235–36, 243–50

Theme and Variations for Orchestra, Op. 42, 229t
Tomorrow, Op. 33, 73, 214, 220–21, 229t (see also *Constant Nymph, The*)
Vier kleine Karikaturen für Kinder, Op. 19, 215
Vier Lieder des Abschieds, Op. 14, 100–2, 231–33, 255n.90
Vier Shakespeare-Lieder, Op. 31, 229t
Violanta, Op. 8, 1–2, 106–9, 117n.78, 123n.84, 126nn.94–95, 136, 145, 171–72, 195n.35, 250n.75
Violin Concerto, Op. 35, 197n.38, 229t, 231–33, 239–42, 243
Violin Sonata, Op. 6, 99–100, 231–33, 255–56
Zwölf Eichendorff Lieder, 100–2
Korngold, George, 16–17
Korngold, Julius, 6–7, 51–52, 57, 66, 214, 225–26, 228–31
Korngold, Luzi, 7–8, 13–14, 15–17, 20–21, 25–27, 26n.15, 57–58, 62–64, 206–7, 212n.3, 224, 241–42, 243–44, 246–47, 248, 251–52
Koster, Theodore, 112–13
Kralik, Heinrich, 243–44
Kretzschmar, Heinrich, 216–17
Krise, Teddy, 35–36, 36n.48
Kulezic-Wilson, Danijela, 174–75

Lack, Russell, 12–13
Lehman, Frank, 83n.2, 117n.76, 118–20, 123–24, 171–73
leitmotif, 7, 133, 134, 147, 153. *See also* Korngold, Erich Wolfgang, thematicism in music of
Lerdahl, Fred, 123–24
Lerner, Neil, 198n.42
Lester, Frankie, 49–50
Levinson, Nathan, 21, 39, 41–42, 61–62, 97–98
Lincoln in the White House, 99–100
Lissauer, Hermann, 85–86, 99–100
Liszt, Franz, 97–98, 100–1, 233
  Mazeppa, 98–99
  Prometheus, 98–99
Little Lord Fauntleroy, 97n.26
Lost Patrol, The, 102–3
Love, Montagu, 213
Lupino, Ida, 77–78

Macario, Anthony, 88n.16
MacEwan, Walter, 61
MacIntyre, Hal, 49–50
MacLaughlin, Joe, 79–80
MacQueen, Scott, 22n.11
Mad Empress, The, 66–67, 81–82

272 INDEX

Magic Fire, 23n.12, 69–70, 87n.13, 192, 212n.3, 226n.47, 233–34, 235–36

Mahler, Gustav, 23, 243–44, 250–51
  Des Knaben Wunderhorn, 100–1
  Symphony No. 1, 180–81
  Symphony No. 2, 236–38

main titles (in film), 96, 98n.33, 100–1, 117–18, 123n.85, 123–24, 137–38, 171–73, 181–82, 229*t* n.a

Majestic, RMS, 1–3, 6–7

Maltese Falcon, The, 112–13

marimba, 111–12, 113–15, 165–66, 176–77n.8, 178–80

Marshall, Brenda, 68–69

Marx, Joseph, 239, 242–43, 243n.41, 244–45

mass culture, value of, 2, 7, 8–9, 11, 84–85, 208–9, 211, 220, 228–31, 250–57

materiality of film sound and music, 17–18, 173, 174–75, 176–81, 183–92, 197–98, 208–9, 210–11

Mattison, Frank, 67–68

McCord, Hal, 41–42, 44, 61–62, 73, 213

Melichar, Alois, 235–36

melodrama (film), 78–79, 137, 193–94, 198–99

melodrama (stage), 174–75

Melton, James, 49n.89

Mendelssohn, Felix, 15–16, 239–40
  A Midsummer Night's Dream, Op. 21 and Op. 61, 1–2, 55–57

metamodernism, 256–57

middlebrow, 9–10, 253–54

Midsummer Night's Dream, A, 13–14, 22n.11, 23–27, 24*t*, 29–30, 37, 38, 39, 55–57, 58–59, 64–65, 72–73, 81–82, 87n.12, 87n.15, 123n.85, 235–36

Mitropoulos, Dimitri, 246–48

modernism, 2–4, 6–9, 10, 11–12, 14–15, 16, 17–18, 19, 21–22, 32–35, 54–55, 125–26, 128–29, 174–75, 184–85, 193–95, 208–9, 214, 215, 220, 233–34, 251–53, 255–56

modernist anxiety, 8–9, 18–19, 54–55, 83–84, 193, 206, 228–31, 233–34, 251–53

modernity, 2–3, 4, 6–7, 8–9, 175–76, 198–99, 202–3, 257

Monroe, Vaughan, 49–50

Monteverdi, Claudio; *L'Orfeo*, 98–99

Moross, Jerome, 29–30, 32–35

Motion Picture Relief Fund, 70

Moviola, 27–28, 28n.22

Mozart, Wolfgang Amadeus, 60, 240n.25, 248n.66, 250–51

multi-track recording, 13–14

Munch, Charles, 246–47

Music Publishers Holding Corporation (MPHC), 73, 75, 76–77

narrative source of music in film, 17–18, 48–49, 174–76, 180–82, 183n.18, 184–85, 189, 192, 210–11, 218. *See also* materiality of film sound and music

Neumeyer, David, 5–6

Newman, Alfred, 30–31, 46

Nietzsche "legend," 21–22, 23–25, 51–52

Nilson, Einar, 222–24

Normandie, 2–4, 24*t* n.d

Novachord, 112–15, 113–15*f*, 165–66, 189–91

Nunó, Jaime, 99–100

Obringer, Roy J., 59–60, 62–63, 64–65, 70, 78–79

octatonic collection, 120–23, 124–25, 196–97, 198*f*

Of Human Bondage, 20n.4, 24*t*, 29n.23, 30–31, 74–75, 76, 85–86, 88n.16, 91–92, 95*f*, 103n.49, 110–12, 113–15, 117–18, 119*f*, 137–40, 140*f*, 142, 143–44, 159, 172–73, 176–77, 179*f*, 187

opera and film music, comparison of, 4–7, 16–18, 128–29, 130–31, 132, 133–34, 136, 137, 145, 168–69, 171–72, 173, 174–75, 254–55, 256–57

orchestral parts (film), 29, 35–36, 116n.74

orchestration, 29–35, 83–84, 110–16

Ormandy, Eugene, 243, 249

Ottley, Roi, 206–7

Outward Bound, 188–89. *See also Between Two Worlds*

Palmer, Christopher, 14

parallel voice-leading, 117–18, 118–19*f*, 120n.82, 186–87

Paramount Pictures, 23, 25–27, 48–49, 57–59, 58n.16, 59n.19, 60n.21, 63–64, 97–98

Parmenter, Ross, 236–38

Pease, Dick, 74

pentatonic scale, 125–26, 127*f*, 153, 227

Peter Ibbetson, 32–35

Pfannkuch, Wilhelm, 239

Phantom Crown, The, 99–100. *See also Juarez*

Plantamura, Ed, 20–21

Platte, Nathan, 40n.56, 41–42, 42n.65, 46, 55–56, 83–84, 85n.7, 97n.26, 102–3

playback. *See* prescoring

Polito, Sol, 169–71

Pöllmann, Helmut, 228, 245

popular culture, value of. *See* mass culture, value of

Pravadelli, Veronica, 193–96, 206
Prawy, Marcel, 239
prescoring, 23–25, 27, 28–29, 58–59, 67–69, 71, 72–73, 74, 75, 77–79, 98–99, 212, 213, 217
previews, 23–25, 42, 46–47, 48, 61–62, 74–75, 76, 78, 89n.18, 97–98, 213, 218
Prince and the Pauper, The, 24*t*, 29–31, 61–62, 103n.49, 110–11, 142–43, 144–45, 146n.30, 151–52, 172–73, 181–82, 229*t*
Prinz, LeRoy, 78
Prisoner of Zenda, The, 46
Private Lives of Elizabeth and Essex, The, 24*t*, 30–31, 67–69, 87n.15, 103–4, 110–11, 118–23, 122–23*f*, 124–25, 125*f*, 131–32, 137, 142–43, 153–54, 155*f*, 159–60, 160*f*, 172–73, 176–77, 180–82, 183*f*, 210–11, 220n.33, 225n.44, 228, 229*t*, 231–33, 255–56
producer-unit system, 36–37
Psycho, 232n.58
Pugni, Cesare; *La Esmerelda*, 72–73, 85n.4

quartal harmony, 125–26, 127*f*

Raab, Leonid, 29–30, 32–35
race (in film), 17–18, 144–45, 175–76, 206–8
Raine, Norman Reilly, 67–68
Ravel, Maurice; *Ma Mère l'Oye*, 196–97
Rebecca, 112–13
Redlich, Hans, 243–44, 245
Reiner, Fritz, 246–47
Reinhardt, Max, 1–2, 1n.1, 37, 38–39, 55–56, 59–60, 63–64, 71–72, 235–36
Reitler, Josef, 239–40, 248n.67
Republic Pictures, 69–70
Riemann, Hugo, 219–20
RKO Pictures, 69–70, 102–3
roadshowing, 22n.11, 31–32, 31–32n.34, 44n.70, 87–88, 87n.15
Robson, Flora, 68–69, 142–43
Roder, Milan, 20–21, 20n.4, 29–32, 31n.32, 33*t*, 102–3, 115–16
Roemheld, Heinz, 20–21, 35n.44, 49–50
Roosevelt, Franklin D., 15–16
Rosenzweig, Alfred, 250–51
Rose of the Rancho, 24*t*, 57–58, 58n.17
Ross, Lanny, 49n.89
Roughly Speaking, 64–65
Rózsa, Miklós, 81–82, 236–38
    Spellbound Concerto, 231–33
Rushton, Richard, 10, 16, 175–76, 194–95, 216–17, 256–57
Russell, Andy, 49–50
Rutz, Hans, 242–43

Saint-Saëns, Camille; Cello Concerto No. 1 in A minor, 79–80, 221n.34
Sampson, Nina, 20–21, 85n.4
Schary, Dore, 108
Schering, Arnold, 219–20
Schneider, S., 79–80
Schoen, Helen, 79–80, 85n.4, 221n.34
Schoenberg, Arnold, 215, 252n.84
Scholl, Jack, 32–35, 35n.41
Schonberg, Harold C., 4n.6, 237n.11, 249–50
Schubert, Franz, 235, 250–51, 252–53
    Impromptu in G-flat Major, D. 889/3, 99–100
    Impromptu in A-flat Major, D. 935, 221n.35
    Symphony No. 8, D.759, 225–26
Schumann, Robert, 196–97
Schwartz, Art, 47, 48
Scores, Phil, 21, 28n.22
scoring sessions, 29, 35–37, 36n.45, 88–90, 91–92
Scott of the Antarctic, 231–33
Sea Hawk, The, 21, 24*t*, 29–30, 31–36, 31–32n.34, 35n.41, 68–69, 85–86, 90–91, 91*f*, 96, 101–3, 104–5, 106*t*, 110–11, 115–16, 117–24, 118*f*, 119*f*, 124*f*, 125–26, 126*f*, 137–41, 138n.18, 140*f*, 142–43, 144–45, 145*f*, 146*f*, 147, 148*f*, 149–52, 150n.35, 151*f*, 159n.43, 159–68, 160*f*, 162*t*, 164*f*, 172–73, 176–77, 178*f*, 180–82, 181*f*, 229*t*
Sea Wolf, The, 24*t*, 30–31, 32–35, 35n.41, 46–47, 54, 70, 108, 110–12, 113–15, 114*f*, 115*f*, 123n.85, 125–26, 127*f*, 137–38, 140*f*, 140–41, 141*f*, 146, 147*f*, 152–53, 159–60, 159n.45, 160*f*, 164–66, 166*f*, 172n.60, 172–73, 176–77, 184–85, 227, 229*t*
Selzer, Eddie, 59–60, 61, 81n.100
Selznick, David O., 41–42, 42n.65, 46, 83–84, 97n.26
shared subjectivity, 186–87, 210–11, 218
Simpsons, The, 256–57
Smith, Stephen C., 81–82
Some Must Watch. See Spiral Staircase, The
Something Wild, 233n.61
sound design, 173, 176–77. *See also* materiality of film sound and music
Spellbound, 97n.26
Spiral Staircase, The, 69–70, 108
spotting processes and notes, 27–29, 41–42, 41n.63, 43–44, 86–87
Star is Born, A, 97n.26
Star Wars, 120n.81
Starr, Herman, 64–65

274 INDEX

Steiner, Max, 20–21, 31n.33, 32n.37, 37–38, 40n.56, 42n.65, 53–54, 64–65, 70–71, 80–82, 93–96, 102–3, 120n.82, 137–38, 183n.18, 219–20, 236–38
Stilwell, Robynn, 184–85
Storm, Jason Ānanda Josephson, 256n.91
Straus, Joseph, 198–99, 202–3
Strauss II, Johann; *Die Fledermaus*, 71–72, 236–38
Strauss, Richard, 8–9, 106–8, 124–25, 135, 182, 243–44
 Also Sprach Zarathustra, Op. 30, 191n.27
 Der Rosenkavalier, Op. 59, 8–9, 180n.13
 Ein Heldenleben, Op. 40, 236–38
 Elektra, Op. 58, 135
 Salome, Op. 54, 131–32, 169–71
 Vier letzte Lieder, Op. posth., 241–42
Stravinsky, Igor, 6n.14, 105n.52, 215
 The Rite of Spring, 6n.14
Strecker, Willy, 243–44, 248
Sullivan, Jack, 213
Swarthout, Gladys, 48–49

Tanner, Michael, 249–50
Taplinger, Robert S., 70
Taruskin, Richard, 4–6, 6n.14, 110n.59, 130–31
Tauber, Richard, 49n.89
Taubman, Howard, 236–38, 247–48
Theilade, Nini, 39
They Made Me a Criminal, 102–3
Thomas, Tony, 13–14, 13n.39, 16–17
timing punches. *See* Korngold, Erich Wolfgang, use of synchronization technology
Toch, Ernst, 4n.6, 29–30, 32–35, 32n.37
Torres, Miguel, 66–67
trailer cues, 30–32, 31nn.32–33, 74–75, 87–88, 213
Turner, Ray, 74

unobtrusiveness of music in film, 211, 219–20
Ussher, Bruno David, 131–32, 137, 219–20

van der Lek, Robbert, 224n.41, 230*t* n.c
van Einem, Gottfried, 243
Vane, Sutton, 188–89
Vaughan, Clifford, 20–21
Vaughan Williams, Ralph, 231–33, 245
 Sinfonia Antartica, 231–33
 Vision of William Blake, The, 231–33
Vaughn, Stephen, 15–16
Verdi, Giuseppe; *Il Trovatore*, 98n.31
vibraphone, 111–12, 154, 164n.49, 165–66, 178n.12, 190n.26

Villa-Lobos, Heitor, 236–38

Wagner, Richard, 133–34, 226n.47, 233–34, 235–36, 252–53
 Die Walküre, 173n.66
 Lohengrin, 32n.35
 Siegfried Idyll, 233, 234*f*
 Tristan und Isolde, 192
Wallace, W. S., 79–80
Wallis, Hal B., 21–22, 23–27, 36–52, 50n.91, 53–54, 61–63, 68–69, 70–71, 88–90, 97–98, 172n.64, 206–7, 212
 cutting notes of, 42, 43–44, 44n.69, 46–47, 46n.76, 68–69
Walter, Bruno, 246–48
Walter, Michael, 5–6
Warner, Jack, 25–27, 26n.15, 36–37, 40–41, 56–57, 61, 66–67, 81n.100, 96, 213, 218
Warner Bros. *See also* Korngold, Erich Wolfgang, contracts of
 Burbank studio, 25–27
 Legal Department, 40–41, 99–100
 Music Department, 20–22, 23–36, 47, 48, 53–54, 77–78, 79–81, 85n.4, 88–90, 98–99, 221n.35, 257
 Research Department, 72–73, 85–86, 85n.4
 Sound Alley, 25–27
 Sound Department, 39, 44, 61–62
 studio personnel of, 16–17, 23–27, 36–37
Warren, Fran, 49–50
Waxman, Franz, 20–21, 80–81, 97n.26, 112–13, 236–38, 241–42
Webb, Roy, 97n.26, 108
Webern, Anton, 1–2, 250–51, 251n.81
Weisenfeld, Judith, 206–7
Welles, Orson, 15–16
Weston, Paul, 49–50
White, Daniel, 128n.97
White, Frank, 112–13
White Flood, 112–13
Whittall, Arnold, 245
whole-tone scale, 125–26, 126n.95, 127*f*
Wieck, Clara, 196–97
Wierzbicki, James, 236–38
Wiesenfreund, Joe, 20–21
Wilder, C. H., 62–63, 81n.100, 81n.104
Williams, John, 11, 83n.2, 120n.81
Wittgenstein, Paul, 202–3
worldbuilding (in film), 84–85, 128–29, 159, 174–92, 216–17
Wright, T. C., 41n.63, 67–69, 70–71, 77–78
Wrobel, William, 232n.58

Zimmer, Hans, 83n.2

The manufacturer's authorised representative in the EU for product safety is Oxford
University Press España S.A. of El Parque Empresarial San Fernando de Henares,
Avenida de Castilla, 2 – 28830 Madrid (www.oup.es/en or product.safety@oup.com).
OUP España S.A. also acts as importer into Spain of products made by the manufacturer.

Printed in the USA/Agawam, MA
August 15, 2025

892047.020